The Fall and Rise of China

Richard Baum, Ph.D.

THE
GREAT
COURSES

PUBLISHED BY:

THE GREAT COURSES
Corporate Headquarters
4840 Westfields Boulevard, Suite 500
Chantilly, Virginia 20151-2299
Phone: 1-800-832-2412
Fax: 703-378-3819
www.thegreatcourses.com

Richard Baum, Ph.D.
Distinguished Professor of Political Science
University of California, Los Angeles

Professor Richard Baum is Distinguished Professor of Political Science at the University of California, Los Angeles, where he specializes in the study of modern Chinese politics and foreign relations. He earned a B.A. in Political Science from UCLA in 1962; an M.A. in Political Science from the University of California, Berkeley, in 1963; and a Ph.D. in Political Science from Berkeley in 1970. He also holds a certificate of achievement in Mandarin Chinese from the Inter-University Program for Chinese Language Studies in Taipei, Taiwan.

Professor Baum has lived and lectured extensively throughout China and Asia. In recent years, he has served as visiting professor and visiting scholar at a number of leading universities, including Peking University; Meiji Gakuin University; The Chinese University of Hong Kong; Delhi University; Leiden University; Princeton University; and Arizona State University, where he was honored as the university's Distinguished Visiting Scholar for 2008.

For many years, Professor Baum was the director of the UCLA Center for Chinese Studies. Throughout his 40-year career, he has served on the boards of several leading organizations in his field, including the National Committee on United States–China Relations and the Joint Committee on Contemporary China of the Social Science Research Council. He has been a consultant to numerous public and private agencies, including the White House, the United Nations, and the Rand Corporation. He is also a frequent commentator on Chinese and East Asian affairs for several leading newspapers, the BBC World Service, Voice of America, CNN International, and National Public Radio.

Professor Baum has written or edited nine books and has published more than 100 articles in professional and popular journals. His books include *China in Ferment: Perspectives on the Cultural Revolution; Prelude to Revolution: Mao, the Party, and the Peasant Question, 1962–1966; China's Four Modernizations: The New Technological Revolution; Reform and Reaction in Post-Mao China: The Road to Tiananmen; Burying Mao: Chinese Politics in the Age of Deng Xiaoping;* and a personal memoir, *China Watcher: Confessions of a Peking Tom.*

Professor Baum is an avid traveler, outdoorsman, and tennis enthusiast. Three of his peak experiences to date have been an ascent of Japan's Mount Fuji by moonlight, exploration of the exquisite Cambodian temple ruins at Angkor Wat, and holding a center-court seat at the Wimbledon lawn tennis championships.

Professor Baum currently divides his time between teaching at UCLA and living and writing in the village of Les Michels in Provence, France. With help from his wife, Karin, a professional restaurateur, and their Basset hound, Millie, he is striving heroically to improve his rudimentary knowledge of French food, wine, cheese, and language. ∎

Table of Contents

Table of Contents

Table of Contents

SUPPLEMENTAL MATERIAL

The Fall and Rise of China

Scope:

This course traces China's tumultuous 200-year journey from collapsing 19th-century empire to aspiring 21st-century superpower. The journey begins with the decline and fall of the Manchu dynasty under the dual stresses of increasing foreign penetration and rising domestic disorder and culminates in China's rise, phoenix-like, from the ashes of radical, revolutionary Maoism to become a globalized, marketized economic—and potential military—powerhouse.

The Demise of the Ancien Régime and the Struggle for Revolutionary Renewal (1793–1945)

The foundational lectures introduce the last days of imperial splendor in 19th-century China and the rising military and mercantile power of an awakening Europe. Two midcentury Opium Wars cripple the Manchu dynasty, rendering it an easy mark for Western penetration and predation. By the end of the century, a series of "unequal treaties" has reduced the once-proud Middle Kingdom to a hollow shell of its former splendor. China is now bankrupt and adrift, at the mercy of foreign interests.

A conservative Chinese Self-Strengthening movement, launched in the 1860s, aims at studying—and emulating—the secrets of Western technological and military prowess; but reactionary Manchu oligarchs, fearful of losing their traditional status, succeed in blocking progressive reform of China's Confucian-dominated educational, cultural, economic, and political institutions. By the end of the century, frustrated reformers begin turning to revolutionary means to effect necessary societal changes.

The moribund Manchu dynasty crumbles in 1912, and for next 37 years, China is wracked by revolution, foreign invasion, and civil war. Externally, a rising imperial Japan is exerting great military pressure on China, while internally, two revolutionary movements fight for political domination: the Guomindang (GMD; a.k.a. Nationalist Party) under Sun Yat-sen and his successor, Chiang K'ai-shek; and the Communists, who rally under the leadership of Mao Zedong.

With Japanese forces preparing to overrun China, the Nationalists and Communists enter into a united front late in 1936, aimed at resisting Japan. Japan attacks in July 1937, easily overrunning the cities of North and East China. Chiang retreats, moving his Nationalist government to Chongqing, deep in China's interior, while the Communists melt into the North China countryside, out of harm's way.

During eight years under Japanese occupation, 1937–1945, the Communists grow stronger, while the Nationalists, beset by rampant inflation, widespread corruption, and incompetent leadership, grow weaker. When the United States enters the anti-Japanese war in December 1941, the tide of battle begins to turn against Japan. In August 1945, the atomic bombing of Hiroshima and Nagasaki brings the war to a sudden, decisive end. With Japan's surrender, Mao and Chiang begin preparations for a final showdown.

The Age of Mao Zedong (1945–1968)

By the end of World War II, the Chinese Communist Party (CCP) has won the loyalty of China's poor peasants, while the GMD has squandered the good will of the urban Chinese. In the civil war that follows, the tide of battle turns decisively in Mao's favor. Beijing falls on January 1, 1949, and Mao declares the birth of the People's Republic of China.

© Corel Stock Photo Library.

The early years of the new regime are devoted to political consolidation and economic recovery. A nationwide land reform program is introduced in 1950, marked by massive land confiscations and violent struggles against "evil landlords." In China's cities, the transfer of power in 1949

Mao Zedong, chairman of the Chinese Communist Party Central Committee, 1935–1976.

witnesses stepped-up political struggles against "reactionary classes," including Guomindang collaborators, foreign agents, and wealthy capitalists.

The outbreak of war in Korea in 1950 puts added strain on China's war-weakened economy while forcing Mao more firmly into Stalin's embrace, thereby hardening the lines of Cold War conflict between East and West.

In 1954, Soviet-style political and legal institutions are imported into China. A new constitution is promulgated, and China officially becomes a "people's democratic dictatorship." Now the CCP launches a program of agricultural collectivization designed to eliminate private ownership of land and other productive assets in the countryside. By 1956, the socialist transformation of the Chinese economy is complete. All rural villages have been collectivized, and all urban industrial and commercial firms have been converted from private to state ownership. But many people resent the power and privileges monopolized by Communist Party members and cadres.

To prevent a Hungarian-style revolt and to assuage the CCP's critics, Mao in 1956 initiates a campaign to "let a hundred flowers blossom." China's intellectuals respond with a torrent of criticism against CCP leadership. Stung by this rebuke, Mao terminates the Hundred Flowers campaign and introduces an Anti-Rightist Rectification movement.

Increasingly concerned with the "revisionist" policies of Nikita Khrushchev in the USSR, Mao in 1958 launches a radical program of social engineering known as the Great Leap Forward. Hastily designed and poorly planned, the Great Leap causes enormous economic hardships. Between 1959 and 1961, upward of 30 million people die of malnutrition and related causes. Seeking to limit the damage, two of Mao's lieutenants, Liu Shaoqi and Deng Xiaoping, begin dismantling the Great Leap. In doing so, they run afoul of Mao, who believes them to be following in Khrushchev's footsteps.

Intent on preventing a restoration of capitalism in China, Mao launches the Socialist Education movement. But many of his comrades have become disillusioned with his radical policies, and they pay little attention to his exhortations. In response, Mao launches the Great Proletarian Cultural Revolution.

Encouraging Chinese students to boldly expose hidden "bourgeois powerholders" in Chinese society, Mao unleashes the Red Guards in the fall of 1966. Schools are dismissed, and young people are urged to "make revolution" against Chairman Mao's enemies. By the spring of 1967, the Cultural Revolution has spread to the CCP itself, with tens of thousands of

Party officials at all levels—including Liu Shaoqi and Deng Xiaoping—being purged. China is in disarray, poised on the brink of anarchy.

Burying Mao (1968–1982)

With the country on the brink of anarchy, Mao in late 1968 calls on the People's Liberation Army to restore order. Millions of urban Chinese youths are sent to rural areas to "remold" themselves through labor. Meanwhile, Sino-Soviet tensions reach the breaking point with an outbreak of shooting along the Manchurian border in March 1969. In midsummer, Soviet officials drop hints of a possible airstrike on China's nuclear facilities.

By 1956, the socialist transformation of the Chinese economy is complete. ... But many people resent the power and privileges monopolized by Communist Party members and cadres.

Convinced that his enemies are trying to do him in, Mao turns against his erstwhile heir apparent, Lin Biao, accusing him of plotting a seizure of power. In a panic, Lin takes flight with his wife and other members of the army high command. Their plane crashes and burns, killing all aboard. Lin is denounced in a nationwide campaign of vilification.

Next, the ever unpredictable Mao, now 80, decides to rehabilitate the disgraced Deng Xiaoping to help revive China's paralyzed political institutions. This irritates Mao's wife, Jiang Qing, and a group of her radical associates, later known as the Gang of Four. Viewing Deng as a rival, they plot to discredit him. But Mao, growing weary of factional struggles, surprises everyone by anointing an unheralded outsider as his successor—Hua Guofeng.

In Mao's final years, the worsening of Sino-Soviet relations presents China's leader with an opportunity to improve relations with the United States. Seeking to enlist American help in containing Soviet expansion, Mao invites a U.S. ping-pong team to Beijing for "friendly competition." This is followed by an invitation to President Richard Nixon to visit China. Although the Sino-American rapprochement is strongly opposed by Jiang Qing, Mao prevails, and the Shanghai communiqué is signed in February 1972.

With Mao's death in September 1976, the succession struggle heats up. The widely despised Jiang Qing and her three radical associates are arrested and charged with conspiring to seize power. With the Gang of Four behind bars, Deng Xiaoping attempts a second comeback, only to have his path blocked by Hua Guofeng, who sees Deng as his principal rival. The two men jockey for position, with Deng enjoying the support of key elder statesmen within the party and army. By 1978, the tide turns in Deng's favor. His ascendancy is confirmed by the CCP Central Committee in November 1978, and a number of sweeping policy initiatives are introduced to reform the stagnant Chinese economy, restore China's shattered legal institutions, and open up China to the outside world.

Mao's death leaves China exhausted and demoralized. Cautiously, Deng sets about reversing Mao's failed economic policies and dismantling the radical legacy of the Cultural Revolution. He rehabilitates large numbers of overthrown cadres, destigmatizes the un-Maoist notions of market competition and profit making, dismantles China's collective farms, and encourages peasants to farm their own family plots. Four Special Economic Zones are opened along China's eastern seaboard, designed to stimulate foreign investment and technology transfer. The age of Mao has ended.

China Rises from the Ashes (1982–2010)
In the early 1980s, a number of senior CCP conservatives criticize Deng Xiaoping's reforms as "capitalist" and accuse members of Deng's reform coalition of fostering "spiritual pollution" in ideology and culture. For the remainder of the decade, the government oscillates uncertainly between reform and retrenchment, resulting in a series of stalled initiatives and partial reforms. Tensions between reformers and conservatives grow stronger, culminating in the January 1987 removal of Deng's liberal-minded protégé, CCP General Secretary Hu Yaobang. Hu is accused by Party hard-liners of being excessively tolerant of "bourgeois liberalization."

In 1989, a number of reform-related stresses and strains converge. The sudden death of Hu Yaobang in April causes thousands of college students to take to the streets in Beijing, demanding that Hu's good name be restored. Party leaders conspicuously ignore the students, accusing their leaders of being unpatriotic and of fomenting turmoil. Insulted, the students redouble their protests. By early May, hundreds of thousands of people—the vast majority nonstudents—fill the streets of Beijing in sympathy with the protesters. With Soviet leader Mikhail Gorbachev due to arrive in Beijing in mid-May, student leaders launch a hunger strike in Tiananmen Square. Enraged by the temerity of the students, senior Chinese leaders vow to put an end to the occupation of Tiananmen Square. Premier Li Peng declares martial law on May 19. A standoff ensues as civilian crowds pour into the streets to block the progress of military convoys.

The students' triumph is short-lived. On June 3, massive waves of government troops, backed by tanks and armored personnel carriers, converge on Tiananmen Square. When civilian crowds try to block their progress, the troops open fire. In the ensuing melee, hundreds of civilians are killed and thousands wounded. When the sun rises over Beijing on June 4, the army has secured Tiananmen Square.

For weeks thereafter, student leaders and others accused of taking part in violence are rounded up and imprisoned. At least two dozen "hooligans" are executed, as a reign of political terror blankets Beijing and other Chinese cities. Meanwhile, Deng Xiaoping congratulates army leaders for their bravery and heroism in defending the government and the party.

Taking advantage of the post-Tiananmen atmosphere of political repression, CCP hard-liners seek to abort Deng's economic reforms. Pointing to the collapse of Communist regimes in Eastern Europe in the last half of 1989, they blame Gorbachev's policy of glasnost for encouraging the spread of bourgeois liberalization. The shocking collapse of the Soviet Union two years later further emboldens them to demand a complete reversal of China's "capitalist reforms."

Though ailing and infirm, the 86-year-old Deng Xiaoping fights back. In January 1992, he embarks on a five-week Southern Tour of China's dynamic coastal cities and Special Economic Zones. Mobilizing support for his reforms at every stop, he disparages those who would reverse them as "women with bound feet." Though he manages to rescue his embattled economic reforms, Deng rules out political reform. Citing the importance of unity and stability as preconditions for China's development, he insists on upholding the four cardinal principles: unquestioning support for the people's democratic dictatorship, CCP leadership, socialism, and Marxism–Leninism–Mao Zedong Thought.

Deng's chosen successor, Jiang Zemin, eases slowly into power, remaining in Deng's shadow until the latter's formal retirement at the end of 1992. Thereafter, Jiang and his chief economic troubleshooter, Vice-Premier (later Premier) Zhu Rongji successfully resolve a series of growing economic problems by taming rampant inflation, marketizing China's state-owned enterprises, and reforming China's dysfunctional banking and tax systems. By the time Deng dies in 1997, China's economy is humming on all cylinders, averaging 10 percent annual growth.

> **The Communist Party maintains its exclusive monopoly on political power, and no dissent is tolerated.**

Early in the new century, Jiang attempts to reform the Communist Party. Introducing his "theory of the three represents," Jiang encourages recruitment of members of China's "new class" of capitalist entrepreneurs into the CCP. Several million capitalists respond to his call.

With Jiang's retirement in 2003, a new generation of "socialist technocrats" assumes power. Led by the new PRC president and party chief Hu Jintao, China's leaders begin to address burgeoning problems of unbalanced economic growth, extreme income polarization, environmental degradation, and bureaucratic corruption. Under the slogan "building a harmonious society," the new leaders begin to restore welfare benefits eliminated during the headlong rush to privatize the economy in the 1990s. Hu pledges to restore tuition-free public education; subsidized health care; unemployment benefits; and retirement pensions for workers, peasants, and migrant laborers.

Though they promote progressive social policies, the new Chinese leaders do not initiate significant political reforms. The Communist Party maintains its exclusive monopoly on political power, and no dissent is tolerated. The mass media in China remain routinely subject to censorship, and all putative challenges to CCP leadership are met with repressive force. Examples of such repression were readily seen during the run-up to the Beijing Olympics of 2008, as dissident journalists, political activists, and social critics were systematically harassed and intimidated.

Meanwhile, China's ongoing economic dynamism has raised concerns of a growing "China threat" in Europe, America, and Japan. The PRC's dramatic rise has generated widespread fears of lost or outsourced jobs and has heightened global competition for energy resources, minerals, and industrial raw materials. Despite repeated Chinese assurances that the country's intentions are entirely peaceful, China is viewed by many as a peer competitor and potential adversary.

Notwithstanding worrisome projections of growing Chinese economic and military power and nationalistic fervor, recent Chinese behavior provides some grounds for cautious optimism. Since joining the World Trade Organization in 2001, China has conformed rather closely with prevailing international norms and standards in its legal, commercial, and financial dealings. China's relations with Taiwan have calmed down considerably since 2005. And China has supported initiatives against nuclear weapons in Iraq, Iran, and North Korea. In all these respects, China is seen as behaving as a "responsible stakeholder." ■

The Splendor That Was China, 600–1700
Lecture 1

Legend has it that the Emperor Napoleon once said of China, "There lies a sleeping giant. Let it sleep, for when it wakes it will shake the world."

For two millennia in the premodern world, the Chinese empire enjoyed cultural and political supremacy. The **Middle Kingdom** dealt with surrounding states as tributaries and regarded all non–Han Chinese peoples as barbarians. A unique combination of advanced water-management techniques, a meritocratic imperial bureaucracy, and a **Confucian** code of virtuous conduct reinforced by laws and unchallenged military prowess enabled the Chinese empire to prosper long after other ancient civilizations disappeared. Though twice invaded by northern barbarians—the Mongols in the 13th century and the Manchus in the 17th—China managed to retain its imperial institutions and culture.

The opening of several **Silk Road** trade routes from the 7th to the 12th centuries brought China into limited commercial and religious contact with peoples and cultures from Central Asia and beyond, but these routes were

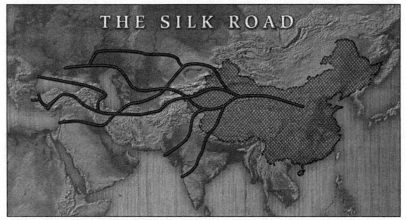

The Silk Road was a network of overland trade routes that linked western China with Central Asia and the world beyond.

largely abandoned following the Mongol Empire's disintegration after 1360. A brief blossoming of Chinese maritime navigation occurred under Ming emperor **Yongle** early in the 15th century, but this age of exploration ended when Yongle's narrow-minded successors decreed an end to oceanic exploration.

From the death of Yongle until the dawn of the modern era, China turned inward, remaining largely indifferent to—and untouched by—the world beyond its immediate periphery. This course spans more than 200 years, from the decline of Chinese imperial power to the contemporary rebirth of modern China. ■

Names to Know

Yongle (1360–1424): The third emperor of the Ming dynasty (r. 1402–1424), who commissioned seven major oceanic expeditions, led by Zheng He. With Yongle's death in 1424, maritime exploration ceased for 400 years.

Zheng He (c. 1371–1433): A Hui Muslim and imperial eunuch, Admiral Zheng launched seven oceanic expeditions between 1405 and 1433. His fleet of 200 six-masted ships reached ports in Southeast Asia, India, Ceylon, the Persian Gulf, Arabia, and the Horn of Africa.

Important Terms

Confucianism: Classical Chinese philosophical doctrine holding that society is best regulated via internalized moral precepts of virtue and benevolence, rather than compulsion.

Middle Kingdom: This literal translation of "Zhongguo" (China) refers to the traditional Chinese belief in a Sinocentric universe.

Silk Road: The network of ancient trade routes linking western China to the Near and Middle East.

Suggested Reading

Hsü, *The Rise of Modern China*.

Huang, *1587: A Year of No Significance*.

Pomeranz, *The Great Divergence*.

Spence, *The Search for Modern China*.

Questions to Consider

1. What were the key sources of Chinese imperial longevity, and which of these were unique to China?

2. Who was Admiral Zheng He, and how did he play a critical role in closing China to the outside world for 400 years?

The Splendor That Was China, 600–1700
Lecture 1—Transcript

Legend has it that the Emperor Napoleon once said of China, "There lies a sleeping giant. Let it sleep, for when it wakes it will shake the world."

Apocryphal, perhaps, but in recent decades this long-slumbering Chinese colossus has begun to stir. Though not yet fully aroused, its immense size and weight have begun to command the attention of its neighbors, near and far.

For some, this awakening giant is a symbol of rebirth and regeneration, inspiring hope and confidence. For others, it's an object of trepidation, its rising strength and growing self-confidence a threat to the very foundations of Western civilization.

What are we to make of this awakening Leviathan, this Gulliver among Lilliputians? How should we understand—and deal with—a rising China? Will it be a friend or a foe? A partner or a competitor? On the answers to these questions will hinge, in no small measure, the final epitaph of our present century, which many observers have already begun to call "the Chinese Century."

This course will not provide definitive answers to these questions. Napoleon's grim warning of a restless, destructive China may prove prescient, or it may be grossly exaggerated.

In either case, we cannot simply take his—or anyone's—word for it. We need to see for ourselves, and then draw our own conclusions.

Before we set out on this journey of discovery, I'd like to tell you a little bit about myself. My name is Richard Baum, and I'm a professor of political science at UCLA. For many years I directed the Center for Chinese Studies at UCLA.

My own introduction to modern China was almost entirely accidental. When I was a senior in college, a long, long time ago, a scheduling conflict led me to enroll in a class with the rather daunting title, "Government and Politics of China." Prior to that time, aside from seeing a few old Charlie Chan movies and enjoying the eggrolls and fortune cookies at Madame Wu's Cantonese Garden in Los Angeles, where I was born, I had had no exposure whatever to anything Chinese.

In my Chinese politics class, the first book we were assigned to read was *Red Star Over China*. It was a gripping tale of the early years of the Chinese Communist Revolution, written by a sympathetic American journalist named Edgar Snow. It included the very first authorized biography of the young Mao Zedong; and it featured a blow-by-blow account of the Chinese Communist Party's epic Long March of the 1930s.

I found it utterly captivating, a real-life adventure of derring-do, with larger than life heroes and villains chasing each other across a war-torn Chinese landscape.

It seemed clear to me then that Mao and his Red Army comrades had been welcomed as liberators by most ordinary Chinese. While outmaneuvering Chiang K'ai-shek's larger, better equipped Nationalist army, the Communists confiscated the property of the rapacious landlord class and distributed it to millions of poor and landless peasants. The peasants, in return, provided the bulwark of popular support for Mao's revolution.

Of course, the true situation turned out to be rather more complicated than that. It was still early days in my education, and I was still a bit naïve. But I was definitely hooked on modern China.

As it turned out, my fascination with the revolutionary adventures of Mao and his top lieutenants has never abated. After graduating from UCLA I went on to went on to get a doctoral degree at UC Berkeley. My doctoral thesis dealt with the bitter factional struggles that broke out between Mao and his comrades in the early 1960s, on the eve of the infamous Cultural Revolution.

Since then, in an academic career spanning four decades, I have visited China more than 30 times. I've traveled extensively throughout the country and lectured at more than a dozen Chinese universities.

Although Mao died before U.S.-China relations were finally normalized in 1979, and I never had an opportunity to meet the legendary chairman face to face, I have had brief personal encounters with three of Mao's latter-day successors: Hua Guofeng, Deng Xiaoping, and Jiang Zemin. And over the years I've met with hundreds of high- and middle-level officials and policymakers. These people play a significant role in the lectures and narratives to follow.

For me, Modern China has been a source of endless fascination, sometimes evoking feelings of profound admiration while, at other times, leaving me feeling bitterly frustrated and outraged. But one thing that China has never, ever been is boring.

Though I will try to maintain a general attitude of scholarly detachment and objectivity throughout these lectures, I will not shy away from revealing my own reactions to major Chinese events and developments. And I will share with you a number of personal anecdotes and observations from my various travels to China.

To place the story of China's awakening in proper historical perspective, the first half of the course will trace the 19th century decline of Chinese imperial power, followed by the early 20th century disintegration of the Empire, and the subsequent struggles among competing revolutionary ideologies and armies that marked modern Chinese history from 1912 until the advent of the People's Republic in 1949. The first half ends with an assessment of Mao Zedong's efforts to radically transform Chinese society after 1949, including both his early triumphs and, more spectacularly, his later tragedies, most notably the Great Leap Forward and the great proletarian Cultural Revolution.

In the second half of the course we examine Deng Xiaoping's effort to reverse two decades of Maoist radicalism. In the late 1970s and '80s Deng introduced a series of rather audacious economic reforms. These reforms set the stage for China's remarkable national revival.

But there was a downside as well, insofar as the unintended social stresses and strains produced by these early reforms led, at least indirectly, to the eruption—and bloody suppression—of massive student protests at Tiananmen Square in 1989.

In the 1990s, under Deng's successor, Jiang Zemin, China recovered from the traumas of Tiananmen and began to open its economy to massive infusions of foreign investment, trade and technology. These latter reforms spurred the dramatic double-digit economic growth that has generally dazzled the world at large.

Politically, however, China's post-Mao leaders proved highly reluctant to relinquish their traditional monopoly of power, and consequently a substantial gap has emerged between China's dynamic, open economy and its rigid, authoritarian political system. In the latter part of the course we will consider the implications of this bifurcation between politics and economics, and we will conclude with an assessment of China's rapidly changing role in international affairs.

The full historical sweep of the course thus spans more than 200 years, from the initial decline in Chinese imperial power to the contemporary rebirth of a self-confident global Chinese powerhouse. The journey from there to here is a fascinating one, filled with a good deal of high drama, and punctuated by a great many unexpected twists and turns. So please fasten your seatbelts, for we are about to embark upon a breathtaking ride.

It is hard for the Western imagination to wrap itself around the idea that as recently as two hundred years ago, the Emperor of China firmly believed that his worldly domain extended to the four corners of the Earth. China was then—as it had been for well over a thousand years—"the Middle Kingdom" (*Zhongguo*), the notional center of the universe. The emperor was the "Son of Heaven" (*Tianzi*). His earthly domain was coterminous with "All under heaven" (*Tianxia*).

Grandiose? Yes, of course. But such imperial hubris was hardly unwarranted. From the founding of the Tang dynasty in the 7th century of the Common Era until the middle years of the Qing (or Manchu) dynasty in the 18th century, Chinese civilization and culture thrived, with only occasional disruptions, the most conspicuous being two foreign dynastic conquests by the Mongols under Genghis Khan in the 13th century and later by the Manchus in the mid-17th century.

But not even the imposition of two foreign dynasties could substantially alter Chinese society and culture. So strong and deeply engrained were the institutions and values of Chinese civilization that the conquerors were gradually absorbed and assimilated by the conquered. Dynasties came and went, but the Middle Kingdom lived on, its grandeur largely undiminished.

By the time the Manchu dynasty fell in the early 20th century, the only visible remaining symbol of Manchu supremacy was the mandatory male queue, or pigtail. In virtually every other respect, the Manchus had become thoroughly Sinified.

In stark contrast to the longevity and majesty of the Chinese empire, throughout most of this same 1100-year period, from roughly 600–1700 C.E., Western civilization lay relatively dormant. From the onset of the Dark Ages following the collapse of the Roman Empire to the first blossomings of the

European enlightenment in the 16th and 17th centuries, the West slumbered while China flourished.

A constellation of factors (institutional, technological, ecological, and cultural) help to explain China's early rise as well as its extraordinary imperial longevity. Some of these factors, such as the philosophical traditions of Confucianism, were unique to China, while others, including mastery of the techniques of wet-rice cultivation and irrigation, were shared with other ancient civilizations. But it was a unique combination of these characteristics that enabled the Middle Kingdom to survive and prosper while other early empires rose, peaked, decayed, and disappeared, one after the other.

To endure for a millennium or even longer, a major civilization requires, first of all, a sustainable natural ecosystem. In China, two great East-West waterways, The Yellow River and the Yangzi River, provided the water needed to nourish and sustain a large-scale agrarian economy.

But China's continental monsoon climate, with periods of intense seasonal rainfall interspersed with prolonged dry spells, meant that farmlands in China were subject to frequent, oscillating cycles of flood and draught. It was not for nothing that the Yellow River, birthplace of Chinese civilization, has for centuries been known as "China's Sorrow."

Under these circumstances, only a sophisticated, well-coordinated system of hydraulic engineering could create the controlled flow of water necessary to support stable, densely populated agricultural communities.

All successful ancient civilizations, including those in Egypt, Mesopotamia, Mesoamerica, and the Indus Valley, had this trait in common: That is, they all had relatively advanced water management systems that included large-scale, centrally-administered networks of irrigation canals, dams, dikes, reservoirs, and sluiceways. China was no exception to this rule.

But it was not sufficient merely to grow enough food to support a large population. To build and sustain an empire, ruling elites had to be able to siphon off substantial amounts of agricultural surplus from rural producers, in the form of taxes, generally paid either in kind or in mandatory corvée labor or both.

These extracted resources were used, in turn, to support the ruler and his retinue of court officials, as well as to maintain a standing army (including periodic military campaigns) and to finance the construction of great urban centers and monumental structures, such as the Great Pyramids of Giza, the Incan temples at Machu Pichu, and the Great Wall of China. And let us not forget the tendency for empire builders in all great civilizations to indulge in the conspicuous consumption of luxury goods—including decorative bronze vessels, ornamental porcelains, gold jewelry, and the like. Such luxury items were produced by urban artisans whose livelihood depended, in the first instance, on the existence of long-distance trade networks, through whose commercialized arteries flowed the resources and the raw materials that were the building blocks of imperial splendor.

But effective irrigation techniques, a taxable farm surplus, a vast network of trade routes, and even a specialized class of urban artisans were still not enough to create an enduring high civilization.

A well-functioning empire also required substantial numbers of competent, honest and loyal court officials, magistrates, and tax collectors.

And this is where China's uniqueness first came into play. For beginning in the 7th century C.E., Tang dynasty officials introduced the world's first civil service system. Designed to recruit the best and brightest young men through a system of standardized, merit-based examinations, China's imperial civil service was, for its time, remarkably progressive, egalitarian, and democratic.

Twice-yearly examinations were open to all males, regardless of birth or wealth. And to reduce the tendency toward nepotism and corruption that were engendered when local economic elites cultivated long-term personal relationships with local magistrates, an avoidance system prohibited civil servants from being posted to their home counties and also mandated the periodic geographical rotation of imperial assignments.

Although the civil service system was nominally open and democratic, there were a few hidden catches.

For one thing, only males could sit for the examinations.

For another, one had to be thoroughly literate in order to pass the exam. And that, in turn, was no trivial matter, since Chinese was an ancient, idiographic language that lacked a written phonetic alphabet. Indeed, a would-be exam taker would have to spend long years memorizing thousands of individual characters and tens of thousands of their combinations.

As for the exam itself, it was a highly stylized exercise in the rote memorization and manipulation of certain classical philosophical texts, and had to be composed in a famously rigid and constrained style of writing known as the "eight-legged essay."

The eight-legged essay was constructed in the following manner: First came a two-sentence opening statement, precisely two sentences, followed by a five-sentence elaboration, precisely so, followed by a preliminary exposition and an initial argument (which had to be constructed in a discrete number of precisely-paired sentences using precise parallel language).

Then came the central argument, followed by the latter argument, the final argument and the conclusion.

And this all had to be done within a prescribed number of words. (And my UCLA students think they have it tough when I ask them to compose an expository essay.)

Because of the difficulty of mastering both the Confucian classics and the rigid format of the eight-legged essay, an aspiring imperial civil servant in China would have to be privately tutored for many years to even have a shot at passing the exam—something that only well-to-do families could normally afford for their privileged sons.

Peasant boys, by contrast, had to work in the fields; there was simply no leisure time for indulging in daily private tutorials. Thus, it is not surprising that the vast majority of successful examination candidates came from the affluent landlord-gentry class.

The subject matter of the civil service examinations consisted largely of ancient philosophical texts, written in the 5th and 6th centuries B.C.E. by the scholar-sage Confucius and a small group of his loyal disciples. Known as the "four books and the five classics of antiquity," these Confucian teachings were aimed at perfecting the moral self-cultivation of the idealized gentleman scholar.

Rooted in traditional ethical principles such as benevolence, propriety, natural harmony, reverence for one's ancestors, and faithful observance of ceremonial rites and rituals, Confucianism prescribed a highly disciplined training regimen for would-be imperial officials.

A successful examination candidate would, of necessity, be an accomplished Confucian scholar.

In the Confucian scheme of things, good governance was rooted in the proper conduct of imperial officials, including the emperor himself. The moral code of Confucianism required conscientious observance of certain well-defined hierarchies of reciprocal, status-based rights and responsibilities.

Thus, for example, Confucian morality mandated that sons should be unconditionally obey their fathers; wives should obey their husbands; subjects should obey the emperor; and the living should revere the spirits of their deceased ancestors.

It was all very precise and orderly; and everyone knew their place—at least in theory.

Given this well-defined system of reciprocal obligations and responsibilities, a smooth-running Confucian society ultimately depended upon each member of an extended family, and of the broader community that encompassed many such extended families, or clans, knowing their proper place in relation to all other community members. There was no concept of universal social equality, and no notion that individual freedom could take precedence over the obligation to enhance the collective welfare of the family.

For such a family-centered, morally-integrated community to function smoothly, its members had to share a common awareness of their mutual obligations and responsibilities. Now, this was all well and good within small, tight-knit village communities, where people were generally connected to one another by kinship or by habitual neighborly interaction.

But what of the non-Confucian others—the unassimilated aliens—who inhabited imperial China's outer regions and border spaces. These outer tribes and nationalities included Mongolians, Tibetans, Muslims, Manchus, and more than 50 other ethnic grouping that did not share the moral traditions and principles of Confucianism.

For these alien others, the emperor's moral authority, and the ethical canons of Confucianism, were insufficient guarantees of interpersonal harmony and social order. Something more was needed.

That something was bureaucratic coercion.

To ensure that people from different parts of the sprawling Chinese empire, that is, strangers unrelated by blood or ancestry, would act in conformity with Chinese norms and practices, punishment for aberrant behavior had to be swift and sure. Criminal conduct had to be well-defined and effectively deterred.

It was the particular genius of China's early emperors and court officials that they recognized the need for both a morally-integrated community of values governing ordinary interactions, and a well-defined set of criminal laws and administrative sanctions to deter and punish aberrant behavior.

Indeed the unique longevity and durability of China's dynastic system owes much to the long-term co-existence of these two very different, but ultimately complementary governing traditions, known in Chinese as Lizhi and Fazhi, respectively Confucian moralism and coercive legalism, which have sometimes been referred to as the Yin and the Yang of effective imperial rule.

Of course, China's dynastic longevity and prosperity also benefited from the fact that for most of its 2000-year imperial history, China was bounded by a collection of smaller, weaker states along its southern, western and northern peripheries.

Toward these lesser states, China's imperial court generally observed a policy of hegemonic tolerance, granting their local rulers substantial autonomy in exchange for ritualized military deference and political obeisance. This Pax Sinica was cemented by the regular gift of valuable national treasures—or tribute—from barbarian kings to the Chinese "Son of Heaven."

In addition to such ritualized tributary relations, routine commodity trade between China and its neighbors, near and far, waxed and waned periodically over the lifespan of the Chinese empire.

Early in the Common Era, a number of overland trade routes were opened linking Western China with the people and cultures of Central Asia and beyond.

Collectively known as the Silk Road, these trade routes reached their zenith during the Tang and Song Dynasties, from the 7th to the 12th centuries C.E.

It was via the Silk Road that Buddhism (from India) and Islam (from Karakorum) first found their way to China. And it was also via the Silk Road that the Venetian explorer Marco Polo first sampled the exotic silks, spices, and porcelains of imperial China.

With the disintegration of the Mongol Empire in the last half of the 14th century, however, control over the Silk Road trade routes became fragmented among contending regional states. As disorder grew at the periphery of China's empire, commerce diminished, and the importance of the Silk Road as a major trade network sharply declined.

This brings us to the question of imperial China's military power. Although Chinese armies were not normally used for territorial conquest, by the time of the Northern Song dynasty (960–1127 C.E.), China's military superiority over its smaller, weaker neighbors was firmly established.

An army of over one million soldiers was supplied by a state-controlled armaments industry that could produce in a single year up to 100,000 tons of pig iron, from which were forged tens of thousands of sets of body armor and as many as 3 million field weapons, mainly consisting of bows, crossbows, and lances.

By clearly underlining the futility of armed resistance to the Son of Heaven, periodic displays of Chinese military might effectively underpinned the empire's tributary system of foreign relations.

The story of China's remarkable imperial longevity, recounted all too briefly in this lecture, is an endlessly fascinating one. But equally fascinating is the improbable tale of spiraling imperial decline that beset China beginning in the late 1700s and culminated in the collapse of the last great Chinese dynasty—the Manchus—in 1911.

In just a little over 125 years, China descended from unsurpassed power to unimaginable impotence, from being the mighty Celestial Empire to being the severely crippled "sick man of Asia." In the next lecture we shall explore the roots of this extraordinary imperial decline.

Malthus and Manchu Hubris, 1730–1800
Lecture 2

> Middle Kingdom complex—a constellation of attitudes marked by extreme cultural self-satisfaction, economic insularity, military complacency, and, above all, a xenophobic contempt for all things "barbarian"—i.e., foreign.

In the mid-1700s, two parallel developments began to undermine China's imperial grandeur: a demographic explosion and the introduction of opium. These factors, combined with the arrogance and complacency of China's ruling elite, precipitated the empire's sharp and tragic decline.

An extended period of peace that began in the mid-17th century led to a decline in domestic mortality rates. It also gave the imperial government the opportunity and resources to improve the nation's water management; this in turn resulted in fewer fatalities from flood, draught, water-borne disease, and malnutrition. Thus China's population doubled in the 18th century, and again in the 19th century. But in this same period, agricultural productivity stagnated, causing a **Malthusian crisis** in which millions of Chinese farmers and laborers lived in dire poverty. Grain surpluses vanished, and agricultural tax revenue dwindled.

In the late 18th century, European demand for Chinese tea, silk, spices, and porcelain rose dramatically. For a time, this trade revenue shored up the imperial treasury. But Europeans brought more than money to China; they also brought opium. English merchants and Chinese middlemen grew rich off this illicit commerce, but the drug wreaked havoc on China's legitimate economy through addiction, inflation, and the destruction of China's favorable trade balance with Europe.

When China finally opened itself to formal trade relations with Europe, several cultural misunderstandings, as well as Chinese xenophobia, soured China's trade negotiations with Britain in 1793. **Emperor Qianlong** ultimately and arrogantly rejected the overtures of Britain's trade representative, **Lord George Macartney**, further weakening the Chinese economy. China's belief in its own superiority was about to be put to the test. ∎

Macartney, Lord George (1737–1806): Irish-born diplomat who led the failed British trade delegation from King George III to the court of Qianlong in 1793. He offended the emperor by refusing to perform the traditional kowtow.

Qianlong (1711–1799): Fifth emperor of the Manchu dynasty. Citing China's "celestial supremacy," Qianlong contemptuously rejected a 1793 request for normal trade relations from Great Britain.

Important Term

Malthusian crisis: A situation in which a population has outstripped its potential productivity.

Suggested Reading

Elvin, *The Pattern of the Chinese Past.*

Hsü, *The Rise of Modern China.*

Huang, *1587: A Year of No Significance.*

Pomeranz, *The Great Divergence.*

Spence, *The Search for Modern China.*

Waley, *The Opium War through Chinese Eyes.*

Questions to Consider

1. What were the main causes of China's dynastic decline?

2. How did the British reverse their unfavorable trade balance with China at the end of the 18th century?

Malthus and Manchu Hubris, 1730–1800
Lecture 2—Transcript

Last time we identified a number of key factors that helped to explain the extraordinary longevity and grandiosity of the Chinese Empire. Let us take just a moment to review these before continuing on our journey.

One factor that contributed to the rise and maintenance of a vast continental empire was China's early mastery of wet-rice cultivation; a second, and closely related factor was the perfection of large-scale water management techniques; third, was the creation of an efficient civil service, with recruitment by competitive examination; fourth, was the adoption of a patriarchal value system that emphasized the obedience of wives to their husbands, sons to their fathers, and subjects to their emperor; and which stressed the wellbeing of the entire family over the rights and liberties of its individual members; fifth, was a well-developed legal code that deterred deviant behavior by prescribing swift and severe punishment for a wide range of crimes and misdemeanors; sixth was the development of advanced metallurgical techniques that sustained the large-scale manufacture of military armaments; and seventh was the fortuitous circumstance of being ringed on three sides by smaller, weaker states willing to pay tribute to the Chinese emperor in exchange for being left alone to enjoy peace and tranquility.

With all these advantages going for it, the question is not so much "How did China become so powerful and remain so dominant for so long," but rather, "Why did the Middle Kingdom collapse so suddenly, and so completely?"

The answer to this question has fueled an entire cottage industry of scholarship among historians of early modern China. Dozens of books have been written, and it still remains enigmatic.

It is a tragic irony of modern Chinese history that the extraordinary success of Imperial China's agrarian civilization, extending over such a long period of time and such a broad expanse of territory, bred habits of complacency, insularity, and arrogance.

Believing China to be self-contained and superior in all things, both material and moral, a succession of Chinese emperors shunned all but the most transient and superficial contacts with the outside world.

Basking in the glow of their own moral and institutional supremacy and superiority, they remained blissfully ignorant of the coming of the Renaissance in post-medieval Europe, and the subsequent dawning of the Age of Enlightenment, with its signature revolutions in science and technology.

Historians searching for the root causes of China's precipitous decline generally start at this point, by taking note of China's extreme ethnocentrism, and its myopic disdain for all things foreign.

But it was not always thus.

For almost 800 years, from Tang dynasty in the 7th century to the early Ming of the 15th century, long-distance oceanic trade and maritime exploration flourished in China. By the 8th century C.E., Chinese traders had sailed to Malaysia, Indonesia, India, Ceylon, and as far west as the Persian Gulf.

By the end of the 8th century, seafaring Chinese explorers had navigated around the Arabian peninsula to the horn of Africa, reaching Somalia, Ethiopia, and Egypt via the Red Sea. By the 9th century, three different maritime trade routes had been opened linking China to East Africa.

The lure of trade also brought Middle Eastern and North African merchants and adventurers to China. By the 12th century, southern Chinese seaports in Guangzhou and Quanzhou were playing host to thousands of foreign travelers, including substantial numbers of permanent settlers.

The high point of Chinese maritime exploration was undoubtedly reached in the early 15th century, under the Yongle emperor of the Ming dynasty. At the outset of that century, seven major oceanic expeditions were mounted by the famous navigator Zheng He.

Seventy-five years before Columbus set sail for the West Indies, Zheng He sailed his massive fleet of more than 200 six-masted Chinese ships, manned by 28,000 crewmen, to ports in Southeast Asia, India, Ceylon, the Persian Gulf, Arabia, and East Africa. Although Zheng He's army was formidable, and though he did not shrink from engaging in displays of military force when confronted by hostile local rulers, his fleet of treasure ships went abroad not as conquerors but as cultural goodwill ambassadors.

Wherever he went, Zheng He liberally dispensed gifts of Chinese silk and porcelain, accepting in return valuable native products from his hosts, including a variety of exotic African animals destined for the imperial zoo in Beijing, where their latter-day descendents still reside. He also brought with him back to China, as guests of the imperial court, emissaries from at least 30 princely states.

Although Zheng He was undoubtedly the most successful maritime explorer and goodwill ambassador in Chinese history, his pioneering journeys ended not in glory but in disgrace.

Following the death in 1424 of Zheng He's patron, the emperor Yongle, a cabal of conservative court officials, decreed an end to Chinese maritime exploration. Fearing Zheng He's growing fame and political influence, they burned all of his nautical charts and shipbuilding blueprints, and allowed his decommissioned treasure ships to rot in the harbor. Zheng himself died on his final voyage in 1433 and was buried at sea.

For the next 400 years China's emperors shunned foreign exploration and contact of any kind. Looking inward, they consigned themselves to an insular, smug self-satisfied existence, an existence that would eventually cost them—and China—dearly.

A similar process of diminishing exposure to the outside world marked China's overland trade contacts with the peoples and cultures of Central and Western Asia.

As we saw in the previous lecture, long-distance trade via the Silk Road flourished from the 7th century on. But with the disintegration of the Mongol Empire in the 14th century, commercial travel via overland routes toward the west became perilous for the Chinese merchants.

And by the time Zheng He's ships were grounded in the 1430s, the Ming dynasty had turned almost totally inward, displaying little or no interest in maintaining contact with the societies and civilizations of Central and West Asia.

Consequently, by the middle of the 15th century, China was effectively cut off from the outside world, first by sea, then by land, and then, perhaps most unfortunate of all, by imperial mandate. It was as if a giant curtain of ignorance had been drawn around the Middle Kingdom.

It would be difficult to exaggerate the negative consequences that would flow from this self-imposed Chinese isolation. Yet this was not the only nor, necessarily, even the most decisive factor that contributed to China's subsequent imperial decline. At least two other important forces were also at work, though historians disagree on the relative importance. First was an unprecedented Chinese demographic explosion and second was the rise of European mercantilism. When these three factors—isolationism, demographics, and European commercial expansion—began to converge in the 18th century, they spelled disaster for China.

Early in the 18th century, around 1710, China's population, which had been relatively stable at between 50 and 100 million for almost a thousand years, suddenly started surging. Within 75 years the population doubled, from 116 million to 242 million. In the century that followed, it doubled yet again.

The origins of this extraordinary population surge can be traced to three interconnected factors. First was the extended period of international peace that followed the Manchu (or Qing) conquest of China in 1644. With the country basically at peace, there was a clear decline in domestic mortality rates. Second, the new Manchu regime, early in its reign, carried out a major campaign to repair long-neglected dykes and irrigation works along the Yellow and Yangzi rivers. The subsequent improvement in water management resulted in fewer fatalities from flood, draught, water-borne disease and malnutrition. Finally, and closely related to the first two factors, there was a significant rise in female fertility, resulting in a substantial and prolonged baby boom.

Demographers are uncertain as to which of these factors was most decisive and in what combinations. But one thing they agree on is that a Chinese population explosion began early in the 18th century and did not abate for more than two centuries thereafter.

Another thing they agree on is that this prolonged population explosion eventually resulted in a Malthusian crisis, as population pressures began to strain the carrying capacity of a traditional agrarian economy.

While population grew dramatically in the 18th and 19th centuries, there was no corresponding increase in total crop acreage under cultivation.

Because of a severe shortage of arable virgin farmland outside of China's major river valleys, the 18th century demographic explosion resulted in a sharp increase in rural population density, and a corresponding reduction, over time, in the amount of land cultivated by the average Chinese farm family. From the beginning of the 18th century to its end, the average farm shrank in size from about 10 acres to less than six acres.

This problem of rising population density was further compounded by the absence of significant innovation in agricultural technology. Because traditional Chinese agricultural and water management techniques, perfected a thousand years earlier, were extremely well suited to China's monsoon climate and riverine ecosystem, a relatively large and stable core population had been sustained from the Tang dynasty right through the early years of Manchu rule.

But as so often happens in human history, success breeds complacency, while also serving to impede innovation and introspection.

Consequently, throughout this extended period of ecological and demographic stability, there were few major technological advances either in production and marketing techniques or in water conservation and management. Consequently few improvements were achieved in the productivity of farms or in the efficiency of farmers.

With a rural population that was rapidly expanding with no new agrarian technologies available to raise farm productivity and with few virgin lands available to lure struggling families to move to greener pastures, Chinese farmers in the late 18th century faced a classic Malthusian dilemma, as a rapidly growing population first caught up with, and then gradually outstripped, the carrying capacity of the land.

The historian Mark Elvin has called this situation a "high-level equilibrium trap," that is, a condition of agricultural impaction characterized by too many people eking out a living on too little land, using traditional means of production and having no place else to go. As farms grew smaller and more and more rural families drifted to the edge of subsistence, grain surpluses vanished and agricultural taxes—which were the main source of imperial revenue—went uncollected.

Almost unnoticed outside the hard-pressed Chinese countryside, the once mighty Manchu dynasty thus began to slip slowly into fiscal decline.

By the time Western merchants began their commercial penetration of China toward the end of the 18th century, the process of fiscal erosion was already well underway. The coming of the West did not, in the first instance, "cause" China's imperial decline, but it certainly accelerated it. Here is, more or less, what happened.

When Western merchants first arrived in force in the late 1700s, rising Chinese commercial profits and customs revenue helped to mask the Empire's fiscal decline from diminished world taxes. With Chinese teas, silks, spices, and porcelains in high demand in Europe, a very favorable Chinese balance of commodity trade helped offset the decline in farm revenues.

By the end of the 18th century, however, a few enterprising British merchants had come up with an ingenious way to obtain the precious Chinese products they needed to satisfy their customers, and to do so without having to expend valuable silver specie in the process.

The key to this magical amplification of British profit was the appearance of a new and highly popular commodity on the Chinese scene called *Papa-ver somni-ferum*, or sleeping poppy—more commonly known as opium.

To be sure, opium was not entirely unknown in China before 1800.

In the declining decades of the Ming dynasty, in the early 1600s, Portuguese traders had brought small quantities of opium paste from Thailand as tribute to the Chinese emperor.

And a certain amount had also been brought in overland from Turkey via the Silk Road.

But when British merchants began smuggling opium in industrial quantities from India to China in the late 1700s, the effects were dramatic. From a mere 200 chests of opium in 1729 (that is, roughly 15 tons of processed opium), imports rose to 75 tons in 1767.

By the 1810s annual imports averaged 340 tons, rising to around 750 tons in the 1820s. In 1839 a total of 3,000 tons of opium (or 6 million pounds) were imported into China.

Demand for the drug was high, and British smugglers and their Chinese middlemen profited handsomely from the growing opium trade. But China's fast-rising addiction to opium had a strongly negative impact on the Manchu dynasty's precarious fiscal stability. With the bulk of the profits from illicit opium trade going to line the pockets of foreign traffickers rather than the treasury of Beijing, China's favorable trade balance began to shrink.

A cascade of adverse knock-on effects followed from this.

As the net flow of silver into the country slowed down, its value on the domestic market increased proportionately. In the 1740s, for example, well before the onset of the opium boom, one *tael* (or a little over an ounce) of silver had a market value of roughly 800 copper coins; by the 1820s, at the height of the opium trade, the value of silver had more than trebled, with one tael of silver now trading for 2,500 copper coins.

For China's beleaguered farmers, already heavily burdened by an emerging Malthusian crisis, this rise in the market exchange value of silver presented a new and potentially crushing hardship. While farmers sold their produce in the market for devalued copper coins, they paid their taxes in silver, which was appreciating in value.

Caught in a classic, inflationary Catch-22, more and more peasants found themselves unable to meet their tax obligations. Increasing numbers of them were being either pushed below the poverty line or forced off the land altogether.

Under the twin forces of a Malthusian-induced farm crisis and an opium-induced reduction of China's favorable trade balance, by the end of the 18th century the Manchu dynasty exhibited the first clear signs of an emerging fiscal crisis.

One early symptom of this was the outbreak in 1796 of a massive tax rebellion among the impoverished settlers in the mountainous regions bordering on the three central Chinese provinces of Sichuan, Hubei and Shaanxi. Known as the "White Lotus Rebellion," it took Manchu armies three years to suppress the rebellious tax protesters.

On the eve of this rebellion, with the Manchu Court in Beijing still basking in its traditional self-satisfaction, the reigning emperor Qianlong received a high-level trade mission sent by King George III of England. The year was 1793, and the occasion for the mission was the Qianlong emperor's 83rd birthday.

Led by Lord George Macartney of Ireland, the British mission was tasked with negotiating a treaty with the Manchu government, one that would permit British merchants to establish a permanent commercial presence in Beijing and grant them freedom to engage in trade in a number of other Chinese coastal cities.

To secure Qianlong's blessing, the British envoy lavished a number of valuable tributary gifts upon him, including ornate mechanical clocks, telescopes, cannon and assorted engineering instruments that were among the most prized fruits of the newly-blossoming English Industrial Revolution.

The record shows that despite Lord Macartney's lavish gifts, he got off on the wrong foot altogether with the Qianlong emperor. For one thing, Macartney insisted on being received with the august title of "imperial envoy," while his Chinese hosts would only acknowledge him only as a common "bearer of tribute."

For another thing, as a product of the European Enlightenment and an emissary of the British Imperial sovereign, Lord Macartney refused to perform the customary, self-deprecating ceremonial kowtow—consisting of three kneelings and nine prostrations—when he approached the emperor. Adding insult to injury, Macartney reportedly dismissed the Manchu emperor's reciprocal gift of a large piece of Chinese jade as a "worthless rock."

Though admittedly amused by the English gifts, Qianlong was nonetheless skeptical of their importance. In a written response to King George's request for "normalized" trade relations, the Son of Heaven noted, rather matter-of-factly, that

> The Celestial Court has pacified the four seas. ... [T]he virtue and prestige of the Celestial dynasty having spread far and wide, the kings of myriad nations come by land and sea with all sorts of precious things. Consequently there is nothing we lack.

Pointing out that no foreigners had ever been permitted to establish a permanent commercial presence in the Imperial capital, let alone enjoy equal standing at the Manchu court, Qianlong dismissed out of hand the British request for a trade mission. His rebuttal was cocky and condescending, to say the least:

> Being so rich in products of all kinds, China has no need of foreign trade. Traditionally people of European nations who wished to render some service under the Celestial Court have been permitted to come to the capital. But after their arrival they are obliged to wear Chinese court costumes, [they] are placed in a certain residence, and they are never allowed to return to their own countries. This is the established rule.

Referring to Britain dismissively as a small island "far away in a remote corner of the earth," the Chinese emperor scolded the British sovereign for his apparent ignorance of Chinese law, and for presuming to take advantage of the hospitality accorded by the Celestial Empire.

> Your envoy's extraordinary requests indicate clearly that many of you Westerners have failed to appreciate our kindness and generosity. ... Your envoy's requests, if granted, would not only constitute a violation of Chinese law but [would] serve no useful purpose for England as well. Knowing how I feel about this, you must abide by my wishes without fail, so both of our peoples may continue to enjoy the blessing of peace. (Dun J. Li, ed., *Modern China: From Mandarin to Commissar*, pp. 41–44.)

This remarkable imperial edict, with its veiled threat, written shortly before the close of the 18th century, at a time when Chinese imperial potency was already beginning to fray around the edges, was in many ways emblematic of China's famous Middle Kingdom Complex—a constellation of attitudes marked by extreme cultural self-satisfaction, economic insularity, military complacency and, above all, a xenophobic contempt for all things barbarian—i.e., foreign. (The two terms were used virtually interchangeably in late imperial China.)

The product of a millennium of economic, cultural, military and institutional superiority, the Middle Kingdom Complex persisted, even as growing evidence of imperial decay became harder and harder to conceal.

(Poor King George! Just a few years after surrendering the American colonies to the independence army of George Washington, the unfortunate British sovereign suffered the further indignity of being rapped on the knuckles like an errant schoolboy by the Chinese Son of Heaven. Small wonder George eventually went mad!)

Though history records that Lord Macartney's mission returned to Britain empty-handed, with precious little to show for having endured Qianlong's humiliating imperial scolding, this was not the end of the story. For with signs of peasant tax protest growing stronger, and with the illicit opium trade increasing unabated, the Manchu dynasty faced a dual crisis of fiscal liquidity and social stability.

The dawning of the 19th century was thus fraught with danger and uncertainty for the Son of Heaven. Notwithstanding Qianlong's haughty and heavy-handed hubris, the Chinese empire found itself sliding dangerously into debt, into denial and, ultimately, into sharp decline. Next time, we will look at the Chinese emperor's urgent efforts to curtail the rising opium trade, and thus halt the Manchu dynasty's accelerating fiscal woes.

As we shall see, however, Chinese claims of Celestial pre-eminence were no longer sufficient to intimidate British opium traders. And when imperial officials in 1839 seized and destroyed more than 20,000 chests of British opium, weighing 1,300 tons, the British Crown responded with a show of military force.

Thus began the First Opium War; and thus ended more than a millennium of Chinese supremacy.

Next time: Barbarians at the Gate.

Barbarians at the Gate, 1800–1860
Lecture 3

> I have heard that the smoking of opium is ... strictly forbidden by your country. ... Why do you let it be passed on to the harm of other countries?
> —Lin Zexu's letter to Queen Victoria in 1839

The British increasingly flouted Chinese law by smuggling larger and larger quantities of opium into the Middle Kingdom. By 1820, opium had surpassed all other commodities as China's chief import. The main port of entry was Canton, on China's southeast coast. As Chinese silver flowed out of the country in ever-larger quantities, the Manchu began executing Chinese opium traffickers.

By 1820, opium had surpassed all other commodities as China's chief import.

In 1839, the Chinese commissioner in Canton seized 20,000 British opium chests and dumped them into the sea. England demanded retribution for the seized opium, dispatching 16 steel-hulled warships and 4,000 soldiers to blockade Canton. Thus began the first of two **Opium Wars**. In 1841, after the Chinese refused to pay compensation and reopen seaports to British trade, British ships attacked Chinese fortifications and wooden warships along the coast. By 1842, British military superiority was clear, and China sued for peace, ending the First Opium War. The British extracted territorial, trade, and financial concessions from China.

By the late 1850s, French, Russian, and American merchants and missionaries joined England in demanding further concessions from China. In October 1856, Chinese soldiers seized a private British sailing vessel and charged the captain with engaging in coastal piracy. Thus began the Second Opium War. When the Manchu refused to provide additional financial indemnities and concessions, British and French forces invaded Beijing, destroying **Yuanmingyuan**. The wanton destruction of Yuanmingyuan remains today as a major symbol of the viciousness of Western aggression against China. The war ended in 1860, and China was forced sign the treaty they had rejected two years earlier as excessively humiliating, granting Europeans additional privileges and concessions. With the conclusion of the Treaty of Beijing, some 1,200 years of Chinese imperial supremacy effectively came to an end. China was now weakened and a tempting target—for both foreign predators and domestic rebels. ∎

Yuanmingyuan, the Manchu Summer Palace in Beijing. The palace was destroyed in 1860, during the Second Opium War.

Elliot, George (1784–1863): Admiral Elliot commanded the British naval force in Canton in 1839–1840. Seeking retribution for Lin Zexu's seizure of British opium, Elliot engaged his warships in a show of military force, precipitating the First Opium War.

Lin Zexu (1785–1850): The imperial commissioner appointed by the Manchu emperor in 1838. Lin sought to suppress the British opium trade in Canton (Guangzhou). His efforts triggered the First Opium War in 1839.

Qishan (1790–1854): The Manchu imperial envoy known as the "manager of barbarians." His diplomatic efforts to limit British military forays in 1840–1841 failed, and he suffered permanent exile.

Qiying (1787–1858): Qiying replaced Qishan as the chief Chinese "barbarian handler" in 1841. He employed dilatory tactics to slow British encroachments. Failing to deter Britain, he was recalled in disgrace.

Important Terms

Opium Wars: Wars launched by European powers in 1839 and 1856 to punish the Manchu government for restricting foreign commercial access to China.

Yuanmingyuan: The Manchu Summer Palace in Beijing, which was destroyed by the British and the French in 1860.

Suggested Reading

Hsü, *The Rise of Modern China.*

Pomeranz, *The Great Divergence.*

Spence, *The Search for Modern China.*

Wakeman, *Strangers at the Gate.*

Waley, *The Opium War through Chinese Eyes.*

Lecture 3: Barbarians at the Gate, 1800–1860

1. What role did opium play in the 19th-century subjugation of China by the West?

2. How did Chinese court officials deal with "barbarian" incursions in the period from 1830 to 1860?

Barbarians at the Gate, 1800–1860
Lecture 3—Transcript

In the last lecture, we previewed the forces that ultimately brought down the Manchu dynasty. This time, we'll look at how the opium trade contributed to the dynastic decline.

As China's fiscal situation worsened in the first few decades of the 19th century, foreign commercial pressures continued to mount.

European traders—and in particular, British traders—were growing increasingly dissatisfied with the commercial rules and restrictions unilaterally imposed by the Manchu court. Just who were these haughty Chinese? Did they not know that Britannia, conqueror of the once mighty Napoleon, now ruled the waves?

Evidently they didn't. Rebuffed in their efforts to negotiate a trade agreement with China, the British increasingly flouted Chinese law by smuggling larger and larger quantities of opium into the Middle Kingdom. By 1820, opium had surpassed all other items of trade as China's chief import.

As the opium flowed in, the silver flowed out. By the mid 1820s, China's overall trade balance, which had been heavily favorable throughout the 18th century, began to turn sharply negative. Between 1831 and 1833, nearly 10 million *taels* of silver flowed out of China (worth almost $14 million at the prevailing exchange rate).

In 1838, an official Manchu estimate placed the number of opium addicts in China somewhere between 2 and 10 million, a figure that reportedly included up to one-fourth of the country's civil servants. A one-day supply of opium in the 1830s cost roughly half the daily wage of a Chinese laborer; and by the mid-'30s, British merchants were netting roughly $18 million a year from the opium trade. Remember, these are 1830s prices. Small wonder the British parliament showed little enthusiasm for curtailing the opium traffic.

But for the Manchu dynasty, it was a different story altogether. Alarmed by the growing prevalence of opium addiction and by the hemorrhaging of silver from the imperial treasury, the Manchu court redoubled its efforts to stamp out the drug trade.

In 1836, the emperor ordered the provincial governor-general in Canton in south China to crack down hard on the sale and use of opium. Over the next two years, the governor imprisoned more than 2,000 Chinese opium dealers, smugglers, and users; in addition, there were daily reports of addicts being publicly executed.

In 1839 the Manchu emperor appointed a new commissioner to oversee the suppression of the Canton drug trade. His name was Lin Zexu. Lin Zexu pursued a policy to deal aggressively with all domestic participants in the opium cycle, while at the same time treating the foreign suppliers of the poisonous drug with a certain amount of leniency and circumspection. Aware of Britain's growing global power and prestige, Lin Zexu hoped to avoid an open conflict, if possible.

Writing to Queen Victoria in 1839, Lin cleverly cited Christianity's own golden rule in an effort to shame the British sovereign into stemming the cultivation, manufacture, and sale of opium:

> I have heard that the smoking of opium is ... strictly forbidden by your country. ... Why do you let it be passed on to the harm of other countries? Suppose there were people from another country who carried opium for sale to England and seduced your people into buying and smoking it; certainly your honorable ruler would deeply hate it and be bitterly aroused. ... Naturally you would not wish to give unto others what you yourself do not want.

There is no record of the British sovereign responding to Commissioner Lin's letter.

In pursuit of his goal of ridding Canton of all opium, Lin Zexu in 1839 ordered all foreigners in the city to surrender their stores of opium within three days; and in addition, he ordered them to sign a pledge that they would never again traffic in the drug.

Violation of this pledge was to be punishable by death. In a gesture intended to sweeten his ultimatum, Commissioner Lin offered a token reward of five and a half pounds of Chinese tea for every opium chest turned over by the foreign merchants.

When the foreigners ignored the commissioner's deadline, Lin threatened to execute two opium merchants. In response, the British reluctantly surrendered more than 1,000 chests (about 75 tons) of opium—which was only around two percent or so of all the opium that was currently stockpiled in Canton's warehouses.

Dissatisfied with the British response, Lin Zexu ratcheted up the pressure. He blockaded a key British trading firm, confining its 350 foreign occupants to the factory compound.

The siege lasted for six weeks, ending only when British merchants agreed to turn over 20,000 additional chests of opium, weighing approximately 1,300 tons—more than two and a half million pounds.

In a classic display of imperial potency, Commissioner Lin's ceremonial destruction of the British opium was carried out in the presence of several high Chinese court officials and foreign dignitaries.

The opium was first dumped into three massive open trenches, each lined with large quantities of salt and lime, where it was then covered with two feet of water. The mixture was then stirred thoroughly, and the resulting slurry was flushed into a nearby creek, where the currents eventually washed it out to sea. Repeating the process several times, it took 500 workers 22 days to complete the destruction of the British opium.

While Commissioner Lin was celebrating his triumph over the opium lords, British merchants were planning countermeasures of their own.

They sent a petition to Queen Victoria's prime minister, Lord Palmerston, urging the British government to demand full compensation for the seized opium. In London and Manchester, a groundswell of patriotic opinion arose, demanding firm governmental action to uphold the trading rights of British merchants abroad—and to sternly repay the deep Chinese insult to British pride.

Amid this rising tide of jingoistic self-righteousness, few British thought to question the propriety—or to note the stunning hypocrisy—of demanding the right to trade freely on foreign markets a substance whose cultivation, sale, and use were punishable by death at home.

Responding to mounting public pressures, in October 1839 Lord Palmerston sent an expeditionary force to blockade Canton's harbor. The force consisted of 16 warships, four armed steamers, 27 transport ships, and 4,000 British soldiers.

The First Opium War was underway; and imperial China would never be the same again.

The British fleet commander, Admiral George Elliot, arrived in Canton bearing a list of Her Majesty's demands. These included: first, full replacement of the destroyed opium (or fair market compensation for it); second, full satisfaction for the "indignities" suffered by British subjects during the Opium seizure incident; third, assurances of the future personal safety of British subjects in China; fourth, a permanent grant of one or more Chinese coastal islands to Great Britain; fifth, the abolition of China's centuries-old trade monopoly in Canton; and finally, repayment of all debts incurred by British merchants as a result of Commissioner Lin's actions.

Pending satisfaction of these demands, Admiral Elliot was instructed to extend his Canton blockade to all the principal ports of coastal China, so as to fully impress the Chinese with Britain's might.

Seeing for themselves the potency of the British warships, with their superior design, their steel-reinforced hulls, their fast cruising speeds, and their powerful artillery shells, the Manchus blinked first.

Having been at peace for a hundred years, China's coastal defenses were badly neglected. Many of the largest cannon were rusted out, having last been used at the end of the Ming dynasty, 200 years earlier; by the same token, the ships of the imperial navy were hopelessly inferior, consisting mostly of wooden warjunks. Recognizing the futility of combat, the Manchus stalled for time.

As the British fleet extended its blockade of China's coast in the fall of 1840, Lin Zexu was removed as imperial commissioner for Canton.

Blamed for failing to deter the British advance, Lin became a convenient scapegoat for the declining fortunes of the Manchu dynasty. For all his patriotic bravura in seizing and destroying two and a half million pounds of British opium, he was rewarded with exile in the remote Chinese northwest territory that is today's Xinjiang Province.

Lin Zexu's replacement, a Manchu imperial envoy named Qishan, now switched to softer tactics. Seeking to ingratiate himself with Admiral Elliot and his staff officers, he agreed to meet the British fleet commander near the mouth of the Yangzi River.

Bearing the official title of "manager of barbarians," Qishan was extremely courteous, even deferential, to the British commander.

Employing flattery and cajolery, he convinced Elliot that the emperor had dispatched an emissary to Canton with instructions to thoroughly investigate British grievances; and he promised that serious negotiations would begin once a determination of the facts had been made. Taking Qishan at his word, Admiral Elliot halted his fleet's advance and reversed its course, returning to Canton.

But Qishan had been bluffing, stalling for time. No Manchu envoy was en route. And in consequence, the credulous Admiral George Elliot was removed from his command. But in an ironic twist of events, the admiral was replaced by his younger, more impetuous cousin, Captain Charles Elliot.

As expected, Charles proved more hard-nosed than his cousin George. And shortly after assuming command, he ratcheted up Britain's demands to include, among other things, permanent British possession of a small Chinese island at the mouth of the Pearl River, called *Xianggang*, or "fragrant harbor." Today, this small island is more familiarly known by its Cantonese name, *Hong Kong*. (Small island indeed!)

When the "manager of barbarians" Qishan balked at Captain Elliot's terms and conditions, Elliot ordered his ships, in a show of force, to destroy a Chinese fortress at Quanbi, southwest of Canton. Qishan's confidence was badly shaken, and he was forced to draft a concessionary document in which he agreed to most of Captain Elliot's demands.

(By this time in the course, most of you will be struggling with the pronunciation of Chinese words and names. This is indeed tricky business. Chinese is a notoriously difficult language, both to pronounce and to render into Romanized spelling, and most people have a hard time remembering Chinese names at first. To assist in this task, you may want to refer to the glossary in the guidebook included with this course.)

The concessionary document drafted by Qishan, at Captain Charles Elliott's insistence, was known as the Quanbi Convention. Its main provisions were first, the permanent cession of Hong Kong Island to Great Britain; second, a cash indemnity of $6 million in silver to be paid to the British; third, equal standing to be given to British and Chinese officials in all business dealings; and fourth, the reopening of Canton to foreign trade.

Having drafted this document under duress, the distraught Qishan delayed signing it. Playing for time, he proposed to submit it to the emperor for approval.

But the Manchu emperor was enraged by the terms of the proposed treaty, which he viewed as a wholesale capitulation to the British; and he refused to sign it. Indeed, he was so angry with Qishan for drafting such a defeatist document that he recalled his chief manager of barbarians to Beijing—in chains—to stand trial for treason. Qishan was subsequently sentenced to death, though his sentence was later commuted to permanent exile.

In any event, the emperor's repudiation of the Quanbi Convention in January 1841 ushered in a new stage in the Opium War. The impulsive Captain Elliot was ordered to relinquish his command to a more senior British officer, the very hawkish Sir Henry Pottinger.

But before Pottinger could reach China to relieve Elliot of his command, the captain, seeking a measure of redemption, boldly undertook a fresh military offensive on his own initiative. In February of 1841 his soldiers captured a series of strategic Chinese fortresses at the mouth of the Pearl River near Canton. He then laid siege to Canton itself, trapping thousands of Chinese fighters in the process. Eventually, Elliott agreed to release the trapped soldiers in exchange for $6 million in ransom.

With the arrival of Sir Henry Pottinger in the summer of 1841, the third and final stage of the Opium War began. The British fleet now sailed north, occupying the port city of Amoy, in Fujian Province, as well as a series of strategic islands and fortresses near the mouth of the Yangzi River. In June of 1842 Shanghai fell to the British fleet. Britain now commanded all maritime access to the southeast coast of China.

Thoroughly defeated, the Manchu emperor decided to cut his losses. He instructed Qishan's successor to negotiate a settlement. When the resulting Treaty of Nanking was signed aboard Pottinger's flagship on August 29, 1842, it represented an almost unimaginably humiliating reversal of fortune for the once proud and mighty Manchu dynasty.

Under the treaty's terms, China not only consented to pay an indemnity of $21 million in silver to Britain (which was far more than the British had demanded just a year earlier), but also agreed to open five coastal cities to British commerce and residency: These were Canton, Amoy (later became known as Xiamen), Fuzhou, Ningbo, and Shanghai.

In addition, the longstanding imperial Chinese trade monopoly was abolished; and Hong Kong Island, a traditional waystation for British merchants en route to Canton, was permanently ceded to Great Britain.

Under a supplemental treaty signed a year later, in 1843, a uniform system of low import duties replaced the punitively high tariffs traditionally imposed on British goods by Chinese customs officials.

Adding insult to injury, British citizens were now granted extraterritorial privileges while residing in Chinese ports.

This meant that Brits were exempt from prosecution under Chinese law.

And finally, Great Britain was granted "Most-Favored Nation" status, which meant that henceforth China was legally obligated to extend to Britain any and all privileges or concessions that might subsequently be granted to other foreign countries.

Having been forced to concede huge chunks of Chinese state sovereignty to the bellicose British, the new chief Chinese barbarian handler, Viceroy Qiying, adopted a policy of appeasement to deal with the British military commander. Defending his approach against criticism by imperial hard-liners, Qiying argued that he was flattering the barbarians precisely in order to get them to lower their guard and, ultimately, to submit to Chinese authority.

In the event, Qiying's soft tactics failed to produce any noticeable change in the foreigners' behavior. On the contrary, Western political and military encroachments increased steadily.

Having failed to manage the barbarians effectively, Qiying was ousted within a year by a group of xenophobic imperial war-hawks. These hard-liners now called on all patriotic Chinese in the treaty ports to stand up to the perfidious "foreign devils." Stirred into action by such patriotic rhetoric, crowds of angry Chinese launched a series of vitriolic attacks against foreigners in Canton and other coastal cities.

In the decade that followed, Western pressures on China increased ceaselessly. Emboldened by the ease with which they were able to gain favorable trade and territorial concessions, foreigners now sought to revise the Treaty of Nanking, to allow them even wider commercial and diplomatic privileges within China.

The new demands, which were a product of joint British, French and American collaboration, included the opening of additional ports to foreign commerce; the establishment of permanent Western ministries in Beijing; and additional across-the-board reductions in import tariffs.

As the frequency and intensity of hostile encounters between Chinese and Westerners increased, the situation became more volatile. All that was required was a single spark.

That spark came in October 1856, when a detachment of Chinese soldiers seized a private British sailing vessel, the *Arrow*, which lay at anchor in Canton harbor. The *Arrow*'s captain, ironically, a Chinese national, was charged with engaging in coastal piracy. British officials rejected the accusation and demanded a formal apology, along with full financial restitution.

When their demands were rejected, the British commenced a naval bombardment of Canton's coastal defenses. The residents of Canton retaliated, burning down several foreign factories. The Second Opium War had begun.

Unlike the war of 1839–1842, which was exclusively a British affair, the Second Opium War involved joint Franco-British military action. In addition, both America and Russia, while not involved in the actual fighting, declared solidarity with the Europeans, justifying this on the grounds that Western civilization had to be defended against the lawless Chinese. As the American envoy William Reed put it in 1857, "The powers of Western civilization must insist on what they know to be their rights, and give up the dream of dealing with China as a power to which any ordinary rules apply."

In December of 1857 a joint Anglo-French force seized Canton. They also captured the local imperial viceroy, carting him off to India in chains, the fourth chief barbarian manager to suffer a cruel fate after failing to halt the advance of the foreigners. (One might even conclude from this that becoming the top Manchu dynasty negotiator was not a particularly promising career move for ambitious imperial officials in mid-19th century China.)

Once they had secured control of Canton, the Europeans sent a note to Beijing, demanding revision of the existing treaties. When their note was returned with a dilatory request for a cooling off period, a joint Franco-British naval force sailed northward.

In a near-replay of Sir Henry Pottinger's northern expedition of 1841, in May of 1858 the Europeans laid deadly siege to the key Chinese forts at Dagu, guarding the entrance to the strategic northeast Chinese city of Tianjin. Belatedly, Beijing now agreed to negotiate.

In the late spring of 1858 the victorious French and British, with the Americans and Russians as their silent partners, drafted a new treaty calling for the opening of 10 more Chinese ports to Western commerce (including this time the island of Taiwan as well as the major Yangzi River port cities of Nanjing and Hankow.)

Additional provisions included permission for nationals of the four countries to reside permanently in Beijing, and the right of foreign warships to enter any port where Western nationals were conducting business. Indemnities totaling 6 additional million taels of silver were paid to the British and French. Western missionaries were to be permitted to travel and proselytize freely anywhere in China. And in a final display of Western arrogance, the sale of opium—unmentioned in the first Opium War—was made legal in China.

Once again, however, the Manchu court balked at accepting such a humiliating document; and they categorically rejected Britain's insistence on signing the treaty in Beijing's Forbidden City, an act which would have set a precedent for foreigners to freely enter the Chinese imperial capital.

The ensuing stalemate lasted 18 months, and was finally broken in the summer of 1860, when a joint British-French expeditionary force, consisting of 41 warships, 143 transport ships, and 18,000 troops, sailed northward from Canton.

Their first objective was to neutralize the Chinese forts at Dagu, which they accomplished with dispatch. Once Dagu's guns were spiked, the expeditionary force sailed upriver to Tianjin unimpeded, where the troops disembarked and proceeded to fight their way to the imperial capital of Beijing, 90 miles to the northwest. In a major show of force, the Franco-British army entered the capital city and proceeded to sack the Imperial Summer Palace at Yuanming Yuan, burning to the ground its magnificent constellation of 200 ornate palaces, pavilions, courtyards, and gardens.

The wanton destruction of the Summer Palace remains today as a major symbol of the viciousness of Western aggression against China. (As a historical footnote, although Yuanming Yuan remained undisturbed and in ruins for the next 120 years, over the past decade or so it has been meticulously restored to its original specifications as a major tourist attraction. But one section of the Old Summer Palace remains unreconstructed. According to a placard erected on the site by the state committee in charge of restoration, a group of European-style palaces in Yuanming Yuan will remain in a state of ruin, as "irrefutable evidence of imperialist powers destroying human civilizations." The government's stated intent in preserving the dilapidated remains was to "encourage the Chinese people to work hard to make the nation strong.")

History buffs might also note that the sacking of the Summer Palace in 1860 was carried out on the orders of the Eighth Earl of Elgin, who was the chief British minister at the time. If that name rings a bell, it is because the Eighth Earl of Elgin was the son of the notorious Seventh Earl of Elgin, who is best known for having looted the ancient Elgin Marbles from Greece early in the 19th century. (Quite a family, those Elgins.)

Soon after the sacking of the Summer Palace, the Manchus signed the treaty they had rejected as excessively humiliating two years earlier. Enacted in Beijing, in October of 1860, its terms were essentially the same as before, with two significant additions. First, the British and French now increased their demand for monetary compensation from 6 million taels of silver to 16 million (worth approximately $22 million). And second, Britain now wrested away from China the Kowloon Peninsula, incorporating it into the newly prosperous Crown Colony of Hong Kong.

With the conclusion of the Treaty of Beijing, some 1200 years of imperial Chinese supremacy effectively came to an end. China was now a humbled and bleeding giant. Although its rulers struggled in vain to maintain a semblance of their former pride and majesty, a weakened Chinese state provided a tempting target for foreign predators and domestic rebels alike. In the next lecture, we shall see how rising peasant unrest in China's rural hinterland further contributed to the fatal weakening of the Manchu dynasty.

Rural Misery and Rebellion, 1842–1860
Lecture 4

> The ruling elite is like the wind, the little people are like the grass. When the wind blows, the grass bends.
>
> — Traditional proverb

A longside the Western military humiliation of China, internal disturbances were emerging in China's rural heartland. The Malthusian crisis begun in the 18th century was intensifying, with tens of millions of farmers driven into debt. Chinese farmers were heavily taxed and intimidated by district magistrates. If a magistrate ignored their petitions, farmers' only recourse was rebellion.

Peasant rebellions were not new in China, and when a series of devastating floods occurred in the early 1850s in North China's Yellow River basin,

Peasants in rural China faced a mounting agrarian crisis in the mid-1800s.

a major uprising—the **Nian Rebellion**—broke out in several provinces. At almost the same time, an even larger rebellion broke out in South China, where a charismatic but mentally unstable young Chinese religious scholar named **Hong Xiuquan** led an uprising of impoverished farmers. At the height of the **Taiping Rebellion** in the mid-1850s, its rebel armies controlled seven provinces and had half a million fighters. When the Taipings tried to conquer North China, their advance failed due to their overconfidence, logistical overextension, and severe winter weather. Weakened by growing internal divisions and rivalries, the Taiping rebels were ultimately subdued in the early 1860s by a combined force of elite imperial troops and European-trained military units.

With the Taipings decisively defeated and Western troops gone from Beijing, the Manchu dynasty would attempt a revitalization. But time would show that agrarian rebellion, combined with the encroachment of Western powers, had fatally weakened the Manchu's hold on the empire. ■

Names to Know

Hong Xiuquan (1814–1864): The charismatic founder and delusional leader of the Taiping Rebellion (1850–1864). Hong believed himself to be the brother of Jesus Christ and ruled the Taiping Heavenly Kingdom until his death in 1864.

Ward, Frederick Townsend (1831–1862): An American soldier of fortune hired to recruit and train foreign mercenaries to help suppress the Taiping Rebellion. Ward was fatally wounded at the battle of Cixi in 1862.

Zeng Guofan (1811–1872): The commander of the imperial Hunan army that defeated the Taiping Rebellion. Zeng later became a leading figure in the Self-Strengthening movement.

Important Terms

laobaixing: Ordinary Chinese people (literally, "old hundred names").

Nian Rebellion (1853–1868): A massive peasant rebellion triggered by the extensive collapse of imperial flood-control works and subsequent famine in the Yellow River region.

Taiping Heavenly Kingdom (1853–1864): A rebel state encompassing several provinces and tens of millions of uprooted peasants, with its capital in Nanjing. Founded by Christian zealot Hong Xiuquan.

Taiping Rebellion (1850–1864): A rebellion begun in Southeast China that was an even greater threat to Manchu rule than the Nian Rebellion.

Chesneaux, *Peasant Revolts in China.*

Hsü, *The Rise of Modern China.*

Pomeranz, *The Great Divergence.*

Spence, *God's Chinese Son.*

————, *The Search for Modern China.*

Wakeman, *Strangers at the Gate.*

Waley, *The Opium War through Chinese Eyes.*

Wright, *The Last Stand of Chinese Conservatism.*

Questions to Consider

1. Why did rural poverty spread so widely in 19th-century China?

2 How did rural unrest contribute to the downfall of the Manchu dynasty?

Rural Misery and Rebellion, 1842–1860
Lecture 4—Transcript

Last time, we saw how Western "barbarians" forced open China's doors in the middle decades of the 19th century. In this lecture we'll see how, coinciding with this Western assault, a mounting agrarian crisis served to foster peasant rebellion in China. Taken together, these two powerful forces—assault from abroad and rebellion from within—served to fatally weaken the Manchu dynasty.

In imperial China, the rural population lived in clustered villages, each of which had its own distinctive local customs, festivals, deities, and temples. Clans (made up of multi-generational, extended family units based on common ancestral lineage) were the social cement that bound rural villages into cohesive communities.

In ancient times there were approximately 100 to 150 distinct, Chinese lineages, each with its own family surname—with names like Wang, Chen, Li, and Zhang being the most common Chinese equivalents of our own Smith, Jones, Johnson, and Williams. Right down to the present day, whenever Chinese refer to "ordinary folk," the term they use, *laobaixing*, literally means "old hundred-names."

Despite the pervasive Confucian norms of patriarchal authority and reciprocal rights and obligations, which we discussed in an earlier lecture, social relations were not always peaceful and harmonious within traditional village communities. For one thing, within a single village there might be two, three, or even more lineages living in close proximity. And it was not uncommon for disputes to break out among them over such things as property boundaries, water rights, tax obligations, and the like.

There were also substantial social class distinctions both between and within lineage groups. The primary measure of socio-economic status in imperial China was land ownership, which was highly uneven in distribution. In some parts of China it was not uncommon for as much as 70 or 80 percent of all land in a village to be owned by a few landlord families, who in turn might either hire laborers to work the land or rent out small parcels to tenant farmers, who were sometimes their own kinsmen.

Notwithstanding the blood ties that sometimes existed between landlords and tenants, land rents commonly exceeded half the family's annual harvest, and were often supplemented by a series of customary fees and corvée labor obligations.

Peasants were thus economically dependent upon members of the landlord-gentry class, who were called (not for nothing) *dizhu*, or "masters of the land." Even those peasants who were otherwise self-sufficient, and who normally earned a sustainable livelihood from farming their own land, were often dependent upon landlords, as dispute mediators, as money-lenders, and as tax intermediaries, and middlemen in their relations with district administrators.

For more than 1,000 years, rural administrative authority was delegated by the imperial court to appointed magistrates, who were recruited from the ranks of degree-holding civil servants. Insofar as district magistrates were the sole formal agents of imperial authority within their jurisdictions, they were "little emperors" in their own right.

Within each district, which generally encompassed several hundred villages, the power of the magistrate was absolute and unchecked. As a well-known traditional proverb put it, "the ruling elite is like the wind, the little people are like the grass. When the wind blows, the grass bends" (Lun Yu, XII:19)

To help administer the functions of local governance—tax collection, law enforcement, the observance of ancestral rituals, record keeping, water management, labor and military conscription, and so forth—each magistrate was entitled to bring with him from his home district, at governmental expense, up to eight or 10 lesser degree-holding scholars who served as secretaries and financial advisors. Ten or more additional district functionaries, mainly clerks, scribes, and notaries, were paid out of the magistrate's own funds.

In addition to these formal agents of district administration, up to several hundred underlings were informally retained by the magistrate in each district, without official pay or title; these latter personnel, including such people as gatekeepers, attendants, runners, jailers, and night watchmen, were expected to earn their keep through side payments collected from their unofficial clients.

Such payments were called "cumshaw" (or "thank-you money," from the original Chinese term *ganxie*, meaning "many thanks"). And they were collected for a variety of services performed on behalf of village residents. The most important of these underling services, most of the time, was that of lobbying district officials on behalf of local residents who needed a favorable judgment or dispensation. Alternatively, villagers would sometimes employ the underlings to help shield them from scrutiny by local officials.

Because more than 90 percent of peasants were illiterate, the magistrate's underlings were often paid to read out official notices and documents, and to write petitions, appeals, and tax protests on behalf of village residents. Insofar as they earned a good deal of their income from such informal representations on behalf of the illiterate peasantry, they were sometimes called "litigation tricksters."

The underlings' place of business, the district headquarters, or *Yamen*, was often a beehive of activity, much of it only marginally legal or official in nature. For most district residents most of the time, the less they had to do with local officials, the better they liked it.

Because there was no administrative transparency or political accountability below the district level, villagers were extremely vulnerable to financial predation and physical intimidation by a magistrate's unscrupulous underlings. In such situations, their only recourse, if petitioning the magistrate failed, was rebellion.

For their part, magistrates were most likely to receive promotions if their districts remained peaceful and peasants voluntarily complied with their tax and corvée obligations. Thus, it was in a magistrate's own self-interest to, for example, have high crop yields in his district.

And this in turn, gave him an incentive, first, to ensure that the district's water works, roads and granaries were maintained in good order; second, to see that public safety was well preserved; and third, to keep exploitation of the peasants down to tolerable levels of discomfort.

If these three tasks were reasonably well performed, then a fourth and most important purpose would be served, namely, reducing the likelihood of peasant rebelliousness.

There can be little doubt that fear of peasant rebellion was a prime motivation for good governance at the district level, as well as a prime deterrent to egregious predation by the magistrate's underlings. Impose too heavy a burden, or exert too heavy a hand, and the peasants might rise up.

It was a precarious political equilibrium, to be sure; but in "normal" times, defined by fairly favorable weather, fairly stable crop yields, fairly effective tax collection and fairly minimal social outlawry, it was an equilibrium that could be sustained by an enlightened, self-interested district magistrate.

(For those who are interested in reading a lightly fictionalized account of a very real district magistrate in Ming dynasty China, I would highly recommend the "Judge Dee" mysteries written by Robert van Gulik.)

It was precisely in order to bolster local social stability that the ideology of neo-Confucianism was vigorously employed by imperial scholar-officials to define the relationship between district magistrates and ordinary villagers.

In the original Confucian social compact, the emperor was obligated to provide benevolent governance to "all under heaven" (*tianxia*) in exchange for unconditional fealty by his subjects. By the time of the Song dynasty, this same set of reciprocal obligations had been extended downward to district magistrates and their constituent village populations. In this manner, the villages below mirrored precisely the social order of the empire above.

Unhappily for the peace and tranquility of the district magistrates, the normal social equilibrium in rural China was subject to a variety of imbalances and disturbances, both natural and man-made. Such disturbances included catastrophic natural disasters; demographic instability (which we discussed in Lecture 2); a rise in predatory behavior by landlords, money-lenders, or a magistrate's local underlings; and the district government's neglect of water works and public granaries.

Any one of these disruptions alone could adversely affect social order in the countryside. In combination, they could generate sharp, sudden, and sometimes devastating shocks to the rural social and political order.

It was a combination of these conditions, compounded by the effects of Western commercial penetration that rendered China increasingly vulnerable to rural unrest in the first half of the 19th century. As Western countries inflicted humiliation after humiliation upon the once-proud Chinese empire, there were simultaneous rumblings of disturbance deep in the rural interior.

After years of grumbling discontent, farmers in many provinces, driven deeper into debt by the progressive devaluation of copper coins relative to silver specie, and unable to pay their taxes, stood at the brink of revolt. Beset by worsening fiscal woes and discredited by their inability to put an end to Western bullying, the Manchus began losing their grip on the countryside.

Rebellion was sparked by a series of natural disasters that began in the early 1850s. Among the worst of these was massive flooding of the Yangzi River, which caused the collapse of dykes along hundreds of miles of the river's densely populated middle reaches, from Chongqing in the west to Hankow east.

The Manchu government was slow to react, and when it did react, its flood relief efforts were meager and inadequate. Consequently, the government was widely blamed for the ensuing loss of life and for the deepening misery of the countryside.

A peasant rebellion followed. Lasting 15 years, the Nian Rebellion at its height engulfed parts of 16 Chinese provinces. The rebels, whose actions were neither centrally directed nor particularly well coordinated, launched frequent raids on rich merchants; they sacked the houses of landlords, executed local gentry and district officers, and opened up prison gates.

In the tradition of peasant brigands everywhere, they distributed confiscated goods to the poor; and they inscribed on their banners the words, "Kill the officials, kill the rich, spare the poor."

Although the Nian rebels employed military tactics and a code of conduct that in some ways foreshadowed Mao Zedong's strategy of "people's war" (about which more will be said in a later lecture), in the end their poorly organized, rag-tag peasant armies were unable to overcome the superior forces and firepower of the imperial army. Still, the very magnitude and duration of the Nian Rebellion—fifteen years—and the enormous cost of suppressing it, took a major toll upon an already weakened Manchu dynasty.

But the most serious internal threat to Manchu rule in the 19th century came not from the Nian rebels, but from the Taipings. The Taiping Rebellion had its origins in the increasing impoverishment of the *laobaixing*, the common people, of southeast China, principally in the two provinces of Guangdong and Guangxi. In these provinces, which comprised Canton's rural hinterland, the effects of the worsening fiscal and agrarian crises began to converge in the late 1840s as a mounting unemployment crisis hit the coastal ports.

Most severely affected were members of Canton's newly marginalized lumpenproletariat. Consisting of hundreds of thousands of coolies, boatmen and porters, their jobs were threatened when Canton lost its status as China's exclusive port of entry for foreign commerce. They were unemployed, and they were increasingly angry.

The leader of the Taipings was a Guangdong native named Hong Xiuquan. Son of a Hakka peasant family near Canton, Hong Xiuquan was an educated young man who four times took and four times failed the imperial civil service examination. After his fourth failure, in 1837, he experienced a nervous breakdown, in the course of which he had a series of visions in which, among other things, an old woman appeared, telling him that he was descended directly from God. He emerged from his delirium obsessed with the belief that he was the younger brother of Jesus Christ.

Hong first encountered Protestant missionaries in Canton during his youth; and he was already familiar with Christian teachings. Now he was driven by his new obsession. He set out to create his own church, with an eclectic blend of Judeo-Christian doctrine that combined elements of Old and New Testament gospel, seasoned with a generous helping of native Chinese mysticism. In the mid-1840s he began to preach his new faith in the remote mountains of Guangxi Province.

Where other disillusioned scholars dreamed of restoring the glory of the Ming dynasty of old, the charismatic Hong Xiuquan aspired to found a new dynasty of his own—which he did, in 1851. He named it, "Taiping Tianguo": the Heavenly Kingdom of Great Peace.

His followers were drawn from the downtrodden masses of the southeast. With rural impoverishment growing steadily, Hong welcomed into his "flock" increasing numbers of uprooted peasants, unemployed coolies, miners, demobilized soldiers, and other members of China's burgeoning underclass.

From the outset the Taiping Rebellion targeted the rich and powerful—landlords, gentry and imperial officials. When the rebels left their Guangxi mountain base and advanced northward toward the Yangzi valley, proselytizing as they went, they attracted a large following among the poor and disaffected.

Wearing their hair unbraided in defiance of the mandatory Manchu style of a single male pigtail, they vented their wrath against the wealthy and the influential. Rich merchants and landlords were put to death; tax registers, land deeds and loan records were burned, and government offices were sacked.

Marching northward through the south-central provinces of Hunan and Hupei, and thence down the Yangzi River, Hong Xiuquan established his

"Heavenly Capital" in Nanjing in 1853. En route to Nanjing, Hong's armies looted the key Yangzi River port of Hankow (today's Wuhan), where they seized 10,000 naval vessels, a million taels of silver, and a huge supply of grain and other provisions.

By this time, Hong's army numbered half a million men, and he effectively controlled a vast land area in central China that included most of Jiangxi, Fujian, Zhejiang, and Anhui provinces, as well as big chunks of Hunan, Hubei, and Jiangsu.

Foreshadowing a revolutionary innovation that would take place under Mao Zedong's rule 100 years later, one of Hong Xiuquan's first official decrees as self-declared emperor was the abolition of private land ownership. A devout (not to say obsessive) Christian, he mandated the destruction of traditional Confucian, Buddhist, and Daoist idols.

Ancestor worship was also outlawed, and men and women were decreed to be equal in all things. Reportedly, up to 100,000 women served in the armed forces of the Taiping Heavenly Kingdom.

After setting up his headquarters in Nanjing, Hong Xiuquan sent an army northward toward Beijing, the imperial capital. By 1854 Hong's forces had advanced as far as the outskirts of Tianjin, less than a hundred miles from Beijing. With the Manchu government in disarray due to the rising pressure of Western forces and the declining morale of the imperial court, it appeared for a time that the Taipings might actually take control of all of China.

But Tianjin was as far as the Taiping forces ever got. Overconfident, logistically overextended, and plagued by severe northern winter weather, they began to falter. In 1855 the expedition's top military commanders were captured and publicly executed by Manchu troops.

By 1856, internal dissention had broken out among Hong's allied military commanders in Nanjing. One local Taiping chieftain harbored ambitions to replace Hong as emperor. In an effort to undermine Hong's claim to be the brother of Jesus, he mimicked Hong's tactics of falling into a trance to "prove" that he enjoyed God's favor. The rebellious chieftain succeeded in recruiting thousands of followers, who honored him as the "Lord of Ten Thousand Years."

In the factional struggles that followed, the spirit and vigor of the Taiping movement were gradually sapped. Hong Xiuquan himself, though victorious over his ambitious rival, began indulging in dissolute behavior to distract him from his growing troubles. As morale deteriorated, the government began to drift, rudderless. And by 1860, the Taiping Heavenly Kingdom had run its course.

In the end, the Taiping's defeat was sealed by a particularly impressive imperial military officer by the name of Zeng Guofan. Zeng commanded the imperial Hunan army; and he was put in charge of operations against the Taipings in the spring of 1860, at almost the same time the British and French were preparing to sack the Summer Palace in Beijing.

With a loyal, well-trained fighting force of 120,000 troops, Zeng and his chief lieutenant, Li Hongzhang, attacked the Taipings at Shanghai and Suzhou, near the mouth of the Yangzi. After scoring impressive victories, they controlled most of Jiangsu Province.

Next they imposed an ever-tightening blockade around Nanjing itself, cutting off Hong Xiuquan's sources of supply. With food and provisions running low, Hong contemplated, and rejected out of hand, the prospect of surrendering to the imperial armies.

Toward the end of their campaign against the Taipings, Zeng Guofan and Li Hongzhang received military assistance from an unexpected and unlikely source, the Western powers. Initially sympathetic toward Hong Xiuquan because of his Christianity and his promise of expanded foreign trade, the British, French, and Americans soon found the Taipings, with their grandiose religious pretensions and their puritanical opposition to the use of opium, not to their liking.

Once the Western powers had tamed Manchu resistance by forcing upon them the humiliating "unequal treaties" of the 1840s, '50s and early '60s, there was little reason for foreigners to seek the overthrow of the dynasty. On the contrary, they now began to realize that their ability to extract further concessions from the Manchus depended largely on the continued survival of the weakened dynasty.

To assist the imperial forces of Zeng Guofan and Li Hongzhang to defeat the Taipings, an American "soldier of fortune" named Frederick Townsend Ward was hired by a wealthy Chinese banker to recruit foreign mercenaries into a new military unit. With 100 demobilized European officers and 200 Filipino seamen making up the mainstay of his new army, Ward supervised the training of 4,000 Chinese recruits, drilling them in European military procedure and supplying them with Western rifles. In 1861 the emperor bestowed on Ward's troops the title of the "Ever-Victorious Army." With that, the foreign-led mercenary forces joined the battle against the Taipings.

Ward's army won a number of battles in the lower Yangzi River region. But in September 1862 he was fatally wounded in battle. Shortly thereafter, a notorious British officer named Charles G. Gorden assumed command of the Ever-Victorious Army.

Leading his troops into battle with a walking stick, Gordon refused to allow his soldiers to loot captured cities, as was the Manchu custom. When a group of mercenaries mutinied, Gordon shot one of the ringleaders and threatened to shoot an additional mutineer every hour until the mutiny ended. It was over inside of an hour.

For his service to the Manchu empire in helping secure the final defeat of the Taipings, Gordon was promoted by the emperor to one of the highest ranks in the Chinese imperial army, and he was decorated with the Yellow Jacket of the Mandarinate. He also earned the sobriquet, "Chinese" Gordon.

For their part, generals Zeng Guofan and Li Hongzhang were also rewarded for their role in defeating the Taipings. Granted high imperial titles, the two men would later distinguish themselves as among the most able and respected Chinese scholar-statesmen of the late 19th century. Together, they played a vital role in fashioning the Manchu dynasty's strategic response to the challenge of Western domination—a response that we shall examine more closely in the next lecture.

As for Hong Xiuquan, after ruling out the possibility of surrender to his enemies, he committed suicide in his Nanjing capital on June 1, 1864. He was 52 years of age. His Taiping Heavenly Kingdom collapsed shortly thereafter.

With the Manchu government having absorbed a series of devastating internal and external shocks, it is perhaps surprising that the dynasty didn't collapse altogether after 1860.

But collapse it did not. With the Taipings now decisively defeated, and Western troops no longer breathing down the necks of the Manchu emperor in Beijing, the dynasty enjoyed something of a respite from foreign aggression.

Indeed, the decade and a half between 1862 and 1875 witnessed a substantial effort to revitalize the tottering dynasty under the reform-minded boy emperor, Tongzhi. Next time we shall examine the Tongzhi Restoration, which was marked by the first significant internal reform efforts of the 19th century, the Self-Strengthening Movement.

The Self-Strengthening Movement, 1860–1890
Lecture 5

> We should carefully watch and learn their superior techniques and also observe their shortcomings. ... If they abandon good relations and break their covenant, we would then have the weapons to oppose them.
>
> — Zeng Guofan, on studying the West

After the Second Opium War and the defeat of the Taiping and Nian rebellions, the faltering Manchu dynasty enjoyed a brief respite. In the early 1860s, scholars sought to redress Chinese vulnerability with respect to the European powers. China launched a series of initiatives aimed at adopting the techniques of Western science and industry while preserving Chinese culture.

Prince Gong's internal reforms, collectively known as the **Self-Strengthening movement**, were introduced to manage rural unrest and to learn from foreigners how to produce modern weapons. Indeed, by the mid-1870s, China was manufacturing thousands of small arms comparable to those used by Europeans.

But the reforms had unintended consequences: Young scholars sent abroad to study Western industrial technology returned and began advocating sweeping educational reforms, including the study of mathematics, astronomy, physics, chemistry, and foreign languages. This rankled many conservative Chinese Confucian scholars, who feared the loss of their traditional lifestyles and intellectual privileges. Within the Manchu court, resistance to reform was led by the powerful **Dowager Empress Cixi**, who conspired at every turn to undermine Prince Gong's proposed reforms.

With reform stalled, China's imperial decline continued unabated—now marked by a highly ambivalent relationship between China and the West, in which Chinese admiration of Western science, technology, and economic progress was offset by deep-seated resentment of Western aggression and bullying. Such ambivalence endured for over a century, flaring up periodically down to the present day.

Between 1860 and 1898, foreign powers established territorial enclaves in dozens of Chinese cities. Japan's more successful modernization and incorporation of Western technology would soon become a threat to the Middle Kingdom. ∎

Names to Know

Cixi (1835–1908): This archconservative dowager empress dominated Manchu court politics in the late 19th century. Operating behind the scenes, she effectively manipulated youthful emperors and undermined all efforts at reform.

Gong, Prince (1833–1898): The principal patron of the Self-Strengthening movement of the 1860s, Gong promoted educational reforms and foreign military technology, thereby running afoul of Cixi.

Important Term

Self-Strengthening movement (a.k.a. **Tongzhi Restoration**; 1862–1875): A reform movement initiated by Manchu Prince Gong, designed to defend China against foreigners by studying the secrets of Western military success.

Suggested Reading

Fenby, *Modern China.*

Hsü, *The Rise of Modern China.*

Spence, *God's Chinese Son.*

———, *The Search for Modern China.*

Teng and Fairbank, *China's Response to the West.*

Wakeman, *Strangers at the Gate.*

Wright, *The Last Stand of Chinese Conservatism.*

1. How did China's early modernizers understand the sources of Western military power?

2. What were the modernizers' prescriptions for overcoming Western technological superiority?

The Self-Strengthening Movement, 1860–1890
Lecture 5—Transcript

After defeating Hong Xiuquan and his Taiping rebels, the Manchus launched a series of initiatives aimed at reviving their tottering dynasty. Launched in the early 1860s, the revival effort was known variously as the "Self-Strengthening Movement" and the "Tongzhi Restoration" (so named after the young emperor Tongzhi, who ascended to the throne in 1862).

The Self-Strengthening Movement was spearheaded by Tongzhi's uncle, Prince Gong. Its centerpiece was a drive to copy the techniques of Western science and industry.

Toward this end, hundreds of Chinese students and scholars were sent abroad to study the secrets of Western military success. But at the same time, and rather contradictorily, their Manchu patrons tried desperately to preserve China's traditional civilization and culture against the onslaught of Westernization.

What they wanted, in short, was to graft modern Western industrial technology neatly onto China's existing Confucian institutions and values, without the former contaminating the latter. This would prove to be a very tall order indeed.

Prince Gong was an arrogant and highly ambitious man. And though he was widely disliked within the imperial court, he enjoyed the trust of his nephew, Tongzhi. With the emperor's backing, Gong initiated a series of profound reforms in domestic and foreign affairs.

In an effort to treat the underlying sources of rural unrest, which had fueled both the Nian and Taiping rebellions, substantial sums of money were appropriated by Prince Gong to repair damaged water works. Devastated farmlands were reclaimed and rehabilitated, and agricultural taxes were reduced or even, in some cases, forgiven altogether.

To deal with growing popular resentment against corrupt officials, a new code of conduct was introduced for civil servants, stressing honesty, personal austerity, and humble demeanor. And to aid in the recruitment of men of practical talent into the imperial civil service, the examinations were revamped to lay greater stress on problem-solving abilities rather than mere memorization of the Confucian classics of antiquity.

In foreign affairs, Prince Gong recognized the importance of modernizing his country's dealings with the outside world. No longer assuming the traditional airs of Middle Kingdom supremacy and invincibility, Gong was well aware of the superiority of Western military technology. To deal with this "weapons gap" he adopted a policy of sending the best and brightest of China's young scholar-officials abroad, to learn the secrets of Western military technology.

Along with Prince Gong, two other officials who were prominent in the movement to learn Western technologies of warfare were (our old friends) Zeng Guofan and Li Hongzhang, military heroes of the suppression of the Taiping Rebellion.

Zeng Guofan was the more senior of the two and the more philosophical of the two. Zeng believed that Western military technology could be comfortably grafted upon China's traditional values and institutions to create an invincible, powerful state. Zeng's disciples called his strategy "using the barbarians to control the barbarians"or, what we might call, "beating them at their own game."

The strategy was outlined in a series of letters Zeng wrote to his former student, Li Hongzhang:

> If we wish to find a method of self-strengthening, we should … regard learning to make explosive shells and steamships and other instruments as the work of the first importance. If only we could possess the superior techniques [of the Westerners'], then we would have the means to return their favors when they are obedient, and … to avenge our grievances when they are disloyal.

> We should carefully watch and learn their superior techniques and also observe their shortcomings. … If they abandon good relations and break their covenant, we should then have the weapons to oppose them.

Like his mentor, Zeng Guofan, Li Hongzhang believed in the superiority of China's traditional civilization and culture. In his view, the only thing China needed to regain its past glory was modern weapons. Li believed that the principal reason for this "weapons gap" lay in the traditional habits of scholarly arrogance and self-indulgence that prevailed within the imperial Mandarinate.

Li Hongzhang noted that Western scholars and officials "use mathematics for reference and exert their energies in deep thinking to make daily increases and alterations" in their weapons. The Western ethos of constant innovation was in contrast to the stagnant self-satisfaction of China's traditional scholars, who in the words of these reformers, sit around "indulging in the inveterate habit of remembering [poetic] stanzas and sentences and practicing fine model calligraphy."

Entrusted by the emperor to supervise the manufacture of European-style weapons, Li Hongzhang established China's first modern arsenals at Ningbo and Foochow. By the mid-1870s these arsenals were producing thousands of small arms generally comparable in quality to the breach-loading Remington rifles used by Europeans.

An ambitious naval shipbuilding program was also launched under Li Hongzhang's direction. But the program was beset from the outset by a series of major obstacles, including a lack of raw materials and insufficient technical talent. There was also rampant corruption in the awarding of construction contracts and in the hiring of overpaid and incompetent foreign advisors. Consequently, naval construction during the Tongzhi Restoration proved to be slow, costly, and wholly inefficient.

Prior to the Tongzhi Restoration, China's Manchu rulers had never recognized other countries as diplomatic equals but only as tributary or vassal states. Consequently, they never felt the need to have a government department devoted exclusively to foreign affairs. The folly of this traditional mode of dealing with Western powers was clearly demonstrated in the diplomatic debacles suffered by a succession of imperial barbarian managers in the course of two opium wars.

To remedy this weakness, Prince Gong established a new imperial department, the *Zongli Yamen* (or Office for General Management) to deal with foreign affairs. To prepare Chinese scholars and officials to interact more effectively with foreigners, Gong promoted the establishment of a new foreign language institute, with instruction offered, for the first time ever in major European languages.

Also for the first time, a few modern schools were opened, with classes offered in mathematics, astronomy, physics, chemistry, and international law. Technologies of communication and transportation were also upgraded with the introduction of the first railroads and modern telegraph lines. In these and other respects, the Tongzhi Restoration planted the first seeds of a genuine Chinese renaissance.

Unfortunately for China, however, not everyone in the court of the young Tongzhi emperor was impressed with Prince Gong's policies or with his emulation of Western techniques. Consequently, an influential group of archconservative Manchu court officials mounted a campaign of resistance and sabotage against the Self-Strengthening Movement.

One key member of the group, the Imperial Grand Secretary Wo Ren, was an ardent defender of orthodox Confucian moral training, and he lashed out sharply against the new thinking. In a famous 1867 broadside directed against the reformers' efforts to emulate foreign science and technology, Wo Ren argued as follows:

> According to the viewpoint of your slave, astronomy and mathematics are of very little use. If these subjects are going to be taught by Westerners as regular studies, the damage will be great. ... Your slave has learned that the way to establish a nation is to lay emphasis on propriety and righteousness, not on power and plotting. The fundamental effort lies in the minds of people, not in techniques. ... From ancient down to modern times, your slave has never heard of anyone who could use mathematics to raise the nation from a state of decline or to strengthen it in time of weakness.

Prince Gong's response to Wo Ren's blind opposition to everything new or foreign was blunt and direct. Addressing the question of defending China against the onslaught of the West, the prince wrote:

> [Wo Ren] considers our actions a hindrance. But if he really has a marvelous plan to control foreign countries ... [we] should certainly follow [his] footsteps. ... [But] if he has no plan other than to use loyalty and sincerity as armor, and propriety and righteousness as a shield, ... and if he says that [lofty] phrases are [sufficient] to accomplish diplomatic negotiations and thereby control ... our enemies, then [we] are indeed skeptical and cannot presume to believe it.

Although Wo Ren was quite outspoken in his opposition to reform, the chief architect of internal court resistance to Prince Gong's proposals was not Wo Ren, but rather the Tongzhi emperor's own mother, the arch-reactionary dowager empress, Cixi.

As regent to the child emperor, Cixi enjoyed enormous power, much of it wielded from behind a famous screen positioned to one side of the imperial throne, from which she would instruct the young emperor on his proper responses.

Cixi had not always been a hard-line reactionary; indeed it was she who, in her role as imperial regent, defied a longstanding Manchu tradition by placing a Han Chinese official—not a Manchu—[named] Zeng Guofan, in command of the army that ultimately defeated the Taipings.

But Cixi was nothing if not supremely ambitious and self-aggrandizing, and she eventually came to realize that if the reformers were successful in imitating Western ideas and innovations, then her own power and influence would be sharply curtailed.

Cixi was a real force of nature; and her behavior was decidedly erratic. At one point she approved the purchase of seven decommissioned British warships, but when the ships arrived in China, staffed by several hundred uniformed sailors under British command, she protested vigorously. When negotiations failed to settle the question of the legal status of the British sailors, she ordered the ships to turn around and return to England.

On another occasion, after Li Hongzhang had recommended the building of a railway line to connect Beijing with other northern Chinese cities, Cixi refused to allow its construction under the pretext that trains were excessively loud and would "disturb the tombs of the emperors."

When construction went ahead anyway, Cixi demanded that the railroad cars be pulled by horse-drawn carts rather than steam engines to ensure that the slumber of her departed ancestors would remain undisturbed.

Cixi's most infamous foible, however, was her alleged embezzlement of 30 million taels of silver that had been set aside by the government to finance construction of modern naval ships.

Aided by a retinue of her loyal eunuchs, she reportedly diverted the construction funds, using them to rebuild the Imperial Summer Palace, which had been sacked and burned in the Second Opium War.

As part of this restoration project, Cixi commissioned the construction of an elaborately hand-carved, double-decked marble pleasure boat. Carved out of a single massive block of marble, the boat was far too heavy to ever set sail.

Indeed, for the past 115 years, Cixi's marble boat has remained moored in the muddy shallows of Kunming Lake, northwest of Beijing. Unable to move, it remains as a painful double reminder of Cixi's corrupt vanity and of the costly failure of the Self-Strengtheners' efforts to modernize the country's defenses.

Because of Cixi's misuse of imperial funds, no new naval warships were put into service in China from the late 1880s until the final collapse of the Manchu dynasty in 1911. One consequence of this lack of naval construction was China's defeat at the hands of a superior Japanese fleet in the Sino-Japanese War of 1894–95.

Was Cixi personally responsible for this humiliating defeat? Probably not. But her extreme vanity and self-centeredness certainly contributed.

For all the Self-Strengtheners' well-intended efforts to raise China's military profile and to modernize its antiquated infrastructure, they ultimately failed to halt the decline of the endangered empire.

There were three key reasons for this failure: First was their own limited understanding of the requirements of modernity. Interested primarily in acquiring Western military technology in order to repulse the Western challenge, they failed to appreciate either the complex upstream and downstream requirements of "out of the box" technologies or the broader institutional and cultural implications of modernization. Even Li Hongzhang, who in many ways was the most forward-looking of the Self-Strengtheners, underestimated the systemic requirements of effective reform. In Li's view (which was shared by many leading Self-Strengtheners of his day), the ultimate goal of reform was to borrow Western technologies merely for their instrumental utility, while carefully preserving Chinese values as the core foundation of empire. In Chinese, their key slogan was: "*Zhongxue weiti, Yangxue weiyong*"—"Chinese learning for the foundation; Western learning for practical use."

The second reason for the Tongzhi restoration's failure was sabotage by Cixi and her ultra-conservative followers. When the Tongzhi emperor fell mysteriously ill and died in 1875, at the young age of only 18 years, Cixi's power increased greatly, while the reformers found themselves progressively marginalized. Indeed, many historians believe that Cixi played a quite active role in assisting her son's death.

In any event, whether by chance or by design, Prince Gong suffered a steady loss of influence after Tongzhi's death. Having been officially chastised three times at the initiative of the dowager empress, he went into semi-retirement in 1884.

As for Zeng Guofan and Li Hongzhang, though they were granted elaborate honors and high official positions throughout the 1870s and '80s, their real power was progressively curtailed by Cixi, who secretly encouraged conservative forces to oppose them at every turn. The third reason for the failure of the "Self-Strengthening" movement was the continued high cost of resisting barbarian incursions.

Though the Opium Wars ended in 1860, foreign powers continued to chip away at Manchu sovereignty and Manchu wealth.

In 1884, China lost a war with France over territorial rights to Indochina. A decade later the Japanese navy, confronting a weak Chinese defense force totally lacking in modern naval vessels, stripped the Korean peninsula and the island of Taiwan from Manchu domination. By the end of the century, more than a dozen "unequal treaties" had been forced upon China by assorted foreign powers, now including Japan.

Further weakening the imperial government was the fact that with import tariffs extremely low (and their collection controlled by foreigners), Western countries were free to flood China with cheap machine-made goods, thereby bringing hard times to China's traditional, labor-intensive textile and clothing industries. In this connection, the idle fantasy of a mid-19th-century British textile mill owner proved prophetic: If he could just "add one inch" to the coattail of every Chinese, he dreamed, "400 million customers would keep the mills of Manchester running forever."

Although increasing numbers of Chinese had come to admire Western science, technology, and economic innovation, they also deeply resented Western bullying and the arrogant attitude of Western entitlement and noblesse oblige that all too often accompanied it.

This ambivalence lay at the very heart of the oscillating, bipolar feelings of respect and resentment, admiration and anger, love and hate, that characterized China's 19th-century response to the West. It was an ambivalence that would endure for more than a century, flaring up periodically, right down to the present era.

Writing in 1949, Mao Zedong captured the essence of this century-long Chinese ambivalence toward the West:

> From the time of China's defeat in the Opium War [wrote Mao], progressive Chinese went through untold hardships in their quest for truth from the Western countries. [Many prominent Chinese intellectuals] looked to the West for truth. … Chinese who … sought progress would read any book containing new knowledge from the West. The number of students sent [abroad] was amazing. … Every effort was made to learn from the West. In my youth, I too engaged in such studies. Representing the culture of democracy, this was called the "new learning."

> But Imperialist aggression shattered the fond dreams of the Chinese about learning from the West. It was very odd—why were the teachers always committing aggression against their pupils? The Chinese learned a good deal from the West, but they could not make it work. … Day by day, conditions in the country worsened, and life was made impossible. Doubts arose, increased and deepened. (Mao, "On People's Democratic Dictatorship")

What the foreigners didn't take by force in the 19th century, they often secured through negotiated leases, concessions, and naked land grabs. Between 1860 and 1898, foreign powers established territorial enclaves in dozens of Chinese cities, from Harbin, Dalian, and Qingdao in the northeast, to Hainan, Shantou, and Beihai in the south.

Capping off this extensive foreign real-estate grab, on July 1, 1898, Great Britain signed a 99-year lease for several hundred square miles of Chinese territory immediately adjacent to the British Colony of Hong Kong. Known as the New Territories, this valuable piece of south China real estate remained in British hands until a little more than a decade ago.

(As a matter of historical interest, it was the approaching expiration date of this 99-year British lease on the New Territories that forced British Prime Minister Margaret Thatcher, in the early 1980s, to enter into negotiations with Deng Xiaoping over the future status of Hong Kong. With Deng unwilling to renew the British lease, which had long been a painful symbol of China's 19th-century humiliation, Mrs. Thatcher had little choice but to agree to return the entire Hong Kong Crown Colony to China. The rest, as they say, is history. In a subsequent lecture we shall examine more closely

China's recapture of Hong Kong, which took place precisely at the stroke of midnight on July 1, 1997—99 years to the minute after the lease on the New Territories was first signed.

Despite continuing predations by foreigners, despite the many failings of the Tongzhi Self-Strengtheners, and despite the sinister machinations of Cixi and her retinue of reactionary palace eunuchs, the Manchu dynasty did not collapse—at least not yet.

On the contrary, in the waning years of the 19th century, just when it looked like the end might be close at hand, the teetering empire seemed to get yet another second wind. Momentarily it steadied itself, as a new and radical program of socio-economic and political reform was urgently enacted by imperial decree.

At this point in the narrative, a brief digression into comparative history will be is in order. The digression begins with a simple but critical observation: In the three decades from 1860 to 1890, while the Manchus were struggling to keep Western institutions and values at arms length, lest they contaminate or otherwise undermine the ideological foundations of the Confucian order, something quite remarkable and quite different was happening in nearby Japan.

Like China, pre-modern Japan had been closed to Western commerce. And when the American naval commander, Matthew Perry, sailed his fleet of menacing Black Ships into Tokyo's harbor in 1853, it was in some ways redolent of Admiral George Elliot's arrival in Canton 14 years earlier.

Like Admiral Elliot, Commodore Perry used his superior weapons and his warships to leverage commercial concessions from the Japanese. Like Elliot, Perry's demands engendered a strong nationalistic backlash on the part of xenophobic Japanese.

But there the similarities end. For one thing, Admiral Perry was not using his gunboats to force poisonous drugs upon an unwilling Japanese population; for another, the traditional Japanese imperial order had long since broken down.

Unlike China under the Manchus, the Japanese state in the Tokagawa era was politically decentralized and evenfragmented, with no single imperial hegemon able to dictate the terms of engagement with foreigners.

When centralized imperial authority was finally reconstituted in 1868, with the Meiji Restoration, the new Japanese emperor shed many of his predecessors' conservative cultural taboos and began to adapt proactively to Western penetration and presence. On the principle that "if you can't beat 'em, join 'em," the Meiji emperor introduced a number of fundamental reforms, many of them conspicuously borrowed from the West.

A modern constitution was adopted, establishing an elected parliament. Modern transportation and communications systems were imported from the West. Universal education was instituted, again patterned after the West. By the turn of the century, a modern urban middle class had begun to emerge in Japan.

Freed from the type of ideological rigidity characterized by Cixi's machinations, which had severely constrained China's Self-Strengtheners, in effect tying one hand behind their backs, if not both hands, Japan's industrial development proceeded with all due speed, without regard for possible contamination effects.

While Cixi was busy building herself a marble pleasure boat, Japanese industrialists were busy building themselves a modern navy.

The striking contrast in the national spirit, or zeitgeist, of China and Japan in the last decades of the 19th century would have enormous downstream consequences for both countries—most of them bad.

By 1895 Japan had far outpaced China in the race to modernize. And within two decades, Japan's leaders would feel strong enough and confident enough to mount a major challenge to Western domination in China.

But all that lay in the future. In the next lecture, we return to the China of the 1890s, as we examine the Manchus last significant attempt to reform China from within. When that effort failed, reform gave way to revolution. Next time: the "Hundred Days of Reform."

Hundred Days of Reform and the Boxer Uprising
Lecture 6

Lecture 6: Hundred Days of Reform and the Boxer Uprising

> When the power of the empire comes from one person, it is weak. When it comes from millions of people, it is strong.
>
> —Reform scholar Wang Kangnian

The self-strengtheners' failure woke up progressive Chinese intellectuals, who began to push for more fundamental changes in Chinese society. In 1898, at the reformers' urging, the young emperor **Guangxu** introduced systemic changes, known as the **Hundred Days of Reform**. He issued 40 imperial edicts abolishing the ancient civil service exams, creating China's first national university, reforming legal codes, promoting foreign trade and economic entrepreneurship, and involving citizens in policy deliberations. The reforms would have changed the face of imperial China.

From 1898 to 1900, the Boxers, a fanatically xenophobic secret society who believed themselves impervious to bullets, rampaged throughout North China.

But just as she had 25 years earlier, the archconservative Dowager Empress Cixi intervened to stop the reforms. She ordered her retainers and eunuchs to raid the emperor's palace and seize the reform decrees. The emperor was imprisoned, and several proreform scholar-officials were banished from Beijing.

Meaningful reform from within was now blocked, and xenophobia flourished under Cixi's rule. Fresh challenges arose, in particular, the **Boxer Rebellion**. From 1898 to 1900, the Boxers, a fanatically xenophobic secret society who believed themselves impervious to bullets, rampaged throughout North China, burning Western churches and slaughtering missionaries and Chinese Christians. In 1900 in Beijing, 10,000 Boxers armed with swords and spears attacked the foreign diplomatic legations for 55 days before 18,000 foreign troops moved in to crush them. In the aftermath of the Boxer uprising, Western powers exacted still greater indemnities from Beijing. ■

Kang Youwei's Audience with Emperor Guangxu Leads to Hundred Days of Reform

After sending five requests to Emperor Guangxu, reformer Kang Youwei was granted a private audience with the emperor in late January 1898. The remarkable conversation, which led to the Hundred Days of Reform, lasted five hours—the longest imperial audience in recorded history. Their conversation was recorded by a scribe and is excerpted below.

Guangxu: Today it is really imperative that we reform.

Kang: In recent years we have … talked about reform … but it was only a slight reform. … The prerequisites of reform are that all the laws and the political and social systems be changed and decided anew.

At this point, Guangxu cast a sidelong glance at the screen next to him, where Dowager Empress Cixi often lurked.

Guangxu: What can I do with so much hindrance?

Kang: Today most of the high ministers are very old and conservative, and they do not understand matters concerning foreign countries. If Your Majesty wishes to rely on them for reform it will be like climbing a tree to look for fish. … If Your Majesty wishes reform, the only thing to do is to promote and make use of lower officials. … The trouble today lies in the noncultivation of the people's wisdom, and the cause … lies in the civil service examinations based on the eight-legged essay.

Guangxu: It is so. Westerners are all pursuing useful studies, while we Chinese pursue useless studies.

Kang: Since Your Majesty is already aware of the harm of the eight-legged essay, could we abolish it?

Guangxu: We could. If you have something more to say you may prepare memorials … and send them here to me later on.

Names to Know

Guangxu (1871–1908): Influenced by liberal intellectuals Kang Youwei and Liang Qichao, this youthful Manchu emperor introduced 40 major domestic reforms in 1898. He was deposed and imprisoned by Cixi following the Hundred Days of Reform.

Kang Youwei (1858–1927): Kang was the leading liberal reformer in the last decades of the Qing dynasty. He persuaded Emperor Guangxu in 1898 to introduce major innovations in education, civil service exams, medical training, and foreign affairs.

Liang Qichao (1873–1929): This student of Kang Youwei worked with Kang to enact the reforms of 1898. Both men fled to Japan in 1898 after Cixi suppressed the reforms and imprisoned Emperor Guangxu.

Important Terms

Boxer Protocol (1901): The treaty that ended the Boxer Rebellion; it exacted large financial indemnities from the Manchus as punishment for their complicity in Boxer attacks on foreigners.

Boxer Rebellion (1899–1900): Insurrection by secret society of "harmonious fists" aimed at killing all foreigners and punishing the Manchus for China's weakness.

Hundred Days of Reform (1898): Abortive effort by Emperor Guangxu to reform the Manchu dynasty from within. Spearheaded by Liang Qichao and Kang Youwei, the reforms were blocked by Dowager Empress Cixi.

Open Door policy (1898): The policy initiated by President William McKinley that was designed to morally restrain foreign powers from dominating China and to maintain equal access among foreign countries.

Suggested Reading

Fenby, *Modern China.*

Hsü, *The Rise of Modern China.*

Preston, *The Boxer Rebellion.*

Schrecker, *The Chinese Revolution in Historical Perspective.*

Spence, *The Search for Modern China.*

Teng and Fairbank, *China's Response to the West.*

Wright, *The Last Stand of Chinese Conservatism.*

Questions to Consider

1. Why did Chinese reformers become radicalized toward the end of the 19th century?

2. In what sense did the Boxer uprising represent the last instance of premodern rebellion in China?

Hundred Days of Reform and the Boxer Uprising
Lecture 6—Transcript

Last time we looked at the Self-Strengthening Movement of the 1860s and '70s and its ultimate failure to halt the precipitous decline of the Manchu dynasty. By the time China suffered its inglorious defeat in the Sino-Japanese war of 1895, the dynasty was in a shambles.

But it still did not collapse—at least not then. In this lecture we shall see how a group of Westernized intellectuals initiated a bold new reform movement in 1898, a movement whose goal was nothing less than a total overhaul of China's moribund economic and political institutions.

The failure of the Self-Strengthening Movement proved particularly frustrating to one group of aspiring reformers. Initially trained in the neo-Confucian tradition of moral philosophy and tributary statecraft, these talented young scholars were severely disillusioned by China's inability to extricate itself from the twin quagmires of European domination and imperial ineptitude.

Some of them had traveled to the West under Prince Gong's program of sending talented students abroad. Others had remained in China, where they gained a growing appreciation for the internal sources of Chinese decay. By the mid-1890s, these two groups of reformers had converged to initiate a lobbying campaign in an effort to gain high level imperial support for fundamental social change.

Leading figures in this coalition of progressive reformers included Kang Youwei, Liang Qichao, Tan Sitong and Wang Kangnian. (These are names we shall be referring to again and again.) Though they emphasized different aspects of China's imperial stagnation, all agreed that mere institutional tinkering and fine-tuning would not do: a fundamental overhaul was needed. Here is Liang Qichao's assessment, written in 1896:

> Those who insist that there is no need for reform say, "let us follow the ancients, follow the ancients." They sit coldly and watch everything being laid waste by following tradition, and yet there is no concern in their hearts. …
>
> Now, here is a big mansion which has lasted a thousand years. The tiles and bricks are decayed and the beams and rafters are broken. It is still a magnificently big thing, but when wind and rain suddenly

come up, its fall is foredoomed. Yet the people in the house are still happily playing or soundly sleeping and as indifferent as if they have seen or heard nothing. Even [the few] who have noted the danger know only how to weep bitterly, folding their arms and waiting for death without thinking of any remedy. Sometimes there are [even] people ... who try to repair the cracks, seal the leaks, and patch up the ant holes in order to be able to go on living there in peace ... in the hope that something better may turn up. These three types of people use their minds differently, but when a hurricane comes they will die together.

For his part, Tan Sitong boldly advocated importing Western institutions and values as China's only hope for reviving the decaying empire. His admiration for the West was enormous, equaled only by his contempt for the superficiality of traditional Chinese scholarship. Writing in 1898, Tan Sitong lamented:

During the last several decades, where have we had a genuine understanding of foreign cultures? When have we had scholars or officials who could discuss them? What [they] mean by foreign matters are things such as steamships, telegraph lines, trains, guns, torpedoes, and machines for weaving and for metallurgy; that's all. [They] have never dreamed of or seen the beauty and perfection of Western legal systems and political institutions. ... All [they] speak of are the branches and foliage of foreign matters, not the roots.

[The] idea of despising our enemies arises because [our officials] think [all foreigners] are still barbarians. This is a common mistake of scholar-officials ... and they must get rid of it. ... We must first make ourselves respectable before we despise others. Now, there is not a single one of the Chinese people's sentiments, customs, or political institutions which can be favorably compared with those of the barbarians.

Other leading reform advocates went further still, advocating a complete makeover of China's governmental system, replacing it with a Western-style parliamentary regime where the people participate in the selection of their leaders. Along these lines, the reform scholar Wang Kangnian wrote:

Chinese who discuss governmental systems speak only in terms of governing the people by a ruler. In the West, however, there are democratic countries ... governed jointly by the ruler and the people. Chinese scholars ... consider [this] strange. [But] what is so strange about it? ...

In general, when the power of the empire comes from one person, it is weak. When it comes from millions of people, it is strong.

As the 19th century wound down toward its close, a 27-year-old emperor, Guangxu, sat on the Dragon Throne in Beijing. Guangxu was deeply disturbed by the prospect of China being dismembered by rapacious foreigners And he was intrigued by the tales of Western-style economic and administrative revitalization in Japan under the Meiji restoration and in Russia under Peter the Great. An avid reader, Guangxu began devouring books about foreign institutions.

Noting the emperor's rising interest in the subject of reform, a well-known scholarly advocate of radical modernization, by the name of Kang Youwei, took it upon himself to persuade Guangxu to underwrite massive reforms. He barraged the emperor with a series of policy recommendations, in the form of written "memorials."

(Today, we would call these memorials "Policy White Papers").

In his heart of hearts, Kang Youwei was what we would call a "utopian socialist."

His ideal world was one in which there would be no separate nations, but a single world government divided into various regions. The central government would be popularly elected. Families and clans would no longer perpetuate themselves over multiple generations, and cohabitation between men and women would be limited to a single year's duration.

All children would be raised in public nurseries and would receive public education from kindergarten through middle school. There would be public hospitals for the sick and public retirement homes for the aged. Public dormitories and dining halls would be made available to all classes and strata according to their working incomes.

Although this was Kang Youwei's ultimate vision for the future, he did not try to impose his utopian views upon Guangxu. Instead, his written memorials to the emperor were far more modest and down to earth.

After sending five such memorials to the emperor, without receiving an affirmative response, Kang Youwei was finally at long last granted that rarest of imperial privileges—a private audience with Guangxu.

Although conservative court officials, led by the irrepressible Cixi, sought to derail this meeting, Guangxu remained adamant, and Kang Youwei got his audience in late January of 1898.

Their conversation was faithfully recorded by a scribe. Here is how it went:

> Guangxu: "Today it is really imperative that we reform."
>
> Kang Youwei: "In recent years we have ... talked about reform ... but it was only a slight reform ... we change the first thing but do not change the second, and then we confuse everything so as to incur failure. ... The prerequisites of reform are that all the laws and the political and social systems must be changed and decided anew."

At this point, Guangxu cast a sidelong glance at the screen next to him, where the ubiquitous Cixi often lurked:

> Guangxu: "What can I do with so much hindrance?"
>
> Kang Youwei: "Today most of the high ministers are very old and conservative, and they do not understand matters concerning foreign countries. If Your Majesty wishes to rely on them for reform it will be like climbing a tree to look for fish. ... If Your Majesty wishes reform, the only thing to do is to promote and make use of lower officials ... and employ them without following tradition. ... The trouble today lies in the non-cultivation of the people's wisdom, and the cause of this lies in the civil service examinations based on the eight-legged essay. ..."
>
> Guangxu: "It is so. Westerners are all pursuing useful studies, while we Chinese pursue useless studies."
>
> Kang Youwei: "Since Your Majesty is already aware of the harm of the eight-legged essay, couldn't we abolish it?"
>
> Guangxu: "We could. ... [Now] you should withdraw and take a little rest. If you have something more to say you may prepare memorials ... in detail and send them to me later on here."

This remarkable conversation lasted for five full hours. In the annals of recorded history, it was the longest imperial audience ever granted.

After the meeting, Kang Youwei and his associates prepared a detailed list of reform proposals. As agreed, the emperor received them; and on June 11, 1898, the reforms commenced.

Over the next three-and-a-half months, more than 40 imperial edicts were issued in rapid succession. The new decrees encompassed a sweeping set of innovations in such areas as higher education, civil service examinations, medical training, and the management of foreign affairs.

Specific mandates included the establishment of China's first imperial institution of higher learning (now called Peking University) and the abolition of the eight-legged essay in imperial civil service examinations. Bureaucratic offices were simplified; non-competitively awarded positions, or sinecures, were abolished; legal codes were improved and rendered comprehensible for the first time ever; and the country's first official daily newspaper was commissioned.

In economic affairs, the commercialization of agriculture and industry were promoted, technological innovation was rewarded, foreign trade was expanded, and a formal process of governmental budgeting was introduced.

In all areas of imperial policy, suggestions were henceforth to be solicited from private citizens with the stipulation that these suggestions should be forwarded to the appropriate administrative departments on the same day as they were received.

In breadth and depth, Guangxu's Hundred Days of Reform were indeed breathtaking.

But the proposed reforms did not go unopposed.

Mobilizing the forces of reaction within the imperial court, the ever-vigilant Cixi pulled out all the stops in her efforts to abort Guangxu's program.

Now in her 60s, and in semi-retirement since 1889, Cixi continued to influence the imperial court from behind the scenes. Alarmed by the radicalism of Guangxu's reforms, and by Kang Youwei's growing influence over the emperor, she devised a scheme to seize power.

On September 21, 1898—exactly 103 days after the first reform decrees were promulgated—a group of ultra-conservative court officials and eunuchs raided the emperor's palace, seizing all documents pertaining to the reforms.

Cixi then announced that Guangxu had suddenly fallen ill, overcome by a mysterious malady that had incapacitated him. How very convenient. This, she said, made it imperative that she herself should assume control of the government. (Not too subtle, perhaps, but nonetheless effective.)

Meanwhile, the emperor was placed under detention and was whisked away to a small island in the Imperial Gardens west of Beijing, where he was kept incommunicado. Cixi's palace coup was now complete, and the "Hundred Days of Reform" came to a sudden, crashing end.

In the aftermath of Cixi's coup, progressive reformers were quickly targeted for arrest. A total of 22 scholars were detained, dismissed from their posts, banished and stripped of all property.

Kang Youwei himself—his writings now officially banned—managed to evade arrest, escaping safely to Japan along with his student, Liang Qichao. However, Tan Sitong, ever the loyal follower of Confucian virtue, remained in Beijing, where he surrendered himself to Cixi, in the process becoming something of an instant martyr.

With the ascent, once more, of Manchu reactionaries to the center of imperial power, the regime took on an ever-stronger tone of atavism, arrogance, and anti-foreignism. Hostility toward all barbarians was officially encouraged, and Western missionaries were accused of committing all manner of abominations, including the boiling and eating of young children.

Xenophobia and nativist superstition now flourished under the reactionary reign of the dowager empress. When a series of natural calamities occurred in 1898 and 1899, Cixi conveniently blamed the foreigners, citing their well-known contempt for Confucianism and for the rituals of ancestor-worship.

By the turn of the new century, a variety of secret societies had become active in China. While each had its own distinctive rituals and belief systems, one thing served to unite them: hatred of the ever-powerful, ever-insidious barbarians.

One such secret society, known as *Yihe Quan*, or the society of "Righteous and Harmonious Fists," called "Boxers" for short, had been in existence for almost a century. The Boxers loathed all foreigners, whom they referred to colloquially as the "hairy ones."

Devoted to the martial arts, they believed that their magical charms and incantations would render them immune to foreign bullets. The Boxers shunned the use of rifles, preferring old-fashioned swords, lances, and fists. In the late 1890s, they decreed that all "hairy ones" must be exterminated, along with their traitorous Chinese collaborators and compradors.

(Compradors, by the way, are the Chinese employees of Western merchants who were used to facilitate relations with local labor organizers and guilds with local merchants and local officials.)

Originally anti-Manchu in orientation (the Manchus were, after all, a foreign dynasty), the Boxers soon found themselves being courted by Cixi and her followers, who shared their antipathy to the "hairy ones." Seeking to co-opt the society of "Harmonious Fists" and thus blunt the Boxers' anti-Manchu anger, she secretly summoned their leaders to Beijing, where she urged them to instruct Manchu court officials in the fine art of boxing.

The rising tide of anti-foreignism broke into the open in 1899, in a north Chinese village near the seaside city of Qingdao, in Shandong Province. Qingdao had recently become a German "sphere of influence," part of the carving up of China in the late 19th century, and local villagers became incensed when their ancestral temple was seized by German missionaries for use as a church. Spurred into action by the Boxers, the villagers attacked the church.

In the spring of 1900 the Boxers, now numbering in the tens of thousands, went on a rampage in Tianjin, southeast of Beijing. They burned churches and shops that sold foreign goods, and they randomly killed Chinese Christians.

On June 13, 1900, a force of over 10,000 Boxers headed for Beijing. En route they brutally assaulted all visible bearers and symbols of Western influence. When they reached Beijing, their first target was the German legation, which they attacked, killing the German minister. Sensing that a decisive blow was about to be inflicted on the foreigners, Cixi now declared war on all foreigners and ordered her imperial officers to collaborate openly with the Boxers.

Soon all the foreign legations in Beijing were under siege, with the imperial court offering a reward of 50 silver taels for each foreign male captured alive.

Trapped within the foreign legations were some 475 Western civilians (including at least 10 foreign ministers of state), along with 450 armed guards, several hundred Chinese servants, and over 2,300 Chinese Christians who had sought refuge from the fanatical Boxers.

Facing near-certain annihilation by the Boxers and their Manchu patrons, the 4,000 besieged inhabitants of the foreign legations held out for 55 days. Ultimately they were saved by a reform-minded Manchu military officer named Ronglu, who refused to order his troops to use their weapons against the foreigners. Instead, Ronglu's soldiers were instructed to discharge a noisy but harmless barrage of rifle fire from guns that remained unloaded.

To lift the siege, an international military force was mobilized in Tianjin. The force took a month to assemble and, when finally assembled, consisted of 18,000 troops, with the largest contingent being Japanese (8,000), followed by Russians (5,000), British (3,000), Americans (2,000), French (800), and a few dozen Austrians and Italians. Setting out for Beijing on August 4, 1900, this allied force reached the beleaguered legations of Beijing 10 days later.

With superior numbers and overwhelming firepower, they quickly overwhelmed the attacking Boxers. By the time the dust settled, 231 foreigners had been killed, along with a substantially larger number of Chinese Christian converts. But Boxer deaths were more numerous by far, numbering well over 10,000. During the entire six-month duration of the Boxer Uprising, an estimated 18,000 Chinese Catholics were killed along with 182 Protestant missionaries.

With the breaking of the siege in Beijing, Western troops throughout north China now went on a rampage of their own in retaliation. In the carnage that followed, German troops proved particularly vindictive. Responding to Kaiser Wilhelm's order, "Make the German name remembered in China for a thousand years, so that no Chinaman will ever again dare to even squint at a German," Kaiser's forces plundered, looted, and slaughtered their defeated foes. Altogether, an estimated 50,000 suspected Boxers were killed by foreign troops.

(For those who savor historical factoids, when American troops participated in lifting the siege of Beijing, it marked the very first time in American history that American troops had fought on Chinese soil.)

(For film buffs, the American role in the 1900 liberation of the foreign legations in Beijing is dramatically and rather shamelessly romanticized in the 1963 Hollywood movie epic, "55 Days at Peking," starring Charlton Heston.)

The peace settlement that followed in 1901, known as the Boxer Protocol, was harsh and vindictive.

A dozen high court officials who had carried out Cixi's policies of assisting the Boxers were either executed or ordered to commit suicide. A few had their sentences commuted, while a number of lesser officials were banished to the outer regions of empire in far off Xinjiang.

Commander Ronglu, the man who had helped save the foreign legations by sparing them live artillery and rifle fire, escaped Western punishment. Later, he would play a pivotal role as Superintendent of Political Affairs in the waning days of the Manchu dynasty.

In addition to the harsh punishments meted out to the Boxers and their Manchu instigators, the foreign powers greatly increased their political and military presence in Beijing. Establishing permanent diplomatic missions in the Chinese capital, the foreigners created what was in effect a "shadow government" that existed alongside the deeply wounded Manchu court.

Finally, adding insult to injury, war reparations totaling 450 million taels of silver (worth approximately $330 million in the U.S.'s current exchange rate) were extracted from the Manchu court by the various foreign powers, to be paid out over a period of 40 years.

(Curiously enough, however, before the reparations could be paid out to foreign governments, the money first had to be borrowed from those very same governments. This was because the imperial Chinese treasury was empty, and the Manchus were forced to borrow the Boxer indemnity money as bonded national debt. The foreigners were thus paid with their own money.

In fact, however, much of the bonded indebtedness was never repaid. A substantial portion of the Boxer funds were later reduced or cancelled outright by the foreign powers.

In this connection, the United States, which played a relatively minor role in suppressing the Boxer Uprising, used a substantial portion of its $24 million share of the Boxer funds to underwrite American-style educational programs and reforms in China and to endow scholarships for talented Chinese students. The balance of the debt was unilaterally forgiven by the United States Senate in two stages, first in 1908 and then again in 1924.

As a condition of receiving their share of Boxer indemnity funds, all foreign governments, at the insistence of the United States, signed an "Open Door" pledge in which they renounced any colonial designs on China and pledged to respect Chinese sovereignty and territorial integrity. This was the famous open-door policy of President William McKinley.

All in all, the Boxer Rebellion was one more inglorious chapter in the century-long humiliation and decline of the Middle Kingdom.

By the end of 1900, with the imperial treasury near empty, with the dynasty in disarray, and with Cixi and her minions blocking all attempts at political modernity, there was little or no chance that progressive reforms would emerge from within the dynasty itself. And as the new century dawned, the initiative for change fell into the hands not of reformers but of revolutionaries.

Next time, the rise of the Chinese Revolution.

The End of Empire, 1900–1911
Lecture 7

In this lecture we witness the final throes of a dying dynasty, and the concurrent rise of the first truly modern Chinese revolutionary political party—the Guomindang of Dr. Sun Yat-sen.

With the collapse of the 1898 reform movement and the suppression of the Boxers, China's government was essentially impotent and rudderless. A group of Western-trained Chinese intellectuals, weary of partial, ineffective reforms, now began to organize themselves in earnest to overthrow the Manchu dynasty and replace it with a progressive, Western-style political movement.

© Prints and Photographs Division,

Dr. Sun Yat-sen.

Their leader was **Sun Yat-sen**, a medical doctor trained in Hawaii and Hong Kong. Unlike the rebels discussed in previous lectures, Sun was distinctly modern and proposed a coherent political plan for China. After leading an abortive uprising in Canton in 1893, Sun was forced to flee to the West, where he formulated his political ideology, the **Three People's Principles**. As the Manchu dynasty grew weaker, Sun's popularity grew both inside China and among overseas Chinese.

The Three People's Principles
(*sanmin zhuyi*)
Written in Chinese

三民主義

民族主義
民權主義
民生主義

Seeking recruits and foreign support, Sun planned at least 10 failed anti-Manchu uprisings between 1906 and 1911. The Chinese Republican Revolution of 1911 began quite accidentally, without any master plan at all, and with its principal architect, Sun, thousands of miles away. A revolutionary bomb exploded unintentionally in October 1911, leading Sun's followers in Hankow (modern Wuhan) to mutiny against the local imperial command, causing the local garrison commander to flee. The rebels found themselves in control of the city, and soon afterward Manchu authority began to crumble throughout the country.

The Chinese Republican Revolution of 1911 began quite accidentally, without any master plan at all, and with its principal architect, Sun, thousands of miles away.

Sun returned to China and christened the Provisional Republic of China, of which he was inaugurated provisional president on January 1, 1912. He also renamed his revolutionary movement the Guomindang, or National People's Party. Without a disciplined, reliable army of his own, however, Sun could not consolidate power. He turned to the former imperial commander in chief, Yuan Shikai. Yuan was willing to collaborate with Sun's Nationalists, but in return Yuan demanded the presidency of the new Republic of China. Sun reluctantly agreed, and he abdicated in Yuan's favor in February 1912, the same month it was announced that the Manchu court had abdicated power to the new republic. ∎

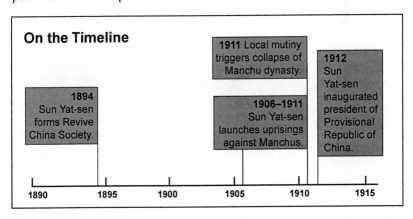

On the Timeline

1894
Sun Yat-sen forms Revive China Society.

1906–1911
Sun Yat-sen launches uprisings against Manchus.

1911 Local mutiny triggers collapse of Manchu dynasty.

1912
Sun Yat-sen inaugurated president of Provisional Republic of China.

1890   1895   1900   1905   1910   1915

Puyi (1906–1967): China's "last emperor." As a toddler, he was placed on the Manchu throne as a figurehead by Cixi in 1908. Puyi was later installed by Japan as the puppet ruler of Manchukuo.

Sun Yat-sen (1866–1925): A medical doctor trained in Hawaii and Hong Kong, Sun led efforts to overthrow the Manchu dynasty. When the dynasty collapsed in 1911, Sun founded China's first modern political party, the Guomindang, and became the first president of the Republic of China. He is revered as the father of modern China.

Yuan Shikai (1859–1916): The last commander of the Manchu imperial army. Yuan transferred his loyalty to Sun Yat-sen after the revolution of 1911, only to seize power from Sun a few months later. Yuan died after an unsuccessful attempt to restore the dynastic system.

Suggested Reading

Bergère, *Sun Yat-sen.*

Fenby, *Modern China.*

Hsü, *The Rise of Modern China.*

Schrecker, *The Chinese Revolution in Historical Perspective.*

Spence, *The Search for Modern China.*

Teng and Fairbank, *China's Response to the West.*

Questions to Consider

1. Did the Manchu dynasty jump, or was it pushed?

2. Why did the revolution of 1911 fail to lead to a viable republican government?

The End of Empire, 1900–1911
Lecture 7—Transcript

Over the past few lectures, we have observed the steady, painful decline erosion of imperial China, from the hubris of the Qianlong emperor to the futility of Commissioner Lin Zexu, from the Opium Wars to Hong Xiuquan's Taiping Heavenly Kingdom, from the sacking of the Summer Palace to the failure of the Self-Strengthening Movement, from the dowager empress's calculated strangulation of the 1898 reforms to the bizarrely atavistic Boxer Uprising.

Through all of this, we watched as imperial China absorbed a staggering number of blows to its sovereignty, to its institutions, to its fiscal solvency and, finally, to the very core of its civilization.

Surely, such a beating could not go on forever. And indeed it did not.

In this lecture we witness the final death throes of a passing dynasty, and the concurrent rise of the first truly modern Chinese revolutionary political party, the *Guomindang* of Dr. Sun Yat-sen.

With the Boxer humiliation serving to deepen the sense of impending imperial doom, last-minute efforts to reform the Manchu dynasty from within gave way to conspiratorial attempts to overthrow it from without.

Now, rebellion was certainly not new in China: the Nians, the White Lotus Rebels, and the Taipings, among others, had all sought the dynasty's demise. Even the Boxers had started out as anti-Manchu rebels.

But none of these primitive rebellions were in any sense of the term "modern." Their leaders were either peasant bandit chieftains or charismatic cultists—people like the delusional Hong Xiuquan. And none of them, save perhaps for the bizarrely superstitious Boxers, had managed to join anti-Manchu anger with the country's growing rage against foreigners.

What was missing in all of these late 18th- and 19th-century insurrections was any effective linkage between rebel demands for such things as tax relief and retribution against rapacious landlords, on the one hand, and a coherent program for ridding China of foreign domination and restoring national pride and dignity, on the other.

The first distinctively modern Chinese rebel to propose a coherent political solution to the twin problems of unrestrained foreign predation and the deepening domestic disorder was Dr. Sun Yat-sen.

A physician by training, Sun was a native of Canton. As you know, Canton was one of the hotbeds of foreign penetration. And resentment against the foreigners was particularly strong there. Also strong in Canton was a sense of Manchu impotence, the inability to maintain order given the presence of the predatory foreigners. In the 1880s, at a time when the dowager empress was tightening her grip on the Manchu court and strangling the reform efforts of the Self-Strengtheners, Sun, then just a teenager, went abroad to study.

He first attended an Anglican missionary high school in Hawaii. Hawaii at the time was still a princely state on the verge of becoming annexed by the United States. He later pursued a medical degree in Hong Kong, where he converted to Christianity in the mid-1880s. This was very fateful both for Sun, himself, and for his party, the *Guomindang*.

While living abroad, Sun was deeply impressed with the cleanliness, the orderliness, and the administrative efficiency of his host societies. During his residency in Hawaii, for example, Sun first became acquainted with American political ideas, the ideas of the Revolution, as well as legal institutions, and the American educational philosophy of John Dewey.

After graduating from medical school, Sun practiced medicine for two years in Hong Kong and Macao. Returning to his native Canton in 1893, he grew increasingly disillusioned with the corruption and decadence displayed by the Manchu bureaucracy.

In this early stage of Sun Yat-sen's political career, he was torn between conflicting reformist and revolutionary impulses. He was highly ambivalent. Do we need to destroy Chinese civilization or to save it? To help resolve this ambivalence, he traveled north to Beijing to seek the advice and counsel of our old friend Li Hongzhang, former commander of the anti-Taiping military forces and leading Self-Strengthening of the 1860s and '70s .

In the 1890s, Li Hongzhang was China's foremost advocate of military modernization. His oversight of the Self-Strengthening Movement and his efforts to introduce modern ships, guns, and industrial infrastructure was very impressive to Sun Yat-sen. But like his mentor Zeng Guofan, Li believed that the key to restoring China's national wealth and powerwas to copy barbarian technology in order to prevent further barbarian incursions. (Use the barbarians to control the barbarians.)

When Sun Yat-sen tried to convince Li Hongzhang that the secret to the wealth and power of Western countries lay not in their battleships, not in their cannon, but in their commitment to the full development of human talent and capability, the free exchange of commercial products, and the full utilization of the earth's natural resources, Li simply ignored him.

And when Sun tried to persuade Li Hongzhang that free universal education and the study of Western law were necessary to reform the Chinese people and perfect their customs, Li refused even to grant him an audience.

Stung by this rebuff, Sun returned to Canton, where a year later, in 1894, he founded a radical anti-Manchu organization, called the "Revive China Society"; in Chinese, *Xingzhong Hui*.

Meeting secretly in Canton, the 112 original members of this society took an oath to expel the Manchus, to restore Chinese rule, and to establish a federal republic, Western in nature. By 1895, overseas branches of the "Revive China Society" had been established in Hong Kong and Honolulu, two places where Sun had undertaken his training.

At this point, in 1895, Sun finally and irrevocably burned his bridges to the reformers' camp. With the aid of 3,000 sympathizers recruited from among the returned students coming back to Canton from abroad and a group of newly-converted Christians, as well as support from local secret societies, Sun plotted to seize control of Canton itself. In the event, however, his plan was leaked to local officials by an informant, a betrayal that resulted in the death of 48 of his followers.

From then on, Sun Yat-sen was a man on the run, literally hounded by the imperial police and ultimately forced to leave the country. Evading several attempts to arrest him (including an 1896 kidnap attempt by imperial Chinese agents in London), Sun traveled widely throughout Europe, refining his revolutionary political ideas, and seeking financial support for his cause.

Ironically, the unsuccessful kidnapping attempt, engineered by Manchu agents in London, made Sun something of a celebrity, giving him access to the drawing rooms and pocketbooks of Europe's polite society, the *haute bourgeoisie*.

While traveling in Europe, Sun alsoformulated the first known version of what would later become his signature political credo, the *Sanmin Zhuyi*, or "Three Principles of the People." The three principles were, respectively, *Minzu* (meaning "Nationalism"); *Minquan* (meaning "People's Rights") and *Minsheng* (meaning "People's Livelihood"). Nationalism, People's Rights, People's Livelihood, the Three Principles of the People of Sun Yat-sen.

Under the first of these principles, Nationalism, Sun called both for the overthrow of the alien Manchu dynasty and for the final removal of all foreign imperialist enclaves and footholds in China—China for the Chinese.

Under the second principle, People's Rights, Sun called for the adoption of four basic democratic political devices: popular election, referendum, recall and people's legislative initiative. He further advocated the separation of five distinct branches of government: the executive branch, the legislative branch, the judicial branch, the police (also known as the control branch) and the civil service (or the examination branch).

Finally, under Sun's third principle, People's Livelihood, he called for equalizing rural land ownership and for regulating the accumulation of private capital. Later, this third principle would be given a more populist spin and would be relabeled, morphing into "land to the tiller," which is perhaps the best known of Sun Yat-sen's Three Principles of the People.

Initially formulated in 1897, Sun Yat-sen's Three Principles of the People were later incorporated as the official political philosophy of the Provisional Republic of China. Though that government was ultimately short-lived, surviving only briefly from 1912 to 1913, the people's Three Principles today remains the governing credo of the Chinese Nationalist Party on Taiwan, the *Guomindang*.

While in his European exile around the turn of the 20th century, Sun Yat-sen's reputation as a revolutionary benefited from a series of reform setbacks in China. The first of these was the collapse of the "Hundred Days of Reform," engineered by the ultraconservative Cixi.

The failure of the "Hundred Days" served mainly to underline the futility of trying to reform the hapless Manchu dynasty peacefully from within. If a further display of Manchu decrepitude were needed, it was provided by the abject humiliation inflicted on China by the foreign powers in the Boxer Protocol of 1901.

As a result of these internal developments, Sun's prestige grew, both inside China and among the burgeoning communities of anti-Manchu Chinese living abroad. In Paris, in Berlin, in Brussels, and in Tokyo, Sun Yat-sen began to gain new and willing recruits to his revolutionary cause.

In 1904 he changed the name of his organization from the "Revive China Society," which suggested a peaceful reform agenda, to the more revolutionary term *Zhongguo Tongmeng hui*, or the "China Alliance Society."

Between 1906 and 1911, the *Tongmeng Hui* attracted several thousand members and affiliates. It was also in this period that Sun began to put his revolutionary ideas into practice, as he organized 10 separate popular uprisings in south China. There was to be no going back. Sun Yat-sen was now a revolutionary.

Unfortunately for Sun and his followers, all of these insurrections ultimately failed, though the final uprising, which took place in Sun's native city of Canton in April of 1911, did generate widespread public sympathy.

(As a historical note to this latter event, Sun's Canton insurrection of April 1911 was later memorialized by a large concrete obelisk erected in one of Canton's main public parks, *Huanghua Gang*. Honoring the memory of 72 revolutionary martyrs who died in Sun's attempt to seize the city, this monument today remains as a major Cantonese municipal landmark.)

Meanwhile, beset by rising revolutionary violence, the beleaguered Manchus belatedly introduced a series of domestic reforms, halfway measures as well as more radical ones, in an attempt to stave off ultimate, inevitable disaster. Between 1905 and 1908, the iron-willed Dowager Cixi, now in her seventies, grudgingly agreed to implement a series of constitutional reforms, which included such things as the final abolition of the much-despised eight-legged essay (it was about time!), the establishment of provincial political assemblies, the reorganization of the imperial bureaucracy, and the introduction of public participation in local administrative affairs and financial planning. In some of these respects she was borrowing the thunder of Sun Yat-sen's populism.

But the reforms were a classic example of too little and too late. Decades of Manchu self-indulgence, negligence, corruption, and reaction were now exacerbated by a series of natural calamities. Between 1909 and 1911 the Yangzi and Han rivers both underwent severe, repetitive flooding, bringing famine to millions.

A morally and fiscally bankrupt regime could offer little in the way of meaningful relief under these circumstances. And tens of thousands of people perished. Close to a hundred thousand rebelled. In the year 1909 alone, 113 local uprisings were reported throughout the country, most of them spontaneous revolts by hungry peasants; a year later, the total jumped to 285.

Much of the violence occurred in the newly-flooded areas along the lower and middle reaches of the Yangzi River—the very same regions where the Taipings had enjoyed their greatest successes half a century earlier.

Anti-Manchu resistance also gathered strength in China's newly-established provincial assemblies, whose locally prominent delegates were increasingly resentful over Manchu efforts to impose centralized control over valuable local industrial assets.

Indeed, it was a rebellion by the Sichuan provincial assembly against a Manchu scheme to nationalize the country's railroads in 1911 that foreshadowed the final ultimate collapse of dynastic system.

Ironically, when the end finally came for the Manchus, it was triggered not by a massive popular insurrection, but by a single, unintentional urban bomb blast. As central government troops were being mobilized to suppress the Sichuan assembly's railroad rebellion, revolutionary allies of Sun Yat-sen's *Tongmeng hui*, who had infiltrated the ranks of the local imperial army in the city of Hankow, hastily pushed forward their plans for an armed uprising.

On October 9, 1911, a revolutionary bomb went off accidentally and prematurely at the headquarters of Sun's military allies inside the Russian Concession at Hankow. Apprised of this rebel bomb blast, the Hankow police mounted a raid on the Russian quarter, where they arrested 32 of Sun's supporters and seized a sizeable cache of weapons and explosives.

Even more important and more devastating, they seized documents that identified a large number of underground revolutionaries among the garrison's officers and men. Their identities revealed, the compromised conspirators decided to strike first.

The rebels, who numbered perhaps as many 2,000 fighters, first attacked the offices of the Manchu governor-general of Hankow. Caught completely by surprise, the governor panicked and fled, along with the local garrison commander. Encountering little resistance, the rebels gained effective control of the city by noon the next day, October 10, 1911.

When the fleeing Manchu governor urged foreign diplomats to send gunboats to bombard the revolutionaries, some foreign consuls flatly refused; others declared their political neutrality; still others simply ignored the request, pretending not to hear.

Thus began the Chinese Republican Revolution of 1911—quite accidentally—without any master plan whatever, and with its principal architect, Sun Yat-sen, thousands of miles away.

In the folklore of China's Xinhai Revolution (so named for the date of the uprising on the Chinese lunar calendar), the seizure of Hankow on October 10, 1911, is celebrated in Taiwan today as "Double Ten Day"—China's National Day, the day that Sun Yat-sen's Republican "David" slew the hated Manchu "Goliath."

In reality, however, the final Manchu collapse was a quite protracted affair, taking place over a much longer period of time; and it was as much the product of decades of festering foreign wounds and domestic political dry-rot as it was a result of revolutionary plan and popular mobilization.

Indeed, it is ironically emblematic of the sudden and unexpected outbreak of the Xinhai revolution that Sun Yat-sen himself was in the United States at the time, on a fund-raising mission. Apparently he was as surprised as anyone by the suddenness of the final Manchu collapse.

With foreign governments now sitting on their collective hands, city after city, province after province, declared independence from Manchu rule. By late November of 1911, three-fourths of China's provincial assemblies had seceded from the Manchu Empire.

Meanwhile, in a desperate effort to stave off total collapse, the Manchus tried to persuade their recently retired Northern military commander, General Yuan Shikai, to assume overall command of what remained of the loyalist armed forces.

Yuan's Northern army (or Beiyang) had originally been organized and trained by Li Hongzhang during the Taiping Rebellion; and it was the best equipped, most modern military force in all of China.

But Yuan Shikai nursed a grudge against the Manchus. Just three years earlier, in 1908, a group of scheming Manchu court officials had forced him into retirement. Still seething from this insult to his pride, Yuan Shikai was in no mood to do the Manchus' bidding. But he was a clever negotiator.

And instead of refusing outright, he dictated a set of strict conditions for his return to military duty. His terms included, among other things, granting himself full power of command over the entire Manchu army and navy and a substantial enlargement of the imperial military budget. The man was looking to increase his own power.

With few, if any, viable options remaining to them, the Manchu regent, a man named Prince Jun, acting on behalf of the six-year-old child emperor Puyi, agreed to Yuan Shikai's terms. On October 27, 1911, Yuan was appointed commissioner in full charge of the imperial army and navy.

Still he was still not satisfied, an he now upped the ante yet again. He demanded that the regime also agree to promulgate a full set of constitutional principles, and that he himself should be named as the emperor's prime minister. Clearly, Yuan Shikai had something more in mind than merely leading troops into battle.

By the end of November 1911, all that was left of the once-mighty Manchu court was the figurehead boy-emperor, Puyi and his regent, Prince Jun. His mother, Princess Jun, and a retinue of loyal family retainers were all that was left.

As for Cixi herself, the incomparably sinister and powerful Manchu Dragon Lady had passed away three years earlier, in 1908, shortly after the death of the Guangxu emperor—and just one day after she succeeded in installing the three-year old Puyi on the Dragon Throne of imperial China.

With Yuan Shikai now in effective command of what remained of both the imperial army and the Chinese government, Yuan cautiously sounded out Sun Yat-sen's revolutionaries about a possible power-sharing arrangement. Communicating through intermediaries, the two rival leaders circled each other warily.

Sun himself had read about the Hankow uprising in a Denver newspaper during his sojourn in the United States. Choosing to remain abroad temporarily, he continued his fund-raising drive.

A month later in November, he left the United States for France, where he redoubled his efforts to secure Western diplomatic recognition and financial support. Returning to China in December 1911, Sun arrived just in time to preside over the birth of the Provisional Republic of China. Meeting in Nanjing on December 29, representatives of the new regime elected Sun Yat-sen as provisional president by a near-unanimous vote of 16 to 1. Three days later, on the first of January, 1912, Sun was inaugurated.

Although he had declared his willingness to share power with Yuan Shikai, Sun's election as provisional president deeply offended Yuan. He had political ambitions of his own, and in a fit of pique, Yuan ordered his lieutenants to break off all negotiations with the republicans.

Recognizing that the provisional republic was extremely fragile, and that it could not long survive without the support of a loyal army, Sun now sought to appease Yuan Shikai to bring him back into the fold.

First he tried to minimize the importance of his own election as provisional president. He even suggested to Yuan's intermediaries that he had agreed to accept the provisional post only in order to reserve the regular presidency for Yuan, himself.

But Yuan was not mollified by this rather half-hearted explanation, and he threatened to order his generals to oppose the new republic and to opt instead for a constitutional monarchy.

In early January of 1912, Sun proposed an arrangement that would ensure a mutually satisfactory transfer of power: In exchange for Yuan's public confirmation of the Manchu dynasty's abdication, and his personal declaration of support for the new republic, Sun Yat-sen would resign as provisional president, thus clearing the way for Yuan to accede to that highly-coveted post. Satisfied with these arrangements, Yuan agreed, and on January 30, the imperial regent, Prince Jun, advised Princess Jun, Puyi's mother, that there were no feasible alternatives to imperial abdication. She thereupon summoned Yuan Shikai to the palace. Her voice heavy with emotion, she announced: "I leave the various matters to your judgment and have no request other than the preservation of the dignity and honor of the emperor."

Two weeks later, on February 12, the abdication was publicly announced. An agreement among the parties to the decree provided that the child emperor Puyi would be given an annual allowance of 4 million taels of silver and would be allowed to live indefinitely in the Summer Palace, along with his mother and a retinue of personal attendants. With that, the 268-year-old Manchu dynasty came to an end, exiting the stage with barely a whimper.

(Film buffs will recall that the last, traumatic days of the Manchu dynasty, and Emperor Puyi's subsequent internal exile within the Summer Palace, are exquisitely depicted in the classic 1987 film by Bernardo Bertolucci, *The Last Emperor*).

As one of their first official acts of governance, the republicans formally moved the seat of Chinese national government from Beijing, whose name means "northern capital," to Nanjing, or "southern capital."

With the abdication now a fait accompli, Yuan Shikai formally announced his support for the new regime. One day later, on February 13, 1912, Sun Yat-sen fulfilled his part of the bargain by resigning as provisional president of the republic.

One month later, Yuan Shikai was duly sworn in as president. Ominously, Yuan took his oath of office not in Nanjing, the Republican seat of government, but in Beijing—symbol of imperial China.

At this point, in the early spring of 1912, there was a single, nominal Republic of China; but there were two rival groups of officials vying for supreme authority, each with a profoundly different vision for China's future. Eyeing each other warily, they set about forming a unified government.

Next time we see how these two groups played out their rivalries on the eve of World War I.

The Failed Republic, 1912–1919
Lecture 8

> When lack of a legal quorum prevented the parliament from convening, Yuan [Shikai] did what any self-respecting autocrat would do; he dissolved the parliament.

China's republican experiment was short-lived: President Yuan Shikai moved to marginalize the Guomindang, buying off some legislators and intimidating others. He arranged the assassination of the GMD's prime minister, Song Jiaoren. By 1913, Sun Yat-sen was again forced into exile. Yuan then set about restoring the Chinese empire, with himself as emperor.

He might have succeeded but for the outbreak of World War I. With the Western powers distracted in Europe, Japan in 1915 presented Yuan with its **21 Demands**, designed to expand its foothold in China. When word of the Japanese demands leaked out, a wave of anti-Japanese, anti–Yuan Shikai nationalism erupted in China. Angered by President Yuan's willingness to capitulate to Japan, Chinese provinces began declaring their independence

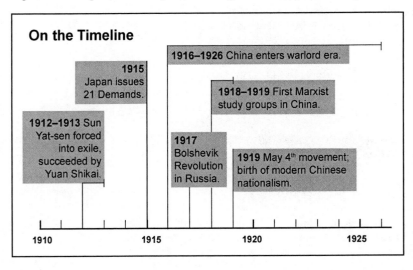

On the Timeline

1916–1926 China enters warlord era.

1915 Japan issues 21 Demands.

1918–1919 First Marxist study groups in China.

1912–1913 Sun Yat-sen forced into exile, succeeded by Yuan Shikai.

1917 Bolshevik Revolution in Russia.

1919 May 4th movement; birth of modern Chinese nationalism.

1910   1915   1920   1925

one by one. Japan's demands could not be implemented, and Yuan's plans for a restored empire were aborted. He died a year later, a broken man.

Soon after, China devolved into an extended period of political fragmentation. Without a strong central government, China's provincial military chieftains—known as warlords—reigned supreme in their regional strongholds. When World War I ended, China, which had nominally joined the victorious Franco-British-American alliance, expected to be rewarded with the return of Germany's concessions in Shandong Province and elsewhere. But the Treaty of Versailles in April 1919 transferred the German concessions to Japan.

Outraged students and workers held mass demonstrations in several Chinese cities. The **May 4ᵗʰ movement,** as these demonstrations were called, lasted for over a month and marked the birth of modern Chinese nationalism. In its aftermath, the New Culture movement deepened the national determination to cast off foreign domination and make China modern, wealthy, and strong. ■

Names to Know

Song Jiaoren (1882–1913): An expert on parliamentary government, Song was the first prime minister of the Republic of China. A year after he orchestrated the GMD's first electoral campaign in 1912, he was assassinated on Yuan Shikai's orders.

Soong Ching-ling (1893–1981): The American-educated second wife of Sun Yat-sen. She was the daughter of Sun's key financial backer, Charlie Soong, and the sister of Soong Mei-ling (Madame Chiang K'ai-shek).

Soong Mei-ling (1897–2003): The younger sister of Soong Ching-ling, and wife of Chiang K'ai-shek. Educated in the United States, she acted as a go-between in the early 1940s, rallying the support of the American people for China's struggle against Japan.

Zhang Zuolin (1875–1928): This Manchu warlord ruled Manchuria from 1916 to 1928, when he was assassinated by a Japanese army officer. His son, Zhang Xueliang, famously kidnapped Chiang K'ai-shek in 1936.

Suggested Reading

Chow, *The May Fourth Movement.*

Hsü, *The Rise of Modern China.*

Meisner, *Li Ta-chao and the Origins of Chinese Marxism.*

Pye, *Warlord Politics.*

Schrecker, *The Chinese Revolution in Historical Perspective.*

Seagrave, *The Soong Dynasty.*

Questions to Consider

1. What was warlordism's legacy in China?

2. How did the May 4th movement affect the course of modern Chinese history?

The Failed Republic, 1912–1919
Lecture 8—Transcript

Today we turn from the collapse of the old imperial order in 1911 to Dr. Sun Yat-sen's bold but ultimately ill-started attempt to create a new republican order in China. Starting out on a promising note, the decade of the 1910s ended grimly for the young republic.

Shortly after the inauguration of the new Republic in February 1912, the victorious revolutionaries of Sun Yat-sen's *Tungmeng hui* reconstituted themselves as a Western-style political party. They called it the *Guomindang*, meaning "Nationalist Party" (abbreviated usually as GMD). Their platform consisted of an elaboration of Sun Yat-sen's Three Principles of the People: nationalism, democracy, and people's livelihood.

Named to run the new party, or to at least to be its titular head, was Sun's long-time ally (and sometimes rival), Song Jiaoren. Song Jiaoren was an outspoken advocate of Western-style parliamentary government.

With Song Jiaoren leading the *Guomindang*'s electoral campaign, China's first parliamentary elections were held in December of 1912, under the rules of a new provisional republican constitution. The party won a resounding majority of seats, a resounding victory, and capped its victory by naming Song as prime minister.

But Yuan Shikai had other ideas and on March 20, 1913—before members of the newly elected parliament could even be certified and seated—Song Jiaoren fell victim to an assassin's bullet at the Shanghai railway station. There was little doubt that Yuan had engineered the assassination, but no hard evidence ever came to light, and the GMD ultimately swallowed this bitter pill with only a mild protest.

With Song Jiaoren's death, the *Guomindang* became virtually rudderless. And when parliament finally convened in April of 1913, Yuan Shikai's supporters shamelessly tried to bribe the *Guomindang*'s majority legislators, offering them each 1,000 British pounds to resign from the party. Some accepted; some refused. But those who refused soon found themselves being hounded by the police. With that, the door began to shut on China's short-lived republican experiment.

Yuan Shikai now set about trying to augment his personal power and undermine that of his rivals. With the national police openly harassing

Guomindang lawmakers and their supporters, Yuan unilaterally revoked the credentials of the remaining GMD-affiliated members of parliament. When lack of a legal quorum prevented the parliament from convening, Yuan did what any self-respecting autocrat would do; he dissolved the parliament.

With Song Jiaoren dead, with parliament dissolved, and with the *Guomindang* now branded as an outlaw party, Sun Yat-sen found himself being forced into exile once again. In August 1913 he fled to Japan, bringing with him hundreds of his fellow *Guomindang* Party activists.

While in Japan, Sun, who was already married with two grown children, took as his second wife the middle daughter of one his key political supporters, a man namedCharlie Soong. Born to a Hakka merchant family on Hainan Island in south China, Charlie Soong migrated to America at the age of 15. Seeking employment as a laborer, he was given food and lodging by a group of Methodist missionaries, who had soon converted him to Christianity.

Returning to China to work as a missionary, Charlie met Sun Yat-sen quite by chance, in 1894, at a Sunday church service in Shanghai. The two men took an instant liking to each other, and soon Charlie Soong quit his mission to join Sun's anti-Manchu crusade.

Charlie Soong had three daughters and two sons—all of whom now called Sun Yat-sen "uncle." Charlie's eldest son, T.V. Soong, was educated at Harvard and Columbia universities.

After he returned to China in the 1920s, his father's political connections enabled him to rise quickly in Guomindang financial circles. In 1928 he became governor of the Central Bank of China, and later he served as Minister of Finance and Foreign Minister in the Nationalist government of Chiang K'ai-shek.

T.V.'s three sisters, Soong Ai-ling (the eldest), Soong Ching-ling, (the middle sister), and Soong Mei-ling (the youngest), were also educated in the United States at Wesleyan College in Georgia.

When Sun Yat-sen went into exile in Japan in 1913, Charlie Soong and his three daughters accompanied him. In Tokyo, Sun hired Charlie's middle daughter, Soong Ching-ling, as his secretary. Despite a 27-year gap in their ages (Sun was 48; Ching-ling was 21), the relationship quickly blossomed into a romance. Evidently, Sun Yat-sen's attachment to Western values was somewhat flexible and pragmatic, for there were some Western moral conventions—such as marital fidelity and monogamy—that he evidently found inconvenient.

Sun and Soong Ching-ling carried on a secretive three-year affair in Tokyo. When her father found out about it, he was livid. And when Sun took Soong Ching-ling as his second wife a bit later on, papa Charlie was so angry that cut off all contact with his dear friend. When Charlie died of cancer in 1918, Sun elected not to attend the funeral.

But the influence of the Soong family endured long after the death of the patriarch. Not only did T.V. Soong go on to become a leading financial figure in Chiang K'ai-shek's government, but his two sisters, Ching-ling and Mei-ling, went on to become the two most influential women in modern China.

In 1925 Soong Ching-ling was widowed by the death of her illustrious husband. A few years later, her sister Mei-ling met and married Sun Yat-sen's Republican protégé, General Chiang K'ai-shek.

When Chiang K'ai-shek subsequently abandoned many of Sun Yat-sen's cherished republican principles, the Soong sisters had a very bitter falling out. Ching-ling cast her lot with Mao Zedong's Communist revolutionaries. Eventually she rose to become vice president of the People's Republic of China. Meanwhile, her younger sister, Mei-ling, was first lady of the Republic of China.

Thus did China's long and destructive civil war eventually come to mirror almost precisely the family quarrel of the Soong sisters, Ching-ling and Mei-ling. I think you'll agree that this is a remarkable story.

Let us now return to Yuan Shikai's cynical coup d'etat against Sun Yat-sen's newborn republican government. When last we encountered Yuan, he had driven Sun into exile. In an effort to legitimize this power grab, Yuan Shikai hired one of Sun's foreign advisors, an American political science professor named Frank Goodnow, to draft a new Chinese constitution. He should have known better than to hire an American political scientist.

Like Yuan himself, Professor Goodnow distrusted direct democracy, believing that the Chinese people were not yet politically mature enough to govern themselves. Consequently, when the new Chinese constitution was finally completed in 1914, it featured a very strong president with virtually unlimited executive authority.

The president was to be elected for a term of 10 years, with no limit to the number of terms he could serve. And he was further empowered to nominate his own successor.

Taken together, these executive prerogatives ensured that Yuan Shikai could, if he so chose, remain president of China for life.

Thus armed with a new constitutional mandate, Yuan Shikai stepped up his drive to restore the dynastic system. First, he revived various Confucian rituals that had been abandoned at the time of the republican revolution, including the imperial rites of ancestral sacrifice performed at Beijing's Temple of Heaven.

He then convened, on his own initiative, a National Congress of Representatives, which voted dutifully—and unanimously—to restore the symbols and ceremonies of the Dragon Throne.

Yuan Shikai might well have succeeded in his grand scheme of dynastic restoration had it not been for the unexpected outbreak of World War I, in August 1914. With the major foreign powers, the Western powers in particular, focusing all their efforts and attention on the war in Europe, Japan now made its move in China.

Japan had nominally entered the war as an ally of France and Britain against the Austro-Hungarian Empire. But Japan's military governors saw an opportunity to expand their own strategic foothold in China. And they grabbed it.

Back in 1900, at the conclusion of the Boxer Rebellion, the major foreign powers had all agreed, at the urging of the United States, to refrain from colonizing China or from seeking exclusive territorial privileges and concessions at the expense of other powers.

Known as the "Open Door policy," this covenant effectively bound the signatories to "share and share alike" when plundering China's national wealth. Very decent of them.

Though cloaked in the loftiest of democratic principles and Christian moral values, such as respect for China's sovereignty and the reaffirmation of America's sacred duty to protect the powerless Chinese against the rapacious Europeans, in reality the Open Door policy was a thinly disguised exercise in calculated self-interest. Some historians have even called it a covenant among thieves.

Fifteen years after the Open Door policy was formally endorsed by the nations of Europe, Japan set about quietly seeking to close the Open Door. Acting on the pretext of assisting allied military operations against German-occupied strongholds in China's Shandong Province, the Japanese government in January of 1915 presented Chinese president, Yuan Shikai, with a shocking document.

Known as the "21 Demands," the document called for China to recognize Japan's paramount commercial and diplomatic interests, not only in Shandong Province, but in Manchuria and Inner Mongolia as well.

In addition, the 21 Demands called for joint Sino-Japanese control of China's infant iron and steel industries, and for Japanese advisors to assume key posts in China's civil administration, as well as in its national army and its police. If fully implemented, the 21 Demands would have reduced China to the status of a virtual Japanese semi-colony.

Badly wrong-footed by the Japanese, Yuan Shikai tried to bargain with them. In exchange for accepting the 21 Demands, Yuan asked for Japan to grant diplomatic recognition to his new imperial regime and to provide substantial financial aid to help modernize China's industrial and military establishments.

Caught between a rock and a hard place, Yuan reckoned (correctly) that given Japan's vastly superior military power, resistance to the 21 Demands would be futile without firm European support. But such support was unlikely to be forthcoming in the midst of a major war in Europe. And so in May of 1915, Yuan Shikai reluctantly accepted the Japanese demands.

But before a final deal could be struck, the contents of the 21 Demands were leaked to the public—we don't know by whom.But there was an immediate angry outcry, as Chinese students, intellectuals, and members of the new commercial bourgeoisie (or middle class) accused Yuan Shikai of betraying China's national honor. Within weeks, a movement to boycott all Japanese goods quickly spread to more than a dozen cities along China's eastern seaboard.

Undaunted by this powerful patriotic backlash, the stubborn, single-minded Yuan Shikai forged ahead with his plan to restore the monarchy. In mid-December 1915 he declared that the following year, 1916, would mark the beginning of a new imperial reign, to be called the "Glorious Constitution" (or *Hongxian*). Presumably, the irony in this was unintended.

In the provinces, opposition to Yuan's imperial restoration campaign rapidly gained momentum. Yunan Province was the first to rebel, declaring its independence from Yuan in late December. This was followed in short order by Guizhou, Guangxi, Guangdong, Zhejiang, Shaanxi, Sichuan, and Hunan.

Urged by his advisors to retire from the presidency and travel abroad, Yuan stubbornly refused. Abandoned by his closest associates, and now— belatedly—overcome with shame and grief, Yuan died unexpectedly, on June 6, 1916. Although the official cause of his death was reported to be uremia, suspicions of murder by poisoning have lingered for more than 90 years.

Natural or not, Yuan Shikai's death brought to a sudden, jolting halt China's brief experiments with both republicanism and dynastic revival.

Thereafter, the country began to slip into chaos and confusion. With no effective central government in place, with the bulk of Sun Yat-sen's republican movement exiled abroad, and with a dozen or more newly independent provinces each going their own way, anarchy now became a distinct possibility.

At this critical juncture, Yuan Shikai's vice-president, a general named Li Yuanhong, a veteran member of Yuan's Northern military clique, attempted to restore some semblance of political order by reviving the 1912 provisional republican constitution of Sun Yat-sen.

His first move was to have himself installed as president; then he would reconvene the elected parliament that Yuan Shikai had unilaterally dissolved four years earlier. But incessant quarreling among provincial governors and military commanders forced Li Yuanhong to abandon his plan.

What happened next is the stuff of Chinese nightmares. Without effective central political leadership able to issue enforceable commands, centrifugal forces spun out of control. The various provinces went their own way, each declaring its own sovereign authority. Although Li Yuanhong and others tried valiantly to maintain the façade of republican governance, the lack of effective central authority fatally undermined their efforts.

By default, political power now gravitated into the hands of provincial military commanders, the so-called *Dujun*. China's warlord era had begun.

Although a nominal central government continued to exist in Beijing under Li Yuanhong, it was powerless to enforce its mandates. Rival cliques of politicians and militarists fought among themselves for the right to make diplomatic and budgetary decisions in the name of the enfeebled republic. As their fortunes waxed and waned, new coalitions and alliances were forged—and just as quickly broken.

The warlords were a strange and colorful lot. One of the more bizarre militarists, Feng Yuxiang, was nicknamed the "Christian General." Before going into battle, he would baptize his troops with a fire hose and inspect their fingernails.

Another colorful warlord, Wu Peifu, was known as the "Philosopher General." He was partial to precious stones and was said to own the world's largest diamond.

A third warlord, Zhang Zuolin, was nicknamed the "Tiger of Mukden." A closeted homosexual whose tastes reportedly ran to very young boys, he nonetheless accumulated five wives and a personal fortune estimated at $10 million—by no means a trivial amount in those days.

Later in the 1920s, Zhang Zuolin would be assassinated by the Japanese militarists in Manchuria; and a decade after that, in 1936, Zhang's son, General Zhang Xueliang, would lead a mutiny against Chiang K'ai-shek on the eve of the Sino-Japanese War—a mutiny that arguably sealed Chiang's and China's fate. (We will have more to say about this remarkable episode later on.)

Within their own bailiwicks, which could be as small as a handful of rural districts or as large as two or three entire provinces, the warlords were a law unto themselves. Commanding personal armies made up largely of peasant conscripts, they were most often men of rather narrow vision and limited ability.

A number of warlords were predators, who got rich by exploiting their own people. Once they had amassed sufficient wealth, many voluntarily relinquished their warlord positions, retiring to the safety of foreign concessions in treaty-port cities, where they could enjoy all the benefits of their ill-gotten gains.

The warlords might have gone down in the history books as something of a mere curiosity, a short-lived feudalistic anachronism. But the decade during which their armies fought for control of China, from 1916 to 1926, was one of the most bloodiest and destructive in modern Chinese history.

Not only were an estimated two million Chinese killed in the senseless internecine wars of this period, but vast numbers of peasants, seeking to escape the continual fighting, were uprooted from the land, becoming a semi-permanent army of impoverished refugees.

It was this vast human migration that inspired Pearl Buck to write her award-winning 1931 book, *The Good Earth*.

Meanwhile, as World War I raged on in Europe, the allied powers, France, England, the United States, and now Japan, were eager to enlist China, at least nominally, in the struggle against Germany and the Austro-Hungarian empire. A key reason for wanting China to enter the war was to facilitate the repatriation of German concessions and property holdings in northeast and central China.

Responding to allied blandishments, China declared war on Germany in August 1917. Almost immediately thereafter, Chinese warlords seized all German and Austrian-controlled properties and assets in the cities of Qingdao, Tianjin, and Hankow.

In consideration for these seizures, the allied powers declared a five-year moratorium on Chinese repayment of indemnities imposed under the Boxer Protocol of 1901. A nice neat little quid pro quo.

Although China was nominally now a member of the victorious triple alliance, when the war ended the allied powers treated China shabbily, not as an equal partner, but as bounty to be distributed among the victors. At the Versailles Peace Conference of April 1919, Chinese representatives were startled to discover that all the territories and assets they had so recently seized from the Germans in Shandong Province had been secretly—and cynically—promised to Japan as compensation for Japan's entry into the war.

Understandably outraged, China's official representatives at the Versailles peace conference demanded the return of Shandong to China. And they further sought from the allied powers a formal commitment to abolish all foreign privileges in China, as well as a formal Japanese renunciation of the 21 Demands. To justify their demands, they invoked President Woodrow Wilson's wartime pledge to uphold the so-called "Fourteen Points," in particular, the Wilsonian commitment to national self-determination, territorial integrity, and "open covenants, openly arrived at."

But it was to no avail; preoccupied with dividing up the larger spoils of war, the allied powers all but ignored China's demands.

Within China, reaction to the hypocritical actions of the victorious allied powers was swift and intense. On May 4, 1919, more than 3,000 students from 13 schools and universities in Beijing gathered at Tiananmen, the famous Gate of Heavenly Peace, which stands at the southernmost portal of the Imperial Palace in the Forbidden City.

The students angrily denounced the perfidious Westerners, as well as the scheming Japanese. For good measure, they also vented their rage at the impotence of the Chinese negotiators in Versailles.

Shouting radical anti-foreign slogans, the demonstrators marched to the residence of China's pro-Japanese vice-minister of foreign affairs, where they proceeded to burn his house to the ground.

When police intervened to disperse the angry crowd, a number of students were arrested and several were beaten. At least one student died of his injuries. The next day, students throughout Beijing declared a strike. Resonant outcries of angry protest occurred in other Chinese cities as well; and in June, factory workers in Shanghai went on strike against all foreign-owned firms. To quell the mounting disorder, the military clique that ruled in Beijing promised to release all imprisoned students and to fire the pro-Japanese vice-foreign minister. In a final act of defiance, China's representatives at the Versailles Conference were instructed not to sign the final peace agreement.

The May 4th movement, as this month-long series of protest demonstrations and strikes was called, was a watershed in modern Chinese history, for it marked the birth of modern Chinese nationalism.

In the course of this movement, large numbers of students, intellectuals, patriotic businessmen, and factory workers expressed their patriotic anger against both the two-faced foreign imperialists and their Chinese lackeys and running dogs. In the immediate aftermath of the May 4th movement, China's deeply-alienated intellectuals began to search for meaningful new solutions to the nagging problems of foreign predation, warlordism, political instability, economic backwardness, and the general bankruptcy of Confucian civilization.

Under the shadow of May 4th, young Chinese students and scholars began to study a variety of foreign philosophies, from democratic socialism to anarcho-syndicalism, from the pragmatism of William James and John Dewey to the hyper-nationalism of Friedrich Nietzsche and the social Darwinism of Herbert Spencer.

Out of the ashes of China's discredited Confucian tradition there also emerged, in the wake of the May 4th movement, the very first sprouts of a new Chinese literary awakening.

Known variously as the "New Learning" and the "New Culture Movement," this Chinese cultural renaissance witnessed the spread of a new vernacular form of writing. First popularized by an American-educated Chinese philosopher and essayist, Dr. Hu Shi, the new vernacular replaced the archaic classic literary style, which required years of tedious study to master, and which bore little or no resemblance to the spoken language.

Because the new written vernacular closely mirrored normal everyday patterns of speech, it was much easier to learn than the classical language. Because of this linguistic simplification, an upsurge in popular education and literacy soon followed, including—for the first time—the education of large numbers of Chinese girls, including, by the way, the Soong sisters.

By the 1920s, a new generation of modern Chinese writers had begun composing their works in the vernacular style, including such literary giants as Lu Xun, Lao She, Mao Dun, and Hu Shi, himself. In terms of literary innovation, the 1920s were China's golden years.

Also active in the May 4th period were a small number of Marxist study groups inspired by the Bolshevik Revolution of November 1917. These study groups began reading the translated works of Karl Marx, Friedrich Engels, and Vladimir Ilyich Lenin.

It was while participating in one of these early Marxist study groups that a young middle-school graduate from Hunan Province received his introduction to the theory of dialectical materialism. Though he was a crude country bumpkin who spoke in a crude southern dialect and dressed rather shabbily, Mao Zedong was destined to make an indelible mark on modern Chinese history.

Next time, we shall examine the origins of the Chinese Communist Party.

The Birth of Chinese Communism, 1917–1925
Lecture 9

> Let us rise and fight together! The revolution is not yet accomplished!
> — The last words of Dr. Sun Yat-sen

While one group of Chinese nationalists gravitated toward Western liberalism, another group was strongly attracted to its Bolshevik antithesis, represented by the triumph of the Russian Revolution. In the theories of Karl Marx and Vladimir Lenin, radical Chinese intellectuals found both an explanation for China's 19th-century misfortunes (capitalists competing abroad for markets, resources, and raw materials) and a prescription for how to end them (proletarian revolution).

China's first Marxist study group was formed in 1918 at Peking University and included 24-year-old **Mao Zedong**. Mao believed that the main force for China's national salvation would be the country's long-suffering rural masses—the peasantry. This went against the grain of orthodox Marxism, which placed its revolutionary hopes on a violent upheaval by the urban working class, the proletariat.

> **Mao believed that the main force for China's national salvation would be the country's long-suffering rural masses—the peasantry.**

In 1920, Lenin's Third **Communist International** (Comintern) sent agents to meet with China's fledgling Marxists and train them in proletarian revolution. Under their tutelage, the Chinese Communist Party (CCP) was formed in 1921.

Meanwhile, Sun Yat-sen, taking advantage of conflict among regional Chinese warlords, returned to Canton and rebuilt the GMD. Recognizing that his failure in 1912 had been due in large measure to the lack of a loyal, well-trained army, Sun placed high priority on organizing and training a revolutionary military force.

In 1921, Sun met with agents of Lenin's Comintern, who became his advisers. Under their influence, he reorganized his Guomindang along Bolshevik lines, and in 1923 he entered into a united front with the fledgling CCP to oppose the "three big evils": warlords, imperialists, and feudal landowners.

With Comintern guidance and Soviet equipment, Sun set up a Peasant Movement Training Institute and a military academy in Canton in 1924. But he died of cancer in 1925, before he could succeed in reunifying China. A struggle for power ensued among Sun's lieutenants, eventually yielding a successor: the strong-willed, right-wing general **Chiang K'ai-shek.** ∎

Names to Know

Chen Gongbo (1892–1946): A founding member of the CCP, Chen quit the party in 1922 and joined the Guomindang. After the Japanese invasion, Chen collaborated with Japan. At war's end, he was tried as a traitor and executed by firing squad.

Chiang K'ai-shek (1887–1975): The leader of the GMD after Sun Yat-sen's death, Chiang led the Northern Expedition to end warlordism. An ardent anti-Communist, Chiang sought to destroy the CCP at all costs—even while tolerating early Japanese encroachments. After World War II, Chiang suffered a humiliating defeat by Mao Zedong's People's Liberation Army (PLA); Chiang fled to Taiwan in December 1949.

Mao Zedong (1893–1976): Political theorist, military strategist, and chairman of the CCP Central Committee from 1935 until his death, Mao adapted Vladimir Lenin's theory of proletarian revolution to the needs of China's rural society. He defeated Chiang K'ai-shek in China's civil war and led the People's Republic of China for 40 years. His radical policies in the 1950s and 1960s caused enormous suffering, leading to major reforms in the 1980s.

Important Term

Communist International (**Comintern**): Organization founded by Vladimir Lenin in 1919 to promote revolutionary movements in colonial and semicolonial countries.

Suggested Reading

Chang, *Wild Swans.*

Chow, *The May Fourth Movement.*

Fenby, *Modern China.*

Hsü, *The Rise of Modern China.*

Meisner, *Li Ta-chao and the Origins of Chinese Marxism.*

Schrecker, *The Chinese Revolution in Historical Perspective.*

Schwartz, *Chinese Communism and the Rise of Mao.*

Questions to Consider

1. What was the appeal of Marxism-Leninism to Chinese intellectuals of the May 4th era?

2. How was Soviet influence manifested in China in the early 1920s?

The Birth of Chinese Communism, 1917–1925

Lecture 9—Transcript

In the swirling vortex of the May 4th movement, all the ambivalent elements in China's long-simmering love/hate relationship with the West were powerfully reproduced and amplified. While one group of Chinese nationalists gravitated toward Western liberalism, another group was strongly attracted to its Bolshevik antithesis, represented by the triumph of the Russian Revolution.

Disillusioned with a century of cruel and callous Western treatment of China, as well as Western hypocrisy at Versailles, a growing number of radical Chinese intellectuals were drawn to the example of the Bolsheviks who, in the name of empowering the toiling masses had successfully thrown off centuries of czarist oppression and seized the property of the ruling classes. For Chinese struggling to overcome a century of national impotence, this was an extraordinary achievement.

Shortly after the Russian revolution, Chinese scholars began translating the works of Karl Marx and V.I. Lenin into Chinese; and a Marxist study group was formed in 1918 under the guidance of a Peking University history professor, who was also the university's head librarian, Li Dazhao.

Part anarchist and part socialist, Li Dazhao believed that for China to regain its lost national strength and energy, patriotic intellectuals would have to replace the pessimism and passivity that had paralyzed the Chinese psyche, with a new spirit of intense mental and physical struggle. Patriotism, he believed, would play a vital role in this national mobilization.

In this belief, Li differed from his principal collaborator, Chen Duxiu. Chen was a Westernized intellectual who, early in his career, wrote that the key to China's national reawakening lay in the twin icons of the Western Enlightenment, which he called "Mr. Science" and "Mr. Democracy."

Where Li Dazhao believed that patriotism was the key to preparing the country for its coming liberation struggle, Chen Duxiu distrusted patriotism as a blind, non-productive emotion, one that could certainly arouse people, but without necessarily enlightening them. And he stressed, instead, the importance of deep self-knowledge and knowledge of society as the essential prerequisites of effective social action.

Together, these two unlikely allies, Li Dazhao and Chen Duxiu—the emotional patriot and the introspective rationalist—founded China's first quasi-Marxist journal, the *Xin Qingnian*, or "New Youth." The year was 1917.

A year later, in 1918, the 25-year-old Hunanese sojourner, Mao Zedong, applied for a job as assistant librarian at Peking University. Armed with a letter of introduction to Li Dazhao from his former middle-school teacher in Hunan, Mao got the job. It would change his life and modern Chinese history, as well.

Right from the start, Li Dazhao's influence on the young Mao was apparent. Like Li, Mao believed that young Chinese intellectuals needed to toughen their minds and bodies for the coming national struggle; and like Li, he was more of a populist than an elitist.

He believed that the main force for China's national salvation would be the country's long-suffering rural masses, the peasantry.

These were not particularly Marxist ideas. Indeed they went against the grain of orthodox Marxism, which placed all revolutionary hopes on a violent upheaval by the urban working class, the proletariat.

In any event, under Li Dazhao's guidance, Mao began to study the Marxist classics in 1919 and 1920. His reading list included *Das Kapital* and *The Communist Manifesto*.

While Marx's predictions of violent class struggle between workers and capitalists clearly appealed to many radical Chinese intellectuals, Lenin's Theory of imperialism made a far bigger impression. The reasons for this were not hard to find.

For one thing, Lenin provided a clear and coherent theoretical explanation for China's 19th century descent into national humiliation and degradation; for another, Lenin's writings contained a powerful revolutionary prescription for how to reverse China's steep decline into national impotence.

Lenin suggested, first, that the global commercial expansion initiated by the Western powers in the 18th and 19th centuries was not merely random or accidental, but was the inevitable outgrowth of the ever-intensifying competition for commercial profits within the advanced capitalist countries of Europe. In Lenin's view, imperial expansion abroad was the direct result of diminishing returns on capital and labor at home.

Both as a source of cheap labor, industrial resources and raw materials, and as a potential market for Western machine-made exports, pre-industrial societies such as China and India were powerful magnets that attracted foreign mercantile capitalists to their shores.

As we saw in our earlier discussion of how China was "carved up" by foreign powers in the half-century following the Opium Wars, the existence of vast, untapped overseas markets, resources and labor made it possible for the Western powers to adopt a mutually tolerant strategy of "share and share alike" in their collaborative exploitation of China's national wealth.

It was this cynical ethos of honor among thieves, dressed up in the lofty, self-righteous moral language of noblesse oblige, that lay at the heart of Europe's agreement to accept President William McKinley's Open Door proposal at the turn of the 20th century.

But that was not the end of Lenin's remarkable theory of imperialism. As overseas European commercial expansion continued apace, he argued, it must eventually lead to the exhaustion of easily-exploitable profit-making opportunities. Once the low-hanging fruit of foreign concessions and extraterritorial privileges had been effectively harvested, commercial rivalries among the imperialist powers would inevitably heat up.

As they began to rub up against one another, the result would be a rise in frictional competition for overseas markets, resources, and labor. In terms of modern game theory, the expansion of capitalism abroad would eventually be transformed from a non-zero-sum game (that is, a win-win situation of mutual gain) into a zero-sum game, where one power's gain was the other powers' loss.

In China, Japan's attempt to impose the 21 Demands in 1915, and thereby secure an exclusive industrial and commercial foothold in China, represented precisely such a transformation from a mutually cooperative game to a highly competitive one. The inevitable end result of such competition, in Lenin's view, was world war.

This, in a nutshell, was Lenin's theory of imperialism: Imperialism is the highest stage of capitalism; and war, in turn, is the highest stage of imperialism. It doesn't take a rocket scientist to comprehend just why this theory would prove so appealing to many radical young Chinese intellectuals of the May 4th era.

But Lenin's theory offered even more. In addition to providing a cogent diagnosis of the reasons for such historical developments as China's 19th century subjugation, the outbreak of World War I, and Japan's increasingly bold attempt to close the Open Door in China, Lenin also provided a timely prescription for putting an end to the predictable evils of imperialist exploitation, predation, competition, and war.

Karl Marx had argued that proletarian revolution was a spontaneous act that could and would only occur when the objective economic contradictions of industrial capitalism had fully intensified and played themselves out. At that point, and only at that point, the exploited industrial workers, having (in Marx's famous phrase) "nothing to lose but their chains," would rise up in revolt against their capitalist slave masters. They would seize the factories and abolish all private property, private property being the ultimate source of their misery.

Precisely because such an uprising could, in Marx's view, occur only when the contradictions of advanced capitalism had become so intense as to create a situation of spontaneous combustion, proletarian revolution could not be a product of purposive human agency, that is, there could be no revolution before its time.

Unlike Marx, however, Lenin was in a hurry. He was not satisfied with such a mechanistic view of revolution. He was unwilling to wait 20, 30, or 50 years for the Russian working class to seize power. His impatience was rewarded by the Bolshevik experience.

In Russia, the revolution of 1917 was an organized, purposive uprising, led by a self-conscious, conspiratorial Communist Party. The Bolshevik experience proved that one didn't need to wait until the internal contradictions of capitalism were fully ripe. One could increase the workers' revolutionary awareness through focused education, propaganda and indoctrination, and thereby enable the proletariat to accomplish its true historical mission.

One could also organize workers into secretive, clandestine cells for purposes of revolutionary agitation. One could, in short, plan and orchestrate a well-coordinated class uprising.

Indeed, this was precisely the stated mission of the Soviet Party. In Lenin's view, the Bolshevik Party was a high disciplined organizational weapon that would be used to hasten the coming of the proletarian revolution.

Now in the view of many historians, this was Lenin's single greatest contribution to the theory and practice of revolution.

In China, where capitalism was still in its virtual infancy, and where the industrial working class made up no more than perhaps two or three percent of the total population, Lenin's prescription for speeding up the historical dialectic by creating a revolutionary Communist Party proved quite appealing. To growing numbers of impatient young Chinese radicals, Lenin's theories seemed virtually tailor-made for China.

Shunned by the bourgeois societies of western Europe and surrounded by forces hostile to Bolshevism, Lenin began to search for revolutionary allies abroad.

Hoping to exploit the radical intellectual ferment of China's May 4th movement, in 1919 the international arm of the Soviet Communist Party, the Third Communist International (more commonly known as the "Comintern"), dispatched several undercover agents to China to explore the possibility of linking up with newborn revolutionary forces there.

What these Soviet agents found in China was a country descending into disorder. There was no national government that could command obedience in the provinces, which were governed by shifting coalitions of regional warlords. They also found in China a situation in which two quite distinct types of revolutionary thinking and organization were developing on separate tracks, quite independent of each other.

The first of these was the small, newly-created Communist movement, the core of which was the Marxist study group at Peking University, organized by Li Dazhao and Chen Duxiu. The other—and at that point, more important— organization, was the newly-resurgent republican movement of Sun Yat-sen.

After fleeing from China in 1913, Sun had lived in exile in Japan. But as China descended into chaos after Yuan Shikai's death, Sun began to look for an opening to re-enter the Chinese political scene. His opportunity came in 1917, when a group of southern provinces, including Guangdong, rebelled against the dissolution of the national parliament in Beijing.

Returning from Japan to his native Canton, Sun began to reassemble the scattered remnants of his failed republican movement. These remnants formed the political base of Sun's reorganized Nationalist Party, the *Guomindang*.

Recognizing that his failure in 1912 had been due in large measure to the lack of a loyal, well-trained republican army, Sun placed high priority on organizing and training a revolutionary military force.

Under the patronage of a sympathetic Cantonese regional warlord named Chen Qiongming, in 1921 Sun proclaimed the birth of a Military Government of the Republic of China, and named himself as commander-in-chief.

It was also in 1921 that Sun Yat-sen had his first fateful encounter with agents of the Third Communist International. A Comintern operative named Maring had been sent by Lenin to seek out potential revolutionary supporters in China. Although Sun was suspicious of Maring's and Lenin's underlying motives, he was clearly attracted by the prospect of gaining Bolshevik financial and military support.

For 20 years Sun had sought Western aid for his republican movement; and for 20 years he had failed. For Europeans and Americans alike, it seemed that the devil they knew (the hapless Manchus and then the inept warlords) was preferable to the devil they didn't know (the visionary nationalist, Sun Yat-sen). There was no small irony in the fact that Sun, a pro-Western liberal, should ultimately be forced to turn for assistance to one of the world's most illiberal, anti-Western countries.

After being expelled from Canton by his erstwhile patron, Chen Qiongming, Sun in 1922 moved his headquarters to Shanghai, where his conversations with Lenin's representatives grew more focused and intense. Determined to remedy the military weakness that had been the source of his undoing a decade earlier, Sun now sought Soviet military assistance. The Comintern was only too happy to accommodate him—for a price.

In January 1923 Sun hammered out an agreement with a Soviet diplomat named Adolf Joffe. In exchange for receiving substantial Soviet military training, weapons, and equipment, Sun agreed to mute his previous hostility toward Bolshevism and to allow the Comintern to advise him in reorganizing his *Guomindang* Party, in order to turn it into an effective Bolshevik-style revolutionary weapon. Though Lenin's Comintern agents readily collaborated with Sun Yat-sen, they were not, at this point, prepared to put all their eggs in Sun's basket.

Even before Maring and Joffe courted Sun Yat-sen, their Comintern colleague, Gregoir Voitinski, had secretly begun liaising with leaders of the new-born Chinese Marxist movement in Beijing.

In 1920, Voitinsky met with Li Dazhao at Peking University. Li, in turn, introduced Voitinski to Chen Duxiu. From all reports, Voitinski was not terribly impressed with these two rather naïve and unsophisticated Marxist enthusiasts. Moreover, at this early stage Li and Chen had recruited relatively few core followers; and their entire Marxist network comprised a few dozen vaguely radicalized members of the Beijing University study group.

Nevertheless, Lenin ordered Voitinski to cultivate Li and Chen, and their followers, and to educate them in Communist doctrine.

Throughout the summer and fall of 1920, Li Dazhao and Chen Duxiu received concentrated instruction in the theory and practice of Bolshevism. In the process, they rid themselves of a good deal of their youthful idealism, bourgeois sentimentality, and romantic nationalism acquired during the May 4th era. They had now become dedicated revolutionaries.

By the late fall of 1920, efforts were underway to organize a bona fide Chinese Communist Party. But the warlords who controlled Beijing were fully aware of the Comintern's subversive intentions. Paid informants and foreign concession police provided a steady stream of information about the comings and goings of key Bolshevik agents.

Alerted that the new Communist Party was about to convene its first National Congress in July of 1921, treaty port police hounded dozens of known or suspected Communists, forcing many to go into hiding. Of the 50 or so original members of the CCP, only 12 managed to attend the founding Party Congress, which was held amid very tight secrecy at a private girl's school inside Shanghai's French Concession.

When the French Concession's foreign police, acting on a tip, raided the girl's school in the middle of the meeting, the delegates fled. Later, they reassembled on a pleasure boat in the middle of the scenic South Lake in neighboring Zhejiang Province. Unhappily, no definitive written record of this first meeting was preserved.

A personal digression, if you will: In 1978, I paid a visit to the Shanghai Girl's School where the first Communist Party Congress had been held in 1921. The building was very hard to find and had no external markings or identifying signage to indicate its historical significance.

I was accompanied on this sojourn by a young Chinese-American electrical engineer, who just happened to be the son of one of the founding members of the Chinese Communist Party, a man named Chen Gongbo. Chen had participated in the very first National Party Congress at this very same girl's school. The front room of the girl's school had been converted into a small historical museum. The elderly proprietor, surprised at receiving an unexpected visit from two Americans, eagerly showed us around. There were some musty old photographs on the walls, including one group photo showing the original participants, including Mao Zedong. But there was no photo of Chen Gongbo.

This was no great surprise, since Chen Gongbo had been condemned as a traitor to China. In 1922, a year after attending the First Party Congress, he terminated his membership in the CCP; and a few years later he joined the rival *Guomindang*. Following the Japanese invasion of 1937, Chen Gongbo collaborated with the Japanese; and at the end of the war he was put on trial for treason. He was executed by a Chinese firing squad in 1946.

So it was no surprise that Chen Gongbo was among the missing persons who had been banished from the Shanghai Girl's School Museum. No photos of him were in evidence, and there was no mention of him in any of the documents on display. After walking around the exhibition hall for a while, I made a remark to the proprietor about Chen Gongbo's conspicuous absence. He became quite animated, and he recounted in some detail the story of Chen's traitorous behavior.

After he finished relating his tale, I gestured toward my companion and I said, "Do you know who this man is?" No, answered the proprietor. "Tashi Chen Gongbo de erzi" I replied. "This is Chen Gongbo's son."

At that point the old man's face reddened noticeably. Gesturing for us to follow him, he unlocked the museum's back room and invited us inside. There we found hundreds of historical photos and documents lying around on tables, in boxes, and in cabinets.

Sorting through a stack of these, he finally pointed with pride to one faded photo—"Here he is," he said eagerly. "Here's Chen Gongbo; see, he's standing next to Chairman Mao."

This incident nicely captures a rather distinguishing characteristic of Chinese communism, to which we shall have occasion to return, and that is, the Communist Party's entrenched habit of erasing from the country's collective memory all favorable references to those party members who were later to be accused of betraying either their country or its leadership.

Eminent "missing persons" of the Maoist era included not only Chen Gongbo but also such top-level party leaders (and erstwhile Maoist comrades) as Wang Ming, Liu Shaoqi, Lin Biao, Zhao Ziyang, and even Mao's own wife, Jiang Qing.

This "missing person" syndrome is perhaps best illustrated by the literal airbrushing of Jiang Qing and the Gang of Four out of all official photos of Mao's funeral service in 1976. It is interesting to note that the traditional-style brick building that once housed the Shanghai Girl's School Museum was bulldozed in the 1990s as part of a major Shanghai urban renewal project. The museum was eventually rebuilt in a larger space, a short distance away, in the upscale Shanghai commercial development known as Xintiandi, where the new museum now stands a few short steps from the local Starbucks.

When I last visited the museum in 2001, none of the original photos or documents from that First Party Congress were on display. Instead, the space was dedicated to an exhibition of the life and times of the late Mme. Sun Yat-sen, Song Ching-ling.

With the Comintern holding the purse strings and providing organizational and logistical guidance, Soviet agents in 1923 began to press for a working coalition, or united front, between Sun Yat-sen's *Guomindang* and Li Dazhao's Communist. Although their long-term objectives diverged profoundly, with Sun favoring Western-style liberalism, while the CCP agitated for proletarian socialism, the two parties shared a strong near-term commitment to eradicating the so-called three evils: warlordism, foreign imperialism, and feudal autocracy.

Under the watchful guidance of a Comintern agent named Mikhail Borodin, an agreement was hammered out between the *Guomindang* and the Chinese Communists in the autumn of 1923. Under its terms, the two parties agreed to share leadership within a single, integrated united front.

Because the CCP at this point numbered a mere 300 members and was still in its infancy, the *Guomindang*, as the united front's senior partner, was given a dominant leadership role in the new organization.

For his part, Sun Yat-sen was able to leverage major concessions from Borodin. For example, as a condition of his agreement to collaborate with the Communists, Sun insisted that the CCP must renounce its party's organizational autonomy and that individual members of CCP should join the *Guomindang* as individuals, not as members of the Communist Party.

Once they had entered the GMD, the Communists would be subjected to Sun's leadership. Though Li Dazhao and Chen Duxiu were skeptical, Borodin pressed them to concede thia point, which they eventually did. Thus was born the *Guomindang*/Chinese Communist United Front.

Moving his headquarters back to Canton in 1924, Sun set up a Peasant Training Institute there. Its goal was to arouse the revolutionary consciousness of the peasant masses. Interestingly, one of Sun's lieutenants at the Peasant Training Institute was Mao Zedong.

In Sun's Canton headquarters, a widening flow of Soviet arms, equipment, and advice helped to lend both discipline and muscle to the forces of the United Front. Under Sun's overall leadership, a modern military institute, the Whampoa Academy, was established in 1925. Its commanding officer was a rising young GMD military star named Chiang K'ai-shek.

Chiang had recently returned from a year of advanced military training in the U.S.S.R. under Bolshevik tutelage. His second-in-command at Whampoa was a rising young Communist political organizer named Zhou Enlai.

Under the watchful eye of Soviet instructors, preparations were made at the Whampoa Academy for a decisive military campaign to liberate China from the grip of warlords, imperialists, and feudal landlords.

But before preparations could be completed, Sun Yat-sen's health began to fade.

Diagnosed with liver cancer, Sun was hospitalized at the American-financed Beijing Union Medical College, where he died in March of 1925 at the age of 58. Shortly before his death, Sun went out of his way to praise the Soviet Union; and he famously exhorted his countrymen, in his "last testament," to ally with all nations "who treat [us] on an equal footing." His last words were, "Let us rise and fight together! The revolution is not yet accomplished!"

Sun's death set off a bitter power struggle within the *Guomindang*, between left- and right-wing factions. Eventually the right-wing, led by Sun's strong-willed protégé, Chiang K'ai-shek, would emerge victorious. But the intra-party split that burst into the open in 1925 was a deep and damaging one; and its effects would continue to be felt for many years to come.

Chiang, Mao, and Civil War, 1926–1934
Lecture 10

A revolution is not a dinner party, or writing an essay, or painting a picture, or doing embroidery; it cannot be so refined, so leisurely and gentle, so temperate, kind, courteous, restrained and magnanimous. A revolution is an insurrection, an act of violence by which one class overthrows another.

— Mao Zedong

In 1925, Sun Yat-sen's death triggered a severe power struggle among senior leaders of the Nationalist Party that took a full year to resolve. Once Chiang K'ai-shek had political and military leadership of the Guomindang firmly in his hands, he quickly prepared a massive military campaign against the warlords.

Chiang launched the **Northern Expedition** in 1926 with the goal of crushing the warlords and unifying China. From the outset, the military campaign was stunningly successful: Within half a year, the Nationalist Army controlled seven southern provinces. But as GMD-CCP united front forces reached the Yangzi River, serious strains emerged between Chiang, the CCP, and left-wing elements within the GMD.

In 1930, the Communists established the Jiangxi Soviet Republic, which by 1934 encompassed a civilian population of more than 3 million people.

When Chiang's troops reached Shanghai, workers there were ordered by their Communist labor organizers to embrace the Nationalist Army as liberators. The workers turned the city over to Chiang without a single shot being fired. But after the Nationalist Army took control of Shanghai in April 1927, it launched a coup against Shanghai's left-wing labor unions, killing or arresting thousands of suspected Communists, and forcing the survivors to flee. Within days, Nationalists killed thousands more Communists in Nanjing, Hangzhou, Fuzhou, and Canton.

In the course of their retreat, the Communists led spontaneous insurrections in Canton, Nanchang, and Hunan. Nationalist forces quickly suppressed these **Autumn Harvest Uprisings**, and the CCP survivors retreated into the mountainous hinterland on the Jiangxi-Hunan border. There, under the leadership of Zhou Enlai, Mao Zedong, and Zhu De, they formed a Red Army and developed a new strategy of revolution, known as people's war.

In 1928, Nationalist forces attacked and forced the Red Army to retreat yet again, to a new headquarters along the Jiangxi-Fujian border. There the Red Army built a mass following among the peasants by confiscating and redistributing the land of wealthy landlords. In 1930, the Communists established the **Jiangxi Soviet Republic**, which by 1934 encompassed a civilian population of more than 3 million people. In that same period, the Red Army fought off four successive campaigns launched by Chiang K'ai-shek. ■

Name to Know

Wang Jingwei (1883–1944): He was initially a leader of the left wing of the GMD, but Wang's disdain for Chiang K'ai-shek led him to collaborate with the invading Japanese in 1937. Wang died in disgrace in Japan at the end of World War II.

Important Terms

Autumn Harvest Uprisings (1927–1928): A series of ill-fated, armed insurrections carried out by the CCP in a desperate attempt to avoid annihilation by Chiang K'ai-shek's Nationalist army.

Jiangxi (Kiangsi) Soviet Republic (1930–1934): The Red Army regional base in South China led by Mao Zedong, Zhou Enlai, and Zhu De.

Suggested Reading

Fenby, *Modern China.*

Meisner, *Li Ta-chao and the Origins of Chinese Marxism.*

Schwartz, *Chinese Communism and the Rise of Mao.*

Short, *Mao.*

Taylor, *The Generalissimo.*

Van Slyke, *Enemies and Friends.*

Questions to Consider

1. Why did the 1923–1927 united front between the GMD and the CCP eventually end in bloodshed?

2. How did the CCP's forced rural exile after 1927 affect its ideological orientation and leadership?

Chiang, Mao, and Civil War, 1926–1934
Lecture 10—Transcript

Last time, we traced the origins and early development of the Communist movement in China; and we saw how the Comintern worked to create a United Front between the new Communist Party and Sun Yat-sen's reorganized *Guomindang*.

In 1925, Sun's death triggered a major power struggle among senior leaders of the Nationalist Party. It took a full year to resolve the conflict. When the dust finally settled, the victor was Chiang K'ai-shek, the conservative commandant of the Whampoa Military Academy.

In a series of Machiavellian political maneuvers, which included an elaborate attempt to implicate one of his top rivals for taking part in a plot to assassinate a second major rival, Chiang successfully neutralized his centrist and his left-leaning competitors.

As a result of such machinations, by mid-1926 Chiang had emerged as the undisputed successor to Sun Yat-sen.

With political and military leadership of the *Guomindang* now firmly grasped in his own hands, Chiang K'ai-shek—who now gave himself the rather lofty title of "Generalissimo," or "Gimo," for short, quickly completed preparations for launching a massive military campaign against the warlords.

Chiang's main military force, the Northern Expeditionary Army, included 7,000 Soviet-trained Whampoa Academy graduates plus 85,000 Russian armed and equipped combat troops, who were mainly recruited from among the impoverished workers and peasants of southern China.

With considerable fanfare, in July 1926 Chiang's Northern Expeditionary Army set out from Canton toward the Yangzi River, some 800 miles to the north. Although Sun did not live to see this epoch-making campaign, it was the culmination of his dream to reunify China under *Guomindang* auspices.

From the very outset, the Northern Expedition proved stunningly successful. Marching northward in more-or-less parallel columns, the well-disciplined, well-equipped troops of Chiang's National Revolutionary Army quickly overwhelmed the ill-disciplined, poorly-prepared peasant conscripts mustered by the panicky regional warlords.

Moving in advance of Chiang's Revolutionary Army, Communist propaganda teams urged the warlords' peasant conscripts to lay down their arms and join the revolutionary cause. Many did so.

To induce the warlords and their field commanders to cease armed resistance, a substantial number of them were offered commissions in the Nationalist Army. At least half a dozen regional militarists and a substantially larger number of their field commanders accepted the offer, changing sides within a matter of weeks.

Within half a year, Chiang's National Army controlled seven southern provinces. With warlord resistance weakening with each passing month, victory became more certain.

But as victory became more certain, the inherent strains and fault lines within the united front became more pronounced. Never more than a marriage of convenience, the United Front now began to unravel.

First to break away from Chiang K'ai-shek's leadership were a group of left-wing *Guomindang* officials who had become increasingly alienated by Chiang's right-wing authoritarian tendencies. Making their headquarters in the newly-liberated Yangzi River city of Hankow, scene of the original Republican revolt of October 1911, this left-wing faction was led by a second former protégé of Sun Yat-sen named Wang Jingwei.

Meanwhile, Chiang led his troops toward Shanghai, 400 miles to the east of Hankow, near the mouth of the Yangzi. The tensions between these two Nationalist leaders, Chiang K'ai-shek and Wang Jingwei, grew steadily sharper in the winter and early spring of 1927.

Also growing deeper and more intense was the mutual distrust and suspicion between Chiang and his increasingly uneasy Communist partners. Some Chinese Communist leaders had warned their Soviet paymasters about Chiang's autocratic tendencies. But the Russians had too much invested in the success of the United Front to change course in midstream; and so they disregarded these early warnings.

By late March of 1927, Chiang's troops had reached the outskirts of Shanghai. As they prepared to enter the city, the Communist-dominated Shanghai General Labor Union launched a general strike. Timed to coincide precisely with Chiang's arrival, some 600,000 industrial workers walked off their jobs, virtually paralyzing the city.

Ordered by their Communist labor organizers to embrace the Nationalist Army as liberators, the Shanghai workers turned the city over to Chiang K'ai-shek without a single shot being fired.

For thousands of foreign nationals living in Shanghai's foreign concessions, Chiang's arrival caused a wave of panic.

They had been led to believe (by Sun Yat-sen's anti-imperialist rhetoric) that a Nationalist victory would spell the end of 90 years of foreign privilege and spheres of influence in China.

To prepare for a possible confrontation, the foreigner powers mustered 42 warships in Shanghai's harbor, manned by thousands of sailors and soldiers. Fearing the worst, the foreigners waited nervously for some sign of Chiang's ultimate intentions.

In the event, they needn't have worried. For unbeknownst either to the terrified foreigners, or to the Communist-controlled labor unions of Shanghai, or to Wang Jingwei's left-wing *Guomindang* government in Hankow, the victorious Generalissimo had entered into secret alliances both with Shanghai's key financial elites and with the city's notorious criminal "Green Gang" (*Qing bang*), a mafia-like secret society that controlled gambling, prostitution, and drug trafficking in the city.

Under the terms of this unholy alliance, all foreigners in Shanghai, along with their properties and privileges, were to be fully protected. In return for such protection, the Green Gang would be allowed to continue operating under Chiang K'ai-shek's patronage.

Because of this cynical quid-pro-quo, the liberation of Shanghai turned out to be largely a matter of business as usual for the city's foreign residents; and the warships in Shanghai harbor were soon taken off ready-alert status, as the foreign community breathed a collective sigh of relief.

But for China's Communists and their local supporters, it was anything but business as usual. Deeply disturbed by Chiang's sharp rightward political shift and by his alliance with powerful financial and underworld interests in Shanghai, Communist Party leaders urged their Comintern advisors to dissolve the United Front.

But before they could act on their fears, Chiang launched a sudden, violent coup against his erstwhile allies.

At 4 am on April 12, 1927, Chiang's army launched a series of coordinated attacks against Shanghai's Communist labor unions. Moving swiftly and brutally, with the aid of civilian goon squads from the Green Gang, Chiang's forces shot suspected Communists on sight, disarmed and beat worker pickets, and arrested hundreds.

When the Shanghai townspeople staged a large protest demonstration the next day, Nationalist troops fired on them, killing 100. By dusk on the evening of April 13, a crippling blow had been dealt to China's fledgling Communist Movement.

Within days of the Shanghai debacle, the systemic liquidation of Communists began in the Nationalist-controlled cities of Nanjing, Hangzhou, Fuzhou, and Canton. Thousands died as the reign of White Terror began.

On April 18, a supremely confident Chiang K'ai-shek announced the formation of a national government in Nanjing—capital of Sun Yat-sen's failed republican experiment of 1912. Meanwhile, 400 miles upriver in Hankow, Wang Jingwei's disheartened left-wing *Guomindang* supporters decided against engaging in an armed confrontation with Chiang's superior forces. As the Soviet adviser Mikhail Borodin put it:

> Since we have been sold out by the reactionaries and … do not have the strength to launch attacks against the imperialists, we have no choice but to stage a temporary, strategic retreat. (Dun J. Lee, ed., *The Road to Communism: China Since 1912*, p. 90).

Although the Comintern's united front strategy now lay in tatters, rendered irrelevant by Chiang's April 1927 coup, the new Soviet leader, Joseph Stalin, was not prepared to declare the policy a failure. Lenin had died three years earlier, in 1924, and a bitter struggle among potential successors had raged thereafter.

Stalin's leading rival, the radical leftist Leon Trotsky, had argued that the united front policy had been a mistake, a rightist error, and that Chiang's anti-Communist Shanghai coup, far from being anomalous or unpredictable, was the inevitable result of Stalin's decision to pressure the CCP into continued cooperation with the reactionary Chiang K'ai-shek.

The Chinese Communists, argued Trotsky, should immediately join forces with Wang Jingwei's left-wing *Guomindang* forces and rise up to make their own autonomous revolution—Chiang K'ai-shek be damned!

For Stalin, this presented a major dilemma for he could hardly acknowledge the failure of the united front policy without validating Trotsky's scathing criticism. Caught between a rock and a hard place, in May of 1927 Stalin naively ordered the CCP to seize control of Wang Jingwei's left-wing regime in Hankow.

But it was already too late for that. With Hankow's demoralized leftists having gone into strategic retreat at the end of April, Chiang K'ai-shek, aided by two powerful northern warlords who had changed sides during the Northern Expedition, easily took control of the city. Deeply distressed by these unhappy developments, the chief Comintern adviser, Borodin, retreated from Hankow to Mother Russia to lick his wounds.

As a historical footnote to these events, Wang Jingwei's deep-seated bitterness toward Chiang K'ai-shek would later play itself out with tragically ironic consequences when Japan's army invaded China in 1937. With Chiang electing to retreat in the face of the overwhelming superiority of the advancing Japanese, Wang Jingwei made a fateful decision to collaborate with the Japanese.

The Japanese militarists were only too happy to exploit Wang's well-known animus toward the Generalissimo; and Wang was rewarded for his defection by being named head of the pro-Japanese puppet government in Nanjing. Like Chen Gongbo before him, Wang Jingwei would be reviled forever afterward in China as a traitor to his country. He died in disgrace in Japan at the end of the war.

Driven from the major cities of central and south China in 1927, the defeated Communists split into three groups. One group followed Borodin's lead and hightailed it to Moscow, where they regrouped under Comrade Stalin's scrutiny, setting themselves up as the CCP Central Committee-in-exile. A second group of survivors from the 1927 coup remained in China's major cities, where they went underground to engage in clandestine revolutionary agitation and propaganda. (They came to be called the "White Area Communists.") A third group abandoned the cities altogether, heading not for Moscow but for the mountainous hinterland of south-central China (where they later became known as the "Red Area Communists").

Among these three groups of Communist survivors, it was the third group that would go on to change the course of modern Chinese history. In the process of escaping from Chiang's campaign of White Terror, this latter group staged a number of ad hoc local uprisings.

On August 1, 1927, a force of several thousand Communists entered the Nationalist-held stronghold of Nanchang, the capital of Jiangxi Province. Seizing temporary control of the city, they held out for three days before they were beaten back by superior Nationalist forces.

A month later a second insurrection took place in neighboring Hunan Province. There the rebels optimistically proclaimed the birth of a Hunan Soviet; but it, too, soon fell before the superior might of Chiang's Nationalists. A third uprising took place in Canton in December, but like the others before it, it was brutally suppressed at a cost of nearly 5,000 revolutionary lives.

Among the survivors of these ill-fated Autumn Harvest Uprisings, as they were called, were men who, decades later, would be inducted into the pantheon of Chinese Communist Party immortality, people like Zhou Enlai, Zhu De, Ye Jianying, Lin Biao, Ho Long, Nie Rongzhen, Chen Yi, Liu Bocheng, and—last but by no means least—Mao Zedong.

From the ashes of inglorious defeat, these men would ultimately fashion an entirely new type of Communist revolution, one with its roots not among the industrial workers of the coastal treaty port cities, but rather among the poor and landless peasants of the vast rural Chinese hinterland.

By the end of October 1927 the remnants of the failed Autumn Harvest Uprisings had begun to converge and regroup along the mountainous border between Hunan and Jiangxi provinces. There, deep in the rugged Jinggang Mountains, they established a revolutionary base. Combining their forces, they created a Red Army.

At the outset, the Red Army numbered no more than a few thousand tattered soldiers, only one-fifth of whom possessed rifles. Not content merely to lick their wounds, however, the Red Army leaders, Zhou Enlai, Zhu De, and the 35-year-old Mao Zedong among them, began to fashion an entirely new strategy of agrarian revolution.

One year earlier, in the spring of 1927, Mao, while on an inspection visit to his native Hunan Province, had written a remarkable essay in which he urged his comrades to pay close attention to the revolutionary anger of China's poor peasants.

"In a very short time," Mao wrote, "in China's central, southern and northern provinces, several hundred million peasants will rise like a mighty storm, like a hurricane, a force so swift and violent that no power, however great, will be able to hold it back. ... They will sweep all the imperialists warlords, corrupt officials, local tyrants and evil gentry into their graves." (*Selected Readings from the Works of Mao Zedong*, p. 30).

To those who argued that Mao's ideas amounted to giving China's crude and backward peasants carte blanche to slaughter landlords, gentry, and government officials willy-nilly, Mao responded:

A revolution is not a dinner party, or writing an essay, or painting a picture, or doing embroidery; it cannot be so refined, so leisurely and gentle, so temperate, kind, courteous, restrained and magnanimous. A revolution is an insurrection, an act of violence by which one class overthrows another. (ibid.)

At the time these lines were written, they did not sit well with the CCP's Bolshevik patrons. According to Marx and Lenin, a socialist revolution was an insurrection of the urban proletariat, the industrial working class.

Neither Marx nor Lenin, nor Stalin after them, believed that peasants had the innate capacity to perceive their own objective class interests, let alone grasp the fundamental truth that it was the system of private land ownership itself that was the real enemy, not merely rapacious local landlords. Only the working class possessed the capacity for such sophisticated consciousness. At best, they argued, peasants could merely serve as auxiliaries of the proletariat, but never, ever as its leading force.

But Mao disagreed. "Without the poor peasants there will be no revolution," he wrote prophetically. (ibid.) Mao's unorthodox views led him to be censured by his superiors within the Communist Party. Indeed, had it not been for Chiang K'ai-shek's bloody coup of April 1927, Mao might have lived out his life in relative obscurity, forever labeled as something of a rabble-rousing heretic. But with the brutal destruction of the party's urban working-class base, Mao got his big chance; and he seized it with both hands.

According to a recent, controversial biography by Jung Chang and Jon Halliday, titled *Mao: The Unknown Story*, Mao set out single-mindedly to grasp supreme power in the Communist Party's Jinggang Mountain stronghold. Skillfully playing his more senior CCP comrades off against one other, he was able to scheme, conspire, betray and blackmail his way to ultimate power. Although this is probably something of an overstatement, there can be little doubt about Mao's single-minded determination or his ruthlessness.

Nor can there be any doubt of his independence of mind. Ensconced in his Jinggang Mountain hideaway with a force of perhaps 10,000 worker-peasant soldiers and a land area encompassing about 200 square miles, including maybe half a dozen villages, Mao was now free to do his thing.

But the Red Army's existence was precarious, and its survival was hardly assured. A series of armed engagements with local bandits and remnant warlord forces made life very difficult for Mao and his colleagues. By the middle of 1928 things were looking quite bleak, as Mao's forces were attacked by pursuing units of the Guomindang.

By the end of the year the Red Army had been forced to abandon its Jinggang Mountain base, moving steadily eastward toward the border between Jiangxi and Fujian. There they made their headquarters in the town of Ruijin where, a short time later, they declared the birth of a new revolutionary government, the Jiangxi Soviet Republic.

With the brilliant Zhu De as his principal military strategist, Mao now began to fashion the essential principles of people's war:

> When the enemy outnumbers you and has superior firepower, never fight merely to hold territory; never stand toe-to-toe fighting a war of attrition;

> —Never enter a battle unless you enjoy clear tactical superiority of at least 5 or even 8:1.

> —Husband your forces; choose carefully the time and place to engage the enemy.

This latter principle was elaborated upon in Mao's famous quatrain composed in the early 1930s:

> The enemy attacks, we retreat;

> The enemy encamps, we harass;

> The enemy tires, we attack;

> The enemy retreats, we pursue.

Recognizing that to wage a successful people's war it was necessary to gain the support of the civilian population in the Red Army's base area, Mao and Zhu De formulated an approach to civil-military relations known as the "fish in water" theory.

In this formulation, the Red Army guerrilla fighters were the fish; while the peasant population in the base area was the water.

Only by carefully cultivating the hearts and minds of the peasants through benevolent treatment, patient persuasion, and leadership by example, could the Red Army fish swim safely in the village water.

The fish in water concept was the key to the Maoists' famous "mass line" style of leadership, which dictated that army officers and party leaders must never coerce the masses into compliance or issue commands from on high.

Rather they must live and work among the people, sweating with them in the performance of menial tasks in order to demonstrate by example their unity of purpose and spirit with the peasants.

In order to set a good example for the masses, Mao and his lieutenants established strict rules of behavior for Red Army soldiers.

As early as 1928, they promulgated a code of conduct containing "three main rules of discipline" and "eight points for attention."

Popularly known as the "three-eight work style," this code spelled out the party's expectations for the treatment of civilians and captured enemy combatants alike. The Three Main Rules of Discipline were: Obey orders in all your actions; Do not take a single needle or piece of thread from the masses; Turn in everything captured. The Eight Points for Attention were: Speak politely; Pay fairly for what you buy; Return everything you borrow; Pay for anything you damage; Do not hit or swear at people; Do not damage crops; Do not take liberties with women; and Do not ill-treat captives.

In a further effort to build a mass base of peasant support for the Communist cause, Mao introduced a program under which Red Army soldiers, when not engaged in combat, would perform various civilian functions as farmers, teachers, militia organizers, and local administrators. This idea of the guerrilla fighter as a jack of all trades (or *duomianshou* in Chinese) rather than a narrow specialist (or *zhuanjia*) became a hallmark of Mao's revolutionary strategy.

Finally, and perhaps most importantly, in the early 1930s Mao launched on an experimental basis what was later to become his signature social program: land reform. Under this program, all farmland and associated property belonging to wealthy landlords and members of the rural gentry were to be confiscated and redistributed to the poor and landless peasants. For the first time, Sun Yat-sen's revolutionary slogan of "land to the tiller" was being translated into a concrete program of social action in rural China, not by the *Guomindang* but by the Communists.

With the rural poor outnumbering the rich by 9 or 10 to one, land reform made good political sense and it contributed in a substantial way to the success of the Communists in mobilizing peasant support.

Notwithstanding their success in mobilizing the peasantry, Mao and Zhu De found their leadership of the Jiangxi Soviet Republic under increasing challenge in the years from 1931 to 1934. Contesting their leadership was the pro-Soviet faction of the Communist Party of China, which under instructions from Joseph Stalin, attempted to wrest command of the Jiangxi Soviet away from the maverick Mao, and to bring it back under Moscow's control.

Also in the early 1930s, the *Guomindang* launched a series of deadly annihilation campaigns against the Red Army's base area in the Soviet Republic.

Despite such challenges, however, the people's war and agrarian reform policies of Mao and Zhu De achieved considerable success.

Between 1931 and 1934, the Red Army added more than 100,000 new recruits to the communist cause, while the territory under their direct control increased from a few hundred to more than 12,000 square miles, roughly the size of the state of Maryland, and encompassing a civilian population of more than 3 million people. Clearly, the Maoists were doing something right.

But they were hardly home free. Far greater challenges lay ahead, including a series of near-disastrous military encounters with Chiang's Nationalist Army, and steadily deepening incursions by an imperial Japanese army determined to reduce China to the status of a defeated colony. Before the 1930s were over, China would descend into the unspeakable hell of a full-blown Japanese invasion.

The Republican Experiment, 1927–1937
Lecture 11

> In its essentials, the Maoist version of people's war was the military equivalent of Muhammad Ali's strategy for subduing a larger, more powerful opponent: "Float like a butterfly; sting like a bee."

While the CCP mobilized peasant support in rural Jiangxi, Chiang K'ai-shek established his Nationalist government in the city of Nanjing. Over the next several years, Chiang—increasingly supported by industrialists, financiers, and rural landowners—turned the GMD from a progressive political organization into an authoritarian one. Although the regime Chiang and his associates established in Nanjing was nominally republican in nature, it proved to be increasingly corrupt and ineffectual.

Meanwhile, Japanese militarists were putting increasing pressure on China. Under Western pressure, Tokyo had withdrawn its odious 21 Demands,

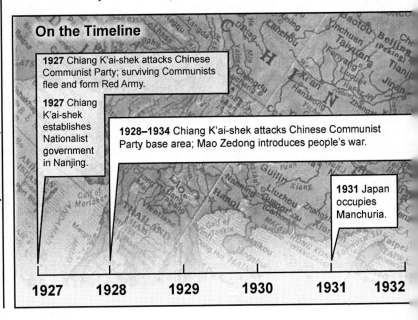

On the Timeline

1927 Chiang K'ai-shek attacks Chinese Communist Party; surviving Communists flee and form Red Army.

1927 Chiang K'ai-shek establishes Nationalist government in Nanjing.

1928–1934 Chiang K'ai-shek attacks Chinese Communist Party base area; Mao Zedong introduces people's war.

1931 Japan occupies Manchuria.

| 1927 | 1928 | 1929 | 1930 | 1931 | 1932 |

and the process of political liberalization had brought to power a new and more progressive Japanese government. But even as Japan was emulating Western political and socioeconomic institutions, Japanese military power was growing steadily. Despite the opposition of Japan's civilian authority, its military commanders openly coveted the rich mineral, industrial, and agricultural resources of Manchuria. In 1931, they invaded Manchuria, setting up a puppet regime with the now 26-year-old Puyi as chief executive. When neither the League of Nations nor the United States forcefully resisted Japan's aggression, Tokyo was emboldened to commit further acts of aggression against China.

Caught between relentless Japanese pressure in the north and a growing Communist movement in the south, Chiang made a fateful decision: He would first concentrate on exterminating the Communists and then resist the Japanese. As he put it, "The Japanese are a disease of the skin; Communists are a disease of the heart." Between 1930 and 1934, Chiang launched four successive encirclement campaigns against the Jiangxi Soviet Republic. But by then, the Red Army was applying Mao's principles of people's war,

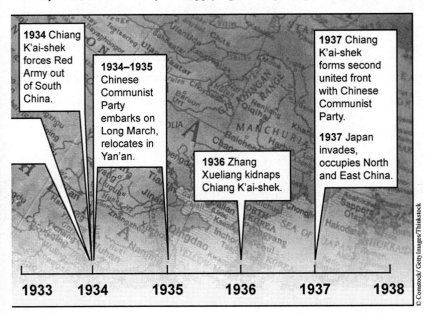

1934 Chiang K'ai-shek forces Red Army out of South China.

1934–1935 Chinese Communist Party embarks on Long March, relocates in Yan'an.

1936 Zhang Xueliang kidnaps Chiang K'ai-shek.

1937 Chiang K'ai-shek forms second united front with Chinese Communist Party.

1937 Japan invades, occupies North and East China.

| 1933 | 1934 | 1935 | 1936 | 1937 | 1938 |

© Comstock/ Getty Images/Thinkstock

141

which allowed them to repel the larger, better-armed Nationalist troops. In its essentials, the Maoist version of people's war was the military equivalent of Muhammad Ali's strategy for subduing a larger, more powerful opponent: "Float like a butterfly; sting like a bee."

In 1934, with half a million GMD troops encircling the Red Army's Jiangxi stronghold, the Communists faced annihilation unless they abandoned the Jiangxi Soviet Republic. In October, 100,000 Communists broke out of the Nationalist encirclement and began the Long March. In 15 months, they covered 6,000 miles of difficult terrain, eventually resettling at Yan'an, in North China. Only one-tenth of those who started the trek completed it. During the Long March, Mao Zedong blackmailed **Zhou Enlai** into giving Mao full command of the CCP, which he held until his death in 1976.

In the fall of 1936, Chiang sent his best-trained army to destroy the Communists in Yan'an. But the officer Chiang chose to lead the campaign, **Zhang Xueliang**, had no interest in fighting fellow Chinese, Communist or otherwise. Ever since Japanese militarists had assassinated his father, the Manchurian warlord Zhang Zuolin, the younger Zhang had been eager to fight Japan. Zhang refused Chiang's orders, instead kidnapping Chiang and demanding a second GMD-CCP united front against the Japanese. Reluctantly, Chiang complied. Fearing a unified Chinese resistance, Japan struck the Chinese heartland in the summer of 1937, igniting World War II. ■

Names to Know

Zhang Xueliang (1901–2001): Son of the assassinated Manchurian warlord Zhang Zuolin, Zhang Xueliang was known as the Young Marshal. He led a mutiny against Chiang K'ai-shek in December 1936 (the Xi'an Incident), demanding a GMD-CCP united front to resist Japan.

Zhou Enlai (1898–1976): The first premier and foreign minster of the People's Republic of China, Zhou was China's foremost diplomat. Ever loyal to Mao Zedong, he was the chairman's right-hand man and chief troubleshooter. Before succumbing to cancer, he paved the way for the Sino-U.S. détente.

Suggested Reading

Chang and Halliday, *Mao*.

Eastman, *The Abortive Revolution*.

Fenby, *Modern China*.

Johnson, *Peasant Nationalism and Communist Power*.

Schwartz, *Chinese Communism and the Rise of Mao*.

Snow, *Red Star over China*.

Sun, *The Long March*.

Taylor, *The Generalissimo*.

Questions to Consider

1. Why did Chiang K'ai-shek's Nationalist government fail to govern effectively from 1927 to 1937?

2. In what respect can it be said that a mutinous act by Chiang's top general in 1936 altered the course of modern Chinese history?

The Republican Experiment, 1927–1937
Lecture 11—Transcript

While the Communists in Jiangxi's Soviet Republic were perfecting Mao's strategic principles of people's war and mass peasant mobilization, Chiang K'ai-shek was busy consolidating his political power. Under Chiang's military-style leadership, the *Guomindang* embraced former warlords, foreign imperialists, wealthy financiers, and criminal gangs. His was a very, very big tent indeed!

In making peace with these unsavory classes and strata, and by co-opting them into his inner circle, Chiang essentially abandoned Sun Yat-sen's "Three Principles of the People," reducing them to hollow cant. Indeed, by the mid-1930s the Nationalist Government had ceased being a progressive political force, resembling more and more closely a classic right-wing authoritarian dictatorship. Although the regime Chiang and his associates established in Nanjing was nominally republican in nature, it proved to be increasingly corrupt, ineffectual, and ultimately repressive.

Dominated by a handful of rich and powerful families closely interlinked by marriage and by overlapping financial interests, including the Soong family dynasty, Chiang's elitist regime never effectively addressed the problems of the country's 500 million impoverished peasants. Nor did it ever learn how to deal with growing urban demands for middle-class political participation.

Ironically, although it was Sun Yat-sen who turned the Nationalist Party into a disciplined, hierarchical organization under Comintern guidance, it was Chiang K'ai-shek who first realized the *Guomindang*'s full authoritarian potential. The city of Shanghai was emblematic of the new regime's elitist zeitgeist. Ruled by an unholy alliance of Nationalist generals, financiers, and underworld chieftains, it was the crown jewel of the Republic of China. By the late 1920s Shanghai had become the playground for the rich and near-rich, a place to enjoy a slice of Europe's *la belle vie* in east Asia. Western social mores and European haute couture were aped wholesale in the new Shanghai. Modern schools and hospitals were built, along with modern theaters, museums, race tracks, gambling parlors and, of course, opium dens.

But while Shanghai's elites were enjoying the good life, all around them, for those who cared to look, there were signs of deepening malaise. Two problems were of particular concern. The first was growing Japanese military pressure in the northeast. The second was a renascent Chinese Communist movement in the south, where Mao Zedong was achieving success in mobilizing land-hungry peasants.

In the early 1920s Japan had experienced a post-war surge of democratic development and international reconciliation. Under Western pressure Tokyo had withdrawn its odious 21 Demands. Internally, the process of political liberalization had brought to power in Tokyo a new and more progressive Japanese government. But even as Japan was emulating Western political and socio-economic institutions, Japanese military power was growing steadily. In 1921 Japan was invited to join the Washington Naval Conference as a full participant, marking its emergence as Asia's first modern great power.

By the middle 1920s, Japanese military commanders were growing increasingly contemptuous of civilian authority. What's more, they were openly coveting the rich mineral, industrial, and agricultural resources of Manchuria. By the end of the decade, a civil-military showdown was looming on the horizon. But by then, hard-line militarists were already in the ascendancy, and they were laying plans to extend Japan's strategic military reach into northeast China.

One thing that concerned them, however, was the Nationalist regime of Chiang K'ai-shek. Having vanquished the warlords and driven the Communists deep into the rural hinterland, Chiang appeared to be succeeding in his effort to create a unified national Chinese government. As he consolidated his Nanjing regime, the Japanese began to consider the relative costs and benefits of early versus delayed military action in China. Their conclusion was essentially that the longer we wait, the more difficult it will be to overcome Chinese resistance.

Making things even more problematic for Tokyo's military planners, Japan's domestic economy faced serious difficulties in the late 1920s. These included a sharp rise in urban unemployment and a deepening agricultural recession. The U.S. stock market crash of October 1929 further exacerbated these domestic strains by triggering a collapse in the Japanese silk market.

Friction between Tokyo and the Nanjing regime had reached a critical point as early as 1928, when a group of Japanese army officers planted a bomb on a railroad car carrying the Manchurian warlord Zhang Zuolin. Zhang was Manchuria's most powerful political and military figure. He had fought against Chiang K'ai-shek during the Northern Expedition, and he was one of only a handful of warlords who refused to be co-opted by the Nationalist regime.

Japan's objectives in assassinating Zhang Zuolin were twofold: The first was their desire to fan the flames of internecine conflict between Zhang's Manchurian army and Chiang K'ai-shek's Nationalist forces. The second goal was to create a general atmosphere of military crisis within Japan, a crisis that would discredit the modern civilian government in Tokyo and give imperial hard-liners the excuse they needed to mobilize for war.

But the militarists' plan hit a snag. The imperialist government in Tokyo, the civilian cabinet, reacted to the assassination of Zhang Zuolin not by giving the army a green light to mobilize for war, but by exerting restraint over Japan's military forces in China.

At that point, rather than abandon their ambitions, the militarists made a fateful decision to act preemptively. On the night of September 18, 1931, they detonated a series of bombs on a railroad track outside the city of Mukden (now called Shenyang), in southern Manchuria.

In the confusion that followed, Chinese and Japanese troops began shooting at each other. Though the civilian cabinet in Tokyo urged restraint, Japanese commanders on the ground pressed their military advantage, attacking the Nationalists' barracks at Mukden and capturing the city itself.

For reasons of his own, Chiang K'ai-shek ordered the commander of his Northeast Army, General Zhang Xueliang, to retreat rather than fight toe-to-toe with the advancing Japanese.

Meeting scant Chinese resistance, the Japanese pressed on. By the end of 1931 all of Manchuria was under their control. But not before the seeds of a bitter conflict had been sowed between General Zhang Xueliang and his commander-in-chief, Chiang K'ai-shek. For Zhang Xueliang was the son of the Manchurian warlord Zhang Zuolin, whom the Japanese had assassinated three years earlier. After his father's death, the younger Zhang had joined the Nationalist Army precisely to fight against the Japanese. So when Chiang K'ai-shek gave him the order not to fight but to retreat, in effect handing his Manchurian homeland over to the Japanese without a struggle. Zhang Xueliang was furious.

As a footnote to this interesting episode, Zhang's bitterness simmered for five long years before it finally burst into the open in December of 1936, when he kidnapped Chiang K'ai-shek and held him hostage in the city of Xian for 13 days. By the time he released Chiang, the course of modern Chinese history had been altered. (We'll return to this fascinating story at the end of this lecture.)

A few months after the Japanese army occupied Manchuria, Tokyo announced the creation a new puppet state there, which they named "Manchuguo" (meaning "Manchu country"). To lend a semblance of legitimacy to this naked act of territorial aggression, the Japanese installed a native Manchurian as chief executive of Manchuguo. As their puppet ruler, the Japanese chose Puyi, the last Manchu emperor, who had first been installed on the Dragon Throne in 1908, at the tender age of 3 by his aunt, the Dowager Empress Cixi. Puyi was now 26 years old.

In response to Japanese actions in Manchuria, the United States government introduced the so-called "Stimson Doctrine," named after Herbert Hoover's Secretary of State, Henry L. Stimson. The new doctrine called for preserving the Open Door in China and stated unequivocally that the United States would not recognize any territorial gains seized by force of arms.

Although it was a very bold statement of moral principle, the Stimson Doctrine was not followed up by any concrete American punitive sanctions against Japan. The doctrine thus lacked real teeth. In the vernacular of the day, it was a "paper tiger." In similar fashion, the League of Nations, created by the victorious allies after World War I to protect world peace, also failed to enact meaningful economic or military sanctions against Japan's aggression in Manchuria. In consequence, Japan's militarists were neither deterred nor punished, with the result that they were further emboldened to commit further acts of aggression against China.

But Japanese military expansion was only one of Chiang K'ai-shek's worries. A second source of concern was the burgeoning revolutionary mass movement being orchestrated Mao Zedong and Zhu De in their Jiangxi Soviet Republic. Caught between relentless Japanese pressure in the north and a growing Communist movement in the south, Chiang made a fateful decision: He would first concentrate on exterminating the Communists then resist the Japanese. As he put it: "The Japanese are a disease of the skin; Communism is a disease of the heart."

Between 1930 and 1934 Chiang launched four successive encirclement campaigns against the Jiangxi Soviet. Surrounding the Communist stronghold with massive numbers of well-armed troops, the Nationalist armies plunged deep into the Soviet base area, looking to annihilate the Communist bandits. But by then the Red Army had begun to practice Mao's principles of people's war, the prime tenet of which was that one should never fight toe-to-toe with a superior enemy force.

Under massive assault by the Nationalist army, Mao's guerrilla fighters pulled back, giving ground willingly, with the Nationalists in all-out pursuit. Soon, the attacking *Guomindang* troops overextended their supply lines, outpacing their logistical support. At that point, the Red Army introduced the tactics of mobile warfare to confuse the enemy and throw them off balance. In its essentials, the Maoist version of guerilla warfare was the military equivalent of Muhammad Ali's strategy for subduing a larger, more powerful opponent: "Float like a butterfly; sting like a bee."

Not only did the highly mobile Red Army seize the tactical initiative against a confused and overextended enemy that had no prior experience with guerrilla warfare, but the Communists also enjoyed the support of the local civilian population. Because of their successful land reform techniques, and because of the Red Army's Three-Eight Work Style, which mandated benevolent treatment of civilian non-combatants, the Communists had truly become "fish in water." The water was the Jiangxi Soviet itself, within which friendly peasants housed Red Army fighters, fed them, and provided them with vital intelligence about enemy troop movements and concentrations.

Though Chiang threw as many as half a million well-armed troops against 100,000 or so lightly-armed Communist defenders in Jiangxi, a combination of superior guerrilla tactics and unanticipated external contingencies, including Japan's 1931 invasion of Manchuria, which temporarily distracted Chiang K'ai-shek, made it possible for the Communists to repel a succession of Nationalist military offensives.

Exasperated by his failed military campaigns, Chiang in 1933 brought in a German military adviser, General Hans von Seeckt, to fashion a new approach to eliminating the Communists. Under Seeckt's guidance, the Nationalists planned their fifth encirclement campaign. They first built a network of airfields and roads around the entire perimeter of the Jiangxi Soviet war zone. They then constructed a ring of brick blockhouses around the Communist base. These interconnected, multi-purpose blockhouses served as defensive fortifications, supply storehouses, field hospitals, and forward operations bases.

Once the outer perimeter was secured, an effective economic blockade was imposed on the Communists. The Nationalist forces would then move forward in limited, measured advances, pausing to consolidate their gains and to create a new ring of blockhouses inside the first one. As Chiang's armies repeated this process several times, the Communists found themselves being squeezed into a smaller and smaller space at the center of their shrinking Soviet Republic. If the Communists were fish in water, swimming in a friendly pond, then the Nationalists were methodically draining the pond to catch the fish.

By mid-1934, the stresses of five successive Nationalist encirclement campaigns had engendered serious internal divisions within the Communist leadership. The most significant of these splits was between the survivors of the 1927 Autumn Harvest Uprisings, including Mao, Zhu De, and Zhou Enlai, and a group of late-arriving Chinese Communists who had been sent to the Jiangxi Soviet from Moscow in 1930, on Stalin's orders. Their instructions were to take control of the Soviet government from Mao.

Dubbed the "Twenty-Eight Bolsheviks" because of their extended sojourn in Moscow after Chiang's bloody Shanghai coup of 1927, these pro-Moscow latecomers viewed the Autumn Harvest veterans, and Mao in particular, with deep suspicion and more than a little hostility. Not surprisingly, their feelings were fully reciprocated by the Maoists.

By the autumn of 1934, the Communists had seen their base area in Jiangxi shrink from 12,000 square miles to a little over 1,500. At that point, the Red Army faced a critical choice: either break out of the tightening Nationalist stranglehold, or stay and die. On October 15 the Red Army executed a hastily-planned, two-pronged escape. With 85,000 soldiers, 15,000 party and government officials, and only 35 women accompanying them, the evacuees managed to break through the Nationalist defense lines in two places, escaping toward the southwest.

Because of the physical risks and hardships involved, the vast majority of Communist women and children, including wives of Red Army soldiers, were left behind. In the ensuing mopping up operations, many of the women who stayed behind were killed by *Guomindang* troops; while thousands of children were either orphaned or permanently separated from their parents.

Thus began the Red Army's fabled Long March. Although it began as an urgent and rather chaotic retreat, and though 90 percent of those who began the march failed to complete it, by the time it ended some 15 months later the Long March had been transmogrified in Chinese popular folklore from a desperate escape to a feat of legendary strategic brilliance and heroism.

In January 1935, the retreating Red Army forces paused to rest in the town of Zunyi, in eastern Guizhou Province. There the Communist Party held an important leadership conference, in the course of which the pro-Moscow "28 Bolsheviks" received a sharp rebuke for having failed to prevent the Red Army's defeat in the fifth annihilation campaign. Their top leader, named Bo Gu, was held responsible for the debacle and was removed from power. With that, the Autumn Harvest veterans assumed control of the party, with Mao Zedong and Zhou Enlai in overall command.

At this point, Mao began to reveal his darker side, including his overweening ambition, his manipulativeness, and his ruthless nature. Not content to share power with Zhou Enlai, the ambitious Mao moved to undermine Zhou's co-equal status through a combination of carrots and sticks, notably including the use of blackmail.

According to one fairly credible account of the events in question, Mao threatened to draft a resolution exposing Zhou's responsibility for Bo Gu's failed military policies during the fifth annihilation campaign. Whether the allegation was true or not, Zhou did not relish a political showdown with Mao; and he blinked first, voluntarily agreeing to take a back seat to Mao.

From that point on, until both men died some 41 years later, in 1976, (within half a year of each other), Mao Zedong completely dominated Zhou, manipulating and intimidating him virtually at will. Also from that point on, Mao assumed full control of the Central Committee of the Chinese Communist Party.

With Mao now in charge of planning for the Long March, the Communists set as their final destination the city of Yan'an in northern Shaanxi Province, some 800 miles to the northwest, as the crow flies. (Of course, being closely pursued over extremely difficult terrain by Chiang's Nationalist armies, the retreating Communists could hardly travel as crows fly; and so the distance they actually covered is estimated not at 800 miles, but 6,000 miles.)

By the time the first scattered units of the Red Army reached Yan'an at the end of 1935, 13 months after they set out, the Communists had traversed nine provinces and crossed uncounted snow-covered peaks, raging rivers, and uninhabitable forests, from Western Guangdong to eastern Tibet.

Of the original 100,000 Long Marchers, only 8,000 reached their destination. The rest, more than nine-tenths of the original Communist force, had either been killed, taken prisoner, or had dropped out along the way.

Having finally reached their Yan'an sanctuary, out of reach of Chiang K'ai-shek's Nationalist armies, Mao's forces rested.

(Now that you've heard the story of this incredibly difficult and harrowing journey, perhaps you can understand why, as a 20-year-old college student, I had been so deeply affected by Edgar Snow's dramatic account of the Long March in his book, *Red Star Over China*.)

Meanwhile, back in Nanjing, at around the same time the Communists were undertaking their arduous Long March, Chiang K'ai-shek and his American-educated wife, Soong Mei-ling, were launching a New Life Movement.

Designed to foster a new spiritual awakening for the Chinese people, the movement drew liberally from both Confucian and Christian moral traditions, seasoned with a small pinch of liberal political rhetoric drawn from Sun Yat-sen's Three People's Principles.

In its bare essentials, the New Life Movement sought to create a new national consciousness based on traditional Chinese virtues of propriety, justice, integrity, and self-awareness. Also receiving stress were such ostensibly Christian values as plain living, personal hygiene, cleanliness, and self-discipline. Chiang once boasted that when properly implemented, the New Life Movement would lead to the "social regeneration of China."

In reality, it did no such thing. Not only were many of the precepts of the New Life Movement essentially a reprise of failed Confucian traditions, they were also highly reflective of Chiang's own deepening right-wing authoritarian tendencies.

The movement offered no economic reforms to ameliorate the poverty of China's long-suffering workers and peasants, and no political framework to allow ordinary Chinese, or their representatives, to participate in deliberating the important issues of the day.

Indeed, at its core, Chiang K'ai-shek's New Life Movement was an attempt to create an orderly, well-disciplined, highly regimented, conformist, and obedient society under patriarchal leadership. As Chiang himself put it, the goal of the movement "is to thoroughly militarize the life of the people. ... It is to make them nourish courage and alertness, a capacity to endure hardship, and especially a habit and instinct for unified behavior. It is to make them all willing to sacrifice for the nation at all times." (ibid)

If this seems to bear more than a passing resemblance to neo-fascism, well, that may not be a pure coincidence.

But even as Chiang was urging his countrymen to discipline themselves and prepare for personal sacrifices, the Japanese were making new advances in China.

In 1932, in response to a growing Chinese patriotic movement to boycott Japanese goods, a shipload of fully-armed Japanese marines came ashore in Shanghai. After a brief exchange of gunfire with Nationalist troops, the Japanese commander ordered an aerial bombardment of the city, followed by a full-scale ground attack on Shanghai's defenders. Three divisions of Japanese soldiers were committed to the battle, which ended in an armistice three months later.

But Japan was only beginning its forays into China. Early in 1933, Japanese forces struck south of their Manchuguo stronghold, attacking Jehol Province, north of Beijing. Then, in the spring of the same year they occupied a strategic mountain pass at the eastern terminus of the Great Wall at Shanhaiguan, less than 150 miles from Beijing.

Soon after, they moved into Hebei Province, south of the Great Wall. Confronted with such audacious acts of Japanese aggression, Chiang K'ai-shek temporized, ordering his outmanned troops to stand down and seek a cease-fire, rather than fight straight on with the Japanese.

Still believing that it was necessary to wipe out the Communists first, before he could take on the full might of Japan, Chiang K'ai-shek took the news of the Red Army's daring escape from Jiangxi quite badly. Determined to catch the Communists at their point of maximum vulnerability, in 1936 he ordered a new all-out assault on Mao Zedong's new headquarters in Yan'an.

But anti-Japanese sentiment had been building steadily in China ever since the Japanese seizure of Manchuria; and in December of 1935 thousands of Chinese students demonstrated in several Chinese cities demanding that Chiang cease his vendetta against the Communists and instead create a national united front to resist Japan.

But Chiang was nothing if not stubborn; and he refused to abandon his plan to wipe out the Communists.

But the man he entrusted with the task to carry out the attack on Yan'an—our old friend Zhang Xueliang—turned out to be a very poor choice indeed. Though he was probably Chiang K'ai-shek's best commanding officer, and though his Northeast Army was the best in all of China, Zhang Xueliang had no stomach whatever for fighting fellow Chinese, be they Communists or otherwise.

Ever since the Japanese militarists had assassinated his father, the Manchurian warlord Zhang Zuolin, the "Young Marshal," as he was affectionately known, had been itching to fight Japan.

And so Zhang Xueliang refused to carry out Chiang K'ai-shek's orders. When Chiang learned of the Young Marshal's refusal to attack Yan'an, the Generalissimo flew to the city of Xian, 100 miles south of Yan'an, to confront him.

What followed was a remarkable turning point in modern Chinese history: Zhang Xueliang turned the tables on his commander-in-chief, kidnapping him in the middle of the night and holding him hostage.

The Young Marshal's demands were simple: Chiang K'ai-shek must call off his planned attack on the Communists and form a second united front with the CCP, directed against the Japanese.

At first the Generalissimo stubbornly refused; but when his wife, the irrepressible Soong Mei-ling, learned of his predicament, she flew to Xian and convinced her husband to agree to the rebels' demands. Reluctantly, the Gimo went along.

And so a second *Guomindang*/Chinese Communist Party, the united front, came into being in December of 1936, a full decade after the first united front had ended abruptly with Chiang's murderous coup in Shanghai.

Observing these events from their base in Manchuguo, the Japanese militarists saw their two worst fears coming true: the termination of the *Guomindang*/Chinese Communist civil war and the formation of a national anti-Japanese united front. In response, in July of 1937 they launched a full-scale invasion of China.

World War II had begun.

"Resist Japan!" 1937–1945
Lecture 12

> In their effort to counteract growing Communist influence in the villages of North China, Japanese commanders pursued a scorched-earth policy of "kill all, burn all, destroy all."

Had Zhang Xueliang obeyed Chiang K'ai-shek's order to attack the Communist stronghold in Yan'an in December 1936, there is little doubt that the CCP would have been wiped out in short order. But Zhang Xueliang rebelled, and the Communists were spared a final, fatal Nationalist assault. In the negotiated truce that followed, the CCP was able to revive itself, regroup, and gradually regain its lost momentum. The CCP went from near annihilation in 1936 to near victory a decade later. While several factors contributed to this reversal, Japan's invasion proved highly instrumental, along with Chiang's inept leadership.

> With her sophisticated good looks, her Christian missionary background, her American education, and her flawless English, Soong Mei-ling was the perfect goodwill ambassador.

In July 1937, Japan seized the Marco Polo Bridge, and Japanese troops swept down from Manchuria. Japanese brutality, epitomized by the Nanjing Massacre, served to rally the people of northern China to the Communist cause. The force of the invasion shocked Chiang, who ordered his troops to retreat. When Japanese troops assaulted the Yangzi River Delta, Chiang moved his capital from Nanjing to Chongqing, 800 miles up the Yangzi River. With foodstuffs and industrial and consumer goods in short supply in Chongqing, inflationary pressures began to mount. Unable to support themselves and their families, hundreds of thousands of impoverished GMD conscript soldiers deserted; countless others survived by preying on civilians in the countryside. To make matters worse, some GMD industrialists and financiers—including members of the Soong family—reaped windfall profits by monopolizing scarce commodities.

By contrast, the CCP adopted a rigid code of ethical conduct for its cadres and soldiers. The Red Army—now called the People's Liberation Army (PLA)—paid great attention to the political indoctrination of its recruits, so that they would not exploit local farmers, steal food or supplies, or abuse peasant women. In this respect, their wartime behavior compared quite favorably with that of their undisciplined—and increasingly predatory—Nationalist counterparts.

© Prints and Photographs Division, Library of Congress.

Soong Mei-ling won U.S. political and financial support for the anti-Japan war effort during her 1943 speaking tour of the United States.

In the early stages of the Sino-Japanese War, President Roosevelt's declared policy of neutrality limited American aid to Chiang, but when Japan attacked Pearl Harbor, Washington poured billions of dollars in military aid into China. In order to keep American goodwill—and material assistance—flowing to Chongqing, Chiang K'ai-shek sought an invitation for his wife, Soong Mei-ling, to visit the United States. With her sophisticated good looks, her Christian missionary background, her American education, and her flawless English, Soong Mei-ling was the perfect goodwill ambassador. By the end of her coast-to-coast speaking tour, she had won the hearts of the American people as well as the U.S. Congress. In the process, she raised tens of millions of dollars in private donations for her charitable fund, United China Relief.

Although the United States was now closely allied with Chiang and the GMD, an American advisory group called the Dixie Mission visited the CCP's Yan'an headquarters in 1944, at Mao Zedong's invitation. Impressed by what they saw there, and put off by Chiang's ineffective leadership, some State Department officials predicted an eventual Communist victory. Popular support for the CCP grew dramatically between 1937 and 1945— CCP membership increased from 50,000 to 1.2 million, while the PLA increased in size from 80,000 to more than 900,000 troops. And when the war against Japan ended, the CCP was in the position to challenge Chiang for control of China. ■

Suggested Reading

Eastman, *The Abortive Revolution.*

Esherick, *Lost Chance in China.*

Friedman, Pickowicz, and Selden, *Chinese Village, Socialist State.*

Johnson, *Peasant Nationalism and Communist Power.*

—*Women, the Family and Peasant Revolution in China.*

Schram, *The Political Thought of Mao Tse-tung.*

Schwartz, *Chinese Communism and the Rise of Mao.*

Seagrave, *The Soong Dynasty.*

Short, *Mao.*

Snow, *Red Star over China.*

Taylor, *The Generalissimo.*

Tuchman, *Stilwell and the American Experience in China.*

Van Slyke, *Enemies and Friends.*

Questions to Consider

1. What unintended role did Japan play in shaping the outcome of the Chinese Revolution?

2. How did Chiang K'ai-shek's wife, Soong Mei-ling, influence U.S. support for China during World War II?

"Resist Japan!" 1937–1945
Lecture 12—Transcript

When Japanese Prime Minister Kakuei Tanaka visited China in 1972 to mark the normalization of Sino-Japanese diplomatic relations, he made a point of apologizing to his Chinese host, Zhou Enlai, for Japan's destructive World War II occupation of China.

But Zhou shrugged off Mr. Tanaka's apology, observing that if it hadn't been for Japan's invasion, "We might still be living in caves in Yan'an." While perhaps a bit hyperbolic, Zhou's response nonetheless contained a substantial grain of truth.

In this lecture we'll see how the Chinese Communists went from the edge of annihilation in 1936 to the brink of victory a decade later. While a number of different factors were involved in this stunning reversal of fortune, the key was the Japanese invasion was a turning point. For it was the sheer brutality of the Japanese invasion—the vast, inhuman destruction of civilian lives and property—that served to unify the rural population in north China under Communist leadership.

By the time the Communists completed the Long March early in 1936, their ranks had been decimated by the pursuing Nationalist armies and by the rigors of their 6,000 mile trek.

They were exhausted, and they were vulnerable.

Had the Young Marshal, Zhang Xueliang, obeyed Chiang K'ai-shek's orders to attack the Communist stronghold in Yan'an in December of '36, there is little doubt that the CCP would have been wiped out in short order.

But Zhang Xueliang rebelled, and the Communists were spared a final, fatal Nationalist assault. In the negotiated truce that followed, the Communists were able to revive themselves, regroup, and gradually regain their lost momentum.

When war with Japan broke out six months later, there was a great deal of initial confusion all around. On July 1, 1937, a minor confrontation took place involving *Guomindang* and Japanese troops at Luguoqiao, the Marco Polo Bridge, a few miles west of Beijing. Though apparently unintended, this incident served to light the fuse of war.

For weeks thereafter, the fuse smoldered, as the two sides engaged in a war of nerves, each side blaming the other for a series of hostile provocations. Meanwhile, both sides stepped up their preparations for war.

At the end of July, Japanese forces took the initiative, decisively seizing the Marco Polo Bridge. At the same time, the government in Tokyo ominously called for a "fundamental solution of Sino-Japanese relations."

Chiang K'ai-shek responded to the Japanese action with a call to war. "The only course open to us now," he said, "is to lead the masses of the country, under a single national plan, to struggle to the end." (J. Crowley, *Japan's Quest for Autonomy*, pp. 338–339).

The massive Japanese assault that followed proved disastrous for the Nationalists. In the first few months of fighting Chiang's forces suffered more than 250,000 battlefield deaths, losing over 50 percent of their most battle-ready troops. Most of the fatalities occurred during the Nationalists' unsuccessful defense of Shanghai, which fell to the invading Japanese in the autumn of 1937.

Aside from the huge number of *Guomindang* military casualties, Shanghai's civilian population also suffered incalculable damage from an unrelenting Japanese naval and aerial bombardment of the city.

After occupying Shanghai and several key cities on the North China Plain, including Shijiazhuang, Baoding, and Taiyuan, the Japanese next trained their sights on the Nationalists' capital of Nanjing. What happened then has been debated by historians for decades.

The Japanese assault on Nanjing began as a conventional military operation, but it quickly degenerated into uncontrolled havoc.

The debacle began when the *Guomindang* general who had sworn to defend Nanjing "to the last breath" suddenly and without warning simply abandoned the city. This left Nanjing's civilian population completely vulnerable, both to the attacking Japanese and to the suddenly leaderless and demoralized Nationalist troops.

The storm of wanton violence that followed was among the worst in modern recorded history. While estimates of total civilian deaths range widely, from a low of 90,000 to a high of 300,000, there can be little doubt of the extreme human cruelty and horror that marked the Nanjing Massacre.

In the six weeks between mid-December 1937 and the end of January 1938, at least 20,000 Chinese women and young girls (and possibly up to three times that many) were raped, mutilated, and killed, some for the mere sport of it, by out-of-control Japanese troops. Grainy motion pictures and still photographs taken by Western missionaries and other eyewitnesses recorded a small portion of the carnage; the diaries of Japanese soldiers documented additional atrocities.

Because the Japanese Emperor Hirohito had personally renounced the international convention governing humane treatment of enemy prisoners, the distinction between captive Chinese soldiers and civilian non-combatants was routinely disregarded by the Japanese invaders; in consequence, tens of thousands of disarmed *Guomindang* troops were slaughtered outright; and an equal number of civilians were killed on suspicion of being disguised combatants.

By the end of January 1938, widespread looting, robbery and arson had left much of the *Guomindang* capital in ruins.

After completing the pacification of Nanjing, the Japanese army conducted an all-out offensive throughout the urban centers of the Yangzi River delta. Forced to retreat up the Yangzi in the summer of 1938, *Guomindang* troops made a major stand at Hankow, where they suffered more than 200,000 casualties, as well as the loss of most of their air force.

By October, the Nationalist forces had been forced to retreat hundreds of miles further upriver, past the fabled Three Gorges into the deep rural interior of Sichuan Province. There they made their headquarters in the teeming riverfront commercial hub city of Chongqing.

Life in Chongqing was difficult for the exiled Nationalist regime, to say the least. From 1939 on, the Japanese bombed the city with chilling regularity, and with devastating results. The Nationalists suffered a severe shortage of weapons, ammunition, and other war matériel, and the *Guomindang*'s military supply routes came under heavy Japanese aerial bombardment.

By 1939 only a single secure overland route linked Chongqing with the outside world, the 715-mile-long Burma Road. Built by tens of thousands of conscripted Chinese laborers, the Burma Road was completed in December of 1938, and it provided a slow but steady trickle of military supplies to the beleaguered Nationalists.

With war matériel, consumer goods, and foodstuffs all in extremely short supply in Chongqing, inflationary pressures began to mount. These pressures were compounded by ill-advised government policies that responded to growing commodity shortages by increasing the supply of money, thereby fueling an inflationary spiral.

Between 1937 and 1942, the face value of Chinese Nationalist banknotes in circulation, denominated in *yuan*, rose 17-fold, while the purchasing power of the *yuan* plunged to less than 3 percent of its former value against the U.S. dollar.

To satisfy its massive need for military manpower, the *Guomindang* forcibly conscripted millions of young men for the war effort. Like other government employees, these military conscripts were paid small, fixed salaries. But with Chinese currency constantly undergoing inflationary devaluation, their pay quickly lost its meager purchasing power.

Unable to support themselves and their families, hundreds of thousands of impoverished *Guomindang* conscript soldiers deserted; countless others survived by preying on civilians in the countryside, stealing from those more helpless and vulnerable than themselves.

Popular morale steadily eroded, while corruption rose to dangerous levels. To make matters worse, a number of well-positioned *Guomindang* industrialists and financiers, including even members of the Soong family dynasty, reaped huge windfall profits by cornering supplies of war-scarce commodities.

Meanwhile, in their rural Yan'an headquarters, 500 miles northeast of Chongqing, the Chinese Communists were reorganizing their forces and refining their message. Able to avoid the brunt of Japanese attacks, which were directed mainly against Nationalist-held cities, rail lines and commercial centers in east and northeast China, the Communists employed their time-tested tactics of people's war against the Japanese invaders.

Mao Zedong and his comrades also substantially altered their land reform practices in this period. In place of the radical policy of confiscating and redistributing the land and property of landlords and rich peasants, the party now adopted a moderate policy of uniform rent reduction. Designed to avoid antagonizing landlords and rich peasants, the new policy was intended to facilitate the mobilization of the broadest possible anti-Japanese patriotic front, including all rural classes and economic strata, including even big landowners. In order to focus popular hostility against Japan, class warfare against the rich was temporarily halted.

In the Communists' drive to mobilize all patriotic Chinese, their cause was unwittingly aided by the Japanese themselves.

In the effort to counteract growing Communist influence in the villages of north China, Japanese commanders pursued a scorched-earth policy of "kill all, burn all, destroy all." Entire villages, suspected of harboring Communist agents, were burned to the ground, their inhabitants slaughtered. As a result of this policy, a deep and abiding rage against Japan took root among the peasants of north China. This rage eventually helped to propel the Chinese Communists to power.

To mobilize peasant support, the Red Army, which was now named the People's Liberation Army (or PLA), paid great attention to the political indoctrination of its recruits, so that they would not exploit local farmers, or steal food and supplies, or molest peasant women. In this respect, their wartime behavior compared quite favorably with that of their undisciplined and increasingly predatory Nationalist counterparts.

Meanwhile, Yan'an served as a magnet for patriotic Chinese from all parts of the country. Between 1937 and 1942, tens of thousands of people made their way to the Communist base area to join the anti-Japanese resistance.

By 1941, the fragile united front between the Communists and the Nationalists had become badly frayed. Never trusting each other, Mao Zedong and Chiang K'ai-shek each sought to take advantage of the other's vulnerabilities and weaknesses. Sporadic armed clashes between the two sides occurred, and were increasing in frequency.

The tensions between them reached the boiling point in July of 1941, when 9,000 Communist troops from the PLA's New Fourth Army were ambushed by a force of 80,000 Nationalist soldiers in the mountains of south-central China. The Communists suffered more than 3,000 killed, while additional thousands were captured and shipped off to *Guomindang* prison camps.

Although from a purely military viewpoint the massacre was an unmitigated disaster for the Communists, they were able to turn it to their advantage. By focusing their propaganda on Chiang K'ai-shek's cold-blooded perfidy and his lack of sincerity in resisting Japan, they were able to generate considerable political capital and sympathy from the New Fourth Army Incident.

With the anti-Japanese war going badly for the Nationalists, the lack of substantial foreign military assistance was proving critical. Although the Soviet Union had provided a certain amount of air defense support against Japan from 1937 to 1939, the conclusion of the Hitler-Stalin non-aggression pact of 1939 meant that Russia was now a nominal ally of Japan; consequently, all Soviet assistance to China ceased.

For its part, in Washington, the Roosevelt administration sympathized with China's plight and provided a certain amount of economic aid to the beleaguered Nationalists. To prop up the *Guomindang*'s plummeting currency, for example, the United States government bought up millions of dollars in devalued Chinese *yuan*, while also providing $40 million in loans to Chiang's government-in-exile in Chongqing.

But American largesse was sharply limited by President Roosevelt's declared policy of neutrality in the Sino-Japanese War.

The first significant boost in U.S. military aid to China came in late 1940, when FDR authorized the informal transfer of 100 U.S. Air Force fighter planes, and their volunteer pilots, to Chongqing.

Nicknamed the "Flying Tigers," the American pilots were commanded by a de-commissioned former U.S. Army pilot named Claire Chennault. Under Chennault's leadership, the Flying Tigers played an important early role in helping to defend Chongqing against Japanese air attacks in 1940 and '41.

But such foreign assistance was just a drop in a very large and very leaky bucket. On the ground in Chongqing and throughout the *Guomindang*-held areas of southwest China, the Nationalists continued to squander both their limited resources and, increasingly, the goodwill of the people they had sworn to defend.

Under these circumstances, the Japanese attack on Pearl Harbor on December 7, 1941, came as a godsend to Chiang K'ai-shek. With the sinking of the U.S. fleet in Honolulu, America could no longer remain neutral in the war in Asia. Now, for the first time, the survival of Free China and the defeat of Japan became vital American national interests.

Suddenly, U.S. financial and military aid began pouring into China. In 1942 alone, Washington provided Chiang with over a billion dollars worth of lend-lease supplies and unsecured loans. At the same time, President Roosevelt named a senior American military officer, General Joseph Stilwell, to be commander-in-chief of U.S. forces in China.

Almost immediately upon arriving in China, "Vinegar Joe" Stilwell came into conflict with Chiang K'ai-shek. Stilwell wanted to reorganize the Nationalist military forces, to get rid of incompetent and corrupt officers and to introduce proper military training and discipline among conscripts. He also wanted Chiang's troops to play a more proactive role in seeking out and engaging Japanese ground forces. In his diary, Stilwell contemptuously referred to the recalcitrant Generalissimo as "the Peanut."

At every turn, Chiang resisted Stilwell's meddling. Expressing his displeasure to FDR, Chiang requested that Stilwell be pulled out of China. When Roosevelt balked, Chiang blackmailed him, obliquely threatening to withdraw from the war effort if Stilwell wasn't recalled.

Since the United States badly needed Chiang's troops (incompetent as they were) to engage the one million Japanese ground forces stationed in China (so that they wouldn't be available to fight American troops elsewhere in the Pacific), Roosevelt reluctantly caved in to Chiang's demand. In October 1944 he pulled Stilwell out of China and replaced him with General Albert C. Wedemeyer. Unlike Stilwell, Wedemeyer was an unabashed admirer of Chiang K'ai-shek.

A second high-level American emissary, Patrick J. Hurley, was also sent to Chongqing to help smooth over relations with the prickly Gimo. Hurley was a one-time coal miner and mule skinner from Oklahoma who had become a lawyer in mid-life. During WW II, Hurley served as FDR's personal representative abroad. In 1944 he was named U.S. Ambassador to China. (As a brief historical footnote, Patrick Hurley used to refer to himself as "General Hurley," though he never held a military commission).

In order to keep American goodwill and material assistance flowing to Chongqing, Chiang K'ai-shek sought an invitation for his elegant and eloquent wife, Soong Mei-ling, to visit the United States. With its strong overtones of soap opera steaminess and seduction, the story of how Madame Chiang secured her invitation raised numerous eyebrows at the time.

Soong Mei-ling's invitation was personally delivered by Wendell Willkie. A wealthy Republican Party patrician, Willkie been defeated by FDR in the 1940 presidential election. Roosevelt had then sent Willkie to China on a good-will mission.

While visiting the Chiangs in Chongqing in October of 1942, the dapper Mr. Willkie was clearly smitten by the flirtatious Mme. Chiang. One evening, while attending a diplomatic reception, Wilkie and Mei-ling slipped quietly out of the reception hall. Wilkie, then 50 years of age, was observed returning to his guesthouse at 4 am.

According to an eyewitness, he looked "very buoyant … cocky as a young college student after a successful night with a girl." That evening, Wendell Willkie invited Madame Chiang to visit the United States.

With her sultry, sophisticated, good looks, her Christian missionary background, her American education, and her flawless, unaccented English, Soong Mei-ling was the perfect "goodwill ambassador" for China. In New York, Chicago, Hollywood, and Washington DC she wowed packed audiences. She also had a private dinner with the Roosevelts at the White House and made a special address to a joint session of the U.S. Congress, where she was introduced by Wendell Willkie.

At Madison Square Garden, Soong Mei-ling was introduced to a capacity crowd as "an avenging angel … a soldier unafraid to fight for justice." To a Hollywood Bowl audience packed with cinematic celebrities including Mary Pickford, Rita Hayworth, Marlene Dietrich, Ingrid Bergman, Ginger Rogers, Shirley Temple, and David O. Selznick, Soong described in vivid detail the horrors of the Japanese "Rape of Nanking." There were few dry eyes in the house.

By the end of her coast-to-coast speaking tour she had won the hearts of the American people as well as the U.S. Congress. In the process, she raised tens of millions of dollars in private donations for her charitable fund, United China Relief.

While Chiang and his media-savvy wife were busy alternately seducing and blackmailing Washington, the Chinese Communists were launching a goodwill mission of their own. Soon after Stilwell's departure, The CCP extended an invitation to a U.S. military advisory group to visit their wartime headquarters in Yan'an.

Against the wishes of a distrustful Generalissimo Chiang, the "Dixie Mission," as the U.S. advisory group was called, set out by airplane from Chongqing. It was July of 1944.

When they reached Yan'an, the Americans were cordially welcomed by Communist leaders, including Mao himself, along with generals Zhou Enlai and Zhu De. The party chieftains took great pains to ensure that their American visitors received a favorable (albeit gilded) impression of Chinese Communism. The image they sought to convey to the Americans was that of the Communist Party as a moderate, progressive, and democratic movement.

After Patrick Hurley was named U.S. ambassador to China, he displayed a keen interest in participating in direct talks with the Chinese Communists. In November of 1944 he flew, unannounced, to the Communists' headquarters in Yan'an. Arriving in a driving rain, he stood stiffly at attention, before deplaning briskly.

Attired in a full-dress army uniform impressively adorned with three rows of military campaign ribbons, which could not have been his own, he paused to have his picture taken with a group of surprised Communist Party leaders, who had been hastily assembled upon hearing of Hurley's arrival. As the rain continued to fall, Ambassador Hurley startled everyone present by emitting a blood-curdling Choctaw war-whoop.

Although he prided himself on his negotiating skills, and though he conducted several rounds of hands-on discussion with top party leaders— and he even escorted Zhou Enlai to Chongqing on one occasion to meet with Chiang K'ai-shek—Hurley nonetheless had only the vaguest understanding of the issues that divided the Nationalists and the Communists; and he made no progress whatever in bridging the vast political and ideological gap that separated them.

As members of the Dixie Mission continued their observations in Yan'an, their findings tended to conflict sharply with those of Hurley and Wedemeyer, who believed that Chiang K'ai-shek and the *Guomindang* represented the one best hope for China's democratic salvation.

In a series of internal memos to Washington, members of the Dixie Mission portrayed the leadership of the Guomindang as corrupt, inept, ineffectual, and alarmingly isolated from the common people. By contrast, they found the Communists to be well-led, highly-disciplined, and uncorrupt.

In one rather prescient memo, a State Department observer attached to the Dixie Mission named John Stewart Service predicted that if present trends continued, with the *Guomindang* becoming increasingly undemocratic, unpopular, and economically irresponsible, the future of China would belong not to the Nationalists but to the Communists.

But Service's memo never reached Washington. It was intercepted—and quashed–by Ambassador Hurley. And for the remainder of the War, Chiang K'ai-shek and his irrepressible wife, Soong Mei-ling, remained the unchallenged American symbols of Free China.

When the war against Japan ended abruptly in August 1945, it was not due to the military efforts of either the Chinese Nationalists or the Communists. It was American air and naval power that proved decisive, culminating of course in the atomic bombing of two Japanese cities.

For their part, the Chinese Nationalists suffered catastrophic losses of manpower, territory, and matériel during the war. But their role in defeating Japan was nonetheless minimal.

General Stilwell had once remarked that Chiang K'ai-shek was far more interested in preserving his forces for the final showdown with Communism than he was in engaging Japanese troops on the battlefield. A number of Western journalists stationed in Chongqing during the war confirmed Stilwell's observation.

With the surrender of Japan, Chiang emerged as a proud—if severely weakened—warrior. Though his image may have been tarnished within China, he had an important ace in the hole: the unwavering support of the United States.

Throughout the Japanese occupation, while Chiang K'ai-shek was husbanding his forces in Chongqing, the Communists in Yan'an were effectively mobilizing mass patriotic resistance to Japan. In the Japanese-occupied rural areas of north China, the Maoists recruited hundreds of thousands of new soldiers and millions of new civilian supporters.

As an indication of the Communists' wartime success, between 1937 and 1945 party membership increased more than 20-fold, from about 50,000 to 1.2 million, while the PLA increased its troop strength from 80,000 to more than 900,000. In that same eight-year period the civilian population under Communist administrative control grew from one million to 95.5 million.

Returning to a point made at the outset of this lecture, it would appear that Zhou Enlai was not greatly exaggerating when he thanked Japanese Prime Minister Tanaka in 1972 for Japan's wartime assistance in helping to bring the Chinese Communists to power. Indeed, without the Japanese invasion, the Chinese Revolution might well have had a quite different outcome.

Next time we'll examine the post-war situation in China and the resumption of civil war between Mao Zedong and Chiang K'ai-shek.

This page has been intentionally left blank.

Chiang's Last Stand, 1945–1949
Lecture 13

We will give Yan'an to Chiang, but he will give China to us.

— Mao Zedong

When the war against Japan ended, there was a brief period in which all sides held their collective breath, uncertain about the future. Could the uneasy truce between Mao Zedong and Chiang K'ai-shek be extended, or would the bitter enemies renew their long-standing civil war, with unknown consequences for China and the outside world?

Chiang K'ai-shek.

Eager to stabilize the situation in China, the United States sent General George C. Marshall to Chongqing to try to convince the CCP and the GMD to form a coalition government. Though Mao and Chiang paid lip service to the idea of a coalition, each set about preparing for the ultimate military showdown. With U.S. airlift support, Chiang's forces reoccupied most of China's major northern and eastern cities from the defeated Japanese. Almost immediately, they began plundering these cities. Inflation surged as GMD officials confiscated properties, factories, and funds and indulged in various vices.

Meanwhile, PLA troops, concentrated in the rural areas of northern and northeastern China, sought to consolidate their control over the countryside. This allowed them to disrupt vital Nationalist rail and communications links, effectively cutting off and isolating the GMD's urban strongholds. Though the Nationalist armies still enjoyed roughly a 2:1 numerical advantage over the PLA, and though their U.S.-made weapons were far superior to anything possessed by the Communists, the bare military odds had begun to narrow rapidly.

When the Soviet Union ended its occupation of Manchuria in 1946, PLA guerrillas fell heir to large numbers of captured Japanese weapons. The CCP-GMD civil war resumed in earnest in 1946, with PLA troops cutting major Nationalist supply lines to the cities of the northeast, thus isolating GMD troops there. Practicing the Maoist strategy of "surrounding the cities from the countryside," the PLA took the offensive in 1947, attacking isolated GMD strongholds one after another. GMD troop morale was severely eroded when Chiang ordered field commanders to blow up their own arsenals, bridges, and food, rather than letting them fall into the hands of the PLA.

Could the uneasy truce between Mao Zedong and Chiang K'ai-shek be extended, or would the bitter enemies renew their long-standing civil war?

By 1948, Nationalist armies began defecting en masse. One by one, China's major cities fell to the Communists during their victorious southward march in 1949. Choosing Beijing as his new capital, on October 1, Mao Zedong ascended a platform atop the Gate of Heavenly Peace at the southern entrance to the Forbidden City. Looking down from the same majestic edifice where a succession of Chinese emperors and court officials had displayed the awesome might of the Middle Kingdom, Mao proudly proclaimed the birth of the People's Republic of China. ■

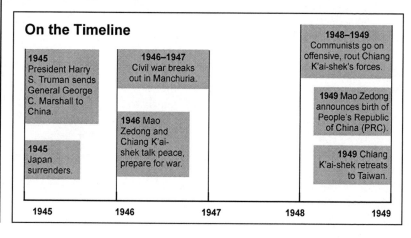

On the Timeline

1945 President Harry S. Truman sends General George C. Marshall to China.

1945 Japan surrenders.

1946–1947 Civil war breaks out in Manchuria.

1946 Mao Zedong and Chiang K'ai-shek talk peace, prepare for war.

1948–1949 Communists go on offensive, rout Chiang K'ai-shek's forces.

1949 Mao Zedong announces birth of People's Republic of China (PRC).

1949 Chiang K'ai-shek retreats to Taiwan.

1945   1946   1947   1948   1949

The Battle of Huai Hai: End of the Road for the Nationalists

The decisive blow to the Nationalists was delivered at the Battle of Huai Hai, which commenced in November 1948. There the Communists surrounded half a million Nationalist troops in the city of Xuzhou, a major railway hub in northwest Jiangsu Province.

The battle was conducted in three distinct phases, over a two-month period. In the course of the battle, five entire Nationalist army groups were decimated, hundreds of thousands of GMD conscripts defected (along with their officers), and vast stores of American-supplied weapons fell into the hands of the Communists.

As the two-month battle ground toward its inevitable conclusion, a PLA advance unit approached the northern bank of the Yangzi, just across the river from Nanjing. Nanjing had been restored as the Nationalist's capital city in 1946 and was bustling with government activity. But with Communists now on the far bank of the river, Nanjing's ruling class experienced massive precombat jitters.

Anticipating an imminent PLA attack, hundreds of high-level Nationalist officials and military officers beat a hasty retreat by air, while thousands of others, less well-connected, jammed onto "dispersal trains" heading south.

Left without an effective government apparatus, Nanjing became chaotic. Chiang K'ai-shek announced that he was stepping down as president, in favor of Vice President Li Zongren.

Before evacuating his Nanjing headquarters in January of 1949, Chiang visited the Sun Yat-sen Memorial Hall, at the edge of the city, one last time. Ascending its 392 steps, he bowed three times before the stately marble likeness of the founder of the Republic of China.

Visibly dispirited, Chiang then flew off to Hangzhou, in preparation for his eventual retreat to the island of Taiwan. Even the habitually upbeat *Time* magazine now observed that Chiang's prestige had "sunk lower than the Yangzi."

Suggested Reading

Barnett, *China on the Eve of Communist Takeover*.

Chang and Halliday, *Mao*.

Esherick, *Lost Chance in China*.

Friedman, Pickowicz, and Selden, *Chinese Village, Socialist State*.

Johnson, *Peasant Nationalism and Communist Power*.

Schram, *The Political Thought of Mao Tse-tung*.

Short, *Mao*.

Snow, *Red Star over China*.

Taylor, *The Generalissimo*.

Tuchman, *Stilwell and the American Experience in China*.

Questions to Consider

1. What were the key determinants of the final outcome of the Chinese civil war?

2. How did the behavior of GMD reoccupation forces influence the popularity of the Nationalists after the Japanese surrender?

Chiang's Last Stand, 1945–1949
Lecture 13—Transcript

When the war against Japan ended, there was a brief period in which all sides held their collective breath, uncertain about the future. Could the uneasy truce between Mao Zedong and Chiang K'ai-shek be extended? Could some sort of power-sharing agreement avert the renewal of hostilities? Or would these two old and bitter enemies renew their longstanding civil war, with unknown consequences for China and the outside world at large?

For the United States, a top priority after the defeat of Japan was to stabilize the political situation in China and prevent an open rupture between the two sides. Toward this end, Ambassador Hurley flew to Yan'an for a second time in the summer of 1945.

Hurley's mission was to coax Mao Zedong to return with him to Chongqing, to hold talks with Chiang K'ai-shek about creating a new coalition government. For their own reasons, both Mao and Chiang were eager to portray themselves to the world (and to the Americans in particular) as cooperative, peace-loving democrats; and so both men readily agreed to Hurley's proposal.

When Mao deplaned in Chongqing in late August (it was his very first airplane flight; he had a well-known aversion to flying), he was duly—if rather coolly—welcomed by the Generalissimo. A famous photo taken on that occasion showed Mao and Chiang drinking a toast together with Hurley.

But even as the two leaders smiled and toasted, Chiang K'ai-shek was preparing to deal a severe blow to Washington's hopes for a coalition government. With major logistical support from the U.S. military transport services, Chiang ordered his armed forces to reoccupy major Chinese cities just as soon as the defeated Japanese forces withdrew. By the autumn of 1945, Nationalist troops had occupied Shanghai, Nanjing, Hankow, Tianjin, and Beijing.

But even as they recaptured these (and other) cities, the *Guomindang* faced a host of new problems. For one thing, Communist partisans in the urban areas (the White Area Communists), rather than actively contesting the *Guomindang*'s return, simply melted away into the countryside, where they began to operate among the peasants—"fish in water."

By way of contrast, the Nationalist forces, lacking any base of popular support in the rural areas, became increasingly ghettoized, confining their operations exclusively within their secure urban enclaves. But even within these urban strongholds trouble was brewing for them.

The *Guomindang*'s re-occupation policies had been hastily conceived and haphazardly implemented, with precious few safeguards against predatory behavior by occupying *Guomindang* forces. Consequently, within a very short time, the recovery of Japanese-held cities and towns degenerated into an undisciplined, opportunistic exercise in looting, profiteering, and embezzlement.

Acting more like scavengers than liberators, *Guomindang* officials grabbed for themselves and their associates all the confiscated Japanese properties, factories, food and funds they could get their hands on. And they further indulged themselves in such pastimes as gambling, opium, and prostitution.

In north China, a foreign reporter noted shocking acts of pilferage committed by occupying officials:

> There has been great confusion in the takeover. ... First there was a scramble for industrial equipment, then for public buildings and real estate, and now government officials are competing for furniture. ... A certain army officer has already taken over several thousand houses. [S. Pepper, *Civil War in China*, p. 26].

Even the Gimo himself was alarmed by the lawless behavior of his representatives. In a letter to the mayor of Shanghai, Chiang wrote:

> It has been reliably brought to my [attention] that the military, political and party officials of Nanjing, Shanghai, Beijing and Tianjin have been leading extravagant lives, indulging in prostitution and gambling, and have forcibly occupied the people's larger buildings as offices under assumed names. ... I have been greatly distressed ... on hearing of such conditions. ... All cases of blackmailing or illegal occupation of ... people's houses must be severely dealt with. ... No culprit is to be harbored by personal favors.

Compounding the problems created by predatory Nationalist officials and army officers was the sharp inflationary surge that followed the *Guomindang*'s reoccupation of China's cities. In many cases, opportunistic officials from

Chongqing brought with them truckloads of Nationalist currency with them when they returned to the eastern seaboard.

Because coastal cities were in dire financial straits due to the collapse of the Japanese puppet currency at the end of the war, Nationalist carpetbaggers (who were euphemistically called "reconversion officials") were able to buy up vast tracts of residential real estate and distressed commercial property at fire sale prices.

These urban predators were also able to reap huge windfall profits by purchasing gold at low fixed prices and then hoarding it while the prices went up. With inflation surging ever upward, by the beginning of 1946 the cost of living index in Shanghai had spiraled to 900 times its pre-war level.

But that was not all. Further compounding the Nationalists' reconversion difficulties was their policy of lenient treatment toward Chinese officials and military officers who had collaborated with the Japanese.

With post-war anger against Japan running very high, the Nationalists were caught on the horns of a dilemma: If they punished all high- and middle-ranking Chinese civil and military collaborators (and there were a lot of them in the occupied areas), they risked driving large numbers of experienced administrators, policemen, and army officers into the arms of the Communists. Yet if they embraced the collaborators, they risked further alienating the general public.

Caught between a rock and a hard place, the Nationalist reconversion authorities tried to have it both ways. Publicly, they renounced former collaborators as criminals and traitors and executed several high-profile quislings. Among those executed was Chen Gongbo, who we first met in Lecture 9.

After defecting from the Communist Party in 1922, Chen Gongbo had become a key associate of the left-wing *Guomindang* leader, Wang Jingwei. Like Wang, Chen despised Chiang K'ai-shek; and after the Japanese invasion the two men decided to collaborate with the Japanese rather than join Chiang's government in exile in Chongqing. After the war Wang died in disgrace in Japan, while Chen was executed in China for treason.

But while a few traitorous "big fish" were publicly fried, the Nationalists quietly and without fanfare went about the task of rehabilitating tens of thousands of lesser-known governmental and civic collaborators, employing them in a variety of official posts to help restore urban services and maintain law and order.

Another famous Japanese collaborator was the last Manchu emperor, Puyi. Puyi was taken prisoner by the Soviet Army in Mǎnzhōu at the end of the war. He remained a captive of the Russians until 1949, when he asked Joseph Stalin to repatriate him to China. He was returned to China the following year, and he spent the next nine years in a Chinese prison camp. In 1959 Puyi was released from custody and was permitted to work as a caretaker in the Beijing Botanical Gardens. He died a natural death in 1967 at the age of 62.

As the Nationalists continued their urban reconversion project in the autumn of 1945, a new and deadly contest was taking shape in China's northeast. At stake was control over Manchuria, heartland of Japan's military-industrial empire in Asia.

Unlike China's eastern seaboard, where the Nationalists enjoyed a strong numerical and logistical advantage in the race to reclaim urban centers from the surrendering Japanese, in Manchuria the Communists held a distinct advantage. They had been conducting guerrilla operations in the Manchurian countryside for years, while the Nationalists had no significant presence there at all.

Though both sides coveted the prize of Manchuria, neither side was immediately able to claim it. Under the terms of the Yalta Agreement of February 1945, signed by Roosevelt, Churchill, and Stalin, the Soviet Union had promised to enter the war against Japan as soon as the European war ended. With Germany's unconditional surrender in May of 1945, Soviet troops marched into Manchuria.

When Japan capitulated three months later, following the atomic bombing of Hiroshima and Nagasaki, over one million Soviet troops were on hand in Manchuria to accept the Japanese surrender.

As stipulated by the Yalta Agreement, the pullout of Soviet forces from Manchuria was due to take place in no more than three months from the date of the Japanese surrender. But as the November deadline drew near, Chiang K'ai-shek found that he didn't have enough troops in place in the Northeast to prevent the Communists from reaping the benefits of the Soviet withdrawal.

Playing for time, Chiang struck a bargain with Joseph Stalin, who agreed to delay the departure of the Soviet forces just long enough for Chiang to airlift half a million of his troops into the major cities of the northeast.

For his part, Stalin used the extra time to systematically loot and plunder the extensive Japanese industrial base in Manchuria. Altogether, Russian occupation troops removed about $2 billion dollars worth of Manchurian plant and equipment. They even pulled up the railroad ties behind them, as they departed by train. About the only thing they left behind were hundreds of thousands of Japanese rifles and assorted small arms, many of which eventually fell into the hands of PLA guerrillas.

Commenting on the post-war Stalinist plunder of Manchuria, one United Nations observer described the scene he encountered there in surrealistic terms, as if a "giant swarm of steel-eating locusts had descended, devouring everything in sight."

With a strong assist from the U.S. air transport service, now commanded by Chiang's old friend Claire Chennault, Nationalist troops reoccupied Manchuria's cities without a struggle. His confidence growing, Chiang now demanded, as a precondition for any power-sharing agreement with the Communists, that all of Manchuria should be recognized as belonging to the *Guomindang*, the Nationalist government.

But the Gimo had overplayed his hand. Even as his forces were re-occupying the major cities of the northeast, 100,000 PLA guerrilla fighters, under the command of General Lin Biao, were infiltrating the Manchurian countryside. Traveling on foot and on horseback, they readied themselves for the forthcoming battle. It was a classic maneuver, straight out of Mao Zedong's theory of people's war.

By November 1945, the two sides were in position for a showdown. At that point, with little or no progress having being made on a coalition government agreement, Ambassador Hurley unexpectedly submitted his resignation. Two weeks later, President Truman dispatched General George C. Marshall to replace Hurley as his special representative in China. Marshall's primary task was to keep the two sides talking in an effort to head off a resumption of all-out civil war.

Marshall remained in China for 13 months. For most of this time, both Chiang K'ai-shek and the Communists' chief negotiator, Zhou Enlai, continued to pay lip service to the American mediation effort, this despite the fact that neither of them had any faith whatsoever in the likelihood of a peaceful resolution of their differences.

In March of 1946, with the icy Manchurian winter beginning to thaw out, Lin Biao's PLA forces attacked a strategic railway junction in southern Manchuria, cutting off the *Guomindang*'s main supply lines to the northeast. With Communist troops in control of the rural countryside and Nationalist forces entrenched in the cities, the stage was set for a showdown.

Unfortunately for Chiang, he mistook the PLA's tactic of avoiding large-scale, pitched battles as a sign of Communist military weakness. His confidence growing, he ordered one of his field commanders to attack and seize the Communist stronghold of Yan'an. It was intended as a major coup, a bold stroke to convincingly demonstrate the *Guomindang*'s invincibility.

Unknown to the Generalissimo, however, the personal secretary of the general in charge of the Yan'an operation was a longtime Communist mole; and he was able to warn the Maoists in plenty of time to allow them to evacuate. By the time the Nationalist forces reached the Communist headquarters, they found an empty nest.

Though Chiang boasted that he had delivered a decisive blow against the "Communist bandits," his was a hollow victory at best. As Mao himself prophetically said, "We will give Yan'an to Chiang; but he will give China to us."

For the second time in a little over a decade, Chiang's obsession with capturing the Communists' Yan'an stronghold had ended in disaster. In 1936, he had been kidnapped by the patriotic "Young Marshal," Zhang Xueliang. A decade later his decision to storm Yan'an resulted in his troops badly over-extending their supply lines and their strategic command-and-control capability.

With the PLA firmly in control of the countryside, the Communists were able to disrupt vital Nationalist rail and communications links, effectively cutting off and isolating the *Guomindang*'s urban strongholds. Though the Nationalist armies still enjoyed roughly a 2:1 numerical advantage over the armed forces of the PLA (roughly 3.7 million soldiers to 1.95 million), and though their U.S.-made weapons were far superior to anything the Communists possessed the bare military odds had begun to narrow rapidly.

With little but frustration to show for his 13-month effort to avert a civil war, General Marshall returned to Washington in January 1947. By then, the PLA had achieved sufficient strength to concentrate its forces for offensive operations against the Nationalist-held urban strongholds. Also by then, the futility of Chiang's strategy of simultaneously trying to recapture and hold all Japanese- and Communist-occupied territories was becoming increasingly apparent.

One of Chiang's more successful strategies during the Northern Expedition of 1926–1927, the co-optation of regional warlords, now came back to haunt him. Several of Chiang's top field commanders were, in fact, aging former warlords, whose allegiance to the *Guomindang* had never been particularly strong, and who were now proving themselves to be rather inept when it came to the politics of urban warfare.

Ignoring Chiang's directives, they imposed their own form of political order, which was often brutal and predatory, on the urban populations they were supposed to be defending against the Communists.

When the PLA went on the offensive in mid-1947, the capital city of Shandong Province, Jinan, was among the first to fall. Over 100,000 Nationalist troops were killed or wounded in an eight-day Communist assault.

Further to the north, Lin Biao, adopting tactics of "sudden concentration and sudden dispersal," amassed a force of 700,000 guerrilla fighters to completely encircle the industrial city of Changchun, in Manchuria's Jilin Province.

Lin's army then launched a siege. Cut off from supplies and troop reinforcements, the *Guomindang* defenders of Changchun ran out of food and ammunition rather quickly; after five months, they defected en masse to the Communists.

Thereafter, the Nationalists' heavily garrisoned cities in the northeast began to fall like so many pieces of overripe fruit. Jinzhou, in Liaoning Province, was the next to go, followed by Mukden (or Shenyang). Altogether, the Nationalists lost 400,000 troops in the battle for Manchuria.

Worse yet for the Generalissimo, whole armies now began to defect to the Communists, as the erosion of popular morale and confidence in the *Guomindang* created a crisis of political will and legitimacy. This further accelerated the Nationalists' military deterioration.

Troop morale was lowered still further when Chiang ordered his field commanders to blow up their own arsenals, bridges, railroad depots, and food stores, rather than letting them fall into the hands of the Communists.

The decisive blow was delivered at the Battle of Huai Hai, which commenced in November of 1948. There the Communists surrounded half a million Nationalist troops in the city of Xuzhou, a major railway hub in northern Jiangsu Province.

The Battle of Huai Hai was conducted in three distinct phases, over a two-month period. In the course of the battle, five entire Nationalist army groups were decimated, hundreds of thousands of *Guomindang* conscripts defected (along with their officers), and vast stores of American-supplied weapons fell into the hands of the Communists.

As the two-month battle ground toward its inevitable conclusion, a PLA advance unit approached the northern bank of the Yangzi River, just across the river from Nanjing. Nanjing had been restored as the Nationalist's capital city in 1946, and it was bustling with government activity. But with the Communists now on the far bank of the river, Nanjing's ruling class experienced massive precombat jitters.

Anticipating an imminent PLA attack, hundreds of high-level Nationalist officials and military officers beat a hasty retreat by air, while thousands of others, less well-connected, jammed onto so-called dispersal trains heading south.

Left without an effective governmental apparatus, Nanjing became chaotic. Chiang K'ai-shek announced that he was stepping down as president, in favor of his Vice President, Li Zongren.

Before evacuating his Nanjing headquarters in January of 1949, Chiang K'ai-shek visited the Sun Yat-sen Memorial Hall, at the edge of the city, one last time. Ascending its 392 steps, he bowed three times before the stately marble likeness of the founder of the Republic of China.

Visibly dispirited, Chiang then flew off to Hangzhou, where he would prepare for his eventual retreat to the island of Taiwan. Even the habitually upbeat *Time* magazine now observed that Chiang's prestige had "sunk lower than the Yangzi."

Further north, PLA troops entered Tianjin in early January 1949. Its inhabitants surrendered without a fight.

Next came Beijing. At the end of January, the Nationalist General Fu Zuoyi surrendered the city—but not before he had first negotiated his own exclusion from the Communists' list of most-wanted war criminals.

Marching six abreast in icy weather, a PLA advance guard marched into Beijing, followed by students bearing portraits of top Communist leaders and soldiers riding in abandoned American trucks. A large portrait of Chiang K'ai-shek, which had hung at the entrance to the Imperial Palace, was replaced by an even larger portrait of Mao Zedong. (Today, 60 years later, it still hangs there, guarding the entrance to the Forbidden City.)

Chairman Mao entered the city in a procession of two dozen motor vehicles. "Today," he remarked to Zhou Enlai, who was riding next to him, "we are going to sit for the imperial examination."

"We should be able to pass it," replied Zhou, ever the obliging yes-man.

In the spring of 1949, with the Communists continuing to sweep down from the north, the Nationalists concentrated their forces along the southern bank of the Yangzi River in preparation for a major defensive stand. Nationalist generals confidently declared the mile-wide, slow-moving Yangzi to be virtually impassible and predicted that the Communists would suffer catastrophic losses if they attempted a crossing.

In late April, however, the PLA surprised the defenders by enlisting the services of thousands of local boat people to ferry them across the river under cover of darkness. When the Nationalist troops on the south bank saw the approaching armada of small fishing boats, many of them simply panicked and fled. The last major natural barrier to the Communist conquest of China had now been breached.

Two days later, Communist troops entered Nanjing, taking the city without a fight. As the civilian population looked on, last-ditch Nationalist defenders blew up the railroad station before stripping off their uniforms to blend in with the civilian crowds.

Seeking to take advantage of the confusion, the Nationalist mayor of Nanjing drove off with 300 million *yuan* in cash; but his chauffeur and bodyguards beat him up and took the money. Meanwhile, roving bands of looters plundered government administrative offices.

The liberation of Nanjing was followed swiftly by the capture of Hankow, which by this time was better known as Wuhan. Meanwhile, two hundred miles downriver, Hangzhou fell, leaving the vital Nationalist stronghold of Shanghai isolated and vulnerable. In Shanghai's outlying rural suburbs, heavy fighting between the Maoist guerrillas and *Guomindang* regulars broke out, creating a massive flood of refugees.

As the PLA tightened its noose around Shanghai, food supplies grew scarce. Within the city a black market flourished, and inflation skyrocketed. Profiteers, thieves, and suspected Communists alike were paraded through the streets in open trucks by Nationalist soldiers before being shot in a public park.

The city fell to the Communists in late May, as PLA forces marched into Shanghai's Foreign Concession, where they hoisted a giant portrait of Mao outside the iconic Great World Entertainment Center, once a symbol of Shanghai's decadent, freewheeling culture of the roaring '20s.

As the victorious PLA continued its southward march, the Communists took Changsha in August, Canton and Xiamen in October, and Chongqing in November. Choosing Beijing as his new capital, on October 1 Mao Zedong ascended a platform atop the Gate of Heavenly Peace at the southern entrance to the Forbidden City.

Looking down from the same majestic edifice where a succession of Chinese emperors and court officials had displayed the awesome might of the Middle Kingdom, Mao now proudly proclaimed the birth of the People's Republic of China.

Meanwhile, a defeated and dispirited Chiang K'ai-shek, having forfeited the trust and confidence of his people, quietly left the Chinese Mainland in December of 1949, retreating to the island of Taiwan, 95 miles off the coast of Fujian Province. The revolution was over. The Mandate of Heaven had changed hands.

In the next lecture we'll examine the early years of the People's Republic of China. The period from 1950 to 1956 has sometimes been referred to as the "golden age" of Chinese communism; and there is truth—some reality—to such a characterization. But it was also a period of increasingly strained relations between the Communist Party and the Chinese people. And as we shall soon see, societal tensions that emerged in these early years would later help to shape the massive national traumas that occurred in Mao's declining years, most notably the Great Leap Forward and the Great Proletarian Cultural Revolution. Next time, the new regime.

"The Chinese People Have Stood Up!"
Lecture 14

Along with their sons, daughters, and even their grandchildren, these former landlords carried with them an indelible political stigma, a scarlet letter that could not be altered or erased—the label of "class enemy." Thereafter, their lives would never be the same.

A few days before Mao Zedong proclaimed the birth of the People's Republic of China, he addressed a political meeting in Beijing. In his speech, Mao famously claimed that "the Chinese people ... have stood up." For all his theatrical dramatics, however, Mao spoke only a half-truth.

To be sure, the upstart Chinese Communist Party had come from nowhere, out of the wilderness, to defeat the much larger, U.S.-backed forces of Chiang K'ai-shek. They had done it by stressing ingenuity, improvisation, and self-reliance, making use of whatever materials they had at hand, while receiving little assistance from the Soviet Union. But though the Chinese Communists won their civil war, they had not yet secured the civil peace. Devastated by more than three decades of revolution, foreign invasion, and civil war, the Chinese economy was a shambles. Having operated in the rural hinterland for more than 20 years, the CCP knew little about how to run an urban economy. Indeed, it would take several more decades for the Chinese people to truly stand up.

Desperately in need of foreign assistance to rebuild China's shattered economy, Mao swallowed his pride and bowed in the direction of the Soviet Union. "Forty years of experience have taught us [that] ... all Chinese without exception must lean either to the side of imperialism or to the side of socialism." With this important statement, Mao established that China would align itself with the "socialist camp," led by the USSR, and would eschew collaboration with the "imperialist camp," headed by the United States.

With the final defeat of the Nationalists in 1949, the CCP set about consolidating its control of the country. The Maoists promulgated a new form of government, the "people's democratic dictatorship," in which the rectification campaign model first devised in Yan'an was applied to Chinese society as a whole. "The people" and their "enemies" were now sharply delimited, with the former category encompassing not just workers and peasants, who formed the core of the party's support base, but also patriotic, law-abiding members of the intelligentsia, the petit bourgeoisie, and even the national bourgeoisie (including patriotic businessmen, managers and entrepreneurs). In extending an olive branch to members of these "impure" classes, the party aimed to enlist their talents in the important task of restoring China's shattered economy. Only the people were granted full rights of citizenship.

Devastated by more than three decades of revolution, foreign invasion, and civil war, the Chinese economy was a shambles.

For those labeled as enemies of the people, the future was decidedly more bleak, as they were earmarked for suppression and dictatorship. A campaign to suppress counterrevolutionaries was launched in Chinese cities in 1950, in the course of which 2.3 million people were detained and 710,000 were executed. In addition, tens of thousands of "bourgeois intellectuals" were subjected to mandatory "thought reform," in which independent thinkers were targeted for harsh criticism.

Two other mass movements were initiated in the early 1950s. The first of these was the Three Anti campaign, which targeted the growing problems of corruption, waste, and bureaucratism among the party's basic level cadres. This campaign was relatively mild and seldom involved coercive struggle. The second campaign—known as the Five Antis—was far more intensive and more coercive. It was designed to expose and punish crimes of bribery, tax evasion, embezzlement, theft of state property, and theft of state secrets by non-Communist industrialists, entrepreneurs, and merchants. In the course of the Five Anti campaign, a pattern was established that would be repeated again and again in mass campaigns over the next two decades: neighbors informing on neighbors, children denouncing parents, workers spying on colleagues, and the compilation of detailed political dossiers on virtually everyone.

In rural areas, a land reform movement was initiated in 1950. Peasants were classified according to their land holdings, and members of the landlord class had their property confiscated. Peasant anger frequently erupted into physical abuse as landlords were paraded before them and "struggled against" for their past crimes. Violence often got out of hand, and upward of 800,000 landlords were killed in the course of the campaign. The confiscated lands were given to poor and lower-middle-class peasants. In this manner, the CCP cemented its popularity among the broad masses of rural dwellers. By 1952, the CCP had penetrated all of rural China, and the landlord class had virtually ceased to exist. ■

The Rectification Campaign Model Developed at Yan'an

Mao Zedong stressed the need to "rectify" the incorrect thoughts and class standpoints of all party members in order to ensure that "correct" ideas and actions would prevail. To do that, all CCP members at Yan'an in the 1940s were required to undergo intensive, group-oriented "study and criticism."

At these sessions, trained cadres would read aloud key party texts, highlighting their main ideas and explaining their significance. Then each participant would be required to "speak from the heart," revealing their innermost thoughts and feelings. In the course of this process of self-examination, party members were expected to acknowledge any lingering doubts or uncertainties they might have about the party's principles and policies. They were further required to expose and criticize any politically incorrect behavior on the part of their friends, family members, and coworkers. Finally, they were required to disclose any errors or imperfections in their own work. This latter process was called "dumping burdens."

Those who unburdened themselves to the satisfaction of the group's leaders were considered "rescued" and were welcomed back into the embrace of the Communist Party. But those who were stubborn or insincere in their self-examinations or who were suspected of harboring reactionary views were subjected to varying degrees of discipline, including incarceration, physical abuse, and even torture.

Suggested Reading

Cheng, *Life and Death in Shanghai.*

Fenby, *Modern China.*

Friedman, Pickowicz, and Selden, *Chinese Village, Socialist State.*

Gittings, *The Changing Face of China.*

Johnson, *Women, the Family and Peasant Revolution in China.*

Lifton, *Thought Reform and the Psychology of Totalism.*

Schram, *The Political Thought of Mao Tse-tung.*

Short, *Mao.*

Questions to Consider

1. How did the CCP consolidate power in the early 1950s?

2. What role did coercion play relative to populist mass mobilization in that period?

"The Chinese People Have Stood Up!"
Lecture 14—Transcript

For decades after the Communist Party's triumph of 1949, historians debated the root causes of their success. Was it mainly due to Mao Zedong's brilliant military thinking and his keen awareness of the importance of mobilizing peasant support? Or was it primarily the result of Chiang K'ai-shek's monumental ego, his inability to limit corruption among his subordinates, and his insensitivity to the concerns of ordinary Chinese?

Or perhaps the key factor was the horrendous devastation caused by Japan's brutal occupation. A cataclysm of such magnitude would have sorely tested the governing capacity of any regime, let alone a brand new, untested Nationalist regime that was already facing a serious domestic insurgency.

Any full and complete accounting of the Communist victory and the *Guomindang*'s defeat must involve some combination of these three factors—at least these three—individually seasoned to taste: Mao's brilliance, Chiang's hubris, and Japan's savage occupation: All played a part.

But one explanation we may comfortably reject out of hand, and that is the notion, advanced in the the United States Congress in the early 1950s, that Free China was lost in 1949 because of the sinister machinations of alleged Communist sympathizers within the United States government, people like John Stewart Service, whose sharply critical wartime appraisal of *Guomindang* corruption and ineptitude were alleged by some in Congress—including Senator Joseph McCarthy—to have shaken America's confidence in Chiang K'ai-shek and thus undermined his chances of success.

Such tortured logic fails to withstand even the most cursory scrutiny. For one thing, the handwriting was already on the wall for the Generalissimo and his government long before President Truman finally, out of sheer exasperation, cut off American aid to Chiang in the summer of 1948. For another thing, China was simply not ours to win or to lose.

It was China's civil war, not ours. A few days before Mao Zedong proclaimed the birth of the People's Republic, he addressed a political meeting in Beijing. In his speech, Mao famously claimed that "the Chinese people ... have stood up." (*Zhongguo renmin xianzai zhanqilai le.*)

For all his theatrical dramatics, however, Mao only spoke a half-truth.

To be sure, the upstart Chinese Communist Party had come from nowhere, out of the wilderness, to miraculously defeat the much larger, U.S.-supplied forces of Chiang K'ai-shek. And to be sure, they had done it by stressing ingenuity, improvisation, and self-reliance, making use of whatever materials they had at hand, while receiving precious little aid, comfort, or assistance from the Soviet Union.

Indeed, Stalin had virtually written off the Chinese Communists' prospects for seizing power. In 1945, for example, following Japan's defeat, the Soviet dictator urged Mao to form a coalition government with Chiang K'ai-shek. Stalin simply didn't believe that Mao could defeat the Generalissimo. Four years later when the Communists emerged victorious from the civil war, Stalin was forced to engage in a rare display of contrition, apologizing for his lack of confidence in his Chinese comrades.

Though the Chinese Communists won the civil war, they had not yet secured the civil peace. Devastated by more than three decades of revolution, foreign invasion, and civil war, the Chinese economy was in a shambles. With at least 30 million more mouths to feed than in 1937, total farm output in 1949 remained well below its prewar peak levels.

As for China's cities, four years of Nationalist mismanagement and corruption had robbed them of their economic dynamism, leaving them awash in demobilized *Guomindang* soldiers, displaced government functionaries, and puppet collaborators—many of whom sought to conceal their shadowy pasts.

Finally, in the immediate post-liberation confusion of 1949, a plurality of political groups and ideologies competed for influence in the intellectual marketplace.

As for the Chinese Communists themselves, having operated in the primitive "mud and shit" of the rural hinterland for more than twenty years, they knew precious little about how to organize and run an urban economy. Indeed, notwithstanding Mao's 1949 boast, it would be several more decades, marked intermittently by Herculean national achievements and horrific national disasters, for the Chinese people to truly "stand up."

In a remarkable speech delivered at the end of June 1949 entitled "On People's Democratic Dictatorship," Mao Zedong acknowledged the difficult, uncharted road that lay ahead. "Soon," he said, "we shall put aside some of the things we know well and be compelled to do things we don't know well." Acknowledging the Communist Party's lack of experience in urban reconstruction, he said:

> Our past work is only the first step in a long march of 10-thousand *li*. Remnants of the enemy have yet to be wiped out.[and] the serious task of economic construction lies ahead … We must learn to do economic work from all who know how, no matter who they are. We must esteem them as teachers, learning from them respectfully and conscientiously. We must not pretend to know when we do not know. We must not put on bureaucratic airs. (*Selected Readings from the Works of Mao Zedong*, p. 313)

Desperately in need of foreign assistance to rebuild China's shattered economy and consolidate its new government, Mao swallowed his pride and bowed long and deep in the direction of the Soviet Union and its "wise leader," Comrade Stalin. It must have been galling for the chairman, for Stalin had essentially written off Mao and his rag-tag guerrilla army throughout the '30s and '40s. Nevertheless, with the Cold War blooming in earnest, Mao was not about to bite the only hand that had both the will and the capacity to feed him: "Just imagine," Mao swooned, "If the Soviet Union had not existed … could we have won victory? Obviously not. … The Communist Party of the Soviet Union is our best teacher, and we must learn from it." (ibid., pp 307, 314).

As far as looking to the West for inspiration or aid was concerned, that was a different matter altogether. Emulating the West had been tried before, more than a half-century earlier, and had been found seriously wanting. As we saw in an earlier lecture, Mao was quite blunt about the role of the West in China's early development. His words, written in 1949 bear repeating here:

> From the time of China's defeat in the Opium War … Chinese progressives went through untold hardships in their quest for truth from the Western countries. [Prominent Chinese intellectuals] … who sought progress would read any book containing new knowledge from the West. … Every effort was made to learn from the West. (Mao, "On People's Democratic Dictatorship")

Yet the results were disappointing. As Western imperialism continued to batter away at China's defenses, eroding Chinese sovereignty and trampling on Chinese pride, admiration turned to anger, and envy turned to resentment. As Mao put it in his same speech:

Imperialist aggression shattered the fond dreams of the Chinese about learning from the West. It was very odd—why were the teachers always committing aggression against their pupil? ... [Then] the Russians made the October Revolution and created the world's first socialist state ... Then, and only then, did the Chinese enter an entirely new era in their thinking ... and the face of China began to change.

If any doubts remained about China's future ideological orientation, Mao quickly dispelled them. Summing up the history of the Chinese Revolution, he said: "Forty years of experience have taught us [that] ... all Chinese without exception must lean either to the side of imperialism or to the side of socialism. Sitting on the fence will not do; nor is there a third road." With this important statement, Mao set China's international compass to point due north, Henceforth China would align itself with the socialist camp, led by the USSR, and would eschew collaboration with the imperialist camp headed by the United States.

Domestically within China, Mao adopted a dualistic policy for dealing with various class enemies, who included former *Guomindang* officers, rural landlords, the urban rich, and other assorted reactionary elements. The policy combined leniency for those who admitted the error of their ways and undertook to conscientiously remold their thinking and obey the government, with iron dictatorship over traitors, diehard reactionaries, and others who had either betrayed or oppressed the laboring masses.

This Maoist dualism was built into the very name of the new government, which was defined as a "People's Democratic Dictatorship" (*Renmin Minzhu Juanzheng*). Its core principle was the grant of full rights of citizenship and participation to all members of the laboring classes, who were collectively designated "the people." On the other hand, those labeled "enemies of the people" would be deprived of all political rights and subjected to ruthless dictatorship by the party-state. If these categories sometimes seemed a bit opaque or overly stereotyped, investigations could be undertaken to resolve any lingering uncertainties. During the Yan'an period the Chinese Communists had gained considerable experience in drawing the line between friends and enemies, and in isolating and controlling the latter.

Throughout World War II, Yan'an had served, as we saw, as a powerful anti-Japanese magnet, attracting Chinese patriots from all over the country, from every possible political persuasion, from illiterate peasants to educated intellectuals, from social democrats to Trotskyites. To bring political unity and discipline to this rather motley mélange of disparate social classes and strata, Mao in 1942 convened a lengthy forum on art and literature. His intent was to establish a unified set of "proper" Communist Party attitudes, values, orientations and work methods, and to inculcate these firmly in all who wished to participate in the Yan'an style of life. Although Mao's immediate focus was the reform of art and literature, the Yan'an Forum was no mere academic seminar on varieties of cultural expression. First, Mao demanded that all artistic and literary works must faithfully reflect the noble political virtues of workers and peasants and must struggle against the exploiting of classes.

Next, Mao stressed the need to rectify the "incorrect" thoughts and class standpoints of all party members in order to ensure that "correct" ideas and actions would prevail. To do that, all party members would be forced to undergo intensive, group-oriented study and criticism. At these sessions, trained cadres would read out key central party texts (often Mao's own speeches), highlighting their main ideas and explaining their significance. Then each participant would be required to "speak from the heart," revealing their innermost thoughts and feelings.

In the course of this process of self-examination, each member of the party was expected to acknowledge any lingering doubts or uncertainties they might have about the party's principles and policies. And they were further required to expose and criticize any politically incorrect behavior on the part of their friends, family members, or co-workers. Finally, they were required to disclose any errors or imperfections in their own work. This latter process was called "dumping burdens."

Those who unburdened themselves to the satisfaction of the group's leaders were considered "rescued," and were welcomed back into the bosom of the party. But those who were stubborn or insincere in their self-examinations, or who were suspected of harboring reactionary views, were subjected to varying degrees of discipline, including, in at least some cases, incarceration, physical abuse, and even torture. For any who might have viewed Mao and the Chinese Communist Party basically as a romantic band of land-reforming liberal democrats, the Yan'an experience would prove to be a real eye-opener.

With the Communists' nationwide victory in 1949, the rectification model of campaigns first devised in Yan'an was applied to Chinese society as a whole.

The people and their enemies were now sharply delimited, at least notionally, with the former category encompassing not just workers and peasants, who were the core of the party's support, but also patriotic, law-abiding members of the intelligentsia, the petit bourgeoisie, and even patriotic businessmen, managers, and entrepreneurs.

In extending an olive branch to members of these "impure" classes, Mao's goal was to enlist their talents in the important task of restoring China's shattered economy. On the other hand, for those labeled as "enemies of the people," the future was decidedly more bleak, as they were earmarked for suppression and dictatorship. Some groups and strata were located uncomfortably on the borderline between the people and their enemies.

One such group was China's so-called "bourgeois intellectuals." Their ranks included tens of thousands of well-educated Chinese who had either worked for the old regime or maintained suspicious foreign contacts, or else simply resisted the party's efforts to impose uniform standards of "correct" thinking on the population at large. These independent thinkers now found themselves labeled as "rightists" and subjected to an intensive process of group-based criticism and confrontation known as "thought reform" (or *sixiang gaizao*).

In the process of thought reform, the intellectuals (many of whom had been educated abroad (by the way being educated abroad was in itself grounds for suspicion), were required to recount their personal histories and to write lengthy, detailed confessions in which they revealed all of their personal contacts and humbly acknowledged their questionable past behavior, including things as trivial as associating casually with foreigners or thinking politically "impure" thoughts. They were often required to go through several successive iterations of their written confessions, until these were judged to be sincere, whereupon they would be liberated and allowed to resume work.

Along with the thought reform of bourgeois intellectuals, a rather more serious campaign of suppressing counterrevolutionaries was launched in 1950. This campaign was designed to root out those groups and individuals who were actively resisting the new regime, including roving bandit gangs (of which there were well over one hundred in the countryside), as well as saboteurs, *Guomindang* spies, arsonists, and assorted other diehard enemies of the people. Punishment for those found guilty was harsh: imprisonment, torture, and in many cases, public execution.

The severity of punishment was intended both to assuage popular feelings of anger against criminals and saboteurs, and to serve as a warning to others. As Mao himself came to put it, when it came to counterrevolutionaries:

> There should be no policy of benevolence. ... As for killings, the principle is that in cases where blood debts are owed or ... when failure to execute would mean popular indignation would go unassuaged, then the death sentence should be carried out without hesitation. (Mao, *Selected Works*, Vol. VI).

A few days after Mao made these remarks, the party's flagship newspaper, *People's Daily*, reported that a massive crowd of 100,000 people had filled Shanghai's Hongkou Stadium "with thunderous shouts and applause" as 300 arch-criminal counterrevolutionaries were publicly executed. Among those executed was the notorious gangster known as "Pockmarked Huang," who was a major figure in the infamous Shanghai Green Gang, the very same criminal gang that had helped Chiang K'ai-shek to suppress the Communists in 1927.

According to the party's own statistics, in the course of the two-year campaign to suppress counterrevolutionaries, over 2 million suspects were detained. Of these, 1.3 million were imprisoned and 710,000 were executed.

While the campaign to suppress counterrevolutionaries wound to a close in 1952, two other mass movements were initiated in the early 1950s. The first of these was a "three-anti" campaign, which targeted the growing problems of corruption, waste and bureaucratism among the party's basic level cadres, many of whom had become arrogant, officious, and politically lazy in the two years since liberation. The Three Anti campaign was relatively mild and seldom involved coercive struggle or detention.

The second campaign on the other hand, known as the "Five Antis," was far more intensive and coercive. It was designed to expose and punish crimes of bribery, tax evasion, embezzlement, theft of state property, and theft of state secrets by non-Communist Party members: industrialists, entrepreneurs, merchants, and even office workers.

In these two campaigns, the Yan'an model of small-group study and self-criticism was employed to rectify petty offenders. But in more serious cases, particularly in the five anti movement, which involved major damage to the state's core interests, harsh punishments were meted out.

In the course of the Five Anti campaign, a pattern was established that would be repeated again and again in Chinese mass campaigns over the next two decades: neighbors informing on neighbors, children denouncing parents, workers spying on colleagues; and the compilation of detailed political dossiers (called *dangan*) on virtually everyone, cadres and *laobaixing* alike.

In the countryside, the first order of business for the new regime, once the suppression of counterrevolutionaries had been completed, was the nationwide implementation of a new land reform campaign. You will recall from an earlier lecture that land reform had been first introduced in the Jiangxi Soviet Republic in the early 1930s, when all land and property belonging to landlords and rich peasants had been confiscated and shared out among poor peasants. Later, during the anti-Japanese war, the land reform program was shelved in favor of a milder, less abrasive policy of rent reduction. But with the resumption of the *Guomindang*/Communist civil war in 1946, land reform was once again introduced in those rural districts controlled by the Communists.

In 1950 the land reform campaign was extended nationwide. It was a complex, multi-stage movement, having both political and economic components. Politically, the goal was to put an end, once and for all, to the traditional rural power structure dominated by the landlord-gentry class. Economically, the goal of the campaign was to stimulate the rapid recovery of agricultural production, which had remained stagnant, or worse, since the mid-1930s.

In the first stage of land reform, work teams composed of urban party members and cadres were dispatched to rural townships and villages around the country. The work teams recruited local peasant activists to form the backbone of a new village peasants' association. Under the watchful eye of the work teams, the peasants associations gathered detailed information about village wealth and property ownership—who owned what, where, and just how they had obtained it. Once this inventory was completed, each family in the village would be assigned a class status (or *jieji chengfen*).

There were four main categories: poor peasants, middle peasants, rich peasants, and landlords. Poor peasants, who comprised around two-thirds of the rural population, were at the bottom of the economic ladder. Their chronic poverty rendered them highly vulnerable to venal landlords and unscrupulous moneylenders, and they were consequently regarded by the Communist Party as the most potentially revolutionary of all rural classes.

Middle peasants accounted for another 20 percent or so of the farm population. They were generally self-sufficient in land and labor, and for this reason they were less likely than poor peasants to harbor deep grievances against local landlords. Because of their ambivalence toward the landlords, the party treated them as a force to be united with but never relied upon.

Rich peasants made up about 10 percent of the rural population. They owned more farmland than they could possibly cultivate themselves. Being relatively well-to-do, rich peasants had little or no enthusiasm for land reform. But insofar as they worked at least part of their own land with their own hands, they had a dual character, as far as the party was concerned, part laboring people, part exploiters.

Finally, landlords accounted for only roughly five percent of the farm population. Drawing their income wholly from land rents and interest on seasonal loans made to poor peasants, they were, by Communist Party definition, an entirely parasitic exploiting class and were thus consigned to the category of enemies of the people.

Once the class status of each family in the village was determined, the results were posted publicly for all to see. At this stage, a number of intermediate categories were recognized (lower-middle peasants, upper-middle peasants, for example), along with distinctions between law-abiding landlords and evil landlords.

The posting of everyone's class status was generally a time of high anxiety, as families receiving upper–class classification knew that their future prospects under the Communist Party would most likely be dim indeed.

Next came the political mobilization of peasant anger and resentment. At this stage, "speak bitterness" meetings were organized by the party work teams. At these meetings, older poor peasants would publicly recount the abuse they suffered at the hands of the evil landlords and their agents in the bad old days before "liberation."

When the villagers' indignation had been thoroughly aroused, the accused landlords and their local agents would then be paraded before the assembled villagers. With hands bound and heads bowed, they were subjected to harsh verbal as well as physical abuse.

At this stage of the movement, many landlords were beaten; and though the party's directives on land reform did not specifically call for killing landlords, executions were clearly tolerated under Mao's 1951 dictum that killing was to be permitted where a blood debt was owed, or where failure to execute would arouse popular indignation.

Altogether, an estimated 15 to 20 percent of all landlords were killed during the land reform movement, between 800,000 and a bit over one million in all. Generally, only the male heads of landlord households were executed, while women and children were spared.

The final stage of land reform involved the ritual burning of old land deeds in a public bonfire and the ceremonial redistribution of the confiscated land to the poor and lower-middle peasant families.

For many, this was a deeply moving experience, and one that clearly contributed to the Communist Party's high popularity among the very poorest two-thirds of the rural population.

By the end of the land reform movement in 1952, rural China's age-old power structure had been completely overturned. The grip of the landlord-gentry class had been broken forever, and the Communist Party, through its leadership of peasants' associations, had penetrated virtually every rural village in China.

As a historical footnote, those minor and law abiding landlords who were spared execution in land reform were generally given a small portion of their former land to subsist upon; and they were expected to demonstrate, through honest labor and obedience to the new government, that they had turned over a new leaf. However, along with their sons, daughters and even their grandchildren, these former landlords carried with them to their graves an indelible political stigma, a scarlet letter that could not be altered or erased— the label of "class enemy." Thereafter, their lives would never be the same.

Earlier in this lecture, we took note of Mao Zedong's 1949 decision to "lean to one side" in the emerging Cold War between the Soviet Union and the United States. In the next lecture, we examine the consequences of Mao's decision to align himself with Joseph Stalin and the USSR.

Korea, Taiwan, and the Cold War, 1950–1954
Lecture 15

If you should get kicked in the teeth [by the Americans], I shall not lift a finger. You'll have to ask Mao for all the help. — Joseph Stalin's warning to Kim Il-sung before the outbreak of the Korean War

By 1949, the Cold War was well underway. The Soviet Union had dropped an iron curtain over Eastern and Central Europe, and President Harry S. Truman had announced the birth of the Marshall Plan, designed to accelerate the economic recovery of Western Europe and thereby counteract rising Soviet power and influence.

After 28 years of civil war and foreign aggression, China badly needed international assistance. Unable to turn to the United States (i.e., the "imperialist camp") because of the deepening Cold War, Mao Zedong went to Moscow (i.e., the "socialist camp") in December 1949. After six weeks of arduous haggling, Mao and Joseph Stalin struck a bargain in February of 1950. Its terms clearly revealed Stalin's ambivalence toward his Chinese "comrades." Stalin extended to Mao credits worth $300 million, half earmarked for the purchase of Soviet military hardware, half for the purchase of Soviet heavy industrial plant and machinery. But to Mao's dismay, the Soviet credits amounted to far less than Stalin had given to the new Communist governments in Eastern and Central Europe in the late 1940s. Worse yet, whereas the aid to Stalin's European satellites had been in the form of outright grants, the credits to China were written up as loans, to be repaid over a 10-year period—with 1 percent annual interest.

The first major test of the Sino-Soviet alliance came in 1950, when North Korea's Kim Il-sung asked Stalin for permission to reunify Korea by force. After a good deal of initial skepticism, both Stalin and Mao approved Kim's plan of attack, and in June 1950, North Korean troops invaded South Korea. The United Nations condemned the invasion, and President Truman ordered the U.S. Navy to patrol the Taiwan Strait to prevent a PRC attack on Taiwan. Under **General Douglas MacArthur**, UN troops repelled the North Korean attack, but Truman and MacArthur disagreed on the aims of the war. When MacArthur's troops advanced to the North Korea–China border in violation of Truman's orders, the Chinese People's Volunteers Army entered the war and successfully repelled the UN forces. A stalemate ensued.

Early in 1951, Truman fired MacArthur for insubordination, and the Chinese side began to show interest in negotiating a cease-fire agreement with the UN command. But Stalin refused to go along. Although neither side was winning the war, the fact that several hundred thousand American troops were bogged down in Korea meant that the United States could not utilize

General Douglas MacArthur, commander of UN forces in Korea, 1950–1951.

these troops to counter Soviet actions in Europe. Consequently, Stalin was content to let the war drag on for another two years, with heavy casualties on both sides but little advantage gained by either. The deadlock was not broken until Stalin died in March 1953, after which a cease-fire was quickly arranged. The cease-fire line was the 38th parallel—an exact reversion to the status quo ante. Three years of deadly warfare had ultimately changed nothing.

In the aftermath of the Korean War, the U.S government sharply revised its strategic calculus with respect to Taiwan. Chiang K'ai-shek was now a vital "free world" ally in the struggle against Communism. Accordingly, in December 1954, President Dwight Eisenhower signed a Treaty of Mutual Defense with Chiang's government-in-exile.

If the Korean War served to bolster Taiwan's relations with the United States, it had a far more negative impact on China's national security. For one thing, China lost the opportunity—perhaps forever—to conclude its civil war by "liberating" Taiwan. We now know that Mao had authorized a cross-Strait invasion of Taiwan in the fall of 1950, which had to be postponed when Truman ordered the Seventh Fleet to patrol the Taiwan Strait. Second, the PRC was condemned as an aggressor by the United Nations for its decision to intervene in Korea. Because of this, China lost its chance to replace the ROC in the United Nations. Two full decades would elapse before China would gain admission to the UN in 1971. Third, as a result of the war, the United States entered into a series of military treaties in Asia designed to

President Harry S. Truman.

contain Chinese Communism, including the U.S.-Taiwan Defense Treaty, the Southeast Asia Treaty Organization, and the ANZUS Pact. Finally, Chinese troops suffered more than 1 million casualties, including 300,000 killed in the last two years of the war, during the prolonged stalemate engineered by Stalin. ■

Suggested Reading

Chang and Halliday, *Mao.*

Fenby, *Modern China.*

Schaller, *The U.S. and China.*

Whiting, *China Crosses the Yalu.*

Questions to Consider

1. Was Mao Zedong's post-1949 alliance with Joseph Stalin (and against the United States) inevitable?

2. How did the Korean War influence Sino-Soviet relations?

Korea, Taiwan, and the Cold War, 1950–1954
Lecture 15—Transcript

As we saw last time, the Maoists' victory in 1949 brought with it two fundamentally new challenges for the Chinese Communist Party: first, to consolidate their political control (by eliminating opposition groups and erstwhile class enemies), and second, to get the economy moving again by distributing rural farmland to peasant families, and by welcoming patriotic urban businessmen, merchants, and entrepreneurs to cooperate with the new regime.

While pursuing these twin domestic goals of political consolidation and economic reconstruction, in foreign policy the Maoist regime cast its lot firmly with the socialist camp. In dire need of economic, technical, and military assistance, Mao swallowed his pride and "leaned to one side," turning to Joseph Stalin and the Soviet Union for help.

By 1949 the Cold War was well underway. The Soviet Union had dropped an "iron curtain" over eastern and central Europe, extending its dictatorial grip, in Winston Churchill's immortal words, "from the Baltic to the Adriatic."

In 1947 President Harry S. Truman intervened to prevent Communist insurgents from toppling pro-Western governments in Greece and Turkey. In proclaiming his Truman Doctrine, the president framed the conflict in southern Europe as a contest between free peoples and totalitarian regimes.

Still later in 1947, President Truman announced the birth of the Marshall Plan, designed to accelerate the economic recovery of western Europe and thereby counteract rising Soviet power and influence in the East.

In that same year (1947), an American career diplomat named George F. Kennan articulated a new strategic blueprint for the United States in its dealings with the Soviets: "The main element of any United States policy toward the Soviet Union must be that of a long-term, patient but firm and vigilant containment of Russian expansive tendencies."

Toward that end, Kennan nowcalled for countering "Soviet pressure against the free institutions of the Western world" through what he termed "adroit and vigilant application of counter-force at a series of constantly shifting geographical and political points." For the next 30 years, Kennan's containment policy would remain the cornerstone of U.S. policy toward the Communist Bloc.

By 1949, Truman had taken the lead in creating a trans-Atlantic anti-Soviet alliance, the North Atlantic Treaty Organization, or NATO. Thus, by the time Mao and the Chinese Communists assumed control of China, the lines of conflict in the Cold War were already clearly drawn. Given the intense hostility between Moscow and Washington, Mao in reality had little choice but to align himself with Stalin and the socialist camp.

Now, it's true that some historians, including Barbara Tuchman and Joseph Esherick, have argued that far from being committed to Stalin from the get-go, Mao was initially inclined to pursue cordial relations with the United States in the middle and late-1940s, and that it was American shortsightedness and intransigence and shortsightedness that prevented this from happening.

In support of this contention, these revisionist historians point to two main pieces of evidence: first, toward the end of World War II, Mao openly expressed a wish to visit Washington DC to talk with President Roosevelt. In conveying this wish to members of the U.S. Dixie Mission in Yan'an, Mao said: "America need not fear that we will not be cooperative. We must cooperate and we must have American help. ... We cannot risk crossing you—cannot risk any conflict with you."

This message never reached President Roosevelt, as its transmission was blocked by U.S. Ambassador Patrick Hurley.

Second, those who support the squandered opportunity theory note that on the eve of the Chinese Communists' victory in 1949, a high-level Maoist emissary held a series of secretive back channel meetings with the outgoing U.S. ambassador to Nationalist China, Leighton Stuart. Among the various subjects discussed at these meetings was the possibility of establishing, some time in the future, diplomatic relations between the United States and the PRC.

The problem with the squandered opportunity hypothesis is that it neglects contextual factors. With respect to Mao's wartime request to visit Washington, for example, there is little doubt that the chairman's primary goal was not to befriend the world leader of the imperialist camp, but rather to drive a sharp wedge between the Americans and Chiang K'ai-shek—a classic application of Mao's patented "united front" tactics, where a less threatening adversary is wooed and cajoled in order to isolate (and ultimately to overcome in defeat) a more immediate and threatening enemy, in this case, the Nationalists.

As for the CCP's 1949 cloak-and-dagger meetings with U.S. Ambassador Leighton Stuart, the chief Communist negotiator at those meetings made it clear that the establishment of cooperative relations between the U.S. and China after the revolution was contingent upon the severance of all U.S. ties to Chiang K'ai-shek.

This was clearly further than the United States government was prepared to go, especially in view of Washington's increasingly tense Cold War relations with Moscow.

Finally, there is scant evidence to support the claim, made by some historians, that Mao was consciously trying to play off the Russians against the Americans, and that he was seeking to escape from a tightening Soviet bear hug by courting American support (a tactic, by the way, which Mao would later successfully use with Richard Nixon).

On the contrary, however, we now know that throughout Ambassador Stuart's meetings with his Chinese counterpart, the Chinese side kept Stalin fully informed about the contents of their discussions; and that it was Stalin, rather than Mao, who proposed that the CCP should keep the door open to possible cooperation with the Americans, even if the U.S. refused to sever its ties with Chiang K'ai-shek.

Ultimately, then, the bulk of the evidence points to the conclusion that Mao's decision to "lean to one side" was almost certainly the product of prevailing geopolitical and ideological realities, including the deepening of Cold War global bipolarity. It was not primarily the result of American blundering and shortsightedness—though, God knows, there was enough of that in the late 1940s and '50s.

In any event, Mao's mild flirtation with the United States ended abruptly with his declaration of "leaning to one side" in 1949. Two months after the declaration of the founding of te People's Republic, Chairman Mao boarded a train for Moscow.

It was Mao's first trip ever outside of China's borders; and it came in the middle of a brutally cold Russian winter. Expecting Stalin to welcome him personally, Mao was greeted at the Moscow train station by a group of second-tier Soviet officials. In fact, Mao was made to wait for an entire week at a suburban Moscow dacha before being granted an audience with the mighty Stalin. Historians have suggested that this obvious slight was intended as a stark reminder to Mao that in any arrangements that might be entered into between the two of them, Stalin was the senior partner, and Mao was the junior supplicant.

Left to cool his heels at the dacha, the chairman expressed his growing impatience: "I have only three tasks here," he complained to an aide. "The first is to eat; the second is to sleep; the third is to shit." (J. Fenby, *Modern China*, p. 364)

With difficulty, Mao swallowed his pride once again. Having already burned his bridges to the United States, he had nowhere else to turn. After six weeks of arduous haggling, Mao and Stalin struck a bargain in February of 1950. Its terms clearly revealed Stalin's ambivalence toward his Chinese "comrades."

In an apparent gesture of fraternal generosity, Stalin extended to Mao credits worth a total of U.S. $300 million. Half of these funds were to be earmarked for the purchase of Soviet military hardware, while the other half was for the purchase of Soviet heavy industrial plant and equipment, including power stations, metallurgical and mining facilities, and railroad stock.

Much to Mao's dismay, the Soviet credits amounted to far less than Stalin had given to the new Communist regimes in east and central Europe in the late 1940s. Worse yet, whereas the aid to Stalin's European satellites had been in the form of outright grants, the credits to China were written up as loans, repayable over a 10-year period—with 1 percent annual interest.

The irony of the Soviet "big brother" charging interest—a device that had been denigrated by Karl Marx as an instrument of capitalist exploitation—on a loan to a fraternal socialist ally was not lost on the thin-skinned Chairman Mao.

Adding insult to injury, there were a number of strings attached to Stalin's rather modest display of Soviet largesse. For example, as a condition of receiving Soviet credits, China was obliged to grant to the Soviet Union a controlling interest in a number of strategic military and industrial facilities in Manchuria—including naval bases, harbors and railroads that had earlier been seized by Soviet occupation forces in 1945. In addition, a number of Sino-Russian joint stock companies were set up for the purpose of jointly exploiting metallurgical and oil resources in Manchuria and in China's northwest border province of Xinjiang.

In yet another bit of irony that could not have escaped the notice of Mao or his colleagues, the terms of the February 1950 Sino-Soviet Treaty of

Friendship appeared to fly in the face of a solemn Soviet pledge, issued in 1918, shortly after the Bolshevik Revolution, to renounce all Russian special privileges and concessions in China that had been extracted under duress by the imperial czarist regime. Now, more than 30 years later, a new imperial Russian regime was picking up, seemingly, where the czars had left off.

Mao clearly resented such Soviet hypocrisy. It was an issue that would smolder for the better part of a decade before erupting into bitter polemics when the Sino-Soviet dispute burst into the open in the 1960s.

On the eve of Mao's return to Beijing in February 1950, Stalin gave him a parting gift: He handed over to the Chinese leader a list of all Soviet spies, moles, and double-agents who had been operating in China.

When senior Soviet intelligence officers learned that Stalin had turned the names over to Mao, they were horrified. A short time later they watched helplessly as Chinese security forces systematically rounded up, tortured, and executed hundreds of their compromised colleagues.

Whatever misgivings Mao and Stalin may have had about their initial encounter, they kept to themselves. For all the outside world knew, Mao and Stalin were the closest of fraternal allies, joined at the hip in the global struggle against "U.S. imperialism and its running dogs."

The first major test of the Sino-Soviet alliance came in the early summer of 1950. For years, tensions had been running high on the Korean peninsula. At the Yalta Conference, the task of liberating Korea from Japanese control had been jointly assigned to the Soviet Union and the United States. Soviet troops would occupy the northern half of the country, down to the 38th parallel, with Americans occupying the south.

This situation of partitioned occupation remained in effect until 1948, when the Americans and the Russians both withdrew their respective occupation forces. Before departing, however, each side set up a "friendly" government in its own zone.

In the north, a Communist regime was established under a pro-Soviet military officer named Kim Il-Song. In the south, a pro-Western regime was installed under Syngman Rhee, an intensely nationalistic, American-educated political activist.

Following the agreed-upon withdrawal of Soviet and American forces in 1948, relations between the two Korean governments became increasingly strained. Both sides advocated reunification—under their own auspices. And each side repeatedly engaged in provocative behavior designed to paint the other side as an aggressor. By 1950 tensions were running extremely high along the 38th parallel.

In North Korea, Kim Il-song was supremely confident that he could quickly prevail in any military contest with the South. But since he was heavily dependent on Soviet military and economic assistance, he could not launch an attack on his own initiative without Soviet consent. In the spring of 1950 Stalin, after a considerable amount of hesitation and waffling, signed off on the North Korean plan of attack.

Although China played no direct role in planning or launching the Korean War, Stalin and Mao exchanged several telegrams about the situation in Korea. Mao, it seems, was initially skeptical, wanting to complete the liberation of Taiwan before unleashing Kim Il-sung in Korea. But once he was convinced that Stalin was going support a North Korean invasion in any event, Mao reluctantly went along.

Although Stalin didn't expect the United States to intervene, he was not willing to risk a Soviet armed conflict with the United States. In a warning telegram to Kim Il-sung, Stalin cautioned the North Korean leader, in no uncertain terms, "If you should get kicked in the teeth [by the Americans], I shall not lift a finger. You'll have to ask Mao for all the help."

Stalin's warning proved prophetic. North Korea's surprise attack came on June 25, 1950, and (at least initially) it was an overwhelming success. Within two days, South Korea's outgunned, outnumbered, troops were in full retreat, with many of them defecting to the North.

On the third day of the war, North Korean troops entered the South Korean capital of Seoul. Within three weeks they had driven down the entire length of the Korean peninsula.

Under intense pressure from the United States, the United Nations unanimously condemned the North Korean invasion as an act of unprovoked aggression. Ironically, it was a vote that was made possible by a Soviet boycott of the U.N.—a boycott that had been launched months earlier when the United Nations failed to oust the Chinese Nationalists in favor of giving their seat to the PRC.

As soon as the U.N. acted to condemn the North Korean aggression, Harry Truman, on June 27, ordered the U.S. 7th Fleet to patrol the Taiwan Strait to prevent either side in the still-smoldering Chinese civil war from taking advantage of the fighting in Korea to launch an attack against the other.

When the UN authorized a police action to repel North Korean aggression, the United States led a multinational military force into Korea, under the command of General Douglas MacArthur—the hero of the Pacific War against Japan. But by the time MacArthur could get substantial UN troops on the ground, the North Koreans had occupied approximately 90 percent or more of the Korean peninsula.

In mid-September 1950, General MacArthur, supported by massive American supplies, transport, and combat troops, launched a surprise amphibious counterattack behind North Korean lines.

The attack on the port city of Inchon caught the North Koreans completely off guard. And the tide of battle soon turned. By early October, the North Korean army was retreating in disarray back across the 38th parallel. In hot pursuit, MacArthur's forces advanced into North Korea, capturing the capital city, Pyongyang, on October 19.

At this point, MacArthur and President Truman had a serious disagreement over how to proceed. MacArthur wanted to march his troops right up to the Yalu River, North Korea's boundary with China. Arguing that Mao wouldn't dare to intervene, the general asserted that "There is no substitute for victory."

Truman strongly disagreed, declaring that the conflict in Korea was a limited war, fought for limited aims, namely, the punishment of aggression and the restoration of the status-quo ante.

By this time, however, Mao Zedong had become deeply alarmed by MacArthur's blatant disregard of Truman's attempt to restrain him.

In early October, Mao gave an order to assemble a Chinese People's Volunteer Army (or CPV) to combat the American-led U.N. forces. In a telegram to comrade Stalin, Mao wrote:

> If we allow the United States to occupy all of Korea, Korean revolutionary power will suffer a fundamental defeat, and the American invaders will run more rampant, [which will] have negative effects for the entire Far East. (Wikipedia, "Korean War")

At the end of October, advance units of the CPV crossed into North Korea. On November 1 they launched a surprise attack on American forces, administering a stinging defeat. The Chinese forces then pulled back, waiting to see if the Americans had gotten the intended message—namely, that any further advance into North Korea would meet with a massive Chinese response.

When MacArthur ignored the Chinese warning, Mao in late November ordered a full-scale military response. Once again, the tide of battle turned decisively, as hundreds of thousands of Chinese volunteers poured across the border into North Korea.

Using controversial human sea tactics, they quickly overran U.N positions, inflicting heavy casualties and forcing a hasty retreat. By January of 1951 the UN forces had been driven back across the 38th parallel.

At that point, early in 1951, Truman fired MacArthur for insubordination; and the Chinese side began to show some interest in negotiating a cease-fire agreement with the United Nations command.

But Stalin refused to go along. Although neither side was winning the war, the fact that several hundred thousand American troops were bogged down in Korea meant that the United States could not utilize those troops to counter Soviet actions in Berlin or anywhere else in Europe. Consequently, Stalin was content to let the war drag on, as it did, for another two years, with heavy casualties on both sides, but with very little advantage being gained by either side.

The deadlock was not broken until Stalin died in March of 1953. Thereafter, a cease-fire was quickly arranged to take effect in July. The ceasefire line was the 38th parallel—an exact reversion to the status quo ante. Three years of deadly warfare had ultimately changed exactly nothing.

But though the Korean War ended in a draw, it nonetheless marked a decisive turning point in China's relations with the United States. Until China entered the war, the U.S. had been reluctant to commit itself to the defense of Chiang K'ai-shek's exiled Nationalist regime on Taiwan. Indeed, on the very eve of the Korean War, the American Secretary of State, Dean Acheson, had conspicuously excluded Taiwan from a list of "vital American interests" in Asia.

In the aftermath of the Korean War, however, the U.S. government sharply revised its strategic calculus with respect to Taiwan. Chiang K'ai-shek was now a vital Free World ally in a struggle against world communism. Accordingly, in December 1954 President Dwight Eisenhower signed a Treaty of Mutual Defense with Chiang's government-in-exile in Taiwan:

> Each party recognizes that an armed attack in the West Pacific Area directed against the territories of either of the Parties would be dangerous to its own peace and safety and declares that it would act to meet the common danger in accordance with its constitutional processes. (TIAS 3178; 6 UST 433–438)

Pursuant to these aims of the U.S.-Taiwan Mutual Defense Treaty, ships from the U.S. Seventh Fleet patrolled the 90-mile-wide waters of the Taiwan Strait to protect Taiwan and prevent the PRC from launching an amphibious attack. For the next 20 years, these naval patrols remained a potent symbol of the U.S. commitment to defend Taiwan. (In truth, however, this symbol was more potent than the reality, since at no time were there more than two very small American naval vessels in the Taiwan Strait at any given time.)

If the Korean War served to bolster Taiwan's relations with the United States, it had a far more negative impact on China's national security. Indeed, the costs to China were enormous.

For one thing, China lost the opportunity—perhaps forever—to conclude its civil war by liberating Taiwan. We now know that Mao had authorized a cross-Strait invasion of Taiwan in the fall of 1950, but it had to be postponed indefinitely when Harry Truman ordered the Seventh Fleet to patrol the Taiwan Strait.

Second, the PRC was condemned as an aggressor by the United Nations for intervening in Korea, although it was a defensive intervention in the first instance. Because of this, China lost any chance to replace the Republic of China in the United Nations. Two full decades would elapse before China would gain admission to the United Nations in 1971.

Third, as a result of the war, the Unites States entered into a series of military treaties in Asia designed to contain Chinese Communism. These included, as we already mentioned, the U.S.-Taiwan Defense Treaty, but also the Southeast Asia Treaty Organization (or SEATO), and the ANZUS Pact, which involved the U.S., Australia, and New Zealand.

Finally, Chinese troops suffered more than one million casualties in the war, including 300,000 killed in the last two years, during the prolonged and ultimately pointless stalemate engineered by Stalin.

But the Korean War was not a total loss for China. On at least two counts the People's Republic scored clear gains. First, the Chinese Communists were able to upgrade their armed forces. During the war, they received substantial Soviet military assistance, including up-to-date Soviet tanks, artillery, and some 3,000 warplanes. Second, by fighting the world's most powerful country to a virtual standstill in Korea, Mao Zedong greatly elevated his and China's stature both within the socialist camp and in the Third World.

Soon enough, Mao would leverage this rising stature both to extract substantially greater economic and military aid from Stalin's successor, Nikita Khrushchev, and to assert China's leadership over the emerging neutralist, nonaligned countries of the Third World.

With the conclusion of the Korean War, China entered an important new stage in its post-revolutionary development, the stage of building socialism. Next time, we'll look more closely at these domestic developments and we will examine the socialist transformation of the Chinese economy.

Socialist Transformation, 1953–1957
Lecture 16

> Writing in July of 1955, Mao strongly criticized those of his comrades who had retreated meekly in the face of pressure from rich peasants to abandon the co-ops. Mao accused these comrades of "tottering along like women with bound feet."

The new stage of China's development began with the promulgation in 1953 of a Soviet-style Five-Year Plan for economic development. Its principal content was a blueprint for achieving the realization of socialism in China. The centerpiece of the First Five-Year Plan was the wholesale Chinese adoption of Stalinist techniques of centralized economic planning and agricultural collectivization and the rapid growth of urban heavy industry.

Joseph Stalin's successor, Nikita Khrushchev, needed China's support in his drive to be recognized as the undisputed leader of the socialist camp. In a display of solidarity with his Chinese "little brothers," Khrushchev generously promised several hundred million dollars in Soviet economic and military aid to China and further agreed to send thousands

Nikita Khrushchev, first secretary of the Communist Party of the Soviet Union.

© Prints and Photographs Division, Library of Congress.

of technical specialists to China to build new industrial facilities. As a result of this fresh burst of Soviet generosity, more than 150 major new industrial projects were initiated in China in the mid-1950s, and several thousand Chinese students were sent to the Soviet Union for advanced training, mainly in engineering and the applied sciences.

Soviet military aid to China also increased: The Soviet Union built several new aircraft and munitions factories in China from 1953 to

1957. Khrushchev also agreed to share Soviet blueprints for an atomic bomb—and to provide China with a prototype nuclear weapon. This fresh burst of Soviet largesse ushered in a new era of Sino-Soviet friendship and cordiality, as the Chinese Communists openly embraced their "big brothers" to the north. And from 1954 to 1957, the Chinese emulated their Soviet senior siblings in almost every respect.

Under the guidance of Soviet advisers, China's urban economy underwent a two-stage transition to socialism. Beginning in 1955, shares in private Chinese companies were purchased by the state, with payment to the former owners amortized over a period of several years. This created an intermediary form of ownership, known as joint state-private ownership. A year later, the second stage kicked in, with all urban industrial and commercial assets now converted entirely into state property. By the end of 1956, virtually the entire urban economy had been nationalized. Although there was a good deal of grumbling among former factory owners and managers, few dared to openly resist the state's takeover of their productive assets.

The coercive aspect of accelerated collectivization meant that there was now—for the first time since 1949—widespread alienation and resentment in rural China.

In the countryside, the process of socialist transformation was more complex and took longer to complete. The process of agricultural collectivization was divided into three sequential stages: **mutual aid**, **cooperative farming**, and **collectivized farming**. In the first stage, several neighboring families formed "mutual aid teams," sharing tools, animals, and labor. In the second stage, four or five such teams were combined, and their property was "invested" in a new cooperative farm. Because these co-ops were voluntary, many rich peasants refused to join, fearing that their assets would be used to subsidize their poorer neighbors.

At this point, Mao stepped in to order the next, higher stage: full collectivization. Writing in July of 1955, Mao strongly criticized those of his comrades who had retreated meekly in the face of pressure from rich peasants to abandon the co-ops. Mao accused these comrades of "tottering along like **women with bound feet.**" Rich peasants were required to contribute their property to the new, larger-scale collective farms.

The coercive aspect of accelerated collectivization meant that there was now—for the first time since 1949—widespread alienation and resentment in rural China. Rich and upper-middle peasant families, accounting for perhaps 20 percent of the rural population, deeply resented their enforced pauperization. Even the poor and lower-middle peasants, presumptive beneficiaries of socialist agriculture, suffered from diminished motivation to work in the new, large-scale, impersonal collectives.

In a classic case of the **free-rider problem,** each family's income depended in substantial measure on the quality of the labor performed by all other farmers in the collective. Hence, the incentive to work diligently was correspondingly diminished for each individual, with the strength of that disincentive being directly proportional to the size of the collective.

Largely as a result of these two factors—resistance to collectivization on the part of rich peasants and the widespread free-rider problem—the tide of collectivization of the mid-1950s failed to yield the anticipated leap forward in farm output. Growth rates barely reached 2 to 3 percent annually—hardly enough to keep pace with China's burgeoning population.

A split now developed between Mao, who wanted to push ahead even faster with economic transformation, and some of his more cautious colleagues, who wanted to take more time to consolidate previous gains. In 1956, these emerging differences were reflected in the speeches and documents of the CCP's Eighth National Party Congress. ■

Important Terms

collective farms (1955–1957): The highest stage of agricultural collectivization, marked by the abolition of private ownership and the large-scale pooling of land and labor among 100–200 families.

cooperative farms (1953–1954): The intermediate stage of agricultural collectivization, marked by the introduction of work points and year-round sharing of land and tools by 20–30 households.

free-rider problem: Classic dilemma posed when all members of a large group share equally in the benefits of membership without adequate monitoring of individual contributions.

mutual aid (1952–1953): The first stage of agricultural collectivization, marked by small-scale, seasonal sharing of tools, animals, and labor by six or eight neighboring families.

"women with bound feet": Classical Maoist reference to conservative cadres who are afraid to boldly innovate.

Suggested Reading

Fenby, *Modern China.*

Friedman, Pickowicz, and Selden, *Chinese Village, Socialist State.*

Gittings, *The Changing Face of China.*

MacFarquhar, *The Origins of the Cultural Revolution,* vol. 1.

Short, *Mao.*

Questions to Consider

1. What were the key policies for the transformation of the national economy in China's First Five-Year Plan?

2. What sociopolitical stresses and antagonisms were engendered in the process of transforming China's national economy?

Socialist Transformation, 1953–1957
Lecture 16—Transcript

In 1953 China entered a new stage of its development. The Korean War was over; land reform was completed; counterrevolutionaries had been suppressed; and the Communist Party was now firmly in control. It was time to move forward.

The new stage began with the promulgation of a Soviet-style Five-Year Plan for economic development. Its principal content was a blueprint for achieving the realization of socialism in China.

The centerpiece of the First Five-Year Plan was the wholesale Chinese adoption of Stalinist techniques of centralized economic planning, agricultural collectivization, and the rapid growth of urban heavy industry. At one level, Mao's embrace of the Soviet model reflected an underlying ideological affinity between the two Communist giants. At another level, it reflected China's dire need of Soviet economic assistance and technical support.

By 1953, China's long, costly involvement in the Korean War had left the country drained and exhausted. In great need of foreign economic and technical assistance, Mao cast his gaze northward. Soon after Stalin died, Mao reminded the new leaders of the Soviet Union that China had born the brunt of the fighting in Korea, and that it was China's heroic sacrifices that had made it possible for the USSR to avoid being drawn into the War. Mao's bottom line was clear: The Russians owed China—big-time.

For his part, Stalin's successor, Nikita Khrushchev, needed China's support in his drive to be recognized as the undisputed leader of the Socialist camp. Like a politician stumping for votes, Khrushchev listened carefully to Mao's pointed reminder about the Soviet-Korean war debt to China. And in a display of solidarity with his Chinese little brothers, Khrushchev generously agreed to revise the terms of Stalin's 1950 Treaty of Friendship and Mutual Aid.

Promising several hundred million dollars in new Soviet economic and military aid to China, the new Soviet leader further offered to terminate Soviet special privileges in Manchuria. Khrushchev further agreed to send thousands of technical specialists to China, at Russian expense, to build new industrial facilities. Mao was pleased.

As a result of this fresh burst of Soviet generosity, more than 150 major new industrial projects were initiated in China in the mid-1950s; and several thousand Chinese students were sent abroad to the Soviet Union for advanced technical training, mainly in the fields of engineering and applied science.

Military aid also increased, as the USSR built several new aircraft and munitions factories in China from 1953 to 1957. In response to Mao's request for Soviet assistance in acquiring nuclear weapons—which Mao treated as an entitlement because of China's enormous Korean sacrifices—Khrushchev agreed to share Soviet blueprints for an atomic bomb and to provide China with a prototype nuclear weapon.

Not surprisingly, this fresh burst of Soviet largesse ushered in a new era of Sino-Soviet friendship and cordiality, as the Chinese Communists openly embraced their big brothers to the north. And from 1954 to 1957, the Chinese emulated their Soviet senior siblings in almost every respect.

In its bare essentials, the Soviet model of socialism called for the elimination of private ownership of the means of production: capital, technology, equipment, and land. Replacing it would be a system of collective and state ownership of all property, with centralized state planning supplanting the corrupt system of bureaucratic capitalism that had characterized Nationalist China.

In 1954 a new Chinese constitution was adopted, largely modeled after the Soviet constitution of 1936. It described a unitary state system similar to the Soviet proletarian dictatorship.

But there was one major difference. Where the Russian system was narrowly based on the notional sovereignty of the working class, the Chinese variant was more broadly inclusive. It welcomed peasants, law-abiding intellectuals, and other patriotic groups and strata under the protective umbrella of a multi-class ruling coalition, called "people's democratic dictatorship."

A number of fundamental rights and freedoms were guaranteed under the 1954 constitution, including freedom of expression and assembly, and the right to vote for local people's deputies. But as we saw in an earlier lecture, such freedoms were reserved exclusively to the people, and were categorically denied to putative enemies of the people.

In a clear departure from the Soviet constitution, the 1954 Chinese charter enshrined "The Thought of Mao Zedong" as the guiding ideology illuminating

China's path to victory in revolution and socialist construction. Slowly but steadily, a cult of personality was taking shape around the dominating, iconic figure of Chairman Mao Zedong.

Under the guidance of Soviet advisors, China's urban economy underwent a two-stage transition to socialism. Beginning in 1955, shares in private Chinese companies were purchased by the state, with payments to the former owners amortized over a period of several years. This created an intermediary form of ownership, known as "joint state-private" ownership. Although this partial buyout was nominally voluntary, in fact company owners had little or no choice but to agree to the terms offered by the state.

A year later, in 1956, the second stage kicked in, with all urban industrial and commercial assets now converted entirely into state property. Over the next two years, annuity payments to former owners were quietly terminated. In most cases, the companies' former managers were permitted to stay on as salaried employees of the state.

By the end of 1956 virtually the entire urban economy had been nationalized. Although there was a good deal of grumbling among former factory owners and managers, few dared to openly resist the state's takeover of their productive assets.

In the countryside, the process of socialist transformation was more complex and took longer to complete. The process, known as collectivization, was divided into three sequential stages: mutual aid, cooperative farming, and full collectivization. The entire process was carried out under the watchful eye of the Communist Party.

In the first stage, which began in 1953, small groups of six to eight neighboring farm families within a single village were encouraged to form seasonal mutual aid teams. These teams would share their farm tools, draft animals and even their labor on a temporary basis during the busiest periods of crop planting and harvesting. Since many (if not most) peasant families still suffered from a shortage of essential means of production, the seasonal sharing of tools, animals, and labor would arguably lead to greater farm output for everyone and would hence increase each participating family's personal income.

For centuries Chinese peasant families had tilled individually small plots of self-owned or rented land. The point of mutual aid was to gradually habituate the peasants to work together in larger groups for the benefit of all. At this preliminary stage of collectivization, all property was still privately owned; and each family was entitled to consume or even to sell, at its discretion, all produce grown on its own land (minus local taxes and mandatory state grain deliveries).

Based on the demonstrated success of mutual aid teams in raising the income of most of their members, most of the time, after one or two harvest cycles the second stage of collectivization was initiated. In this stage, the cooperative aspects of farm production were extended, along with the size of the basic farming group.

Now, instead of six or eight families aiding each other on a temporary seasonal basis, 20 or 30 families, comprising 100 to 200 people, were grouped together in a cooperative farm, on a year-round basis. At this stage, all productive property, including land, animals, and tools, remained privately owned, at least in theory, but now the property was permanently invested in the cooperative.

In the new form of semi-socialist, semi-private ownership, family income was determined by a combined calculus that included, first, a return proportional to the assessed share value of the assets invested in the co-op, that is, land, tools, and animals of a particular family; and second, was a return proportional to the family's actual labor contribution (which was based on the number of work points earned by each family member during any given farming cycle).

Like mutual aid, the cooperative farms were expressly intended to be voluntary in nature. Coercion in the recruitment of new members was strictly forbidden. Unlike mutual aid, however, peasant families were not free to sell or consume the crops grown on their own piece of land. The harvest now belonged to the co-op as a whole, with the profits shared out according the dual criteria of the size of investment shares owned and work points earned (the former favored well-to-do farmers, while the latter favored those with many able-bodied laborers).

Where the mutual aid teams had been largely successful in fostering an attitudes of shared responsibility and welfare, the results of cooperative farming were more mixed. On the plus side, the year-round pooling of land, labor, tools, and animals, involving 20 or 30 households, made possible both a more well-defined division of farm labor and larger, more efficient economies of scale in farm production.

Moreover, from the Communist Party's ideological perspective, the cooperative farms, by reducing (though not eliminating) the return on private investment, also encouraged the socialist habit of working for the benefit of the entire group, rather than one's own individual self-interest.

The main problem with the principle of voluntary membership was that the co-ops tended to attract mainly the poor, less self-sufficient families in the village. Drawn by the prospect of sharing the land and assets of their better-off neighbors, poor and lower-middle peasants flocked to join the co-ops.

But an entirely different calculus guided the behavior of more affluent families in the village. If they joined the co-op, they would lose half the return on their family property, while having to make up the loss by earning work-points through ordinary labor. This meant that the well-to-do would, in effect, be subsidizing those with few productive assets of their own. Under such circumstances, to be a rational rich or upper-middle peasant, joining a co-op was not a particularly attractive option. Why join?

Why indeed? After a full year of cooperative farming, the results bore out the logic of calculated self-interest. Poor peasants flocked into the co-ops, while rich and upper-middle peasants held back, preferring to go it alone. Consequently, rural China began to polarize into two distinct economic strata: the first comprising hundreds of thousands of so-called "paupers' co-ops," those with impoverished members whogenerally possessed low quality land, few draft animals, insufficient labor power, and low levels of technical skill.

The second stratum was made up of a much smaller number of relatively affluent, self-sufficient farm families. These upscale farmers had no inclination to join the co-ops.

By the spring of 1955 Mao was becoming increasingly distressed by this polarization of wealth in rural China. His concern centered primarily on the emergence of a new class of affluent rich peasants, who were flourishing outside the boundaries of the socialist economy.

Adding to the chairman's worries was the fact that in some provinces, well-off peasants who had initially been persuaded to join the co-ops were now demanding to leave, and to take their property with them. Worse still, local cadres in some provinces were allowing them to do so.

In response to these dual tendencies of rising class polarization and the abandonment of cooperative farming by the well-to-do, Mao Zedong put his foot down in the summer of 1955.

Originally, the cooperative farms were intended to be created and consolidated gradually,over a period of several years before giving way to the third and highest stage of full-scale agricultural collectivization. But when the co-op movement stalled early in 1955 and began to actually reverse itself, moving backward toward private farming for rich and upper-middle peasants, Mao Zedong stepped in.

Writing in July of 1955, Mao strongly criticized those of his comrades who had retreated meekly in the face of pressure from rich peasants to abandon the co-ops. Mao accused these comrades of "tottering along like women with bound feet." (This was a phrase Mao would use over and over again to decry the conservatism of anyone he deemed guilty of the sin of "Right opportunism").

Arguing that the nationwide co-op movement was taking (in Mao's words) "tremendous strides forward," the chairman chastised his comrades for wanting to "wait and see" before pushing ahead with the next stage of collectivization. As for the dissolution of thousands of existing co-ops, Mao argued that allowing them to dissolve "caused great dissatisfaction among the masses and was altogether the wrong thing to do." (all quotes from Mao, *Selected Readings*, pp. 316–339)

To counteract the "rightist error" of "going too slow" and permitting the "drastic dissolution" of the co-ops, Mao suggested that there would soon be a dramatic upsurge in mass enthusiasm for collectivization in the Chinese countryside. The masses, he said, are demanding it. They are eager to realize the full fruits of socialism. Having spoken his piece, the chairman then sat back to measure the impact of his words.

The impact was not long in coming. Within two months, a "high tide" of collectivization had emerged. Throughout the countryside, rural officials read the chairman's words as a mandate for accelerating the process of collectivization.

Originally expected to take four or even five years to complete, the timetable for third-stage collectivization was moved up by anxious officials who were afraid of being labeled as "women with bound feet." If one was going to err in the process of collectivization, it was clearly safer politically to err on the side of excessive enthusiasm. If one valued one's career, too much, too soon was far better than too little, too late.

By February of 1956, more than half the villages in China had been pushed willy-nilly into the higher stage of collectivization—a full two years ahead of schedule and in many cases without ever having gone through the intermediate co-op stage. By the end of 1956, more than 90 percent of China's 500 million peasants had been organized into collective farms. It was, as Mao had predicted, a "high tide" of socialism.

But it was a very problematic high tide, at best. In pushing China's peasants into these new, larger and more fully-socialist farms, local officials throughout the country had routinely violated the Communist Party's longstanding principles of voluntarism, patient persuasion, and leadership by example.

With cadres up and down the line anxious to prove their enthusiasm for socialism, rich and upper-middle peasants were no longer offered a choice. Now they were ordered to join the collectives, and their land and other property was now subject to total confiscation.

Those who balked were punished. In many cases, recalcitrant well-to-do peasants, rather than give their family assets up to the collective, went on a massive binge of "conspicuous consumption," slaughtering and eating their farm animals, chopping down their trees for firewood, and spending their savings on food and drink.

The collective farms were large, impersonal units of production. Far larger than the co-ops that preceded them, each new collective encompassed, on average, 100 to 200 families—roughly 500 and 1,000 people. In most cases, a collective farm was physically coterminous with the village itself, so that the administration of village and collective farm were effectively merged into one.

Within each collective, the distinction between mine and thine was largely obliterated. All major productive property (land, tools, and farm animals) was collectively owned. All income was distributed according to work points, based on the socialist distribution principle of "from each according to his ability, to each according to his work; he who does not work, nor shall he eat."

No longer was income partly based on shares of property investment. Indeed, the only vestiges of private property that remained were the tiny, scattered garden plots within a family's courtyard, called "self-retained lands," or "private plots," which were used to grow vegetables to supplement the family's diet, along with one or two chickens and the occasional pig raised within the family's compound. All else was owned in common.

The coercive aspect of accelerated collectivization meant that there was now, for the first time since 1949, widespread alienation and resentment in rural China. Having been deprived of the means of earning their own independent livelihood, rich and upper-middle and rich peasant families, accounting for perhaps 20 to 25 percent of the rural population, deeply resented their enforced pauperization. Even the poor and lower-middle peasants, presumptive beneficiaries of socialist agriculture, suffered from diminished motivation to work in the new, large-scale, impersonal collectives.

In a classic case of what economists call the "free-rider problem," work points earned by each collective farm member had their cash value determined by the net value of the farm's total harvest. Thus, each family's income depended, in substantial measure, on the quality and quantity of the labor performed by all other farmers in the collective.

With as many as 500 or 600 able-bodied peasants in a single collective, personal responsibility was very difficult to assess and monitor let alone to assign to individuals or families. Hence, the incentive to work diligently was correspondingly diminished for each individual. The strength of that disincentive was being directly proportional to the size of the collective: The bigger the collective unit, the weaker the incentive to work hard.

Under this system, people tended to just go through the motions in their fieldwork. Content to free-ride on the efforts of the others, they paid scant attention to the quality or efficiency of the work performed.

Largely as a result of these two factors—resistance to collectivization by rich-peasants and a widespread free-rider problem—the "high tide" of collectivization of the mid-1950s failed to yield the anticipated "leap forward" in farm output. Indeed, agricultural production limped, rather than leapt forward, with growth rates barely reaching 2 or 3 percent annually, hardly enough to keep pace with China's rapidly burgeoning population.

Parenthetically, it should also be noted that this very same free-rider problem has doomed large-scale collective farming to failure everywhere in the socialist world. Whenever individual reward is determined by group effort, the incentive to work hard and the ability of group members to monitor each other's performance diminishes in proportion to the size of the group. (Just recently, it has been made clear that Israel's famous rural Kibbutzim have been failing in large numbers for precisely this reason.)

Despite clear evidence that free-riders were undermining the effectiveness of China's collective farms, Mao steadfastly denied that there was any such problem. In his belief system, the worker-peasant masses could be educated to understand the benefits of working for the good of the collective, rather than for themselves. "Serve the people," was Mao's oft-repeated mantra.

But the reality of the free-rider problem was not lost on the chairman's close associates, in particular Communist Party Vice-Chairman Liu Shaoqi and Party General-Secretary Deng Xiaoping, the number two and number five ranking officials in the Communist Party hierarchy.

Both Liu Shaoqi and Deng Xiaoping recognized the disincentive effects of large-scale collectives. A decade later, during the Cultural Revolution, such awareness would cost both men dearly, as Mao accused them of "taking the capitalist road." In Mao's view, the failure of the collectives, and later the massively larger rural people's communes, was due to sabotage by rich peasants and counterrevolutionaries, rather than to the flawed motivational logic of collectivization itself.

Notwithstanding the lack of a major leap forward in agriculture, the year 1956 marked an important turning point in China's post-revolutionary development. In that year, the transition to socialism was basically completed. Landlords, counterrevolutionaries, rich-peasants, and rightists had been dealt a severe blow; and private wealth and property ownership were largely a thing of the past.

Although agricultural growth was painfully slow, the industrial economy had surged as a result of Soviet aid. Consequently, between 1953 and 1956, the economy as a whole expanded at a reasonably healthy rate of six-and-a-half percent annually.

In a generally celebratory mood, Chinese Communist Party leaders convened the Eighth National Party Congress in September of 1956. It was the first such Congress to be held since the founding of the PRC.

For most of those in attendance, there was a palpable sense of satisfaction in the achievements of the past half-dozen years. Speaker after speaker praised the fruits of China's economic and political transformation. For most party cadres, it was a time to bask in the ostensible superiority of socialism.

Many leaders now called for an extended period of economic relaxation, consolidation, and adjustment to correct existing flaws and imbalances in the socialist system. Rather than pushing impulsively ahead, they believed it was necessary for the country to catch its collective breath.

In a rare display of self-satisfaction, party Vice-Chairman Liu Shaoqi confidently declared that the question of "who will win in the struggle between socialism and capitalism … has now been answered."

That was a fateful statement that he would come to regret.

In a similar vein, the official resolution of the Eighth Party Congress stated that henceforth the country's principal task would shift from winning victory in the struggle between the proletariat and the bourgeoisie, to redressing economic imbalances between "the advanced socialist system" and the "backward forces of production." In other words, class struggle was now to be superseded by economic development as the country's number one priority.

But not everyone present at the 1956 Party Congress shared this general mood of optimism. Chairman Mao was growing decidedly uneasy with the prevailing attitude of complacency and self-congratulation displayed by his top lieutenants. In the next lecture we will examine the sources of Mao's rising dissatisfaction and the controversial measures he took to address them.

Cracks in the Monolith, 1957–1958
Lecture 17

> We have given our blood, sweat, toil and precious lives to defend not the people, but the bureaucrats who oppress the people and live off the fat of the land. They are a group of fascists who employ foul means, twist the truth, band together in evil ventures, and ignore the people's wish for peace.
>
> — From an anonymous pamphlet entitled *J'accuse*,
> written during the Hundred Flowers movement

By the fall of 1956, the twin pillars of China's socialist transformation—the Sino-Soviet alliance and the socialization of the national economy—were basically complete. But soon afterward, the facade of national harmony and well-being began to show cracks; and by 1957, a series of deepening domestic and international fault lines could no longer be ignored.

Shortly after Nikita Khrushchev famously denounced Stalin's "cult of personality" in 1956, a group of Mao Zedong's own close comrades—including Zhou Enlai, **Liu Shaoqi**, and **Deng Xiaoping**—began to downplay the role of individual leaders in their speeches and writings; and at the Eighth Party Congress, they collaborated in excising from the Chinese constitution all references to the guiding role of "the thought of Mao Zedong."

Mao had other reasons for concern as well. Throughout the Communist bloc, the fall and winter of 1955–1956 had brought a general relaxation of heavy-handed Stalinist policies toward intellectuals. Khrushchev was the trendsetter in this liberalization movement, promising Russia's creative intellectuals greater freedom of expression.

In China, intellectual ferment was also on the rise. After years of rigid ideological and political control, Chinese writers, teachers, scientists, and students were growing visibly restless. Dusting off an ancient Chinese aphorism, CCP leaders introduced a new policy of tolerance toward China's "thinking class." Under the slogan "Let a hundred flowers blossom; let a hundred schools of thought contend," they encouraged intellectuals to speak their minds and pledged to listen carefully. Thus began China's **Hundred Flowers campaign**. Although it was initially proposed by Premier Zhou Enlai, the campaign was soon appropriated by Mao Zedong.

The CCP sponsored a series of open forums in May and early June of 1957, in which they sought to engage intellectuals in open debate. At around the same time, a new form of political expression—called *dazibao*—made its debut on billboards and walls on Beijing's college campuses. Using *dazibao*, intellectuals started to express themselves—cautiously at first, but then with growing boldness. Among other things, they accused Communist Party officials of being doctrinaire, arrogant, opportunistic, and corrupt; some even directly criticized Chairman Mao.

Stung by the mounting intensity and ferocity of the intellectuals' attack, Mao struck back, instituting the **Anti-Rightist Rectification movement**. Mao instructed his associates to punish all those who had dared to attack the party. Led by Deng Xiaoping (who had evidently opposed the liberal Hundred Flowers policy from the outset), the new movement witnessed a harsh crackdown on China's "bourgeois intellectuals." Hundreds of thousands of non-Communist teachers, writers, scientists, and artists were now subjected to intensive "criticism and struggle." Teachers were paraded in front of their students, made to wear dunce caps identifying their alleged crimes, and forced to sign confessions. Tens of thousands were beaten; many were imprisoned; and more than a few died, some by their own hand. Moreover, the majority of those who were labeled as rightists were dismissed from their jobs and sent to the countryside to be reformed through physical labor. Much later, Deng Xiaoping estimated that up to half a million people were falsely accused and punished as rightists in the course of the rectification movement, which continued until 1958.

Meanwhile, China's relations with the Soviet Union grew increasingly strained. Mao believed Khrushchev's brand of socialism was leading not

> Teachers were paraded in front of their students, made to wear dunce caps identifying their alleged crimes, and forced to sign confessions.

to Communism but to a rebirth of bureaucratic capitalism in the USSR. Terming this alarming trend **modern revisionism**, Mao began to contemplate a dramatic break with the Soviet model.

Worried about the spread of revisionist influences within his own Party, Mao in the fall of 1957 expanded the targets of the Anti-Rightist Rectification movement from the bourgeois intellectuals to the Communist Party itself. By the time the movement ran its course in 1958, over 1 million party members and cadres had been investigated, reprimanded, put on probation, or expelled from the party for their alleged rightist errors. By the spring of 1958, Mao's thinking had undergone a profound shift toward the left. He now began to envision an entirely new form of socialist economic construction based on the twin ideas of "continuing the revolution" and liberating the subjective energies of the Chinese masses: The Great Leap Forward was at hand. ■

Names to Know

Deng Xiaoping (1904–1997): A veteran CCP leader and economic pragmatist, Deng introduced sweeping market reforms after Mao Zedong's death. Twice purged as a "revisionist," Deng supplanted Hua Guofeng as China's top leader in December 1978. Best known for his 1962 slogan: "It doesn't matter if the cat is white or black, so long as it catches mice."

Liu Shaoqi (1898–1969): A CCP organizational specialist and one of Mao Zedong's top lieutenants, Liu become Mao's heir apparent in the mid-1950s. Teaming with Deng Xiaoping to dismantle Mao's Great Leap Forward in 1961–1962, Liu was later accused of "taking the capitalist road." He was purged by Mao in 1966 and died in captivity in 1969.

Important Terms

Anti-Rightist Rectification movement (June 1957–1958): The struggle against "bourgeois intellectuals" and wayward CCP members following the termination of the Hundred Flowers campaign.

dazibao (**big-character posters**): Large hand-written posters, often anonymous, espousing political principles or accusing others of wrongdoing. Widely used in the Hundred Flowers movement and later during the Cultural Revolution and Democracy Wall period.

Hundred Flowers campaign (1956–1957): Mao Zedong's invitation to Chinese intellectuals to freely air grievances. When complaints turned to attacks on the CCP, Mao launched the Anti-Rightist Rectification movement.

modern revisionism: The Maoist charge that Nikita Khrushchev and his successors abandoned revolutionary Leninism in favor of peaceful coexistence and restoring capitalism in the USSR.

Suggested Reading

Chang, *Wild Swans*.

Chang and Halliday, *Mao*.

Cheng, *Life and Death in Shanghai*.

Fenby, *Modern China*.

Lüthi, *The Sino-Soviet Split*.

MacFarquhar, *The Origins of the Cultural Revolution*, vol. 1.

Pan, *Out of Mao's Shadow*.

Schram, *The Political Thought of Mao Tse-tung*.

Shambaugh, *Deng Xiaoping*.

Short, *Mao*.

Questions to Consider

1. What were the main issues in Mao Zedong's dispute with Nikita Khrushchev?

2. Did Mao set a trap for China's intellectuals when he initiated the Hundred Flowers movement?

Cracks in the Monolith, 1957–1958

Lecture 17—Transcript

As we saw in the last lecture, by the fall of 1956 the twin pillars of China's socialist transformation—the Sino-Soviet alliance and the socialization of the national economy—were more-or-less completed. But soon afterward, the facade of national harmony and well-being began to show cracks. And by 1957 a series of deepening domestic and international fault lines could no longer be ignored or papered over.

Unlike the majority of his comrades, Mao Zedong was not satisfied with the situation in 1956. Due to the unexpected stagnation of farm production, the urban industrial sector was running short of investment funds. Mao wanted to speed up the pace of industrial development, which would require extracting even more resources and revenues from the collective farming sector. The economy was seriously out of balance, and Mao knew it.

Meanwhile, in Moscow, Nikita Khrushchev suddenly and without warning launched a verbal attack on Joseph Stalin. In a secret speech delivered to the 20th Congress of the Soviet Communist Party in February of 1956, Khrushchev denounced Stalin for having carried out a series of purges within the party in the 1930s, for having executed large numbers of Soviet citizens, for deporting national minorities from their homelands, for causing the great famine of the early 1930s, and for widespread, egregious violations of the principles of socialist legality.

But perhaps Khrushchev's most telling critique of "comrade Stalin," at least as far as Mao Zedong was concerned, was his denunciation of Stalin's "cult of personality"—the carefully-cultivated, glorified image of god-like benevolence, omnipotence, and invincibility that surrounded the late Soviet dictator.

Suddenly, alarm bells started going off in Mao's own, supremely egotistical mind. The chairman had reason to be concerned. Shortly after Khrushchev's attack on Stalin's "cult of personality," a group of Mao's own close comrades, including Zhou Enlai, Deng Xiaoping, and Liu Shaoqi, began to downplay the role of individual leaders in their own speeches and writings. And at the Eighth Party Congress they collaborated in excising from the Chinese constitution all references to the guiding role of Mao Zedong's "Thought"—this just two years after they had inserted that language in the constitution.

Mao was upset; but he evidently consented to this downgrading; for he had no wish to openly contradict Khrushchev at this point, on this issue—at least, not yet.

But Mao had other reasons for concern as well. Throughout the Communist bloc, the fall and winter of 1955 and early 1956 had brought a general relaxation of heavy-handed Stalinist policies toward intellectuals. Khrushchev was the trendsetter in this liberalization movement, promising Russia's creative intellectuals greater freedom of expression.

Taking their cue from Mother Russia, intellectuals throughout the Soviet bloc began to voice their pent-up frustrations. By the time Khrushchev gave his de-Stalinization speech in February of '56, teachers, writers, artists, and students throughout eastern and central Europe were calling for a roll-back of repressive Stalinist policies.

In Moscow, Warsaw, and Prague, factory workers joined with dissident intellectuals in calling for greater freedom. In Budapest, massive street protests, some involving as many as 200,000 people, paralyzed the country's hard-line Stalinist leadership.

Fearing the spread of chaos, Nikita Khrushchev sent in hundreds of Soviet tanks and 17 divisions of combat troops to crush the Hungarian revolt. More than 3,000 people died in the ensuing crackdown.

In China, intellectual ferment was also on the rise. After years of being subjected to rigid ideological and political controls, Chinese writers, teachers, scientists and students were also growing visibly restless. With one eye on the worsening situation in eastern Europe, the Eighth Party Congress in September of 1956 held out an olive branch to China's alienated intellectuals.

Dusting off an ancient Chinese aphorism, party leaders introduced a new policy of tolerance toward China's thinking class. Under the slogan, "Let a hundred flowers blossom; let a hundred schools of thought contend," they encouraged the intellectuals to speak their minds and pledged to listen carefully and conscientiously to their opinions and grievances. Henceforth, they promised, intellectuals would be treated with dignity and respect, as valued members of China's socialist community.

Thus began China's famous "Hundred Flowers" campaign.

Although it had been initially suggested by Premier Zhou Enlai in the summer of 1956, the campaign was soon appropriated by Mao Zedong himself. In the fall of 1956 Mao expressed his belief that by encouraging China's wary and reserved intellectuals to express themselves openly and freely, without fear of reprisal, they would be able to "shed their burdens," psychologically.

Relieved of their anxieties, they mightparticipate more eagerly and enthusiastically in the cause of building socialism. Such, at any rate, was the theory behind the "Hundred Flowers" campaign. In practice, however, things turned out rather differently.

Conditioned by years of shoddy treatment at the hands of the Communist Party, China's intellectuals initially failed to respond to Mao's invitation to "shed their burdens." Having been once bitten, they were twice shy. As one scholar put it, "Experience has shown that [party] policy could change suddenly, with today's license becoming tomorrow's [prison] sentence." (Benton and Hunter, *Wild Lily, Prairie Fire*, p. 13). Sensing a possible trap, the intellectuals held back, refusing to expose themselves.

After waiting in vain for the intellectuals to respond to his invitation, Mao decided that even stronger assurances were needed to coax them into participating. In a famous speech delivered in late February of 1957, entitled "On the Correct Handling of Contradictions among the People," Mao affirmed the need for vigorous intellectual debate and criticism.

Once again employing a floral metaphor, he called for unfettered intellectual "blooming and contending" in China. Arguing that "Plants raised in a hothouse are unlikely to be hardy," the chairman sought to reassure China's intellectuals that the bulk of their concerns belonged to the category of benign contradictions among the people, rather than antagonistic contradictions with class enemies.

To coax the intellectuals out of their shells, the CCP sponsored a series of open forums in May and early June of 1957, in which they sought to engage intellectuals in open debate, hoping thereby to clear the air. At around the same time, a new form of political expression, called *dazibao*, or "big-character posters," made its debut on billboards and walls on Beijing's college and university campuses.

Now, at last, the intellectuals began to express themselves, cautiously at first, but then with growing boldness. Often choosing to hide behind a protective shield of anonymity (or pseudo-anonymity), poster-writers began to direct a growing stream of criticism at Communist Party cadres and bureaucrats. Among other things, party officials were scored for being "doctrinaire," "arrogant," "undemocratic," "opportunistic," "officious," and just plain "corrupt."

One anonymous law student at People's University in Beijing complained bitterly that the Communist Party's promises of a just and democratic future under socialism had been betrayed:

> I hold that the socialism we now have is not genuine socialism … Genuine socialism should be very democratic, but ours is undemocratic. … [Under Communism] A man is judged not by his virtues and abilities, but by whether or not he is a party member. … Even desks and wastebaskets are distributed according to one's party status. … Once I was ill and needed medical care, but I had to be of the 13th rank to qualify. How could I climb to the 13th rank?

Another critic wrote an anonymous pamphlet with the title, "*J'accuse*" (I accuse), invoking the spirit of the famous 1898 broadside by the French writer Emile Zola. In it, the critic bemoaned the unprincipled opportunism and opulent lifestyle of high-level party officials:

> A great many cadres are enjoying a luxurious life of banquets and villas. Why should I live so frugally? How many people have learned to fake obedience, bow to the leadership, [and] turn their backs on the masses, [in order to] become high-ranking officials? …
>
> [It seems] we have given our blood, sweat, toil and precious lives to defend not the people, but the bureaucrats who oppress the people and live off the fat of the land. They are a group of fascists who employ foul means, twist the truth, band together in evil ventures, and ignore the people's wish for peace.

Not even Mao himself was immune from criticism. One essayist asked rhetorically,

> What does it mean when the Communists say they suffer so that the people may not suffer, and that they let the people enjoy things before they do the same? … These are lies. We ask: Is Chairman Mao, who enjoys the best things in life, … having a hard time? … That son of a bitch. A million shames on him.

Warming up to his task, this critic then went on to skewer the chairman:

> Our pens can never defeat Mao Zedong's party guards and his imperial army. When he wants to kill you, he doesn't have to do it himself. He can mobilize your wife and your children to denounce you and then kill you with their own hands! Is this a rational society? This is class struggle, Mao Zedong style! (ibid., p. 63).

Stung by the mounting intensity and ferocity of the intellectuals' attack, Mao sat back and waited. Then he struck back. In early June a substantially revised version of the chairman's February speech was issued. The new version was considerably more confrontational and hard-line than the original.

Where the February speech had stressed the importance of free "blooming and contending" among competing ideas, Mao now added a stern warning against sabotage by class enemies, including counterrevolutionaries, rich-peasants and rightists. In Mao's newly revised view, China's overthrown class enemies remained unreconciled to their defeat; and they constituted a dangerous threat to the socialist cause.

In emphasizing the need to remain vigilant against class enemies, Mao directly contradicted the Eighth Party Congress's formal conclusion that class struggle was "essentially over" in China. On the contrary, the chairman now claimed, "The class struggle between the proletariat and the bourgeoisie … will be long and tortuous and at times very acute. … In this respect, the question of whether socialism or capitalism will win is really not settled."

After warning against the "frenzied attacks" of counterrevolutionaries and rightists, Mao went on to enumerate six criteria to be used in distinguishing between the "fragrant flowers" of healthy debate and the "poisonous weeds" of noxious capitalism. The flowers, he said, should be lovingly and carefully nurtured, while the weeds should be pulled ruthlessly out at the roots:

> What [asked the chairman] should be the criteria … for distinguishing between fragrant flowers and poisonous weeds? … Broadly speaking, we consider the criteria should be as follows:
>
> (1) Words and actions should help to unite, not divide, the people of our various nationalities;
>
> (2) They should be beneficial, not harmful, to socialist construction;

(3) They should help to consolidate, not weaken, the people's democratic dictatorship;

(4) They should help to consolidate, not weaken, democratic centralism;

(5) They should help to strengthen, not discard or weaken, the leadership of the Communist Party;

(6) They should be beneficial, not harmful, to international socialist unity.

Of these six criteria, [concluded the chairman,] the most important are the socialist path and the leadership of the party. (Mao, *Selected Readings*..., p. 378)

Having clearly narrowed the limits of free speech for intellectuals, Mao next instructed his associates to punish all those who had dared to attack the party. And in the summer of 1957 an "Anti-Rightist Rectification movement" was launched.

Led by Deng Xiaoping, who had evidently opposed the liberal "hundred flowers" policy from the outse), the new movement witnessed a harsh crackdown on China's bourgeois intellectuals.

In a throwback to the repressive days of the Yan'an Forum of 1942, hundreds of thousands of non-Communist teachers, writers, scientists, and artists were now subjected to intensive criticism and struggle. Teachers were paraded in front of their students, made to wear dunce caps identifying their alleged crimes, and forced to sign confessions. Tens of thousands were beaten; many were imprisoned; and not a few died, some by their own hand.

Aside from the denunciations, beatings, and detentions, the majority of those who were labeled as rightists were dismissed from their jobs and sent down to the countryside to be reformed through physical labor. Much later, Deng Xiaoping would estimate that up to half a million people were falsely accused and punished as rightists in the course of the rectification movement, which continued until 1958.

In recent years, a debate has raged among scholars over whether Mao deliberately led China's intellectuals into a trap, enticing them to expose their true feelings as a prelude to cracking down on them. Supporting this hypothesis is the fact that the chairman had been known, on occasion, to disarm his adversaries with praise before pouncing on them. And on more than one occasion, he had set elaborate traps for his colleagues to test their loyalty.

On the other hand, there is no direct evidence of Maoist pre-meditation in 1957. Indeed, the conciliatory tone of his February speech had the air of sincerity. Moreover, Mao's initial soft line had been opposed by several of his top comrades at the time, including both Liu Shaoqi and Deng Xiaoping, who complained that the chairman was courting disaster by encouraging intellectuals to criticize the party.

But Mao persisted. And when his conciliatory gestures produced an avalanche of criticism, he lost a great deal of face with those comrades who had been skeptical from the outset—to the point where, by 1958, he actually began to consider retreating from the frontline of policymaking. So, was Mao baiting a trap for the intellectuals? To coin a phrase, "You pays your money and you takes your choice."

Whatever the truth of Mao's motivation, his relations with Nikita Khrushchev were showing clear signs of strain. Shortly after Khrushchev's February 1956 de-Stalinization speech, China's flagship daily newspaper, the *People's Daily*, published a lengthy, unsigned theoretical article which defended Stalin as an "outstanding Marxist-Leninist fighter" and refuted Khrushchev's verbal attack on Stalin's "cult of personality." While acknowledging that Stalin had made some serious mistakes, the *People's Daily* article defended the historical contribution of strong leaders: "Marxist-Leninists hold that leaders play a big role in history. ... It is utterly wrong to deny the role of the individual, the role of forerunners and the role of leaders." Though Mao did not personally write this article, he did sign off on it.

In the aftermath of the Hungarian revolt of 1956, Mao's relations with the Soviet Union leader grew even more strained. He sharply criticized the Russians for sending Soviet tanks into Budapest without first consulting with other members of the Socialist camp. In Mao's view, such Soviet unilateralism violated the spirit of fraternal consultation and deliberation, and was symptomatic of Khrushchev's growing attitude of "great-nation Chauvinism."

At a November 1956 meeting of the Chinese Communist Party Central Committee, Mao openly voiced his concern over the implications of Khrushchev's February speech; and for the very first time he issued a critique of another one of the Soviet leader's recent ideological pronouncements, to wit, Khrushchev's claim that in the era of nuclear weapons, socialism could achieve victory peacefully, through parliamentary means, without necessitating revolutionary armed struggle.

To Mao, the idea of a "parliamentary road to socialism" smacked of heresy, since it contradicted directly a principal axiom of Lenin's theory of imperialism, namely, the inevitability of war. In an obvious angry fit, Mao complained to his comrades:

> The Sword of Stalin has been abandoned by the Russians. ... As for the sword of Lenin, has it too now been abandoned? ... In my view, it has ... to a considerable extent. ... Khrushchev's report ... says it is possible to gain political power by the parliamentary road, [and that] it is no longer necessary for all countries to learn from the October Revolution. Once this gate is thrown open, Leninism by and large is thrown out.

Now, up to this point, Mao's quarrel with Khrushchev had been kept separate and distinct from his rising alarm over the nefarious activities of rich peasants and bourgeois intellectuals at home. But over the next few months, these two different concerns would begin to converge.

Increasingly, Mao viewed Khrushchev's abandonment of the Leninist principles of revolution and war as the flip side of China's own intensifying class struggle. To these twin heresies, Mao now affixed a new label: he called them "modern revisionism" (*xiandai xiuzheng zhuyi*).

Mao defined "modern revisionism" as the abandonment of core Marxist-Leninist principles, and he traced its origins to a resurgence of bourgeois ideology and liberalism in post-revolutionary socialist society.

Addressing his comrades in mid-May of 1957, at the height of the Hundred Flowers "blooming and contending" in China, Mao signaled a shift in his thinking: "Over the past few months everyone has been repudiating [ideological] dogmatism, but [we have] done nothing about revisionism. ... Now we ought to pay attention to repudiating revisionism."

As far as is known, this was the first instance of what would later emerge as a full-blown Maoist obsession with preventing a capitalist restoration in China—an obsession that would eventually envelop China in an orgy of revolutionary extremism.

As Mao's unhappiness with Khrushchev intensified, so too did his impatience with the strategy of blindly imitating the Soviet model of socialism. Characterized by central planning, agricultural collectivization, and rapid urban industrial growth, the Soviet model had become bogged down in China.

Rich peasants were sabotaging the collective farms, agricultural productivity was stagnating, and the resulting lack of extractable revenues from the countryside was hampering the country's urban-industrial growth. Moreover, in the aftermath of the divisive Anti-Rightist Rectification movement, China's industrial experts—engineers, scientists, and technicians—had become demoralized, showing little enthusiasm for socialism. In Mao's view something needed to be done to jump-start the moribund economy.

As we saw in the last lecture, at the Eighth Party Congress in 1956, Mao's colleagues had opted for a prolonged period of economic "consolidation and adjustment" to resolve existing economic problems and put the economy back on a sound footing. But Mao was far from satisfied with such a conservative game plan. For him, more of the samewas not the answer; it was precisely the problem.

As his anger at Khrushchev grew more intense, along with his frustration with China's rich peasants and bourgeois intellectuals, Mao began to point the finger of suspicion at those of his colleagues who had exhibited skeptical attitudes toward the "high tide" of agricultural collectivization in 1955 and '56.

Worried about the spread of revisionist influences within his own party, Mao in the fall of 1957 expanded the targets of the Anti-Rightist Rectification movement from the bourgeois intellectuals to the Communist Party itself. By the time the movement ran its course in 1958, over one million party members and cadres had been investigated, reprimanded, put on probation, or expelled from the party outright for their alleged rightist errors.

By the spring of 1958, Mao's thinking had undergone a profound shift toward the Left. He now began to envision an entirely new form of socialist economic construction, based on the twin ideas of continuing the revolution and liberating the subjective energies of the Chinese masses.

There would be no more emulating the old Soviet model; there would be no more relying on bourgeois intellectuals for economic and technical progress; there would be no more advancing at a snail's pace, "tottering around like women with bound feet"; and there would be no more nay-saying. The chairman had made up his mind.

A "Great Leap Forward" was at hand. For the next three years, Mao would apply the lessons of people's war to the struggles against nature. Objective limits on economic growth would be overcome through mass mobilization.

With proper motivation and leadership, said Mao, there was no mountain that the Chinese people could not climb, no obstacle that they could not surmount. When the chairman confidently proclaimed that China would overtake Great Britain in a little more than a decade, the people believed him. No one dared to say "no ... that's impossible."

The result was catastrophic.

Next time, the Great Leap Forward.

The Great Leap Forward, 1958–1960
Lecture 18

When the Chinese men's table tennis team won the world championship in 1958, their victory was officially attributed to "the emancipation of mind wrought by the [Great Leap's] mass education in socialist relations and values."

In 1958, Mao Zedong attempted to dramatically accelerate China's economic development with the **Great Leap Forward**. Distrustful of Khrushchev's revisionism, Mao abandoned the Soviet model of socialist construction and struck out in an uncharted direction, hoping to leapfrog the Russians and beat them to the promised land of Communism. It was an audacious gamble. And it failed, miserably.

It was an audacious gamble. And it failed, miserably.

Despite China's severe shortages of capital and technology, Mao believed that given the proper ("red") ideological motivation and leadership, China's peasant masses could overcome all obstacles to economic development. The first major innovation, at the end of 1957, mobilized of tens of millions of collective farmers during the winter season, when the demand for field labor was low. The peasants were put to work building large-scale water conservation projects—dams, reservoirs, dykes, and canals.

In some cases, as many as 10,000 peasants were transported to a single work site. Since the distances involved were great, temporary barracks were erected at the work sites, where the laborers would remain for weeks or months at a time. To maintain discipline and morale among the work force, a rudimentary military-style regimen was introduced: Workers arose at dawn to recorded bugle calls, ate their meals in communal canteens, and marched in step to the work sites. Participating laborers received no monetary compensation for their work—only meals, housing, and transportation were provided. The entire enterprise was portrayed in the state media as a "people's war against nature." This, in turn, set a militaristic tone for the entire Great Leap Forward.

To facilitate mass mobilization of labor, peasants were organized into huge, impersonal **rural people's communes**, each with an average size of more than 20,000 people. To prove their ideological superiority, communes distributed income according to need, rather than labor. Innovations in farming techniques began to be widely reported and popularized. Almost immediately, claims of doubled or even tripled, crop yields were reported in the party press, as rural officials competed to meet and exceed established norms of crop production.

With the new, larger size of the people's communes, it became possible, at least in theory, to broadly diversify the rural economy. By introducing a large-scale division of labor involving thousands of peasants, the people's communes were to become entirely self-sufficient. Perhaps the most notorious example of rural economic diversification during the Great Leap Forward was the campaign to create large amounts of high-quality steel in **backyard blast furnaces**. Working day and night, China's mobilized peasants smelted scrap iron of all kinds—including tools, bicycles, and household utensils.

Mao Zedong and Nikita Khrushchev. Distrustful of Khrushchev's "revisionist" policies, Mao chose to diverge from the Soviet model of development.

239

In their eagerness to please Mao and demonstrate the superiority of China's new "shortcut to Communism," Chinese officials made grossly exaggerated claims of China's various economic miracles. But the Great Leap could not be sustained. With the first heavy summer rains of 1958, many of the water conservation structures constructed the previous winter began to fail, inundating hundreds of thousands of acres of cropland. The 1958 experiment with farming innovations also proved a failure, as did the backyard steel furnaces. Although large amounts of scrap metal were successfully melted down and forged into crude steel, the resulting products were unusable. To make matters worse, the obsessive drive to keep the furnaces firing around the clock had created a severe shortage of fuel for cooking and heating, as well as massive soil erosion.

By the winter of 1959, the Party Central Committee—and even Mao himself—recognized that something had gone seriously wrong. Although Mao gave ground on some of the particulars of the Great Leap, he was too stubborn to acknowledge failure. In the face of a growing crisis, a few of Mao's lieutenants began to raise their voices in dissent. And in the summer of 1959, their newfound courage presented Mao with the single biggest challenge of his career to date. ■

Important Terms

backyard blast furnaces (1958–1959): Indigenous kilns used in rural areas to smelt crude steel during the Great Leap Forward. Most of the steel was unusable.

Great Leap Forward (1958–1962): Mao Zedong's ill-fated attempt to reach Communism ahead of the USSR by relying on subjective factors—mass ideological mobilization, selfless devotion to labor, and "red" leadership. This movement resulted in great famine and 30 million deaths.

rural people's communes: First introduced in 1958, these communes encompassed as many as 10,000 families, all of whom shared equally in communal income and contributed voluntary labor to backyard steelmaking and other nonagricultural tasks.

Suggested Reading

Chang and Halliday, *Mao*.

Fenby, *Modern China*.

Friedman, Pickowicz, and Selden, *Revolution, Resistance, and Reform in Village China*.

Gittings, *The Changing Face of China*.

Li, *The Private Life of Chairman Mao*.

Lüthi, *The Sino-Soviet Split*.

MacFarquhar, *The Origins of the Cultural Revolution*, vol. 2.

Schram, *The Political Thought of Mao Tse-tung*.

Short, *Mao*.

Questions to Consider

1. Why did Mao Zedong abandon the Soviet model of socialism in 1958?

2. To what extent were the radical innovations of Mao's Great Leap Forward planned in advance, as opposed to being spontaneous experiments?

The Great Leap Forward, 1958–1960
Lecture 18—Transcript

In this lecture we look at Mao Zedong's effort to dramatically accelerate China's economic development by undertaking a "Great Leap Forward." Distrustful of Khrushchev's revisionism, Mao abandoned the Soviet model of socialist construction. And in 1958 he struck out in a new and uncharted direction, hoping to leapfrog the Russians and beat them to the promised land of communism.

It was an audacious gamble. And it failed, miserably.

For various reasons, the Soviet model had not proved to be a very good fit for China. For one thing, Soviet-style socialism spawned economic free-riders, as we saw. For another, it was ill-suited to China's demographic and economic conditions. China had little advanced technology for industrial development; few world-class scientists and engineers; little virgin land to bring under cultivation; and a massive, unskilled rural population that was still using thousand-year-old farming techniques.

The Great Leap began not as a grandiose blueprint for human social engineering, but as a series of ad hoc responses to specific developmental problems. The programs of the Great Leap were often improvised and experimental; and some of them made reasonable sense, at least in theory. All too soon, however, the enterprise spun out of control.

The first major innovation, introduced at the end of 1957, involved the mobilization of tens of millions of collective farmers during the slack winter season, when the demand for field labor was sharply reduced. Instead of sitting around in their villages through the long Chinese winter, peasants could be put to work building large-scale water conservancy projects—dams, reservoirs, dykes, and canals.

The concept was rather simple and dated back to ancient imperial times: Large-scale water conservation projects meant higher, stable crop yields; and stable crop yields meant greater tax revenues for the state.

Since China was short on both investment capital and advanced technology, but long on raw, unskilled human labor, idle male laborers were conscripted from the villages to do the heavy work of building water management projects using whatever simple tools they had at hand—shovels, picks and hoes.

In some cases, as many as 10 thousand peasants, from up to a dozen or more villages were transported to a single work-site. Since the distances involved often exceeded 10 or 15 miles, they were too great to be traveled on foot in a single day. So temporary barracks were erected at the work sites, where the laborers would remain for weeks, or even months at a time, returning home only infrequently.

To maintain discipline and morale among the work force, a rudimentary military-style regimen was introduced: Workers arose at dawn to recorded bugle calls, ate their meals in communal canteens, and marched in step to the work sites, their tools over their shoulders like rifles.

Once there, they synchronized their labor to the sharp, regular rhythms of work chants. Participating laborers received no paid compensation for their work, though meals, housing and transportation were provided free of charge.

Perhaps inevitably, this new, militarized form of large-scale, labor-intensive conservation work was compared to the Red Army's conduct of people's war during the Yan'an period. In fact, the entire enterprise was now portrayed in the state media as a "people's war against nature." And this, in turn, set a militaristic tone for the entire Great Leap Forward to followed.

One key feature of the water management campaign was the marked absence of expert scientific or technical input. Blueprints were done on-the-fly, often by inexperienced draftsmen; surveying was slipshod; material specifications were mere approximations, based on crude estimates of load-bearing capacities and structural requirements.

The fact that many of these huge projects later failed or collapsed because of design or construction flaws did not immediately dampen the regime's enthusiasm for the triumph of the human spirit. In the can-do ethos of the Great Leap Forward, expert scientists, engineers, and technical intellectuals were denigrated as useless, impractical bookworms, while the politically mobilized "red" peasants and cadres were given credit for achieving amazing feats of creativity and daring.

With millions of male laborers living on construction sites, often for months at a time, the spring of 1958 saw a growing shortage of able-bodied farm workers in the villages.

As the busy spring planting season approached, women were mobilized to work in the fields. To conserve household labor, domestic chores were now collectivized. Instead of each woman cooking for her own family, a few women would prepare meals for everyone in the village. Childcare was also managed on a communal basis, with a few village grannies keeping watch over all the local children. Care for the elderly, sick, and disabled was similarly arranged on a largescale basis.

The net effect of all this was to free up large numbers of women from the demands of household domestic chores, enabling them to participate in farm labor while the men were away working on conservation projects. Chinese propagandists praised the new system for having liberated Chinese women from household drudgery. But if it was women's liberation, it was a rather strange type of liberation, involving the swapping of one kind of drudgery for another.

By the late spring of 1958, several of these ad hoc innovations had become more-or-less permanent fixtures in China's collective farms. Communal dining halls were now the norm. They were lauded in party newspapers as a breakthrough for their Communist spirit of literally "serving the people."

In some areas, rural cadres began to experiment with enlarging the scale of the existing collective farms by amalgamating as many as 10 or even twenty neighboring villages to form a single, integrated administrative unit, with populations as high as 10,000 or even 20,000 people.

The mass media were quick to applaud such experiments as the "first sprouts of communism." And Mao himself was delighted with the sudden upsurge of enthusiasm for these things that he called "newborn socialist things."

On an inspection tour of rural Henan Province in the early summer of 1958, Mao visited one of these newly amalgamated large-scale collectives. Impressed by the evident enthusiasm of the local peasants and cadres, Mao asked for the name of their new organization. *"Weixing renmin gongshe,"* came the answer—the "Sputnik people's commune."

On Mao's return trip to Beijing, a reporter from the *People's Daily* asked the chairman for his impression of this new Sputnik commune. Mao's five-word response—*"Renmin gongshe hao!"* (people's communes are good!)—appeared the next day as a banner headline on the masthead of Communist Party's flagship newspaper.

All over China, rural officials now hastened to emulate the Sputnik experience. Mao had said, "people's communes are good," and now, suddenly, they began to pop up everywhere like mushrooms after a spring rain.

Suddenly, all roads to Weixing were jammed with officials converging from all parts of the country, seeking to learn the secrets of organizing and running a people's commune. Just what was a people's commune? And how did it work?

Along with the dramatic enlargement of China's collective farms, extraordinary claims of unprecedented crop yields began to appear in the official media. In areas where people's communes had been formed relatively early, the summer wheat harvest in 1958 was said to have virtually doubled from the previous year. New breakthroughs in productivity were reported almost daily as a wave of unbridled optimism spread like wildfire.

New innovations in farming techniques now began to be widely reported and popularized. A revolutionary method of planting rice, called "deep plowing and close planting," was promoted in the summer of 1958.

The theory behind it was that if two tons of rice could be grown on a given plot of land by planting the seedlings 12 inches apart, at a depth of six inches, then far larger yields could, in principal, be achieved by planting the young seedlings twice as close together, at twice the depth, and with twice as much fertilizer added per acre of rice.

To facilitate deep plowing, a new, larger type of farm plow was introduced, the "two wheel, two-share plow." Pulled by two fully grown men or a water buffalo, it could dig a furrow up to 18 inches deep.

Almost immediately, claims of doubled or even tripled crop yields were reported in the party press, as rural officials across the country competed among themselves to meet and exceed established norms of per-acre production.

A famous photo printed in the *People's Daily* showed a group of children playing happily on the top of a thick, rich plot of mature rice plants. The plants in the photo were as thick as a straw mattress, and they easily supported the weight of the frolicking children.

With the new, larger size of the people's communes, it now became possible, at least in theory, to broadly diversify the rural economy. By introducing a large-scale division of labor involving thousands of peasants, the communes could, it was argued, become entirely self-sufficient—not merely in food production, but in industry, commerce, education, and military training as well. No longer bound by the conventional technocratic constraints of the old Soviet model, China was blazing a new and original pathway to the future.

Perhaps the most famous example of rural economic diversification during the Great Leap was the notorious campaign to create large amounts of high-quality steel in backyard blast furnaces. Here again, the idea was to substitute large-scale, mobilized human labor for the scientific, technical, and capital requirements of making steel in modern urban factories. In launching the new campaign, Mao declared that his goal was to surpass Great Britain in steel production within 15 years.

Throughout the countryside, millions of peasants were conscripted to build small-scale clay, brick-and-mortar kilns. Operating around the clock, the kilns were fired to superheated temperatures. To keep the furnaces blazing, all available rural fuel supplies were consumed. Whole forests were denuded of trees; and all available household heating and cooking coal was requisitioned.

To supply the needed pig iron, scrap metal was collected in every village, including old farm tools, bicycle parts, household pots, pans, and utensils. Anything and everything metallic was fed into the furnaces. Nothing was spared, not even family woks.

Working night and day, China's mobilized peasants produced almost three million tons of backyard steel in 1958, approximately 15 pounds of steel for every man, woman, and child in rural China. The sudden spike in output represented a 30 percent increase in the country's total steel production for 1958. A few months later, an obviously exuberant Chairman Mao revised his goal of catching up with Great Britain from 15 years down to only three.

And still the innovations kept coming. One problem that had long plagued rural China was the prevalence of grain-consuming pests—birds, rats and insects. As part of the Great Leap, a "people's war" was launched to eliminate the four leading crop-eating pests.

In this new campaign, sparrows were designated public enemy number one. To reduce the sparrow population, a low-cost, labor-intensive strategy was devised.

Millions of peasants, mainly women, children and the elderly, were mobilized to bang pots and pans and wave sticks and brooms outdoors. The resulting din frightened the sparrows out of the trees and fields, and into the air. Unable to land because of the intense noise, they would eventually drop from exhaustion, whereupon they were set upon by the crowds of people and strung onto garlands, which were then displayed as trophies. Those who killed the most sparrows were given commendation as an advanced worker, or "Sputnik." Tens of millions of sparrows were killed in this way.

By the mid-summer of 1958, a national euphoria was in evidence. Fueled by extreme claims of success in the "people's war against nature," and amplified by an overactive Communist propaganda machine, China's leaders began to believe that they had discovered a shortcut to Communism—the ultimate Nirvana.

By the end of 1958, the country's 750,000 collective farms had been consolidated and merged into just 23,000 people's communes, each with an average size of 25,000 people. In the excitement of the moment, it escaped notice that many (if not most) of the communes had been set up in haste, without much planning or preparation.

With Mao already engaged in a contest of egos with Nikita Khrushchev, the Chinese leader was eager to prove the superiority of China's newly discovered pathway to Communist perfection. To bolster China's claims that the people's communes would hasten the arrival of pure Communism, Mao gave his blessing to a new system of income distribution to pay China's communal farmers. Instead of receiving payment proportional to the work they performed, as in the past, commune members now would receive the bulk of their income based on the Communist distribution principle of "to each according to his need," that is "free supply."

In the new system, income entitlements were calculated for different demographic categories, for men, women, children and the elderly, on the basis of their average daily caloric requirements. At the conclusion of each harvest, 70 percent of the commune's distributable income would be handed out according to these entitlements, without regard to labor contribution. Only 30 percent was awarded on the basis of work actually performed.

To ensure that all remnants of capitalism were thoroughly eradicated in the new communes, the small private plots and domestic animals that individual families had been permitted to retain for their own private use under collectivization were now communized. And rural free markets, where peasants had traditionally sold or bartered their surplus produce, were summarily abolished. Across China, the "wind of Communism" was blowing with gale force.

To spur even greater increases in farm output, emulation contests were held throughout the countryside. First, the members of one commune would pledge to double their grain output at the next harvest. Then a neighboring commune would counter-pledge to raise their grain harvest by, say, 125 percent, and so on. Those communes that met or exceeded their pledges were awarded the honorary title of "Sputnik."

By August of 1958, Central Party leaders had become dizzy with success. Believing that food was abundant, they ratcheted up communal quotas for mandatory grain procurement by the state.

Local officials, who were painfully aware that many of the reports were grossly exaggerated, were nonetheless obligated to fulfill the new, higher quotas. Clearly reluctant to offend their superiors, they lied to them, inflating their harvest estimates while squeezing every last drop of grain out of the hapless peasants, who were forced to tighten their belts just to survive. The result was a national orgy of official exaggeration and unreality at the very top of the food chain, while at the bottom of the chain, hundreds of millions of peasants began to suffer shortages.

The engine driving this entire upward spiral of inflated expectations was Mao Zedong himself. By the late summer of 1958 Mao had gone all in in his competition with Khrushchev, in effect betting the house on the success of the Great Leap. Because of this, he could not countenance the loss of face that would accompany any acknowledgment of failure. Aware of the intensity of Mao's feelings, his lieutenants dared not question his judgment or dampen his enthusiasm.

Meeting in August of 1958 at the seaside resort of Beidaihe, not far from Beijing, Chinese leaders basked in their ostensible success. China's 1958 grain harvest had, it was estimated, exceeded 450 million tons, surpassing even the United States. And party leaders were told that the country could produce as much rice as it wanted to. Mao even went on record as suggesting that everyone should eat not three meals a day, but five.

By summer's end, the party's propagandists were proclaiming unprecedented breakthroughs in every realm of human endeavor from steelmaking and gain production to medical science and even athletic competition. On the ground in the provinces, however, the gap between rhetoric and reality was becoming painfully apparent. Although the initial crop harvest in the summer of 1958 was, in fact, larger than average, a number of serious problems had begun to emerge.

When the first heavy summer rains fell in 1958, many of the dams, canals, dikes, and reservoirs constructed in the previous winter began to fail, causing inundation of hundreds of thousands of acres of cropland. Of the 500 largest reservoirs under construction in the winter of 1957–58, more than 200 were abandoned within two years.

Nor did the Great Leap's water conservation failures end there. In 1975 a huge dam built in 1958 in Henan Province during the height of the Leap collapsed, causing an estimated 200,000 deaths—the largest single dam disaster in human history.

The main causes of failure were inadequate engineering know-how and the routine use of substandard construction materials. The Maoist emphasis on mass mobilization over careful planning, on ideological "redness" over technical expertise, had created not miracles, but vast misfortune.

The 1958 experiment with close planting and deep plowing also proved a failure. Rice seedlings, it turned out, could not be successfully transplanted at a depth of more than 10 inches. It tended to kill the delicate seedlings. And doubling the application of fertilizer per acre tended to burn the young seedlings, rather than nourish them.

It was later revealed that the famous *People's Daily* photo that showed children playing on a thick bed of close-planted rice had been faked by local cadres for the benefit of visiting party dignitaries.

The backyard steel furnaces were the next to fail. Although large amounts of scrap metal were successfully melted down and forged into crude steel, the resulting products were unusable. The steel's composition was not standardized, its smelting temperatures varied widely, its chemical alloys were impure, and its tensile strength was so poor that it tended to crack under stress. Once again, the ascendancy of "red" ideology over "expert" planning and engineering had led to failure.

To make matters worse, in the obsessive drive to keep the backyard furnaces firing 24/7, the reckless denuding of forests and underbrush from rural hillsides created a severe shortage of fuel for cooking and heating, as well as a massive problem of soil erosion. The effects of these environmental disasters are still being felt in rural China today, some 50 years later.

The systematic elimination of grain-devouring sparrows was also of dubious value. Though millions of sparrows were killed, it turns out that the tiny birds devoured their weight in insects. Without sparrows to control the insect population, crop damage was even greater than before.

On top of all this, the much-vaunted "free supply" system introduced in the people's communes also turned out to be a failure. With 70 percent of a commune's income distributed to members without regard for work performed, the free-rider problem worsened considerably.

The communes were so large, and so impersonal, that it was virtually impossible to monitor individual work performance, let alone to punish those who failed to pull their weight. Under such circumstances, the incentive to work diligently was further diluted. Field management was done carelessly, planting was haphazard, and mature grain was left to rot in the fields.

The combination of deeply flawed technical innovations, diminished incentives to work hard, and a false sense of economic abundance and personal entitlement added up to a recipe for catastrophe. With Mao still basking in his late-summer euphoria, urging people to eat five meals a day, communal granaries in the autumn began to run dangerously low, and meals served in communal kitchens became plainer, sparser, and less appetizing. As one peasant recalled, "At first an individual got 18 ounces of food a day, but later there was so little grain in our store[house] that they reduced it to nine ounces. With that you couldn't even make steamed buns, so they made a soup, a kind of gruel." (J. Becker, *Hungry Ghosts*, p 172)

Complaints began to pour into newspapers around the country, bemoaning the poor quality of communal food and the careless indifference of communal cooks. Rice stalks, wheat chaff, and pieces of corn husk now found their way into communal meals with increasing regularity. And the gruel got thinner and thinner.

By the end of the year, the bubble of irrational exuberance had begun to burst. Crop yields in the second half of 1958 were much lower than in the first half. And the adverse effects of the wasteful backyard steel campaign and the ill-advised free supply system were beginning to be felt.

Yet quotas for compulsory grain delivery to the state remained unrealistically high. When peasants complained that they couldn't meet their inflated grain quotas, Mao accused them of "hoarding and dividing" surplus grain among themselves. And he ordered rural cadres to search their homes and seize the grain.

Caught uncomfortably between the demands of their superiors and the frantic pleas of the commune members, local cadres did as they were told. In many areas, they hired thugs to search peasants' homes for concealed grain, beating up anyone who resisted. In a number of cases, sympathetic rural cadres committed suicide rather than comply with such inhumane orders.

By the winter of 1959, the Party Central Committee—and even Mao himself—recognized that something had gone seriously wrong. At a meeting in late February, Mao grudgingly acknowledged that leftist excesses had created problems. He now ordered a reduction in compulsory steel and grain quotas and a readjustment of the free supply system to strengthen work incentives in the people's communes.

Although Mao gave ground on some of the particulars of the Great Leap, he was too stubborn to acknowledge failure—especially to Nikita Khrushchev. And so, even as the grain supply situation became progressively worse, Mao unilaterally stepped-up China's exports of grain to the Soviet Union in repayment of Stalin's 1949 loan.

In the face of a growing crisis, a few of Mao's lieutenants began to question the inflated claims of success. Previously afraid to speak out for fear of offending the chairman, they now began to raise their voices in dissent. And in the summer of 1959 their newfound courage presented Mao Zedong with the single biggest challenge of his career to date.

Next time, Defense Minister Peng Dehuai confronts Chairman Mao.

Demise of the Great Leap Forward, 1959–1962
Lecture 19

> Grain scattered on the ground.
> Potato leaves withered.
> Strong young people have gone off to make steel.
> Only children and old women harvest the crops.
> How can they pass the coming year?
> Allow me to raise my voice for the people.

> —Poem composed by Peng Dehuai on the eve of his meeting
> Mao Zedong about the failure of the Great Leap Forward

The bubble of unreality that enveloped China during the Great Leap Forward caused a number of senior party leaders to question the wisdom of the entire enterprise. As reports of peasant hunger and malnutrition began to filter up to Beijing from the provinces, a few bold souls dared to speak out. The most fearless of these was China's plain-speaking minister of national defense, **Peng Dehuai**.

In truth, people were beginning to starve in large numbers.

Hearing reports of severe rural hardship, Peng made an inspection tour of people's communes in a number of provinces in the late fall and winter of 1958. He was dismayed to find that conditions on the ground did not resemble the idyllic portrait being painted in the party's media. He discovered widespread malnutrition, cadres beating exhausted peasants, poorly run communal dining halls, and backyard furnaces squandering resources.

At a Central Committee meeting in the summer of 1959, Peng sent Mao Zedong a five-page "letter of opinion" detailing the findings from his inspection tour. He noted that the "habit of exaggeration" had spread throughout the country in the summer of 1958 and that "tremendous harm" had been done when reports of "unbelievable miracles" were published in the party press. People had become "dizzy with success," he said, believing that "communism was [just] around the corner." He went on to note that despite the masses' initial enthusiasm for the people's communes, many communal dining halls had been poorly run; the backyard steel furnaces had "squandered material and financial resources"; and in general, the Great Leap had been launched hastily, without a "plan for achieving necessary balance."

Mao devised a two-pronged strategy to isolate his Defense Minister. First, he circulated Peng's letter of opinion to everyone present, to test their loyalty to his leadership. Next, he convened a full plenary session of the conference, in

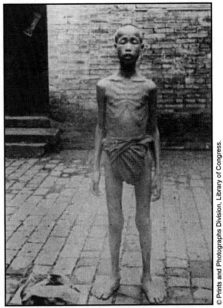

Malnourished boy. China's Great Leap Forward led to widespread famine and 30 million deaths.

which he threatened those who dared "waver at this crucial point in time." Peng, famous for his short temper, erupted in anger, and the two had a heated exchange that ended in shouting and profanity. At Mao's initiative, Peng and his small inner circle of supporters were officially charged with having formed an "anti-party clique" and were subjected to varying degrees of punishment. Peng was stripped of his post as defense minister and placed under house arrest in Beijing.

With opposing voices thus silenced, in the last half of 1959 the "leftist wind" picked up new momentum and cadres at all levels once again displayed exaggerated support for the Great Leap. Throughout the country, grain procurement targets were ratcheted upward yet again. Forced to surrender more and more of their meager harvest to the state, peasants became desperate; meanwhile, local cadres became more coercive than ever in their efforts to meet grain delivery quotas. Although the regime announced record new increases in grain production in 1959, the harvest had actually dropped by 30 million tons from the previous year. Yet in the face of growing food shortages, Mao insisted that the problem was not declining grain production, but willful sabotage.

In truth, people were beginning to starve in large numbers. In the summer of 1959, one top party official conceded that 25 million people were suffering from severe malnutrition. By the end of the year, peasants in many provinces had been reduced to eating the bark off trees. When children died, parents hid their bodies, not reporting the deaths, so that they could continue to get the child's meager food ration. In a few of China's poorest provinces, instances of cannibalism were documented.

In late 1960, Mao retreated to the "second line" of leadership, allowing his top lieutenants, Liu Shaoqi and Deng Xiaoping, to mitigate the damage done by the Great Leap. They divided the communes into smaller units and eliminated the free supply system. They also ended the backyard steel program and reintroduced family ownership of small garden plots and domestic animals. Rural free markets were permitted to reopen, and families were encouraged to supplement their income with sideline occupations. By 1962, China saw the first signs of economic recovery. ∎

Names to Know

Kang Sheng (1898–1975): The sinister head of Mao Zedong's internal security and intelligence apparatus, Kang gained influence by compiling confidential dossiers on thousands of party officials from the 1930s to the 1970s.

Peng Dehuai (1898–1974): An outspoken PLA general and China's defense minister, Peng was purged by Mao Zedong in 1959 for criticizing the Great Leap Forward.

Suggested Reading

Chang and Halliday, *Mao.*

Fenby, *Modern China.*

Lecture 19: Demise of the Great Leap Forward, 1959–1962

Friedman, Pickowicz, and Selden, *Revolution, Resistance, and Reform in Village China.*

Li, *The Private Life of Chairman Mao.*

MacFarquhar, *The Origins of the Cultural Revolution,* vol. 2.

Schram, *The Political Thought of Mao Tse-tung.*

Short, *Mao.*

Zheng, *Scarlet Memorial.*

Questions to Consider

1. Why is the "Peng Dehuai affair" regarded as a turning point in CCP history?

2. How did Mao's lieutenants manage to bypass him in their efforts to mitigate the damage done by the Great Leap Forward?

Demise of the Great Leap Forward, 1959–1962
Lecture 19—Transcript

The bubble of unreality that enveloped China during the Great Leap Forward caused a number of senior party leaders to question the wisdom of the entire enterprise. As reports of peasant malnutrition began filtering up to Beijing from the provinces, a few bold souls dared to speak out. The most fearless of these was China's plain-spoken Minister of National Defense, Peng Dehuai.

Peng was a war hero. He had been the commander-in-chief of Chinese forces in the Korean War. Born into a poor peasant family, he had known famine in his own childhood. Two of his siblings had starved to death. With little formal education, Peng Dehuai was widely respected as an able, candid and forthright leader who stood up for what he believed in. He had crossed swords with Mao on more than one occasion in the past, and he was not afraid to challenge the chairman.

Hearing reports of severe rural hardship, Peng made an inspection tour of people's communes in several provinces in the late fall and winter of 1958. He was dismayed to find that conditions on the ground did not resemble the idyllic portrait being painted in the party's own media. Revisiting his own native village in Hunan Province, Peng observed the deteriorating economic conditions at first hand. Peasants were being worked to the point of collapse. Cadres were beating people who failed to fulfill their grain quotas. Many women had stopped menstruating prematurely as a result of overwork and undernourishment.

Responding to this, Peng Dehuai sent an urgent cable to Mao Zedong in Beijing, requesting that Mao further reduce grain quotas and predicting a massive famine if something were not done to ease the plight of the peasants.

After receiving Peng's cable, Mao visited his own home town of Shaoshan, also in Hunan Province—his first such home visit in more than three decades. Conditions there were bleak, but the local peasants were so in awe of Mao—and so intimidated by their local cadres, who were eager to please the chairman—that they did little other than genuflect to the brilliance and authority of the chairman. When Mao asked if the communes were popular with the masses, they responded enthusiastically. Only one brave soul mustered the courage to "speak truth to power": "If you hadn't come to Shaoshan," he said, "we would all have starved to death."

Mao responded to this poignant revelation in cavalier fashion, suggesting that people should "be more thrifty with [their] food." They should eat less in the winter, he advised, and a bit more in the spring and fall. Though Mao kept his irritation at Peng Dehuai locked within himself, his behavior in 1959 became increasingly erratic and bizarrely erotic as well. Long known as a promiscuous womanizer, Mao greatly enjoyed the company of pretty young peasant girls. At the chairman's behest, a private lounge, complete with oversized bed, was built adjacent to the main dance-floor in the Communist Party's leadership compound in Zhongnanhai, in central Beijing.

At Saturday night dance parties throughout the spring and summer of 1959, Mao, now in his mid-60s, would take teenage girls—often three or four at a time—into his private lounge for sexual orgies. According to his personal physician, Li Zhisui the chairman seldom bathed or brushed his teeth, and he emitted a rather foul odor. But Mao never permitted himself to reach a climax. Like many Chinese emperors before him, he feared that it would diminish his potency. Evidently, Mao's sexual appetite was greatest when he was under the most intense political stress. By the early summer of 1959, the stress had been building steadily, and a confrontation between Mao and his outspoken defense minister seemed increasingly likely.

The setting for their epic showdown was Mt. Lushan, a famously scenic mountain resort in Jiangxi Province, near a picturesque bend in the Yangzi River. There, for six weeks in July and early August of 1959, Mao presided over a working conference attended by 100 top party and state officials, including Peng Dehuai. Peng initially tried to beg off from attending the meeting on grounds of fatigue. But a personal phone call from Mao persuaded him to attend. On the eve of the meeting, Peng composed a poem in the classical style of Peking opera verse. In it, he revealed his profound dissatisfaction with Mao's Great Leap Forward:

> Grain scattered on the ground.
> Potato leaves withered.
> Strong young people have gone off to make steel.
> Only women and children harvest the crops.
> How can they pass the coming year?
> Allow me to raise my voice for the people.
> (J. Domes, *Peng Dehuai*, p. 93)

When the party's leadership conference began at Lushan on July 2nd, Mao divided up the participants into six regional groups. Peng Dehuai was assigned to the Northwest group. In the first few group meetings, Peng voiced his concerns over falsified grain statistics and bemoaned the fact that China was continuing to export grain into Russia despite the famine.

But his colleagues were uneasy, reluctant to join in his criticism, afraid to challenge Mao's judgment and authority. Instead, they heaped ritualistic praise on the Great Leap and dutifully noted the masses' "great enthusiasm" for the people's communes.

Peng was growing alarmed. Surely his comrades knew that something was greatly amiss in the countryside. But none were willing to express their doubts on the record.

Now he changed his tack. Acutely aware that his base of support was dwindling to practically nothing, Peng decided to present his contrarian views directly to Mao. On July 14 he sent the chairman a five-page handwritten "letter of opinion," detailing the findings from his recent provincial inspection tour.

Deferring at the outset of his letter to Mao's superior wisdom, Peng Dehuai took great pains to reassure the chairman that the Great Leap was a "great achievement," and that it had brought "more gains than losses." Choosing his words carefully, he skirted around the issue of malnutrition, never using the words "famine" or "hunger."

(Now here it should be noted that the habit of using humble, self-deprecating language when addressing the emperor had been cultivated by imperial Chinese court officials over many centuries. Recall, for example, the Imperial Grand Secretary Wo-ren's reference to himself as "your unworthy slave" in his memorial to the emperor opposing the Self-Strengthening movement of Prince Gong in the 1870s. And a bit later on we'll see that the Tiananmen student demonstrators of 1989 adopted a similar tactic of ritualized imperial genuflection on at least one occasion prior to the bloody crackdown of June 3, 1989.)

In any event, After Peng Dehuai completed his obligatory verbal kowtow to the emperor, he got down to the point. He noted that the "habit of exaggeration" had spread throughout the country in the summer of 1958 and that "tremendous harm" had been done when reports of "unbelievable miracles" were published in the party press. People had become "dizzy with success," he said, believing that "communism was [just] around the corner."

This, in turn, led officials throughout China to engage in even more gross exaggerations of their production claims, which in turn led to the ratcheting further upward of compulsory grain quotas. "We considered ourselves rich," said Peng, "while actually we were still poor. ... For a long time," he said, "it was not easy to get a true picture of the situation."

Peng Dehuai went on to note that despite the masses' initial enthusiasm for the people's communes, many communal dining halls had been poorly run; the backyard steel furnaces had "squandered material and financial resources"; and in general, the Great Leap had been launched hastily, without a "plan for achieving necessary balance."

Peng's conclusion was that the wave of "leftist tendencies" that had accompanied the implementation of the Great Leap had "caused considerable damage to the socialist cause."

Although Peng Dehuai concluded his "letter of opinion" with the obligatory acknowledgment of Mao's brilliance in blazing a path filled with "great achievements" en route to a "bright future," there could be no denying the deeply critical message that he had conveyed to the chairman.

Alert to the potential danger posed by Peng Dehuai's "sugar-coated" challenge, Mao devised a two-pronged strategy to isolate his defense minister. First, he set out to test the loyalty of each person in attendance at the Lushan conference.

To accomplish this, Mao personally circulated Peng's letter of opinion to everyone present. By gauging their reactions, he could see who was steadfastly in support of Mao's leadership and who was not.

Sensing what Mao was up to, Peng urgently requested to have all copies of his letter retrieved, claiming that it was a private missive intended for Mao's eyes only. The request was denied.

Next, to prevent potential defectors from conspiring behind his back in small group meetings, Mao convened a full plenary session of the Lushan conference. Speaking to the assembled party leaders on July 23, he addressed head-on the question of rising dissatisfaction with the Great Leap.

By turns humble, rambling, introspective, egotistical, sarcastic, and downright intimidating, Mao confronted his chief critic, Peng Dehuai:

> Now that you've said so much, [the chairman began,] let me say something. ... People say we've become isolated from the masses, but the masses still support us. ... [Some comrades] are wavering. ... They [pay lip service], affirming that the Great Leap and the people's communes are good and correct. ... But we must see on whose side they [really] stand. I would advise them not to waver at this crucial point in time. [Their] brinksmanship is rather dangerous. If you don't believe me, [just] wait and see what happens.

Having said this, Mao paused for effect. Casting his gaze in the general direction of a group of top PLA generals seated in the conference hall, he laid down the gauntlet: "If the People's Liberation Army won't follow me," he said, "then I will go down to the countryside, reorganize the Red Army guerrillas, and organize another People's Liberation Army."

Pausing yet again for effect, he continued: "But I think the Army will follow me." At that point, several Chinese generals stood up and shouted their pledges of allegiance to Mao.

When Mao finished speaking, Peng Dehuai's famously short temper erupted. He accused Mao of despotism, comparing him to Stalin in his later years; and he warned that "if the Chinese peasants were not so patient, we'd have another Hungary [on our hands]."

The gloves were off, and Mao now responded in kind, accusing Peng of being a rightist, of sabotaging the people's democratic dictatorship, and of attempting to organize an opposition faction within the Communist Party.

Things turned even uglier when Mao attempted to cut short the defense minister's retort, at which point Peng angrily reminded the chairman of a quarrel they had had two decades earlier, during the anti-Japanese War: "In Yan'an," shouted Peng, "you [messed with] my mother for 40 days. Now, I've been [messing with] your mother for only 18 days, yet you want to call a halt—but you won't [get away with it]." Actually, he didn't say "messed with:" There was a much cruder peasant word that he used. He then stalked out of the room. (Salisbury, *The New Emperors*, p. 184; Schram, loc. cit)

The defense minister had overplayed his hand. Several key leaders who had initially been inclined to endorse his criticism of the Great Leap, including such senior figures as Zhou Enlai, Liu Shaoqi and Marshal Zhu De, now backed off, intimidated by the chairman's display of full-bore combativeness. Mao had won.

Leaving the conference hall after his confrontation with Peng, Mao bumped into the still-fuming defense minister. "Let's have another talk," suggested the chairman. "There's nothing more to talk about," replied the war hero. "No more talk."

In the days that followed, no one ventured to speak out in Peng Dehuai's defense. At Mao's initiative, Peng and his small inner circle of supporters, including the PLA chief of staff, a deputy foreign minister, and Mao's own longtime political secretary, were officially charged with having formed an "anti-party clique," and they were subjected to varying degrees of punishment. Peng himself was stripped of his post as defense minister and placed under house arrest in Beijing.

The lessons of Peng Dehuai's abject defeat at the hands of Mao were not lost on anyone in the party's leadership circle: First, it was clearly safer to err on the side of leftism than on the side of rightism. And second, despite Mao's open invitation to his colleagues to "speak out" freely and openly, challenging the chairman could be extremely hazardous to one's political health. As a senior Chinese diplomat put it, "After Lushan the whole party shut up. We were all afraid to speak out."

One big reason that Mao was able to intimidate his critics so consistently and so effectively—aside from his famous mercurial temper and iron will—was his chief of internal security, Kang Sheng. Ever since the mid-1930s, Kang Sheng had been entrusted by Mao with the task of compiling secret dossiers on all party leaders at or above the provincial level.

Knowing that such career-damaging "black materials" existed, and that Mao would not hesitate to use them to destroy his colleagues, was a huge deterrent to would-be critics. In this respect, Kang Sheng was Mao's chief enabler, in much the same way that Lavrentiy Beria had been Joseph Stalin's principal enabler. Without such loyal and utterly ruthless security chiefs, both Stalin and Mao might not have enjoyed such apparent invincibility.

With opposing voices thus silenced, in the last half of 1959 the leftist wind picked up new momentum. Since it was now politically risky (if not downright suicidal) to oppose rash advances, cadres at all levels once again displayed exaggerated support for the Great Leap.

Throughout the country, grain procurement targets were ratcheted upward yet again. Sputnik competitions once again yielded absurd claims of unprecedented crop yields. And communal kitchens were ordered to reopen after having been shut down in the spring.

Forced to surrender more and more of their meager harvest to the state, peasants became desperate. Meanwhile, local cadres became even more coercive than ever in their efforts to meet grain delivery quotas. In the search for concealed food, many peasants were tortured and beaten to death. Although the regime announced record new increases in grain production in 1959, the reality was that the harvest had actually dropped by 30 million tons, almost 15 percent of the total, from the previous year. Yet in the face of growing food shortages, Mao insisted that the problem was not declining grain production but willful sabotage.

According to the chairman, rich peasants were undermining the people's communes by burying their food supplies deep underground, eating only thin gruel and turnips during the day, when officials were inspecting the villages, while feasting on their hidden treasures at night. In truth, people were beginning to starve in large numbers. In the summer of 1959, one top party official, Bo Yibo, conceded that 25 million people were suffering from severe malnutrition. By the end of the year, peasants in many provinces had been reduced to eating the bark off the trees.

Large numbers of people were suffering from scurvy, while the stomachs of malnourished men, women, and children became grotesquely distended. When children died, parents hid their bodies, not reporting the deaths, so that they could continue to get the child's meager food rations. In a few of China's poorest provinces, instances of cannibalism were documented. Here is one firsthand report from Anhui Province. It is not for the squeamish:

> The worst thing that happened during the famine was … that parents had to decide [who] would be allowed to die first. They … could not afford to let their sons die, but a mother would say to her daughter, "You have to go and see your granny in heaven." Then they stopped giving the girl food, just giving her water.
>
> [When the girls died] the families would swap the body of their daughter for that of a neighbor. Five or seven women would agree to do this among themselves. Then they would boil the corpses into a kind of soup. [They] had learned to do this during the famine of the 1930s. [And they] accepted it as a kind of "hunger culture." (Becker, *Hungry Ghosts*, p. 138)

And still Mao refused to change course. He had silenced his critics, but in the process he had also shut down the regime's most vital feedback mechanisms—debate and criticism—which were now needed more than ever to prevent an arrogant, willful dictator from indulging his utopian fantasies. To distract himself from his troubles, Mao now spent more and more time with comely young peasant girls at his Saturday night dance meetings in Zhongnanhai.

But such distractions could not alter the basic situation, which turned even worse the following year. By 1960 there was nothing left to buffer the long-suffering peasants from debilitating disease and agonizing death. By the end of that year, people in some places had been reduced to eating clay soil in the hope of filling their empty bellies. By the spring of 1961, more than 30 million Chinese had died of malnutrition and related diseases. Here is a description from a peasant woman in Anhui Province:

> All the trees inside the village had been cut down. And nearby trees were all stripped of their bark. I peeled off the bark of a locust tree and cooked it as if it were rice soup. ...

> More than half the villagers died ... between New Year and April [of 1960]. ... When people died, no one collected the bodies. The corpses did not change color or decay because there was no blood in them, and not much flesh. (ibid., pp. 136–137)

No longer able to deny reality, Mao made a symbolic display of empathy with the hard-pressed peasants. He announced that he would temporarily stop eating meat.

But he continued to insist that the difficulties were only temporary, and that they were the product not of his own wrongheaded policies, but of rich peasant sabotage and three consecutive years of bad weather and catastrophic natural disasters. Yet through it all, in the face of severe famine, Mao callously continued to export millions of tons of Chinese "blood grain" to the Soviet Union.

Although Mao's colleagues dared not oppose his policies, they knew that unless things changed soon, there was a very real danger of regime collapse. And so they quietly began taking matters into their own hands.

In late 1960 and 1961, Mao's second in command, party Vice Chairman Liu Shaoqi, joined with Deng Xiaoping and others to address the most egregious causes of the famine. Even Zhou Enlai, who had never openly opposed Mao, and never would, was sympathetic (In this connection, it has been reported that Kang Sheng had a great deal of "black material" on Zhou Enlai, which may explain Zhou's well-known aversion to crossing swords with Mao).

In any event, after the Lushan Plenum, Mao "voluntarily" retreated to the second line of party policymaking; and he allowed Liu Shaoqi and Deng Xiaoping to try to rescue China's devastated rural economy.

Over the next two years, Liu and Deng adopted a number of emergency reform measures. First, they drastically reduced the size of the people's communes, dividing each one into roughly three smaller-sized units. To strengthen local production responsibility and to overcome the endemic free-rider problem, they restored the accounting functions of the pre-1958 collective farms (which were now called "production brigades"), so that peasants from each village would be held responsible for their own production results, including both profits and losses, rather than simply folding these into the commune's general accounts as before.

When the incentive effects of this partial decentralization of accounting and income distribution proved insufficiently motivating, Liu and Deng went even further. In 1961 they shifted ultimate responsibility for income, profits, and losses down to the level of the old co-operative farms (which were now called "production teams"), consisting of just 20 to 30 families.

To generate additional food and income for hungry peasants, Liu and Deng also restored to individual families the right to own small private plots of land and small domestic animals, which had been confiscated when the communes were first formed in 1958. They also permitted families to engage in private sideline occupations (such as brick-making or tool repair) to supplement their meager agricultural income. And to spur local commerce, they reopened rural free markets, which had been shut down as "remnants of capitalism" in 1958.

By 1962, Liu and Deng had strengthened material incentives even further, by "contracting production to individual households." Under this system, each family was allocated a piece of village land to cultivate for itself. After delivering a fixed quota of compulsory grain to the state, each family was free to consume or sell or trade the remainder of their output, as it saw fit. Under this policy, there would be no more free riding on the collective, since each family was fully responsible for its own success or failure, profit or loss.

By 1962, the reform policies of Liu Shaoqi and Deng Xiaoping had brought about the first clear signs of an economic recovery. The worst of the famine was over, and throughout the countryside, hundreds of millions of peasant survivors began to pick up the pieces of their shattered lives. But for the Communist Party, the job of restoring its badly damaged reputation and credibility had just begun.

"Never Forget Class Struggle!" 1962–1965
Lecture 20

> It doesn't matter if a cat is white or black, so long as it catches mice.
> — Deng Xiaoping, in 1962, defending the shift to a more pragmatic,
> rather than ideological, approach to economic development

In the early 1960s, Liu Shaoqi and Deng Xiaoping began restoring the Communist Party's traditional top-down, bureaucratic decision-making procedures. Liu and Deng favored careful planning, centralized leadership, and cautious advance over spontaneous mass mobilization. They also quietly rehabilitated thousands of party members who had been wrongfully persecuted during the Anti-Rightist Rectification. Finally, reversing Mao Zedong's preference for ideological "redness" over technical expertise, they invited China's much-maligned intellectuals to once again contribute their ideas and talents to China's economic construction—this time without fear of reprisal. Defending these pragmatic policy changes in 1962, Deng explained the shift to a more practical, scientific approach to economic development by famously stating, "It doesn't matter if a cat is white or black, so long as it catches mice."

In the early 1960s, Mao's anger at top lieutenants Liu and Deng was increasing. Mao's contempt for Nikita Khrushchev had been building since 1959, when the Soviet leader openly pursued détente with the United States, repudiated Lenin's theory of inevitable war, and reneged on his pledge to provide China with a prototype of an atomic bomb. By 1962, Mao's wrath at Khrushchev had begun to converge with—and spill over onto—his growing distrust of Liu and Deng. (Mao would later confirm this convergence when he scathingly referred to Liu as "China's Khrushchev.")

Lumping Liu and Deng together with Khrushchev, Mao in 1962 launched a blistering attack on "creeping revisionism" and demanded an intensified class struggle to prevent the restoration of capitalism at home and abroad. At the Central Committee's Tenth Plenary Session, he unveiled a new rural mass campaign of ideological education and indoctrination called the

Socialist Education movement. Its goal was to immunize peasants against Soviet-style revisionism.

But Liu and Deng had a very different view of what was wrong with China and how to fix it. In their view, the failures of the Great Leap had created not an urgent need for renewed class vigilance, but rather widespread desperation, demoralization, and an epidemic of petty corruption. Responding to conditions of extreme hardship, those rural dwellers with tradable resources—such as money, official position, and control over collective assets—had utilized these assets to secure their own advantage. In the lax atmosphere that enveloped the countryside in the wake of the Great Famine, even gambling and prostitution—which had been stamped out in the early 1950s—reappeared in rural China.

By the end of 1964, Mao had lost patience with Liu and Deng. At a party work conference in December, he angrily confronted Liu, accusing him of undermining the Socialist Education movement by altering both its goals and its means. In January of 1965, Mao expressed his displeasure in a Central Committee directive that made the unprecedented allegation that the central aim of the Socialist Education movement was "to rectify powerholders within the [Chinese Communist] Party who take the **capitalist road**." While no individual party leaders were singled out as "capitalist roaders," viewed in the context of his rising irritation with his top lieutenants, there could be little doubt that the chairman's primary target was his second-in-command and heir apparent, Liu. ∎

Important Terms

capitalist road: Mao Zedong's mid-1960s allegation that many of his comrades were ignoring class struggle and following a "revisionist" path, leading to a restoration of capitalism in China.

Socialist Education movement (a.k.a. **Four Cleanups movement**; 1962–1965): Mao Zedong's attempt to launch a mass campaign to inoculate peasants, workers, and cadres against class enemies seeking a "capitalist restoration."

Suggested Reading

Baum, *Prelude to Revolution.*

Chang and Halliday, *Mao.*

Fenby, *Modern China.*

Friedman, Pickowicz, and Selden, *Revolution, Resistance, and Reform in Village China.*

Gittings, *The Changing Face of China.*

Li, *The Private Life of Chairman Mao.*

MacFarquhar, *The Origins of the Cultural Revolution,* vol. 3.

Schram, *The Political Thought of Mao Tse-tung.*

Shambaugh, *Deng Xiaoping.*

Short, *Mao.*

Questions to Consider

1. Why did Mao Zedong object so strenuously to the dismantling of his radical policies in the early 1960s?

2. How did Mao express his unhappiness?

"Never Forget Class Struggle!" 1962–1965
Lecture 20—Transcript

In the early 1960s, Mao watched with growing discomfort as Liu Shaoqi and Deng Xiaoping dismantled his cherished Great Leap Forward—brick by brick, backyard steel furnace by backyard steel furnace, communal dining hall by communal dining hall. Though they paid lip-service to the chairman's "wise" policies and leadership, in practice they increasingly ignored him.

Later, Mao would complain that throughout the early 1960s, Liu and Deng "treated me like a dead ancestor at a funeral. ... [They] never came to consult me."

In this lecture we'll examine Mao's rising anger at his top lieutenants. We'll see how the chairman increasingly identified their post-Great Leap reforms with the heretical policies of Nikita Khrushchev. Lumping Liu and Deng together with Khrushchev, Mao launched a blistering attack on "modern revisionism" and he demanded an intensified class struggle to prevent the restoration of capitalism at home and abroad. In doing so, he set off a series of profound shock waves that would erupt a few years later into China's tumultuous Cultural Revolution.

Not only did Liu Shaoqi and Deng Xiaoping reverse the prevailing leftist tendencies within the people's communes, they also poured cold water on Mao's cherished technique of using mass campaigns to generate radical social change. Favoring careful planning, centralized leadership, and cautious advance over spontaneous mass mobilization and frenetic people's wars against nature, Liu and Deng restored the Communist Party's traditional top-down, bureaucratic style of decision-making.

But they went even further than that. They quietly rehabilitated thousands of party members who had been wrongfully persecuted during Mao's Anti-Rightist Rectification campaign of 1957–1958. And finally, reversing Mao's well-known preference for ideological "redness" over technical "expertise," they invited China's much-maligned intellectuals to once again contribute their ideas and talents to China's economic construction—this time, without fear of reprisal.

Defending these pragmatic policy changes in 1962, Deng Xiaoping explained the shift to a more practical, scientific, and results-oriented approach to economic development by famously invoking a feline metaphor: "It doesn't matter if a cat is white or black," he said, "so long as it catches mice."

But if Deng was thus indifferent to the color of the economic cat, Chairman Mao decidedly was not. As he watched Deng and Liu reversing his policies, Mao grew increasingly incensed at their evident lack of concern for ideology, and their indifference to considerations of class conflict. As one of Mao's key supporters would put it a few years later, using a different metaphor, the chairman believed that "It is better to have a socialist train running late than a capitalist train running on time." Better, in other words, to be poor than to be bourgeois.

In January of 1962 Mao began to fight back. At a work conference attended by 7,000 party cadres—the largest such convocation in party history— he delivered a lengthy speech in which he bemoaned the lack of mass mobilization and the emphasis on bureaucratic procedure that had come to dominate the party's work style since the Great Leap.

Employing his patented, indirect style of attack, Mao alleged that "certain comrades"—a favorite generic target of his—"are afraid of the masses ... [they are] afraid that the masses' views ... will differ from those of the leading organizations. ... They [even] suppress the masses. ... This attitude is extremely evil."

Harping on a theme that he had first raised when he abruptly cancelled the Hundred Flowers Movement in 1957, Mao spoke of the continued existence of class struggle in the ideological field: "The reactionary classes which have been overthrown," he said, "are still planning a comeback." And then he added a brand new warning: "In socialist society, new bourgeois elements may still be produced ... There are some people who adopt the guise of Communist Party members, but they in no way represent the proletariat— instead they represent the bourgeoisie. Our party is not pure."

At the conclusion of the working conference, Liu Shaoqi gave his own view of the situation. The remarks he had prepared for the occasion were moderate and conciliatory in tone, and had been circulated in advance to members of the Politburo for comments and suggestions.

But after hearing Mao's speech Liu hastily revised his remarks. And when he delivered his speech it took Mao—and everyone else at the meeting—by surprise. In it, Liu Shaoqi attacked the policies of the Great Leap Forward. Using language even stronger than that used by Peng Dehuai two-and-a-half years earlier, he candidly charged that "People do not have enough food, clothes, or other essentials." And he acknowledged that "Agricultural output, far from having risen in 1959, '60, and '61, dropped tremendously. ... Not only," he said, "was there no Leap Forward, but [there was] a great deal of falling backward."

Rejecting Mao's explanation that the failures of the Great Leap were due mainly to bad weather and natural calamities and the activities of rich peasants, Liu stated that as far as he was aware, in most rural areas there had been no serious bad weather from 1959 to 1961. And then he went on to assert that the many difficulties encountered during those years were 70 percent due to human error and only 30 percent due to natural causes—a precise reversal of Mao's own assessment, which was 70 percent due to natural causes and 30 percent to human error.

Liu further rejected Mao's claim that with respect to the Great Leap Forward as a whole, out of 10 fingers, "mistakes are only one finger, while achievements are nine fingers." When Mao interrupted him to insist that the achievements were genuine, Liu stood by his statement.

According to participants at the meeting, Mao had been caught completely off guard by the tone and content of Liu's remarks. To minimize the damage to his own prestige, Mao immediately ordered his new defense minister, the sycophantic General Lin Biao, to give a speech defending the Great Leap.

Lin had replaced Peng Dehuai after the Lushan plenum; and he now proceeded to fawn obsequiously over Chairman Mao's wisdom and the brilliance of his leadership:

> In times of trouble, [Lin enthused,] we must rely even more on the ... leadership of Chairman Mao, and trust [his] leadership even more. ... Facts prove that [our] troubles spring precisely from our failure in many instances to act according to Chairman Mao's directives. ... In the past, whenever our work was done well, it was precisely [because] Chairman Mao's thought was not interfered with.

Sitting backstage while Lin delivered these remarks, Mao was pleased. "What a good speech," he remarked, addressing his personal physician, Dr. Li Zhisui, who was seated next to him. "Lin Biao's words ... are simply superb," he continued. "Why can't other party leaders be so perceptive?"

After Lin finished his effusive praise, Mao took the stage once again. Now feeling more relaxed and expansive, he issued an ostensibly contrite self-criticism in which, with evident humility, he asked his comrades to hold him personally responsible for any failings that might have occurred in the Great Leap.

But to many of those in attendance, Mao's confession did not ring true. It had a staged, theatrical quality to it; and his contrition seemed mainly designed to silence his critcs, to pre-empt them, rather than to accept personal blame for the horrific disasters of the previous three years.

Following the conclusion of this pivotal meeting, Mao viewed Liu Shaoqi, and by extension Deng Xiaoping, with barely disguised contempt. Previously, he had interpreted their efforts to rescue the Chinese economy from the leftist excesses of the Great Leap mainly as errors of judgment and policy but not as evidence of counterrevolutionary intent. Now, however, his doubts about Liu and Deng began to merge with his growing fears about the effects of Khrushchev's insidious counterrevolutionary revisionism.

By this time (early 1962), Mao's anger at Khrushchev was approaching the boiling point. A series of pointed Soviet barbs had deeply irritated the chairman. It wasn't bad enough that Khrushchev had belittled the people's communes, repudiated Lenin's doctrine of inevitable war, and proclaimed the existence of a parliamentary road to socialism. But the Soviet leader had also begun to seek détente with the head of the imperialist camp, the United States of America.

Khrushchev's reasoning in pursuing rapprochement with the United States was that in the age of nuclear weapons, world war would have no winners, only losers, and was thus unthinkable.

In Mao's view, however, nuclear war was not only thinkable, but it was also winnable. Referring to nuclear weapons as paper tigers, Mao challenged the Soviet leader to be more, rather than less, confrontational toward U.S. imperialism. Indeed, at the height of his Great Leap euphoria in 1958, Mao had boasted that "the East Wind prevails over the West Wind." And he had even boasted that in the event of a nuclear war, China could suffer 100 million casualties and still emerge victorious.

Khrushchev, on the other hand, was appalled by the radical excesses of the Great Leap and of Mao's rhetorical excesses as well. He was afraid that Mao might just be naïve or delusional enough to drag the Soviet Union willy-nilly into a nuclear war with America.

In 1959, he responded to Mao's reckless adventurism by reneging on his earlier promise to share Soviet nuclear secrets with China and to provide Mao with a sample atomic bomb. A year later, in 1960, he unilaterally withdrew all Soviet technical advisors from China, leaving hundreds of industrial projects half-finished. And for good measure, the Soviet advisors took all their blueprints with them when they left.

Mao's growing anger at Khrushchev was expressed in a series of nine "open letters" addressed to the Central Committee of the Soviet Communist Party. Written intermittently between 1960 and 1964, the nine letters clearly reflected Mao's view that Khrushchev was restoring capitalism in the Soviet Union. This restoration was, in Mao's view, marked by the emergence of a new class of bureaucratic elites, made up of party officials, government technocrats, and industrial intellectuals.

Comprising a new bourgeoisie, members of this elite class enjoyed high salaries, special housing and shopping privileges, access to the best schools for their children, and private summer homes, or *dachas*. Completely "divorced from the [laboring] masses," they had, in Mao's view, lost sight of the original goals of the Bolshevik Revolution. At their head marched Nikita Khrushchev, who was derisively labeled, in one of the latter nine CCP "open letters," as a "phony Communist."

By 1962 Mao's wrath at Khrushchev had begun to converge with and spill over onto his growing distrust of Liu Shaoqi and Deng Xiaoping. Later, Mao would confirm this convergence when he scathingly referred to Liu Shaoqi as "China's Khrushchev."

In September 1962 Mao launched a counter-offensive against creeping revisionism. At the Central Committee's tenth plenary session, he unveiled a new rural mass campaign of ideological education and indoctrination, which he called the "Socialist Education movement." Its goal was to inoculate China's peasants against the deadly virus of capitalism.

In the speech launching the new movement, Mao addressed the issue of continuing class struggle in China, making clear its link to Soviet revisionism:

> Do classes exist in socialist countries? [he asked rhetorically.] We can now affirm that classes do exist, and that class struggle undoubtedly exists. ... We must acknowledge this ... and admit the possibility of the restoration of the [overthrown] reactionary

classes. We must raise our vigilance and properly educate our youth and our cadres. ... Otherwise a country like ours may head in the opposite direction. ... From this moment on, we must talk about [class struggle] every year, every month, every day, at conferences, at party congresses ... and at each and every meeting.

As Mao envisioned it, the new Socialist Education movement would be mainly didactic in nature. Party-organized work teams would travel throughout the countryside conducting education in class struggle among the basic-level cadres and peasants, reminding them of the evils of the old landlord-dominated society, warning them against the pernicious machinations of rich peasants, and reinforcing the party's traditional ethos of serving the people.

The goal was to provide immunization against what Mao called "the sugar-coated bullets" of the bourgeoisie. Here is how he himself put it:

It has been proved that the enemy cannot conquer us by force of arms. However, the flattery of the bourgeoisie may conquer the weak-willed in our ranks. There may be some Communists ... who cannot withstand [such] sugar-coated bullets. ... We must guard against such a situation.

But Liu Shaoqi and Deng Xiaoping had a very different view of what was wrong with China and what was needed to be done to fix it. In their view, the failures of the Great Leap had created not an urgent need for more class vigilance and struggle, but rather, widespread desperation, demoralization, and an epidemic of petty corruption.

With tens of millions of peasants having starved to death, and hundreds of millions more suffering from varying degrees of malnutrition, by 1962 socialist morality had broken down badly, especially in the rural areas of the country.

Responding to conditions of extreme hardship, those rural dwellers with tradable resources, such as money, official position, or control over collective assets, had utilized these assets to secure their own advantage. In areas hard hit by famine, village cadres had routinely solicited bribes from peasants in exchange for allowing them, for example, to withhold grain from compulsory delivery to the state.

Sometimes the bribes were made in cash, sometimes in goods, sometimes in labor donations, and sometimes in female sexual favors. Often, bribes in the form of sex, or cigarettes, or other scarce commodities were widely offered to village cadres who tallied work points, or who dispensed fertilizer, or who weighed harvested grain, or dispensed job assignments. In addition, many rural cadres misappropriated collective funds, for example, using money earmarked for welfare payments to build private homes or to finance banquets or weddings.

In the lax, everyone-for-himself political atmosphere that enveloped the countryside in the latter stages of the Great Famine, even gambling and prostitution, which had been stamped out altogether in the early '50s, made their reappearance in rural China.

To Liu Shaoqi and Deng Xiaoping, the root cause of this rural moral decay was not counterrevolutionary sabotage by a few scheming rich peasants and class enemies, but wholesale organizational laxness and indiscipline within local party branches. Only when the party cleaned its own house could it restore its reputation for integrity and set a good example for the peasantry.

Unlike the populist Mao, who wanted to light a fire under the peasants to criticize capitalist tendencies from the bottom up, Liu and Deng were instinctive elitists. They believed in strict party discipline. For them the preferred method of rectifying corrupt rural cadres was to dispatch work teams to conduct investigations behind closed doors, away from the prying eyes and ears of the *laobaixing*.

By the end of 1964, Mao had clearly lost patience with Liu and Deng. At a party work conference in December of that year, he angrily confronted Liu, accusing him of undermining the Socialist Education movement by altering both its goals and its means. In Mao's view, corruption was not the main problem, capitalism was. And the solution was not closed-door investigations by elitist work teams but mass mobilization of the peasantry.

In January of 1965 Mao's displeasure was expressed in a Central Committee directive entitled "Some Problems Currently Arising in the … Socialist Education Movement." In this important document, Mao made the unprecedented allegation that the central aim of the Socialist Education movement was "to rectify power-holders within the [Chinese Communist] Party who take the capitalist road." Power-holders! While no individual party leaders were singled out as "capitalist roaders," Mao's comments were clearly directed toward the very highest levels of the CCP, including the Central Committee itself.

In the five-and-a-half years that had elapsed since Peng Dehuai was purged at the Lushan plenum, this was the first time that Mao had directly suggested that any of his closest associates might be hidden counterrevolutionaries. Viewed in the context of his rising irritation with his top lieutenants, there could be little doubt that the chairman's primary target was his second-in-command and heir apparent, Liu Shaoqi.

But Liu could not be toppled as easily as Peng Dehuai. For one thing, he and Deng Xiaoping were still formally in charge of the party's day-to-day operations, while Mao remained on the second line of leadership. For another thing, Liu and Deng were extremely popular; they had many powerful friends and supporters within the party apparatus, people who would not sit still for another Peng Dehuai-style Maoist purge. And finally, discontent with Mao's growing obsession over class struggle was becoming more widespread both inside the party and among the disillusioned Chinese intelligentsia.

Thus, as Mao readied himself for the final showdown, he had to proceed cautiously, preparing his moves with all the skill and deliberation of a consummate chess player.

Now, in the interest of full disclosure, and before we proceed to examine the consequences of Mao's attack on Liu and Deng, I must tell you that I was the one who first uncovered many of these developments. Back in 1967, while I was a graduate student studying Chinese in Taiwan, I accidentally stumbled upon a cache of Communist Party Central Committee documents hidden away in the reading room of the Taipei Institute of International Relations. The documents had recently been seized by Republic of China commandos during a guerrilla raid on the Chinese mainland; and they were marked "top secret." I had no idea what was in them, but I certainly wanted to find out.

I tried to convince the institute's librarian to let me read the documents, but he was most reluctant to let them out of his sight. In the end he let me translate them for him into English but only on condition that I would make no copies, take no notes, and remove anything from the library when I went home in the evening. I readily agreed to these conditions, and I began to translate the documents.

Within the first few minutes I realized that I was in possession of a veritable goldmine of hitherto unknown information detailing many of the events I have described in this lecture. Most importantly, the documents clearly revealed the growing schism between Mao and his lieutenants, Liu Shaoqi and Deng Xiaoping.

Of course, by 1967 Western scholars were already well aware of the existence of this schism, for the Cultural Revolution was already well underway. And Mao had already criticized Liu Shaoqi in public. But no one had uncovered direct evidence of its origins and early development. Here in my hands was the smoking gun, the trigger that had set off Mao's Cultural Revolution. I could hardly contain my excitement.

Just before I finished translating the documents I made one of the most fateful decisions of my young life. I hid the original documents in a zippered inner compartment of my briefcase before leaving the Institute for the evening. My plan was to take the documents over to a nearby U.S. Naval Hospital in Taipei, where a friend of mine had once let me use the hospital's Verifax— precursor to the Xerox machine. If everything went well, I would be able to photocopy the documents and return them first thing the next morning, before anyone was the wiser.

By then I was running on pure adrenalin, and in my chemically-induced excitement I never stopped to consider the consequences that would follow if I got caught with a set of stolen, top secret Communist documents in an authoritarian state ruled by Mao's arch-rival, the rabid anti-Communist dictator, Chiang K'ai-shek.

If I had thought about it, I probably wouldn't have done it. But the gods must have been smiling for I didn't get caught, and I was able to return the purloined documents without incident the next morning.

Having survived this harrowing adventure unscathed, I focused my attention on the extraordinary revelations contained in this documentary treasure trove. For the next several years, the information unearthed in these documents fueled my entire academic career. By the time I was finished with them, I had completed a doctoral dissertation, four research articles, and two books, including the definitive study of the Socialist Education movement. Looking back on these events more than 40 years later, I have to admit that I was a very fortunate young man.

Next time, we'll look at the origins and immediate antecedents of Mao's tumultuous Cultural Revolution. We'll see how Mao carefully plotted his revenge against Liu, Deng, and other alleged capitalist roaders within the Chinese Communist Party hierarchy.

"Long Live Chairman Mao!" 1964–1965
Lecture 21

During the revival of the Hundred Flowers campaign from 1961 to 1963 ... a large number of new literary works had been published—many of them in apparent violation of Mao's cherished style of socialist realism.

To prepare for his coming struggle with "revisionists" and "capitalist roaders" within the CCP, Mao Zedong needed to enlist the support of the PLA. But the debacle of the Great Leap and the purge of revered war hero Peng Dehuai had seriously undermined army morale. Thus as his first order of business, Mao entrusted to Defense Minister **Lin Biao** the task of leading a campaign to revive Mao's flagging personality cult.

In 1964, Lin launched a mass movement within the PLA to study the thought of Chairman Mao. To promote the movement, Lin personally edited a collection of Mao's pithiest precepts, aphorisms, and homilies, which he packaged into a pocket-sized paperback entitled *Quotations from Chairman Mao Zedong*—more popularly known as the **Little Red Book**.

All military units were required to hold regular study sessions, in which selected passages from Mao's Little Red Book would be collectively recited, analyzed, and sermonized upon. Akin to the worship of deities in fundamentalist religious schools, the study sessions focused on Mao's strategic brilliance and god-like qualities of omniscience, omnipotence, and benevolence. The mantra "Long live Chairman Mao! A long, long life to Chairman Mao" had its origins in this campaign, as did the practice of starting public meetings with the phrase "Chairman Mao teaches us."

With the Mao-study campaign unfolding on a massive scale within the army, the next target audience in the campaign to revive Mao's personality cult was the younger generation. In 1965, PLA political instructors were sent out to schools, universities, and local branches of the Communist Youth League throughout the country to promote group study of the Little Red Book.

While spreading Chairman Mao's thoughts among the younger generation, the Maoists also began to attack what they called "unhealthy tendencies" in cultural and literary circles. In the Maoist view, all art and literature must be in the style of **socialist realism**, glorifying the worker-peasant masses and vilifying class enemies. But during the revival of the Hundred Flowers campaign from 1961 to 1963, a large number of literary works appeared that were critical of Mao's radicalism.

Many writers populated their works of fiction with **middle characters—** characters who were neither perfect prototypes of the "new socialist man" nor degenerate, bloodthirsty villains. Unlike the simplistic cardboard cutout figures of the socialist realism school, these flawed, yet recognizably real figures struggled on a daily basis with complex political situations and moral ambiguities. Heroic solutions were seldom available to them, so they did the best they could. Indeed, their imperfect behavior gave them a distinctly human quality with which readers could identify.

To avoid incurring Mao's wrath, Chinese intellectuals revived a literary tradition that had been practiced widely in ancient imperial times. Disguising their criticisms of Mao and his policies as historical allegories, fictionalized parables, or satire, they produced a veritable blizzard of politically incorrect works of art and literature. Satirical articles hinted at Mao's penchant for indulging in "great empty talk" and forgetting what he had said.

Perhaps the deepest literary affront to Mao during this period was a modern Peking opera by **Wu Han,** entitled *Hai Rui Dismissed from Office*. When the opera was first written and performed, it received a positive review from Mao, but the chairman's wife, Jiang Qing, had a very different take on it. In Jiang's view, the story of Hai Rui was a reactionary allegory for Peng Dehuai's 1959 dismissal. Both men had been widely esteemed for their integrity and courage; both had confronted local tyrants in an effort to redress wrongs inflicted on peasants; both had petitioned the emperor to relieve peasant burdens; and both had been fired for their efforts. Jiang eventually persuaded Mao that the opera was an indirect defense of Peng Dehuai—and a slap in the face of the chairman. Now utterly convinced that representatives of the bourgeoisie were attacking him from all directions, Mao was ready to take action: The Great Proletarian Cultural Revolution was about to begin. ∎

Chairman Mao Reforms "Revisionist" Educational System

As another element of Mao Zedong's critique of revisionism in the cultural sphere in the 1960s, he turned his celebrated wrath against China's educational system. Back in the mid-1950s, China had modeled its educational system closely upon that of the Soviet Union. It was a hierarchical system, based on rigorous competitive examinations at every level, and offered two distinct educational tracks: an elite academic track and a broad-based vocational track. But now, in the mid-1960s, the Soviet model fell into Maoist disrepute, and the chairman began to severely criticize the "erroneous methods" being used to educate China's children. Complaining that the Soviet system stressed book learning at the expense of more practical forms of education, Mao urged a shortening of the school curriculum and for classroom education to be combined with two years of hands-on vocational training in a factory or farm, or in military training. The idea was to put all students in direct, daily contact with the day-to-day hardships of ordinary workers and peasants.

Mao's critique of the educational system also included an attack on the existing school curriculum, which he felt required students to study too much. "This is exceedingly harmful," said the chairman, "and the burden is too heavy. It puts students in a constant state of tension. ... The [school] syllabus should be chopped in half. ... It is evident that reading too many books is harmful."

Names to Know

Lin Biao (1907–1971): A senior PLA general and longtime confidant of Mao Zedong, Lin became defense minister after Peng Dehuai's purge in 1959. Lin died in a plane crash in 1971 following an alleged attempt to assassinate Mao.

Wu Han (1909–1969): A playwright, historian, and deputy mayor of Beijing. His writing group published essays critical of Mao Zedong in 1961–1962. His 1961 opera *Hai Rui Dismissed from Office* was an allegorical criticism of Mao's 1959 purge of Peng Dehuai.

Hai Rui Dismissed from Office: An allegorical 1961 opera by Wu Han likening the purge of Peng Dehuai to the Ming dynasty emperor's dismissal of a loyal minister, Hai Rui.

Little Red Book (a.k.a. ***Quotations from Chairman Mao Zedong***): A collection of Maoist sayings and writings that was distributed widely to soldiers and students in 1964 and 1965.

middle characters: Literary reference in the early 1960s to ordinary people who are neither heroes nor villains; tacitly antithetical to socialist realism.

socialist realism: The Stalinist notion, endorsed by Mao Zedong, that art and literature should glorify the working classes and expose the evil machinations of class enemies.

Suggested Reading

Chang and Halliday, *Mao.*

Fenby, *Modern China.*

Li, *The Private Life of Chairman Mao.*

MacFarquhar, *The Origins of the Cultural Revolution*, vol. 3.

Schram, *The Political Thought of Mao Tse-tung.*

Short, *Mao.*

Questions to Consider

1. Why did Mao authorize the mass publication and circulation of the Little Red Book in 1964–1965?

2. What was the significance of Wu Han's *Hai Rui Dismissed from Office*?

"Long Live Chairman Mao!" 1964–1965
Lecture 21—Transcript

If Mao was going to neutralize Liu Shaoqi and Deng Xiaoping and generate the political traction necessary to achieve his goal of defeating modern revisionism, he first needed to burnish his own image. In the parlance of modern political science, the chairman needed to activate his base. To achieve this, he turned first to his defense minister, Lin Biao, and the People's Liberation Army.

Lin was a sycophantic follower of Chairman Mao, and he had vigorously defended Mao against Liu Shaoqi's verbal assault at the conference of 7,000 cadres in 1962. Now, two years later, Lin Biao was put in charge of a nationwide campaign to revive Chairman Mao's flagging "cult of personality."

While Lin's absolute devotion to Mao was beyond reproach, the loyalty of the PLA as a whole was more problematic. Two things had served to erode the army's faith in the chairman.

First was the Great Famine of 1959–1961. Although the PLA's 3.5 million soldiers had been effectively insulated from the devastation of the three hard years, many of them had family members who suffered badly in the great famine. Secret documents obtained by Taiwanese espionage agents on the mainland confirmed that the fallout from the Great Leap had seriously undermined troop morale.

Moreover, the army's esprit de corps, and its faith in Mao's leadership, had also been sorely strained by the Peng Dehuai affair. A number of high-ranking PLA staff officers had been appalled by Mao's cruel treatment of Peng. If the chairman intended to wage a successful struggle against revisionists and capitalist roaders within the party, he would need to count on the full, unwavering support of the military.

In 1964, with Mao's blessing, Lin Biao launched a mass movement within the PLA to "Study the Thought of Chairman Mao." To promote this movement, Lin personally edited a collection of Mao's pithiest precepts, aphorisms, and homilies, which he packaged into a handy pocket-sized paperback entitled *Quotations from Chairman Mao Zedong*—more popularly known as the "Little Red Book."

All military units were required to hold regular study sessions, in which selected passages from the Little Red Book would be collectively recited, analyzed, and sermonized upon. Akin to the worship of deities in fundamentalist religious schools, the study sessions focused on Mao's strategic brilliance and his god-like qualities of omniscience, omnipotence, and benevolence.

The mantra "Long Live Chairman Mao! A long, long life to Chairman Mao" (*Mao zhuxi wansui Mao Zhuxi wanwan sui!*) had its origins in this campaign, as did the practice of starting every public meeting with the phrase, "Chairman Mao teaches us ..." (*Mao zhuxi jiaodao women ...*)

Although some senior military leaders balked at the adulation being heaped upon Mao, few dared openly to object. One of those who did was the PLA's chief of staff Lo Ruiqing. Lo's immediate predecessor had been purged as a member of Peng Dehuai's anti-party clique in 1959.

Lo was himself incredulous. He viewed the national fetish of reciting quotations from the Little Red Book as "a needless exercise in forced memorization." "If Mao Zedong Thought is the most advanced and creative form of Marxism-Leninism," he asked rhetorically, "then does this mean there is no room for improvement?" For all his skepticism, Lo was rewarded a year later by being dismissed.

With the Mao-study campaign now unfolding on a massive scale within the army, the next target audience in the campaign to revive Mao's personality cult were members of China's younger generation. In 1965, PLA political instructors were sent out to schools, universities and local branches of the Communist Party Youth League throughout the country to promote group study of the Little Red Book. Later, during the Cultural Revolution, these army-led study groups would become the backbone of China's youthful Red Guards.

Now, while it's been widely noted that the nationwide Mao study campaign of 1964–1965 produced millions of overzealous revolutionary youngsters, it is also true that many young people took a calculated, opportunistic approach to this campaign, using it to advance their own personal careers and agendas.

One young man, whom I later met in Hong Kong, told me this personal story: As the son of a former landlord growing up in a remote rural area of Guangdong Province, his future prospects had looked very dim. Whenever a new political campaign came along, he was singled out for struggle as a typical class enemy.

Then, in 1965, the mass Mao-study movement began, and a competition was held among young people in his village to see who could memorize and debate most persuasively the "Thought of Mao Zedong." Realizing that he had nothing else to lose, he poured himself into the study of Mao's Little Red Book, memorizing chapter and verse. He handily won his village's Mao-study contest and the commune-wide competition that followed. He then traveled to county headquarters, where he bested all other local contest winners. As his prize, he won an all-expense-paid trip to the provincial capital of Guangzhou, where a province-wide competition was to be held.

However, this young man had other plans. Using his expense money, he boarded a train to a small fishing village near the Hong Kong border, where he bribed a Chinese border guard to look the other way as he entered the water and swam to safety in Hong Kong. Despite 15 years of intensive ideological indoctrination, the spirit of individual entrepreneurship was evidently alive and well in rural China.

The Maoists, while spreading Chairman Mao's thoughts among the younger generation, also began to attack what they called "unhealthy tendencies" in cultural and literary circles. During the revival of the Hundred Flowers campaign in the early '60s while Mao was in retreat on the second line of leadership, a large number of new literary works had been published, many of them in apparent violation of Mao's cherished style of socialist realism.

The chairman's absolutist views on culture, which date back to the 1942 Yan'an Forum, mandated that all writers and artists should be unambiguously reflecting the class struggle and the standpoint of the proletariat in their works, glorifying the heroic qualities of workers, peasants, and soldiers, while vilifying the evil deeds of counterrevolutionaries, reactionaries, and rightists.

But in the new era of intellectual liberalization that characterized the reign of Liu Shaoqi and Deng Xiaoping in the early '60s, many writers populated their works of fiction with ordinary characters, characters who were neither perfect prototypes of the "new socialist man" nor degenerate, bloodthirsty villains.

Unlike the simplistic cardboard cutout figures of the socialist realism school, these flawed, yet recognizably real "middle characters," as they were called, struggled on a daily basis with complex political situations and moral ambiguities. Heroic solutions were seldom available to them, so they did the best they could. Indeed, their imperfect behavior gave them a distinctly human quality with which many readers could readily identify.

But Mao strongly objected to the ambiguous portrayal of the everyday lives of ordinary people. And in 1964 he launched a counterattack against authors who wrote approvingly of "middle characters" in their works.

In Mao's view, the favorable literary depiction of moral uncertainty and compromise served to undermine the proletarian will that was essential to achieving victory in the struggle against revisionism. As one left-wing propagandist put it in a literary journal of this period,

> What sort of people are these so-called "middle characters"? According to their advocates, they are people from among the masses ... who are midway between good and bad, advanced and backward ... who vacillate between the socialist and capitalist roads. ... It is even said that people in this state constitute the great majority of the masses.

> [But] the people are the makers of history and the masters of the new society. To describe the great majority of them as middling and colorless, dullards who are indifferent and phlegmatic. ... Does this not expose the hostile [class] standpoint of those who make such assertions?

In a parallel attack on intellectuals who urged adoption of a relaxed attitude toward class struggle in the philosophical realm, Mao lashed out at a group of educators who had popularized a school of thought known esoterically as "two combine into one."

The man who bore the main brunt of the Maoist attack was a veteran Communist Party philosopher named Yang Xianzhen. Yang was a Central Committee member who had made the mistake in his academic lectures of placing roughly equal emphasis on both struggle and reconciliation in the handling of contradictions under socialism.

In philosophical circles, the principle of peaceful class reconciliation was known as "two combine into one" (*er he he yi*), while its dialectical opposite, the principle of unremitting class struggle, was known as *yi fenwei er* ("one divides into two").

In the language of modern-day game theory, "two combine into one" was a formula for achieving a win-win, or positive-sum outcome, while "one divides into two" was a formula for zero-sum, winner-take-all struggle and conflict resolution.

In his lectures, Yang Xianzhen showed no particular preference for one as opposed to the other of these contrasting principles, which he viewed as complementary rather than antagonistic. But it was Yang's great misfortune to have supported Peng Dehuai's critique of the Great Leap Forward back in 1959. Mao hadn't forgotten; and he clearly hadn't forgiven. Now it was payback time.

In the summer of 1964, Mao was shown a newspaper article summarizing Yang Xianzhen's lectures. His reaction was swift and decisive:

> Yang Xianzhen believes that two combine into one, and that synthesis is the indissoluble tie between opposites. [But] what indissoluble ties are there in this world? Things may be tied [together], but in the end they must be broken apart. ... You have all witnessed how two opposites, the Guomindang and the Communist Party, were combined into one on the Chinese mainland. Their synthesis looked like this: Their armies came, and we devoured them. We ate them bite by bite. ...
>
> "One divides into two" [said Mao,] is [proper] dialectics. [But] "two combine into one" is revisionism.

In March of 1965 Yang Xianzhen was denounced as a "representative of the bourgeoisie inside the party, a tool of Peng Dehuai, and a mini-Khrushchev."

No matter that the case against him was grossly exaggerated, if not wholly fabricated the wording of the denunciation embodied a perfect Maoist ideological trifecta, lumping together the "revisionist" Khrushchev, the "anti-party" Peng Dehuai, and the "bourgeois power-holder" Yang Xianzhen into a single, one-size-fits-all conspiracy.

Next Mao turned his celebrated wrath upon China's educational system. Back in the mid-1950s, during the first five-year plan, China had modeled its educational system closely upon that of the Soviet Union. It was a hierarchical system, based on rigorous competitive examinations at every level. And it offered two distinct educational tracks: an elite academic track for high-achieving students and a broad-based vocational track for ordinary students.

But now, in the mid-1960s, the Soviet model had fallen into Maoist disrepute, and the chairman began to severely criticize the "erroneous methods" being used to educate China's children.

Complaining that the Soviet system stressed book learning at the expense of more practical forms of education, Mao urged a shortening of the school curriculum from 12 years to nine, with formal classroom education melded in with two years of hands-on vocational training in a factory or a farm or in a military unit. The idea was to put all students—not just the less talented ones—in direct, daily contact with the day-to-day hardships and struggles of ordinary workers and peasants and soldiers.

Mao's critique of the educational system also included an attack on the existing school curriculum, which, he said, required students to study too much.

"This is exceedingly harmful," said the chairman, "the burden is too heavy. It puts students in a constant state of tension. ... The syllabus should be chopped in half. ... It is evident that reading too many books is harmful."

He then went on to attack the prevailing examination system:

> Our present method of conducting examinations is a method for dealing with the enemy. ... It is a method of surprise attack, asking oblique or strange questions. ... I am in favor of publishing [exam] questions in advance and letting the students study them and answer them with the aid of books.

> At examinations, whispering into each others' ears and taking other people's places ought to be allowed. If your answer is good and I copy it, then mine should be counted as good. [These things] used to be done secretly. Now let them be done openly. ... Let's give it a try.

Finally, Mao directed his animus at the bourgeois life-styles enjoyed by China's ivory-tower intellectuals. To counteract their sedentary, cerebral life-styles, Mao proposed a drastic remedy: "We must drive actors, poets, dramatists, and writers out of the cities," he said, "and pack them all off to the countryside. ... Whoever does not go down will get no food."

As we saw in a couple of earlier lectures, Mao's mercurial moods and periodic, intense outbursts could be quite unnerving and intimidating to those around him. Particularly in the aftermath of the Anti-Rightist Rectification and the Peng Dehuai affair, few intellectuals had the fortitude to openly criticize the chairman. Eschewing open opposition, they now turned instead to a more subtle and indirect mode of criticism.

To avoid incurring Mao's wrath, Chinese intellectuals in the early '60s revived a literary tradition that had been practiced widely in ancient imperial times. Disguising their criticisms of Mao and his policies as historical allegories, fictionalized parables, or satirical they produced a veritable blizzard of politically incorrect works of art and literature.

A case in point is provided by a much-praised, award-winning painting that appeared on the back cover of the Communist Youth League's flagship magazine, *China Youth*, at the end of 1964.

The painting, which appeared to be a typical example of Mao's preferred style of socialist realism, depicted happy, healthy Chinese peasants working diligently to secure a bountiful harvest in a golden-colored field overflowing with tall, abundant wheat stalks waving in the breeze. In the background, against a landscape of purple-grey hills, were three large piles of harvested wheat with a red flag protruding prominently from each of them. In the foreground were scattered individual stalks and husks of wheat lying randomly on the ground.

After winning various awards for socialist realism, the painting was suddenly removed from exhibition early in 1965, and the issue of *China Youth* that featured it was withdrawn from circulation.

What had happened? It seems that when a local cultural watchdog took a magnifying glass to the painting, some hitherto unseen anomalies were revealed. For one thing, the contour of the hills in the background of the painting appeared to resemble the supine corpses of Vladimir Ilich Lenin and Mao Zedong, respectively. For another, one of the flag staffs protruding from the three piles of harvested wheat was broken—snapped in half, with its red flag drooping on the ground.

Now, one of the key loyalty tests during the famine years of 1959–1961 had been the demand that cadres faithfully uphold the "three red flags"— the Great Leap Forward, the people's communes, and the general line for socialist construction. The fact that the middle flag, representing the people's communes, was broken in half in the painting and dragging on the ground, suggests that the artist was making a political statement.

But the piece de resistence was the randomly scattered wheat stalks and husks in the foreground of the painting. By scrutinizing them closely, one could make out a string of Chinese characters formed by the not-so-randomly fallen stalks: *Jiang Jieshi wan sui!*—"Long Live Chiang K'ai-shek."

One can only wonder at the fate of the unfortunate artists who painted this prize-winning landscape.

Carefully disguised works of biting political criticism, parody, and satire also appeared in the Chinese mass media in this period. Three senior Beijing-based Communist Party propaganda workers were particularly active in producing such satirical works. Their names were Deng Tuo, Liao Mosha, and Wu Han. Beginning in 1961, these three men, using a collective nom de plume, wrote over 100 articles in the Beijing journal "Front Line" (*Qianxian*), under the generic heading, "Notes from a Three-Family Village."

In one fairly typical column, entitled "Great Empty Talk," the three writers observed:

> Some people have the gift of the gab. They can talk endlessly on any occasion, like water flowing from an undammed river. After listening to them, however, when you try to recall what they have said, you can't remember a thing. ... As chance would have it, my neighbor's child once imitated the style of some great poet and put into writing a lot of "great empty talk." ... He wrote a poem called "Ode to Wild Grass," which is nothing but great empty talk. The poem reads as follows:
>
> > The Venerable Heaven is our father
> > The Great Earth is our mother
> > And the Sun is our nanny
> > The East Wind is our benefactor
> > And the West Wind is our enemy.
>
> Although such words as heaven, earth, mother, father, sun, the East Wind, benefactor, and enemy catch the eye, they are used to no purpose here and have become mere clichés. ... Therefore, I would advise these friends, those people given to engaging in great empty

talk to read more, think more, say less and take a rest when the time comes for talking.

Now, in view of Mao's well-deserved reputation for making long-winded, rambling speeches at party conferences, it did not take much of an imagination to see in this essay an oblique criticism of the chairman himself. Particularly telling was the embedded poem, which came perilously close to ridiculing a 1958 verse by Chairman Mao himself, in which he famously boasted that "the East Wind prevails over the West Wind." Was Mao's most famous poem an example of "great empty talk"—a "mere cliché"?

A second illustration of the subversive impact of the authors of "Notes from a Three Family Village" involved a column they wrote entitled "A Cure for Forgetfulness." In it, they argued that when someone suffers from repeated memory lapses and is unable to speak sensibly, then it is necessary to refrain from criticizing or correcting him.

Instead, the recommended treatment was to "pour dog's blood on the head of the afflicted person, then pour cold water over him in order to stimulate him." Or, alternatively, "one could use the shock treatment of beating him over the head with a special bludgeon." Once again, this came very close to being an indirect attack on Mao himself. It certainly didn't resemble any legitimate psychiatric advice.

But perhaps the deepest literary affront to Chairman Mao during the Hundred Flowers revival in the early '60s was a modern Peking opera entitled "The Dismissal of Hai Rui" (*Hai Rui baguan*), written by a Peking University professor, Wu Han, who was also a member of the "Three Family Village" writing group.

A noted playwright and historian in his own right, Wu Han had become prominent in Beijing political circles, and he had risen to become a deputy mayor of the city. His opera, written in 1961, was about a famous historical figure, a Ming dynasty official named Hai Rui, whose deep and abiding concern for the plight of oppressed peasants was legendary in China.

In the mid-16th century, at a time of serious national famine, Hai Rui had stood up to the local tyrants who had unlawfully seized land from the peasants, returning the land to its rightful owners. For this Hai Rui had received praise from the Ming emperor. But when he later pleaded with the emperor to relieve the peasants' unreasonable tax burdens, Hai Rui was rewarded for his efforts by being unceremoniously sacked and banished.

When Wu Han's opera was first written and performed, it received a positive reviews, including from Mao, who voiced the opinion that "the play is good; Hai Rui was a good man."

But, the chairman's wife, Jiang Qing, had a very different take on it. Jiang Qing was Mao's fourth wife. In the early 1930s she had been a minor, B-movie actress in Shanghai. When the Sino-Japanese War broke out, she left Shanghai and headed for Yan'an, where she first seduced and then married Chairman Mao, against the advice of his comrades, who believed her to be a gold-digging harlot. As a condition of their marriage, Jiang was prohibited from ever participating in politics.

When Jiang Qing first saw "The Dismissal of Hai Rui" performed in 1962, she found it offensive, and she tried to have it banned. But she was turned down cold by leaders of the cultural establishment, who chastised her for violating her "no politics" marriage contract.

In Jiang's view, the story of Hai Rui was a reactionary allegory. As she saw it, Wu Han's interpretation of the circumstances surrounding Hai Rui's dismissal paralleled all too closely the circumstances of Peng Dehuai's 1959 dismissal. Both men had been widely esteemed for their integrity and courage, both had confronted local tyrants in an effort to redress wrongs inflicted on peasants, both had petitioned the emperor to relieve peasant burdens, and both had been fired for their efforts, their reputations destroyed by imperial fiat.

Pointing out these parallel circumstances to her illustrious husband, Jiang Qing eventually persuaded Mao that the opera was, in fact, an indirect defense of Peng Dehuai—and a slap in the face of the chairman. Now utterly convinced that representatives of the bourgeoisie were attacking him from all sides, Mao's long-smoldering anger reached the point of combustion. He was ready to stop talking, and to start acting. The Great Proletarian Cultural Revolution was about to begin.

Mao's Last Revolution Begins, 1965–1966
Lecture 22

Before leaving his Hangzhou hideaway, [Mao Zedong] wrote to his wife in Shanghai, telling her that there would soon be "great disorder under heaven." It was a most prescient forecast.

In the autumn of 1965, Mao suddenly disappeared from public view. Calculating that he could not launch an effective attack against his adversaries from the nation's capital, where they enjoyed the strong support of the Communist Party bureaucracy, he had left Beijing for a villa in Hangzhou. With a brain trust consisting of his wife, Jiang Qing, his defense minister, Lin Biao, his security chief, Kang Sheng, his chief theoretician, Chen Boda, and the Shanghai municipal party leader Zhang Chunqiao, the now 72-year-old chairman mapped out his campaign.

The opening salvo was delivered on November 10, 1965, when Yao Wenyuan, a young left-wing propagandist in the Shanghai party organization, published a biting critique of Wu Han's opera, *Hai Rui Dismissed from Office*. An instant chill of anxiety went through the Beijing literary establishment. Most deeply disturbed, aside from Wu Han himself, was Wu's boss and principal patron, Beijing mayor **Peng Zhen**.

At first, Peng (a close associate of Liu Shaoqi and Deng Xiaoping) instructed Beijing's newspapers not to reprint the article. But under pressure from Zhou Enlai, he relented. Peng had a mitigating editor's note added to the article and also had Wu Han write a self-criticism, acknowledging his failure to understand that "proletarian literature and art must serve contemporary politics." In defending Wu and opposing publication of Yao's article, Peng had revealed his loyalty to Liu and Deng. In 1966, Mao labeled Wu's opera a **poisonous weed**, and members of Peng's close circle began to feel the heat as well. Moving in for the kill, Mao convened a Politburo meeting at which a strongly worded circular was adopted, announcing Peng's dismissal. The document further suggested that Mao intended to go after even bigger fish. "People of Khrushchev's ilk," it read, are still "nestled in our midst." Accordingly, it is necessary to "repudiate and strike down all counterrevolutionary revisionists." Mao instructed Liu to announce the official verdict on his old friend Peng.

Shortly after the dismissal of Peng, political agitation commenced on the campus of Peking University. On May 25, 1966, a philosophy instructor named **Nie Yuanzi** wrote an inflammatory *dazibao* accusing the university's president of suppressing the revolutionary masses on the campus. Mao sided with Nie, making her an instant left-wing heroine and inspiring radical students elsewhere to follow her example.

As factional disturbances increased in frequency and intensity in Beijing's high schools and colleges in the late spring of 1966, Liu Shaoqi and Deng Xiaoping dispatched work teams to sort through the conflicting claims of rival groups. At Peking University, the work team supported the beleaguered president and strongly criticized unruly student rebels as hooligans. Informed of this latest turn of events in early July, Mao was livid. It was time for him to join the battle in person.

Mao boarded his private train for Beijing, where he proceeded to shake the Chinese political establishment to its very foundation. Mao strongly criticized the work teams, arguing that they had suppressed the masses and terrorized rebellious students at *Beida* and elsewhere. A week later, Mao ordered the work teams to be withdrawn. Henceforth, the Cultural Revolution in schools and universities would be conducted by the revolutionary students themselves, with their leaders selected from below by students and teachers rather than being appointed from above by central authorities. When they learned of Mao's order, Liu and Deng were deeply distressed. Mao had tested his two top lieutenants by stirring up trouble, and they had failed the test—just as Peng had failed the test Mao had set for him earlier in the year.

Shortly after this incident, Mao wrote a personal note to a student in Beijing, praising him for helping to form a rebel organization at his middle school. The insurgents there had called themselves **Red Guards**. Mao congratulated the young man, and to convey his approval, he coined a new battle cry: "To rebel is justified!" Mao's words were reprinted in

> **Henceforth, the Cultural Revolution in schools and universities would be conducted by the revolutionary students themselves.**

student newspapers across the country, quickly becoming the most famous rallying cry of the Cultural Revolution.

In the course of several public appearances by the chairman in August and September of 1996, he received more than 1 million ecstatic young Red Guards. Wearing olive-drab military-style uniforms adorned with bright red armbands and waving copies of the Little Red Book, the students excitedly chanted "Long live Chairman Mao! A long, long life to Chairman Mao!" Mao's embrace of the Red Guards would soon lead China's impressionable students to undertake a succession of ever more daring—and ever more violent—actions. ∎

Names to Know

Nie Yuanzi (b. 1921): A female philosophy instructor, Nie put up a wall poster at Peking University in May 1966, challenging the university's ban on wall posters and mass meetings. Mao Zedong endorsed her poster, praising her as a "true revolutionary."

Peng Zhen (1902–1997): A veteran CCP revolutionary and mayor of Beijing. Peng was purged by Mao Zedong in 1966 for protecting Wu Han against leftist criticism. He was rehabilitated by Deng Xiaoping in 1978.

Important Terms

Beida: Nickname for Peking University, a contraction of *Beijing Daxue*.

poisonous weeds: Mao Zedong's 1957 characterization of art and literature that served to undermined socialism, CCP leadership, or Marxism-Leninism.

Red Guards (a.k.a. ***hongweibing***): High school and college students mobilized by Maoists in 1966 to launch attacks on "bourgeois powerholders."

Suggested Reading

Chang and Halliday, *Mao*.

Fenby, *Modern China*.

Li, *The Private Life of Chairman Mao*.

Ling, *The Revenge of Heaven*.

MacFarquhar, *The Origins of the Cultural Revolution*, vol. 3.

Schram, *The Political Thought of Mao Tse-tung*.

Questions to Consider

1. Why couldn't Mao Zedong rely on the party organization to unmask and criticize his detractors?

2. How did Mao initially orchestrate his attack on Peng Zhen and other "bourgeois powerholders" in 1965–1966?

Mao's Last Revolution Begins, 1965–1966
Lecture 22—Transcript

As a prologue to Mao's Cultural Revolution, his first move was a rather unexpected one. In the early autumn of 1965 the chairman suddenly disappeared from public view. Speculation mounted: Was he ill? Was he dead? One rumor had him suffering from Parkinson's disease, another the he had suffered a stroke.

In fact, Mao had quietly left Beijing. He calculated that if he could not launch an effective attack against his adversaries from the nation's capital, where Liu Shaoqi, Deng Xiaoping, and their allies enjoyed its strongest support from the Communist Party bureaucracy, then he'd have to go elsewhere. Indeed, Mao would later complain that Beijing was controlled so thoroughly and so tightly by his enemies that "no needle could penetrate, no drop of water could enter."

To bypass the regular party apparatus, Mao left the capital and moved his temporary headquarters to his private villa in the resort city of Hangzhou, near Shanghai. There, he gathered around him a group of loyal left-wing supporters. It was November of 1965, and Mao was now 72 years old.

With a brain trust consisting of his wife, Jiang Qing, his defense minister, Lin Biao, his security chief, Kang Sheng, his chief theoretician, Chen Boda, and the Shanghai Municipal Party leader Zhang Chunqiao, the chairman now mapped out his coming campaign.

The opening salvo was delivered on November 10, 1965. On that date, a young left-wing propagandist in the Shanghai party organization, by the name of Yao Wenyuan, published a biting critique of Wu Han's opera, "The Dismissal of Hai Rui."

Yao's article, which appeared in a Shanghai newspaper, accused Wu Han of "using the past to ridicule the present." Specifically, Wu Han was charged with manipulating historical events in a veiled attempt to "demolish the people's communes and restore the criminal rule of the landlord class." And his play was now labeled a big "anti-party poisonous weed."

Implicit in Yao Wenuyan's critique was an even more serious charge: namely, that Hai Rui was, in reality, a stand-in for the disgraced Marshal Peng Dehuai, and the vindictive emperor, by extension, was a stand-in for Mao Zedong.

With the publication of Yao Wenyuan's attack, an instant chill of anxiety went through the Beijing literary establishment. Most deeply disturbed, aside from Wu Han himself, was Wu's boss and principal patron, the mayor of Beijing, Peng Zhen. A member of the party's inner Politburo elite, Peng Zhenwas a close associate of Liu Shaoqi and Deng Xiaoping. He had also been a patron of Wu Han and the "Three Family Village" writing group. Was Mao now preparing to go after Peng? Was the mayor being set up for a fall?

In an obvious dilemma, Peng Zhen went into defensive mode. First, he stalled for time. He ordered Beijing's newspapers not to reproduce or even to mention Yao Wenyuan's article.

But when Zhou Enlai pressured him to reverse this directive, Peng Zhen instinctively knew that the premier was speaking on Mao's behalf. So he lifted the publication ban and he ordered the *People's Daily* to reprint Yao's article, accompanied by a mitigating editor's note in which he tried to limit the damage by explaining that the controversy surrounding Wu Han's opera was entirely academic in nature, not political. He added a caveat to the effect that if there were any political errors in the opera's underlying libretto, then they were due to the author's inadequate understanding of history rather than any subversive political intentions or motives.

To deflect further attacks from the left, Peng Zhen urged Wu Han to write a pro-forma self-criticism, acknowledging that he had failed to fully understand that "proletarian literature and art must serve contemporary politics." Wu Han dutifully obeyed.

Mayor Peng undoubtedly hoped that the incident would quickly blow over. But Mao was just getting started. Convinced that Peng Zhen had trivialized Wu Han's errors in order to protect himself from criticism, Mao held the Beijing mayor's feet to the fire. In December of 1965 he instructed Peng to conduct a thorough investigation into Wu Han's misconduct and to report back his findings in two months' time. "What I want to know," demanded Mao, "is whether Wu Han is truly anti-party, anti-socialist."

It must have been an agonizing two months for Peng Zhen, knowing that Mao was putting him to the test. Assembling a small group of five veteran Beijing politicians and propaganda specialists, Peng and his colleagues tried hard to defend Wu Han against the charge of lèse majesté.

When their completed Outline Report was delivered to the party Central Committee on February 12, 1966, Mao's suspicions were confirmed. Peng Zhen was shielding Wu Han, downplaying the seriousness of his mistakes.

That was all the chairman needed to know. At a Politburo meeting held in Hangzhou, Mao labeled "The Dismissal of Hai Rui" as a "poisonous weed," and personally denounced Wu Han for being "no better than a member of the Guomindang."

Peng Zhen was now in very deep doo-doo. Mao had set a trap for him, and he had stepped right into it.

Fearful of Mao's intentions, Peng Zhen tried to distance himself from the "Three-Family Village" writing group. He sent Wu Han on an inspection trip to the provinces of agricultural products, while Deng Tuo, another member of the group, was quietly sacked as editor of the *People's Daily*, a sacrificial lamb.

Despondent over his sudden disgrace, however, Deng Tuo committed suicide. Thereafter, his immediate boss and chief literary patron, the party's head of propaganda, Lu Dingyi (who had helped to prepare Peng Zhen's February Outline Report) suffered an anxiety attack so severe that he took indefinite medical leave, spending the next several months convalescing at a clinic in faraway Guangdong Province, the farther away from Beijing, the better.

Meanwhile back in Beijing, Liu Shaoqi himself was beginning to feel the heat. Seeking a brief respite from the capital's increasingly volatile political climate, he took his wife on a three-week state visit to south and and southeast Asia in early April 1966. But Mao was ready for Liu's evasive maneuvers. And within two days of Liu's departure, the chairman denounced Peng Zhen and his entire Beijing Municipal Party Committee by name, calling for their dismissal. For good measure, he demanded Lu Dingyi's dismissal as the head of the central propaganda department. Peng was now thoroughly isolated, so much so that even his oldest friends stopped returning his phone calls.

Moving in for the kill, Mao now convened an enlarged Politburo meeting. It was early May. At his initiative a strongly-worded circular was adopted, announcing Peng Zhen's dismissal and the reorganization of the entire Beijing Municipal Party Committee. The document further suggested, although it was oblique, that Chairman Mao intended to go after even bigger fish. "People of Khrushchev's ilk," said the May 16 circular, are still "nested in our midst." Accordingly, we must "repudiate and strike down all counterrevolutionary revisionists."

In a characteristically perverse and cold-blooded twist of the knife, Mao instructed Liu Shaoqi, who had just returned from his trip to east and south Asia, to announce the official verdict on his old friend, Peng Zhen.

Peng's downfall marked the climactic end of the first stage of Mao's "Great Proletarian Cultural Revolution" and the beginning of its even more dramatic second stage. In this new phase, the chairman would bypass altogether the regular Communist Party apparatus—which he by now thoroughly distrusted—and instead appeal directly to the young people of China, who were the spiritual heirs of the May 4th movement.

Having been thoroughly indoctrinated in "The Thought of Mao Zedong," China's students would now be entrusted to carry out the struggle against bourgeois power-holders and revisionists.

Shortly after Peng Zhen's dismissal, political agitation commenced on the campus of the venerable Peking University. Founded during the Hundred Days of Reform in 1898, Beida, as the university is commonly known, is China's oldest institution of modern higher education. It was there that the young Mao Zedong first studied Marxism with the CCP's co-founder, Li Dazhao. And it was there that the largest student demonstrations took place during the May 4th movement. In late May, 1966, Beida once again became a hotbed of political agitation.

The purge of Peng Zhen had placed the president of Peking University, a man named Lu Ping, in a difficult situation. On the one hand, Lu Ping felt obligated to demonstrate his loyalty to Mao by showing support for the new Cultural Revolution. On the other hand, Lu was a leading member of the Beijing academic establishment, and he had little or no enthusiasm for yet another chaotic mass movement.

To resolve his dilemma, he did what many Chinese officials before and since did: He paid lip service to the need for a thorough exposure and removal of bourgeois power-holders, while at the same time arguing that class struggle should be conducted in a restrained and orderly manner, without mass meetings, without public denunciations, and without wall posters.

In the Maoist parlance of the time, Lu Ping was "waving the red flag to oppose the red flag." That is, he was displaying a leftist banner to distract attention from his rightist intentions. It was a gambit that would be employed repeatedly, with varying degrees of success, in hundreds and thousands of schools, universities, offices, factories, and farms around the country over the next few years.

On May 25, a middle-aged female philosophy instructor named Nie Yuanzi and a group of her leftist friends put up a *dazibao* outside the Beida students' dining hall. In it, they directly challenged Lu Ping's ban on wall posters and mass meetings:

> To hold meetings and post *dazibao* are militant mass methods of the best kind. But you ... prevent [the masses] from holding meetings and putting up posters. ... You manufacture various taboos and regulations ... to suppress the masses, in order to sabotage the Cultural Revolution. We warn you. ... You are daydreaming! Now is the time for all revolutionary intellectuals to go into battle ... and to resolutely wipe out all monsters, demons, and counterrevolutionary revisionists of the Khrushchev type.

Upon learning of Nie Yuanzi's attack, Lu Ping fought back. He mobilized members of the university's Communist Youth League branch to respond with wall posters of their own, denouncing Nie Yuanzi as a renegade and a rightist. (Rightist? If the label seems a little strange in this context, given the very radicalism of Nie's rhetoric, just remember that in Mao's China it was always safer to attack one's opponents as rightists rather than leftists—even if those labels were rendered meaningless in the process).

Pressing his counterattack, Lu Ping hauled Nie Yuanzi and her associates in front of an audience of university administrators, teachers, and party members. There the rebel leaders were harshly interrogated and accused of attempting to undermine party leadership.

Observing these events from the outside, the vast majority of Beida students were in a quandary. While they revered Chairman Mao on the one hand, they didn't dare disobey the commands of their own University president and party committee. So most of them opted to take the safer course, the path of least resistance: They stayed out of the dispute.

But when the Beida establishment stepped up its attack on Nie Yuanzi, many students felt pressured to show their support for President Lu and the party committee—mainly out of an instinct for self-preservation, rather than any firm conviction. So they fell into line with the Beida establishment, and Nie Yuanzi's radical faction was soon isolated.

Meanwhile, in his luxurious villa in the scenic West Lake district of Hangzhou, Mao listened intently as messengers informed him of the latest events at Beida. It didn't take very long for him to draw his own conclusion: Nie Yuanzi was a true revolutionary; Lu Ping was a bourgeois reactionary. Signaling his support for the rebel faction at Beida, Mao hailed Nie's *dazibao* as "China's first Marxist-Leninist Big Character Poster."

With Mao's endorsement, Nie Yuanzi now went, literally overnight, from being a "right-wing renegade" to being a left-wing heroine. The very next day, the *People's Daily*, which was now operating under left-wing editorial control as a result of the purge of Lu Dingyi and the firing and suicide of former editor Deng Tuo, published a ringing endorsement of Mao's call to deepen the Cultural Revolution. Under the banner headline "Sweep away all Demons and Monsters," the editorial excitedly noted:

> The scale and momentum of the Great Proletarian Cultural Revolution ... have no parallel in history. ... Facts eloquently prove that Mao Zedong's thought (once it takes root among the masses) becomes a moral atomic bomb of colossal power.

A day later, the same newspaper stressed the life-and-death nature of the current class struggle:

> Like two armies facing each other in battle, the antagonistic world outlooks of the proletariat and the bourgeoisie are locked in a struggle which invariably results in one vanquishing the other. Either you crush me, or I crush you. Either the West Wind prevails over the East Wind, or the East Wind prevails over the West. There is no middle road.

Was this mere empty talk? Perhaps, but even empty talk can have consequences. Such authoritative articles, appearing in the Communist Party's flagship newspaper served to trigger a virtual tsunami of radical student activity at Beida, as well as on other nearby college and high school campuses. Suddenly, rebellious students in every Beijing school were writing wall posters and convening frenzied accusation and struggle sessions against local power-holders—from college presidents and principals to classroom teachers and office administrators.

At Beida, a group of student rebels seized President Lu Ping and a group of his colleagues. They stuck pointed dunce caps on their heads and forced them to kneel while the frenzied students spattered black ink on their faces, beat and kicked them, and then paraded them around the campus in disgrace.

Caught completely off guard by the mounting chaos, the Central Committee of the party, still under the day-to-day direction of Liu Shaoqi and Deng Xiaoping, played it strictly by the book. In cases of serious or widespread disorder, the standard operating procedure of the party was to send out work teams to investigate. And so Liu and Deng dispatched a number of work teams to schools and universities throughout Beijing to examine the nature and circumstances of the rising factional turmoil. Their mandate was to identify the source of the problem and then to fix it.

As agents of the party establishment, the work teams tended to be inherently conservative in outlook. Habitually accustomed to upholding hierarchical authority and party discipline, they weren't very likely to support rebellious students who were denouncing, and often physically abusing, established authority. It must have been very disorienting for them.

Unprepared for such anti-establishment turmoil, most of the work teams instinctively instinctively by upholding the status quo. In some cases they expelled rebellious student leaders. When the work team at Beida investigated the violent humiliation of President Lu Ping, their report characterized the incident as unprincipled hooliganism.

Informed of this latest turn of events in early July, Mao was livid. It was time for him to join the battle in person. But before leaving his Hanzhou hideaway in early July, the reclusive chairman wrote to his wife in Shanghai, telling her that there would soon be "Great disorder under heaven." It was a most prescient forecast.

Mao re-entered the Chinese political scene with a splash, quite literally. On July 16, 1966, after several months of absence, his photo was spread across the front page of the *People's Daily*—swimming in the Yangzi River. It was the first time the chairman had been seen in public since November. According to accompanying press reports, Mao had swum 15 kilometers (roughly nine-and-a-half miles) down the Yangzi in 65 minutes—almost four times as fast as the world record for that distance.

Eyewitnesses told a somewhat different story. As candidly described by Mao's physician, Li Zhisui, the chairman had not really swum at all, but rather had simply floated downstream on his back, taking advantage of a rather rapid current, his bloated belly causing him to bob up and down like a cork.

No matter how he did it, Mao was definitely back. He was physically vigorous, and he was hopping mad.

Shortly after his Yangzi River swim, Mao boarded his private train for Beijing, where he proceeded to shake the Chinese political establishment to its very foundations.

No sooner did Mao return to the capital on July 18 than Liu Shaoqi urgently sought a private meeting with him. The request was denied. Mao was shunning him. The following day at an informal party meeting, Mao strongly criticized the work teams, arguing that they had suppressed the masses and terrorized rebellious students at Beida and elsewhere. "We must not restrict the masses," he exhorted.

A week later Mao personally ordered the work teams to be withdrawn. Henceforth, the Cultural Revolution in schools and universities would be conducted by the revolutionary students themselves, with their leaders selected from below by students and teachers rather than being appointed from above by central authorities. (It is interesting to note that we can see in this a clear recapitulation of Mao's earlier anger at Liu and Deng for using elitist work teams to prevent mass peasant mobilization during the Socialist Education movement. This was a clear recapitulation of Mao's deepest worries about his lieutenants.)

When they learned of Mao's order, Liu Shaoqi and Deng Xiaoping were deeply distressed. Liu's daughter reported that she had never seen her father so upset, not without reason I might add.

Mao had tested his two top lieutenants by stirring up trouble. Then he sat back to watch how they deal with it. And they had failed the test, just as Peng Zhen had failed the test Mao had set for him earlier in the same year.

At Mao's initiative, the decision to withdraw the work teams was publicly announced on July 29 to a packed audience of 10,000 students in Beijing's Great Hall of the People. On stage were seated Liu Shaoqi, Deng Xiaoping, and Mao's ever-faithful lap-dog, Zhou Enlai.

At Mao's behest, Liu issued a vaguely worded self-criticism, in which he accepted personal responsibility for any errors committed by the work teams.

But his apology was perfunctory, half-hearted, and he claimed that the errors in question were inadvertent, the result, as he put it, of an "old revolutionary facing new problems."

Seated backstage, out of sight, Mao snorted to his doctor, seated next to him, "Old revolutionary? What old revolutionary? Old counterrevolutionary is more like it." When Mao's physician heard that, he shuddered, for he knew that Liu Shaoqi was done for.

Shortly after this incident, Mao further fanned the flames of rebellion when he wrote a personal note to a young high school student in Beijing, praising him for helping to form a rebel organization at his middle school, which was attached to Beida's sister institution, the prestigious Tsinghua University.

The insurgents at the high school had called themselves *hongweibing*—"Red Guards." Mao congratulated the young man; and to convey his approval, he coined a new battle cry: *"Zaofan youli!"*—"To rebel is justified!" Mao's words were reprinted in student newspapers across the country, quickly becoming the most famous rallying cry of the entire Cultural Revolution.

On August 5, the *People's Daily* published a short essay by Mao Zedong, entitled "My first *dazibao*." In it, Mao charged that the party's work teams had "suppressed revolutionaries, stifled dissenting opinions, and … imposed a white terror." To rectify such "poisonous" behavior, Mao exhorted the masses to "Bombard the Headquarters" [of the bourgeoisie].

Three days later, on August 8, Mao made a rare public appearance in Tiananmen Square, where he greeted thousands of gleeful, adoring young students. It was the first of several such meet-and-greet events to be held by the chairman in August and September of 1966.

In the course of these public appearances, Mao received over one million ecstatic young Red Guards. Wearing olive-drab military-style uniforms adorned with bright red armbands, and waving copies of the Little Red Book (compliments of Lin Biao and the PLA), the students excitedly chanted "Long live Chairman Mao! A long, long life to Chairman Mao!"

At one of these mass receptions, a female student named Song Binbin spontaneously removed her own armband and handed it to the chairman. On it, the characters *"Hong-wei-bing"*—Red Guard—were printed in gold letters on a field of crimson. Mao smiled broadly as he put it on. He was now an honorary Red Guard. The students were ecstatic.

Next time we shall see how Mao's symbolic embrace of the Red Guards emboldened China's impressionable students to undertake a succession of ever more daring—and ever more violent—actions. The Cultural Revolution was about to get very ugly, and on a very large scale.

The Children's Crusade, 1966–1967
Lecture 23

At heart I was struggling with myself. Our principal had been very good to me. ... [If I] turned against him ... I would be acting against my own conscience. ... On the other hand, if I wanted to enter a university, I needed "political capital," which I could acquire only [by attacking] the powerholders.

— A high school student, after witnessing
the brutal beating of his principal

In August 1966, Mao Zedong unleashed the Red Guards. At a Central Committee meeting that same month, Liu Shaoqi and Deng Xiaoping were criticized and demoted. Lin Biao replaced Liu as Mao's heir apparent, and top leftists, including Mao's wife, **Jiang Qing**, were named to head a new Central Cultural Revolution Small Group. Mao's decision to include Jiang in the new group raised a number of eyebrows, since it violated the CCP's long-standing ban on her participation in politics. Although Mao and Jiang's relationship was quite stormy and they had stopped living together years earlier, Jiang became a major player in the Cultural Revolution—and a key member of the so-called Shanghai Clique.

We were intoxicated with our own power. We were Chairman Mao's "little red generals," and we were immortal. Who would dare to oppose us?

With Mao having sounded the call for a nationwide student rebellion, the Cultural Revolution entered its most turbulent stage yet. In September 1966, fall classes were cancelled in all Chinese schools and universities to allow students across the country to form Red Guard detachments and go forth to "make revolution." Almost immediately, differences of opinion emerged over who was eligible to join the Red Guards. With no central directives available to resolve the question of who was eligible to join, competing organizations of Red Guards sprang up in many schools and universities. To bolster their contention that they were true revolutionaries, students from "bad" class backgrounds often exhibited behavior that was more radical and destructive than that of the "naturally red" students.

Groups of Red Guards humiliated, imprisoned, and tortured thousands of teachers and administrators. Thousands were beaten to death—no one knows just how many—and suicides were common. Once they had finished struggling against their school officials, Red Guards were instructed to "destroy the **four olds**." The rampaging students burned books, smashed works of art, and defaced religious icons. They

Jiang Qing and Mao Zedong. Jiang, Mao's fourth wife, became a powerful leader of the leftist Shanghai Clique.

were also given free railroad passes to link up and exchange revolutionary experiences with counterparts from other areas, which led to a good deal of petty vandalism and other inappropriate behavior. As one former Red Guard said, "We were intoxicated with our own power. We were Chairman Mao's 'little red generals,' and we were immortal. Who would dare to oppose us?"

In the winter of 1966–1967, the Cultural Revolution spread to factories and farms, as rival factions took to the streets to settle their differences. The first major city to experience a systematic assault by the mobilized industrial workers—who called themselves **revolutionary rebels**—was Shanghai. In January 1967, a city-wide organization of 100,000 leftist factory workers confronted a 20,000-strong militia organization set up by the municipal government. The insurgents surrounded city hall, and a tense standoff ensued, with each group claiming to represent the true revolutionaries. Mao and Zhou Enlai personally intervened, praising the rebellious factory workers for correctly "grasping revolution." Thereafter, the entire municipal government apparatus was reorganized.

In the aftermath of the Shanghai uprising, radical Red Guards and revolutionary rebels throughout China began to seize power in factories, offices, commercial establishments, schools, and universities, in emulation of their Shanghai compatriots. As the scope of working-class participation broadened, the motives of participants became murkier and less principled. With violence beginning to edge over into anarchy, Mao intervened once more. In the spring of 1967, he ordered all schools reopened, all Red Guards back to school, and all workers back to work.

Meanwhile, the power struggle in Beijing was entering a new stage. Encouraged by members of the Central Cultural Revolution Small Group, radical students at Tsinghua University captured Liu Shaoqi's wife, Wang Guangmei, and publicly humiliated her in a mass rally. Liu was also taken captive; suffering from untreated diabetes and pneumonia, he died of medical neglect in 1969. Peng Dehuai also died in captivity, after being brutalized by Red Guards. At Zhou Enlai's behest, Deng Xiaoping avoided prison and was exiled to a small township.

The Chinese Communist Party was being systematically shattered—its leaders brutalized, its morale crushed. Slowly but surely, Mao's radical minions were pushing the country toward the brink of anarchy. ∎

Name to Know

Jiang Qing (1914–1991): Mao Zedong's fourth wife and a former movie actress, Jiang met and married Mao in Yan'an in 1938. She became China's culture czar during the Cultural Revolution, instigating Red Guards to attack "powerholders." She was convicted of murder and treason in 1980 and hanged herself in her prison cell in 1991.

four olds: The Red Guards were mobilized in 1966 to destroy "old habits, old ideology, old customs, and old culture."

revolutionary rebels: Nonstudent activists in the Cultural Revolution, including workers and peasants.

Suggested Reading

Chang, *Wild Swans*.

Chang and Halliday, *Mao*.

Cheng, *Life and Death in Shanghai*.

Fenby, *Modern China*.

Gittings, *The Changing Face of China*.

Li, *The Private Life of Chairman Mao*.

Ling, *The Revenge of Heaven*.

MacFarquhar and Schoenhals, *Mao's Last Revolution*.

Questions to Consider

1. Why did the Red Guard movement break down into unprincipled factional conflict?

2. How did Jiang Qing and her radical colleagues contrive to expand mass attacks on suspected class enemies?

The Children's Crusade, 1966–1967
Lecture 23—Transcript

In August of 1966 Mao unleashed the Red Guards with a series of carefully-orchestrated personal appearances at Tiananmen Square. Feeding on the mass frenzy of the adoring students, Mao spurred his "little red generals" into action. In this lecture we shall see how Mao's patronage caused the Red Guard movement to grow dramatically in the summer of 1966, and then to run off the tracks and out of control in the fall of that year. By the follwing winter of 1967, China was poised on the brink of anarchy.

In between meeting and greeting multitudes of ecstatic young Red Guards at Tiananmen Square, in the first half of August 1966, Mao was chairing an important plenary session of the Party Central Committee. It was the first full plenum to be held in four years since Mao launched the Education Movement in 1962. Although the party constitution called for annual plenary sessions, Mao hadn't wanted to convene the party's supreme decision-making body until he was assured of controlling both its agenda and its outcome. Now, that time had come.

With legions of eager, excited young students packing the rafters of galleries above the main floor of the Great Hall of the People, the Central Committee meeting was dominated thoroughly by the leftists. Speaker after speaker denounced Mao's putative adversaries, including Peng Zhen, the "Three Family Village," and the work teams controlled by Liu Shaoqi and Deng Xiaoping. Not surprisingly, the final communiqué adopted by the plenum represented a decisive victory for the Maoists. Liu Shaoqi and Deng Xiaoping were demoted in rank, while Peng Zhen and Lu Dingyi were dismissed outright, along with PLA Chief of Staff Lo Ruiqing. (You may recall that a year earlier, Lo Ruiqing had sharply criticized Lin Biao for ordering the army to memorize the Little Red Book.)

To fill the leadership vacuum created by these prominent demotions and dismissals, the plenum appointed leading members of Mao's left-wing brain trust—Lin Biao, Jiang Qing, Kang Sheng, Chen Boda, and Zhang Chunqiao—to head up a new Central Cultural Revolution Small Group (or CCRG, for short). And Lin Biao was now designated to replace Liu Shaoqi as Mao's successor.

Mao's decision to include Jiang Qing in the new Central Cultural Revolution directorate raised a number of eyebrows, since it clearly violated the CCP's longstanding ban on Jiang's participation in politics. Although Mao had stopped living with Jiang years earlier, and though their relationship was quite stormy—she was furious at his constant womanizing, and he resented her penchant for political intrigue—Jiang nonetheless quickly became a major player in the Cultural Revolution and a key member of the so-called "Shanghai Clique."

A decade later the four leftist leaders of this Shanghai Clique, Jiang Qing, Zhang Chunqiao, Yao Wenyuan, and an unheralded young factory security worker named Wang Hongwen, would be imprisoned and universally reviled as the infamous "Gang of Four." But that would come later. For now, in the late summer of 1966, the leftists were flying high.

With Mao having sounded the call for a nationwide student rebellion, the Cultural Revolution entered its most turbulent stage yet. In September, fall classes were cancelled in all Chinese schools and universities to allow students across the country to form Red Guard detachments and to go forth to "make revolution."

Almost immediately, differences of opinion emerged over who was eligible to join the Red Guards. Students from the so-called "good" class, or good backgrounds, namely, the offspring of workers, peasants, soldiers, cadres, and revolutionary martyrs, argued that they alone should have the right to be Red Guards, insofar as they had been "born red," or naturally "red."

Other students, from bad or questionable class backgrounds, such as intellectuals, rich peasants, and the petty bourgeoisie countered by arguing that one's revolutionary purity depended not on the accident of one's birth, but on one's manifest political attitudes and behavior. You are what you do, they said, not what you were born.

With no central directives available to resolve this question of who coud join and who couldn't, competing organizations of Red Guards sprang up in thousands of schools and universities.

To bolster their contention that they were the true revolutionaries, students from "bad" or "impure" class backgrounds often exhibited behavior that was more radical and destructive than that of their "naturally red" cohorts, who were under less pressure to prove their revolutionary merit. Imitating Nie Yuanzi and her Beida comrades, these "impure" students waged fierce and often brutal struggles against their unfortunate teachers and school administrators.

In many cases, the students' political actions conflicted with their personal feelings. One young Red Guard from Fujian province told of his personal dilemma when one of his favorite teachers was attacked by his Red Guard faction. His account is both vivid and disturbing—so disturbing, in fact, that some of you may wish to skip over it:

> The heaviest blow to me was the killing of my ... beloved teacher, Chen Gude. He had been imprisoned ... and tormented by class bullies ... I was powerless to stop them, and [besides,] it was reactionary even to try to protect someone. ...
>
> Over 60 years old and suffering from high blood pressure, Teacher Chen was dragged out at 11:30 a.m. [After being] exposed to the hot sun for more than two hours, ... he was beaten with fists and broomsticks ...
>
> He passed out several times but was brought back to consciousness each time with cold water splashed onto his face. He could hardly move his body. His feet were cut with glass and thorns. But his spirit was unbroken. He shouted "Why don't you kill me? Kill me!"
>
> This lasted for six hours, until he lost control of his bowels. Then they tried to force a stick into his rectum. He collapsed for the last time.
>
> They poured cold water on him again—but it was too late. ... The killers were stunned momentarily, for this was ... the first time they had ever beaten a man to death. ... People began to run away, one after another. ... The school doctor was summoned. [Terrified,] the doctor wrote on the death certificate: "Death due to a sudden attack of high blood pressure." (K. Ling, *Revenge of Heaven*, pp 11–12)

Some students were sickened by what they saw and tried to avoid taking part. After witnessing the brutal beating of his high school principal, one student wrote:

> At heart I was struggling with myself. Our principal had been very good to me. ... [If I] turned against him ... I would be acting against my own conscience. ... On the other hand, if I wanted to enter a university, I needed "political capital," which I could only acquire [by attacking the power-holders].

Throughout the late summer and autumn of 1966, similar scenes were played out at tens of thousands of schools across the country, as teachers and administrators were systematically subjected to humiliation, physical abuse, and torture. Thousands were beaten to death—no one knows just how many—and suicides were common.

How to explain all this madness? In numerous memoirs and reminiscences of the events of this period, former Red Guards have acknowledged the brutality of their own behavior, yet without being able to satisfactorily explain how the boundaries of conventional civility had been so easily breached.

Clearly, peer group pressure and the absence of adult supervision were important factors, much as they had been key factors in William Golding's fictionalized account of adolescent brutality in his vivid novel, "Lord of the Flies." In the case of the Red Guards, mass hysteria was an additional factor. A psychological contagion had been induced by the students' frenzied devotion to Chairman Mao. In giving vent to their most destructive impulses, they truly believed they were acting on behalf of their living deity.

In such a hyper-charged atmosphere, the license to defy authority interacted with immature youthful absolutism and overactive teenage hormones to create an explosive, potentially deadly mix. Nowhere was this combustibility demonstrated more clearly—or more fiercely—than in the Red Guards' violent conflicts with rival groups of rebel students.

Like the Sharks and the Jets in the musical "Westside Story," the "born red" students and the "impure" students in each school vied with each other to see who could be the most revolutionary. At first their competitiveness was expressed verbally, shouting at each other quotations from the Little Red Book. But before long it became intensely physical. And within a year, open warfare between rival Red Guard factions would destroy whatever unity of principle and purpose may have notionally existed at the outset.

Once the Red Guards had finished struggling against their own school officials, they were instructed by Mao's leftist "brain trusts" on the Central Cultural Revolution Group to go forth and "Destroy the Four Olds." The "Four Olds" were defined as old thinking, old culture, old customs and old habits. And students were given a free pass to "smash" them, quite literally.

Responding to the call, roving bands of youngsters, some as young as 14 or 15, ransacked homes, shops, and offices, burning "old" books, defacing works of art, smashing religious icons, and generally making mayhem. They even tore down street signs and renamed them, "Anti-Revisionism Street," and "Eradicate Capitalism Avenue."

Urban traffic patterns were rendered chaotic when the Red Guards decided that a red light should mean "go," and a green light, "stop." The world was, quite literally, being turned upside down in China.

In the fall of 1966 Red Guards were given a free pass on the nation's railroads and bus lines. Encouraged to "link up" and "exchange revolutionary experiences" with their counterparts from other provinces, they roamed the country freely in groups, forming alliances with like-minded youngsters from other areas.

In a highly repressive society where young people normally enjoyed precious little autonomy or freedom expression, the "linking up" movement unleashed more than just revolutionary impulses. The students also engaged in a good deal of petty vandalism, licentious sexual activity, and just plain hooliganism. As one former Red Guard later told me, "We were intoxicated with our own power. We were Chairman Mao's 'little red generals,' and we were immortal. Who would dare to oppose us?"

As the Red Guards responded to Chairman Mao's call to "Bombard the headquarters," Mao's wife, Jiang Qing, was busy carrying out her own brand of revolution. Appointed to head the cultural subgroup of the Central Cultural Revolution Group, she became a one-woman censorship board—a virtual czar of culture.

Under her direction, all Western music and films (and many Western musical instruments) were banned as bourgeois, and traditional Chinese songs and operas were categorically banned as "feudal remnants." In their place, Jiang Qing personally compiled a list of "approved" films, music, and theatrical works. Eight—and only eight—model revolutionary operas and ballets were authorized for performance during the Cultural Revolution. All were highly political and militant in content, bearing names such as "The Red Detachment of Women," "Taking Tiger Mountain by Strategy," and "The Red Lantern."

Mme. Mao also had a major impact on the world of fashion. From 1966 on, any form of personal expression of individuality in fashion, couture or clothing was prohibited. Women were instructed to dress plainly and austerely, in simple green or blue military-style uniform jackets, with baggy trousers and flat shoes. Hair was worn either in austere page-boy cuts or in pig-tails, hidden under PLA-style peaked caps. Makeup and jewelry were forbidden altogether.

What few people knew at the time was that while Jiang Qing was relentlessly stamping out bourgeois culture among the Chinese masses, in the privacy of her own private villa in the south of China, she freely indulged her own taste for Western films, fashions, and accoutrements. As a former movie actress, who had once played in an Ibsen film, she had particular fondness for Greta Garbo movies.

As autumn deepened in 1966, and student rebelliousness began to get seriously out of hand in many areas, frustrated party and government leaders in the provinces began to mobilize their local constituents to resist the unruly students. Fighting fire with fire, they shouted revolutionary slogans of their own, claiming to be the true leftists, while painting the young rebels as fraudulent opportunists who were waving the red flag.

To resist the conservative backlash, the Maoists in November put out an order to their followers all over the country to mobilize members of the working class to repel what they called the "frenzied counterattacks" of the power-holders. No longer confined to schools, universities, and cultural institutions, the Cultural Revolution now spread to industrial and commercial enterprises.

The first major city to experience a systematic assault by the mobilized industrial workers, who called themselves "revolutionary rebels," was Shanghai. In early January 1967, a city-wide organization of 100,000 left-wing factory workers confronted a 20,000-strong militia organization set up by the Shanghai municipal government. The insurgents surrounded city hall, a building on Shanghai's famous Bund. A tense standoff ensued, with each group claiming to represent the true leftists.

When two local members of the Central Cultural Revolution Group, Zhang Chunqiao and Yao Wenyuan, arrived on the scene and endorsed a "seizure of power" by the radical workers against the municipal authorities, they were strongly denounced by the proestablishment militia. A standoff ensued.

At this critical juncture, Mao Zedong and Zhou Enlai intervened personally. Praising the rebellious factory workers for correctly "grasping revolution," they sealed the fate of Shanghai's political establishment. Within a matter of days, three-quarters of the members of the Shanghai municipal party committee and government were dismissed outright. Four of them later died as a result of injuries suffered during the confrontation. Thereafter, the entire municipal governing apparatus was reorganized.

In mid-January Mao formally approved this transfer of power, and thereby brought into existence a new form of popular governance, which he referred to as the "Shanghai People's Commune."

Loosely modeled after the Paris Commune of 1871 (when Parisian workers had rose up to seize control of their city), the new Shanghai Commune turned out to be a fiasco. With no clear lines of command, no well-demarcated functional jurisdictions, little or no administrative experience, and no discipline whatsoever, the victorious insurgents made what can only be called a proper hash of things. Their constant quarreling over the spoils of victory made any form of rational governance impossible.

For the second time in less than a decade, Mao was forced to backtrack on his vision of creating a revolutionary people's commune. Now he proposed a less radical, more highly structured form of government, which he called the "revolutionary committee."

In this new model, political and administrative authority would be wielded by a single unified committee composed of three evenly weighted constituencies: First were the representatives of the rebellious masses, the workers and students; second were former cadres and officials who had "passed the test" of loyalty to Chairman Mao; and third were representatives of the People's Liberation Army. Military participation was deemed essential for the maintenance of discipline and order.

In the aftermath of the Shanghai uprising, radical Red Guards and revolutionary rebels throughout China began to seize power in factories, offices, commercial establishments, schools and universities, in emulation of their Shanghai compatriots.

In many places, rebellious workers used the pretense of "making revolution" to press for higher wages or to demand the abolition of the exploitative system of labor contracts, under which millions of temporary workers enjoyed no job security and no welfare benefits. Some simply were seeking revenge against their factory managers, foremen, or co-workerswho had done injury to them in the past.

As the scope of working class participation broadened, the motives of the participants became murkier, less principled, and more patently self-interested. With all sides loudly proclaiming their loyalty to Chairman Mao, it become extremely difficult, if not impossible, to tell which groups (if any) were truly revolutionaries, and which were merely waving their red flag.

As violence mounted early in 1967 and began to edge over into anarchy, Mao intervened once again. In the spring of 1967, he ordered all schools to be reopened, and he instructed itinerant Red Guards to return to their home schools to resume classes. At the same time, workers were told to make revolution only in their spare time, in their own factories after completing their daily eight-hour work shifts.

To restore order in those work units that had been hardest hit by factional violence, Mao ordered Lin Biao to dispatch PLA propaganda teams to the most trouble-plagued units, where the mandate was to "support the leftists."

For reasons already mentioned, this was easier said than done. More often than not, the army propaganda teams, at a loss to determine who were the real revolutionaries and who were opportunistically "waving the red flag," opted to uphold the established power-holders. Like the work teams of Liu Shaoqi and Deng Xiaoping before them, the army propaganda teams were reluctant to hand power to unruly insurgents, who often conducted themselves like hooligans.

Meanwhile, the power struggle in Beijing was entering a new stage. Encouraged by members of the Central Cultural Revolution Group, radical students at Tsinghua University demanded to "drag out" Liu Shaoqi and his wife, Wang Guangmei, to face the wrath of the masses. Although Zhou Enlai tried to protect Liu and Wang by refusing to grant the students access to them, the rebel students outsmarted them. They devised a clever ruse to trick Wang Guangmei into coming out into the open.

An elegant woman from a well-to-do family, Wang Guangmei had worked as an interpreter for the U.S. military in Chongqing during the anti-Japanese War. Her beauty, grace, and charm, while widely admired within China, were a source of great irritation—and envy—to Jiang Qing.

Of more immediate political relevance was the fact that Wang Guangmei had led a work team to Tsinghua University in June of 1966. Under her guidance, the work team had suppressed the rebel faction and defended the local party establishment. Now it would be payback time.

One day in the early spring of 1967 Wang Guangmei was lured out of her residence by an anonymous phone caller who claimed that her daughter, Pingping, had been badly injured in a traffic accident. Alarmed, Wang rushed to the hospital, where she was grabbed by a group of Tsinghua students who had cooked up the incident as a hoax.

The rebels took Wang Guangmei back to the campus of Tsinghua University, where they forced her to put on her own elegant silk evening gown that she had worn while on a state visit to Indonesia with her husband the previous year. Jiang Qing had seen a photograph of Wang decked out in her fancy gown, accented with an expensive string of pearls, high heels, bright red lipstick, and fashionable coiffure. And Jiang had been livid. Now was the time for her revenge.

After forcing Wang to don the silk dress, her student captors added silk stockings and high-heeled shoes. Then they draped a string of white-painted ping-pong balls around Wang's neck, representing the pearl necklace that she had worn, and slashed a wide streak of bright red lipstick across her face, from cheek to cheek.

Wang remained defiant as they led her away to a mass struggle meeting on the Tsinghua University campus. There she was given a mock trial in front of hundreds of students, who shouted epithets at her, including "whore" and "harlot."

Shaking with fear and anger, Wang refused to bend to the will of her tormentors. After several hours, she was allowed to return home. One rebel later wrote that Jiang Qing "[told] me … to humiliate Wang Guangmei. … We could insult her any way we wanted."

A few months later, Liu Shaoqi himself was dragged out to face a kangaroo court of Red Guards. As he attempted to speak, he was shouted down by the crowd, which rained blows down on his head. He was punched, kicked, and forced to assume the painful "flying sparrow" position, with knees bent and arms outstretched to the rear.

Later, Liu was sent away to the city of Kaifeng, in Henan Province, where he was kept in solitary confinement for two years. Suffering from diabetes and pneumonia, contracted during his long incarceration, Liu was denied medical care. He died in November 1969 on a surgical gurney, alone and naked in a bare, unheated room in a Kaifeng prison hospital. The cause of death was medical neglect.

Other top leaders and their families were similarly brutalized in 1967. Bo Yibo, one of the Communist Party's most senior economic planners, was beaten into unconsciousness at a mass rally in Beijing's Workers Stadium. After being subjected to torture during a prolonged Red Guard interrogation, the former PLA Chief of Staff Lo Ruiqing was permanently paralyzed in a failed suicide attempt.

Peng Dehuai, Peng Zhen, and other erstwhile "capitalist roaders" were driven around Beijing in the back of an open truck, wearing dunce caps and placards denouncing them. At a series of mass rallies in athletic stadiums, they were beaten senseless.

Peng Dehuai later died of his cumulative injuries, as did Lo Ruiqing. So too did the famous Long March veteran, Marshal He Long. Even Mao's oldest comrade, Zhu De, co-founder of the Red Army, in 1928, was repeatedly beaten and struggled against.

As for Deng Xiaoping and his family, Deng's son, Pufang, broke his back when he jumped (or was pushed) off the roof of a building during a brutal interrogation by militant Red Guards. He remained paralyzed for life. Deng Xiaoping himself, it should be noted, avoided serious physical harm when he and his wife were sent to the relative safety of a remote rural township at Zhou Enlai's behest. At least some of the time, Zhou did what he could to protect his old comrades.

But it was not nearly enough. The Chinese Communist Party was being systematically shattered; its leaders brutalized; its morale crushed. Slowly but surely, Mao's radical minions were pushing the country toward the brink of anarchy.

The Storm Subsides, 1968–1969
Lecture 24

By the late winter of 1969, the rustication movement had witnessed the largest human migration in Chinese history. Within six months, more than 10 million youngsters, ranging in age from 14 to 23, were sent from Chinese cities to rural areas and remote border regions.

As China descended into wider and deeper disorder in 1967, two questions began to occur to people: Just what did Chairman Mao know about the extent of the spreading violence and cruelty? And why didn't he do anything to stop it? Without doubt, Mao had personally set in motion the chaotic events of 1966–1967. Moreover, he had not lifted a finger to protect his oldest and closest comrades from extreme physical abuse and even violent death. Based on the testimony of Mao's personal physician, Li Zhisui, the chairman was an aloof and cold-blooded deity, a philosopher-king who professed deep devotion to the popular masses but showed little concern for flesh-and-blood human beings. It is entirely possible that Mao, living inside this imperial cocoon, did not fully comprehend the destructive consequences of his pronouncements.

But there was one person who clearly understood and appreciated the chairman's power to unleash the fury of the masses: Jiang Qing. It was she and her leftist allies who led the brutal assault against the powerholders. Driven partly by pent-up resentment at the party elders who had barred her from politics for 30 years and partly by personal ambition and an evident intoxication with political power, she relished playing the role of patron saint to the Red Guards.

By the spring of 1968, China was perched on the thin edge of anarchy. Governing bodies in virtually all Chinese provinces and municipalities were being replaced by new revolutionary committees, many of which were paralyzed by disputes over who had the authority to do what. To instill a greater sense of discipline, military officers were appointed to fill the top positions in most of the revolutionary committees. Meanwhile, Red Guards and revolutionary rebels throughout the country routinely ignored Beijing's urgent requests to reconcile their factional differences and create a "great unity." Resisting all entreaties from above, the rebels engaged in increasingly large-scale, destructive acts.

In 1968, Red Guards looted PLA armories and turned whole cities into battlegrounds. In Wuzhou, Guangxi Province, rival Red Guard factions armed with light artillery, antiaircraft guns, mortars, and machine guns skirmished in streets, in government buildings, and in private homes: 2,000 buildings were destroyed, and 40,000 inhabitants were left homeless. Also in Guangxi Province, the spring of 1968 brought reports of gruesome forms of ritualized violence, including acts of cannibalism, where one group of rebels would ceremonially carve up and then devour the vital organs of their slain enemies.

> **After repeated Maoist calls for unity and discipline went unheeded, in August 1968 Mao authorized the use of military force to suppress unruly Red Guards.**

Red Guard violence now took on an international dimension. In June 1968, rebels stormed the North Vietnamese consulate in Nanning. Another group of roving rebels looted trains carrying Soviet arms to North Vietnam. After repeated Maoist calls for unity and discipline went unheeded, in August 1968 Mao authorized the use of military force to suppress unruly Red Guards. Thousands of PLA-led **Mao Zedong Thought Propaganda Teams** entered schools, factories, and villages. In some places they encountered rebel resistance, but for the most part they brought factional violence to a rapid halt.

In a move designed to permanently disband the Red Guards, Mao revived the program, first introduced during the Great Leap Forward, to send large numbers of urban middle-school students **up to the mountains and down to the villages**. While earlier rustication movements in China had been short-term in nature, this one was to be permanent. Ten million urban students were sent down to villages to learn humility, industriousness, and plain living from the peasantry. The vast majority of these young people would henceforth be classified as rural inhabitants and not be allowed return to their urban homes. Because of this, and because precious few of the sent-down youths would ever have an opportunity to pursue formal education again, they have been referred to as China's lost generation.

After the Red Guards had been dispersed to the countryside, the next step in restoring political and administrative normalcy in China was to rebuild the badly damaged Communist Party apparatus. By 1969, Lin Biao's PLA—which largely survived the Cultural Revolution unscathed—dominated 23 of 29 provincial revolutionary committees. At the Ninth Party Congress in April 1969, almost half the newly elected Central Committee members were military officers, and Lin himself was formally anointed as Mao's designated successor. Jiang Qing and three other members of the radical Central Cultural Revolution Small Group were also elevated to the Politburo. Soon enough, these two factions would become serious rivals for political power. For now, however, they were allies, each with a major stake in defending the legacy of the Cultural Revolution. Ahead lay the daunting task of restoring a traumatized nation's faith in a badly damaged Communist Party. ∎

Important Terms

Mao Zedong Thought Propaganda Teams: Led by the PLA, these disciplinary teams entered schools and factories throughout China in August 1968 to suppress factional violence and punish recalcitrant Red Guards and rebels.

up to the mountains, down to the villages (*shangshan, xiaxiang*): The Maoist rustication movement of late 1968 that urged urban youths to resettle in the countryside to learn humility and discipline from peasants.

Suggested Reading

Chang and Halliday, *Mao.*

Fenby, *Modern China.*

Friedman, Pickowicz, and Selden, *Revolution, Resistance, and Reform in Village China.*

Li, *The Private Life of Chairman Mao.*

Ling, *The Revenge of Heaven.*

MacFarquhar and Schoenhals, *Mao's Last Revolution.*

Pan, *Out of Mao's Shadow.*

Short, *Mao.*

Zheng, *Scarlet Memorial.*

Questions to Consider

1. Why did Mao Zedong finally decide to curb Red Guard violence and chaos, and what methods did he use?

2. Why did the People's Liberation Army emerge as such a powerful political actor at the end of the Cultural Revolution?

The Storm Subsides, 1968–1969

Lecture 24—Transcript

Last time we saw how Red Guards and revolutionary rebels used—and abused—their Maoist mandate to destroy the "Four Olds," to attack capitalist roaders, and to seize local power throughout the country. In this lecture we examine the consequences of their actions.

As China descended into wider and deeper disorder in 1967, two questions began to occur to people: Just what did Chairman Mao know about the extent of the spreading violence and cruelty? And why didn't he do anything to stop it?

Without doubt, Mao had personally set in motion the chaotic events of 1966 and '67. His Olympian latest instructions had spurred the Red Guards to "bombard the bourgeois headquarters," "expose all demons and monsters," "seize power," and "drag out" the capitalist roaders. Those were his slogans.

Moreover, he had not lifted a finger to protect his oldest and closest comrades from extreme abuse, both physical and verbal, and even violent death (only Zhou Enlai had intervened in this way, and only to a very limited extent). Based on the testimony of Mao's personal physician, Li Zhisui, the chairman was an aloof and cold-blooded deity, a philosopher-king who professed deep devotion to the popular masses but showed little concern for flesh-and-blood human beings. Seated on high, far above the *sturm und drang* of mortal life, not even his closest comrades—including his own wife—could see him without an appointment.

It is entirely possible that Mao, living inside this imperial cocoon, didn't fully comprehend the destructive consequences of his Delphic pronouncements. But there was one person who clearly did understand and appreciate the chairman's power to unleash the fury of the masses. That was his wife, Jiang Qing. It was she, more than anyone, aided by her leftist allies in the Central Cultural Revolution Group and the Shanghai Clique, who led the brutal assault against the power-holders.

Driven partly by pent-up resentment at the party elders who had barred her from politics for 30 years, and partly by personal ambition and an evident intoxication with political power, she relished playing the role of "patron saint" to the Red Guards—a role that, as a former actress, she played to the hilt.

As a historical footnote, more than a decade later, in 1980, when Jiang Qing was put on trial for her actions during the Cultural Revolution, she refused to accept any personal responsibility for the violence of the Cultural Revolution: "I was [just] Chairman Mao's lap dog," she demurred. "When chairman said bite, I bit."

Whether as a mere lapdog or as master architect, Jiang Qing was certainly at the forefront of the mounting chaos. When army propaganda teams intervened to support local power-holders against rebel insurgents in the spring of 1967, Jiang Qing was furious. Later that summer she took her revenge: She instructed her Red Guard followers to direct their anger against alleged capitalist roaders inside the People's Liberation Army. Thus unleashed from on high, radical students began trespassing onto a number of restricted army bases to confront military power-holders. Now the army itself was under direct orders from Mao not to use force in defending themselves against the revolutionary students. Thus the army sat on its collective hands, offering no resistance to the onslaught of the Red Guards.

Once they realized that the army would not stop them, they stopped arguing and debating and began breaking into PLA armories. With soldiers looking passively on, the Red Guards hauled away large quantities of military weaponry and equipment. When outraged PLA commanders began sending urgent messages to Beijing expressing their alarm, Mao finally intervened. He personally rescinded Jiang Qing's instructions and issued orders prohibiting Red Guards from entering any more army bases. But the damage had already been done. And soon afterwards, the pilfered weapons were used in a series of deadly civil wars involving pitched battles between the radical Red Guards and their factional rivals.

As early as the spring of 1967 a group of senior party leaders tried to stop the spiraling madness before it got out of control. Appealing directly to the Central Cultural Revolution Group, China's former agricultural minister, Tan Zhenlin, spoke out on behalf of the dissenting party officials. But when Jiang Qing and her leftist comrades rudely dismissed his concerns and gave him short shrift, the very thin-skinned Tan Zhenlin exploded with anger: "Your purpose is to get rid of all [the] old cadres. ... They made revolution for decades, yet [now they] end up dying, with their families broken. This is the cruelest struggle in the history of our party."

When Tan's outburst elicited no response, he sent a personal note to Lin Biao: "I have come to the end of my tether," he said. "I am ready to die to stop them." Another member of the dissident group, the highly prestigious and much decorated Foreign Minister Chen Yi, said of the Cultural Revolution that "[it] is one big torture chamber."

But such *cri de couer* went for naught. For all their efforts in trying to halt the madness, Tan Zhenlin and Chen Yi were both purged for having instigated a so-called "February Adverse Current." It seemed that there would be no stopping the leftist juggernaut. By the spring of 1968, China was perched on the thin edge of anarchy. Governing bodies in virtually all Chinese provinces and municipalities were being replaced by new "three-in-one" revolutionary committees. But many of these new committees were themselves paralyzed by disputes over who had the authority to do what and to whom.

To instill a greater sense of discipline, military officers were now appointed to fill the top positions in most of the new revolutionary committees, generally at the expense of the quarrelsome revolutionary masses. Meanwhile, Red Guards and revolutionary rebels throughout the country routinely ignored Beijing's urgent requests to reconcile their factional differences and create a "great unity." Resisting all entreaties from above, the rebels engaged in increasingly large-scale, acts of destruction. In a major escalation of factional violence, whole cities now became battlegrounds. In Wuzhou Municipality, in the southern province of Guangxi, a pitched battle occurred in April 1968 between two rival alliances of rebel organizations, the Grand Army and the Alliance Command, each with several thousand fighters.

Using light artillery, antiaircraft guns, mortars, and machine guns seized from PLA arsenals, the two sides skirmished in streets and alleys, in government buildings and private homes. In two weeks of heavy fighting, more than 2,000 buildings in Wuzhou were laid waste and 40,000 inhabitants were rendered homeless. Eventually, the Alliance Command routed the Grand Army, taking 3,000 prisoners in the process.

The unfortunate captives were systematically interrogated and tortured, after which the victors staged three mass executions by firing squad. More than 300 bodies were dumped into shallow graves at a local cemetery. Other corpses were thrown into the West River, where the current carried them downstream. For weeks afterward, bloated corpses from the civil war in Guangxi were seen floating in the harbors of Hong Kong and Macao, three hundred miles downriver.

Also in Guangxi Province, the spring of 1968 brought fresh reports of particularly gruesome forms of ritualized violence, including acts of cannibalism, where one group of rebels would ceremonially carve up and then devour the vital organs of their slain enemies. Here is one contemporaneous eyewitness account of cannibalism in Binyang County, Guangxi. It is not for the squeamish or faint of heart:

> After lighting their kerosene lamps, the hunters searched for victims. … Once they had seized their prey and indulged in some small talk, one of them would sit on the body of a victim … while another cut open the stomach with a five-inch knife. The liver popped out with a little squeeze or kick. … Cutting away the lung and some other adjacent body parts, they then searched for the gut. At that point someone went home to fetch garlic and rice wine. After boiling the liver … seven or eight people sat around a table … and silently consumed the liver by the light of the stove. Some used chopsticks, and some simply ate with their hands.

According to local records, over 3,000 people in Binyang County were killed in 1968. Red Guard violence now took on an international dimension reflecting of the growing schism between Beijing and Moscow and also between Beijing and Moscow's allies in Hanoi, North Vietnam. In June 1968, a band of armed Red Guards stormed the North Vietnamese consulate in Guangxi's capital city of Nanning, forcing the startled Vietnamese diplomatic staff to evacuate the building. The young Chinese rebels screamed anti-revisionist, anti-Soviet slogans as the diplomats fled the building. Other roving groups of rebels, anxious to get hold of heavy weapons, derailed and looted a number of Soviet military trains carrying weapons and war matériel to Hanoi for use in the war against the U.S.-backed South Vietnamese government.

By the late spring of 1968, Mao himself was becoming seriously alarmed over the escalating violence. With large-scale disorder spreading to several provinces, Mao instructed Zhou Enlai to send a directive to the PLA's military headquarters in Guangxi, demanding that law and order be restored immediately throughout the province.

But there were no accompanying orders to use force if necessary. And so the warring factions ignored the order, with the PLA sitting on its hands they refused to lay down their arms and stop their attacks. Shortly afterward, a second directive was issued from Beijing, more serious than the first. This time it bore Mao's personal imprimatur, warning that the rebels' continued refusal to obey orders would be "severely punished." But again there was no order to the army to use force if necessary, and again there was no sign of compliance by the warring factions.

By this time, Chairman Mao's words had begun to lose their once-magical potency. The genie of mass anarchy was out of the jar, and the only institution capable of pushing it back inside—the People's Liberation Army—had been ordered to refrain from defending itself by force. They were still sitting on their hands.

Three years earlier, in 1965, Mao had called for class struggle to be waged to the bitter end. And he had heaped scorn on the philosophy of class reconciliation and moderation, known as "two combine into one." (We talked about that in an earlier lecture.) But in the intervening three years, Mao had seen the bitter fruits of his thesis on class struggle devolve into widespread, unprincipled chaos. Finally, he had had enough. It was now time to combine two into one.

On July 27, 1968, Mao took the dramatic step of summoning five of the most recalcitrant student leaders, including the philosophy instructor Nie Yuanzi of Beida and another young firebrand Kuai Dafu of Tsinghua, to a 4 am emergency meeting at the Great Hall of the People. Now Mao used to keep people off guard by summoning them at the last minute to these middle of the night meetings. He seldom slept, and nobody knew when his summons would come. And so it kept on everyone on their toes. This particular meeting went on for several hours, with the chairman sternly exhorting the fractious students to stop their fighting and unite for the greater good. The students continued to bicker, however, and the meeting ended with their mutual antagonisms and recriminations undiminished.

A few days later, on August 1, 1968 (which just happened to be the 40th anniversary of the founding of the Red Army) Mao issued a directive authorizing the PLA to suppress factional conflict by force, if necessary, finally. A few days later, the first contingent of so-called "Mao Zedong Thought Propaganda Teams" arrived on the campus of Tsinghua University. Commanded by uniformed PLA officers, the propaganda teams were tasked with restoring order and imposing military discipline over the unruly Red Guards.

In a symbolic gesture of the chairman's personal support for this PLA disciplinary initiative, on August 5 Mao sent a highly-publicized gift to the Tsinghua University propaganda team, a basket of fresh mangoes. The next day, the entire front page of the *People's Daily* was given over to the news of Mao's "precious gift of mangoes." The message was clear: The chairman had decreed an end to factional conflict; the PLA was taking control; and force would be used to quell the violence if necessary. Having outlived their usefulness to the chairman, he had signed the order to silence them.

All over China, tens of thousands of Mao Zedong Thought Propaganda Teams entered schools and universities in August 1968. In some places they encountered rebel resistance. But for the most part they brought factional violence to a rapid halt. Under a new slogan—"purify class ranks"— revolutionary committees across the country began to cull the fractious students and rebel workers from their ranks, subjecting them to considerable verbal abuse and humiliation. In a move designed to permanently disband the Red Guards, Mao now revived a program, first introduced during the Great Leap Forward, to send large numbers of urban middle-school students "up to the mountains and down to the villages." While earlier rustication movements in China (known generically as *xiaxiang* or "down to the village") had been short-term in nature, a year or two at most. This time it was to be permanent.

Intended as a form of compulsory mass re-education, rustication was accompanied by a Maoist admonition to the sent-down youths to learn humility, industriousness, and plain living from the peasantry. (As we will see subsequently, Lin Biao would later accuse Mao of cruelly betraying the Red Guards with this order, turning them into cannon fodder once they had exhausted their usefulness to him. That's for a later lecture.)

Notwithstanding the punitive aspect of the rustication movement, it was packaged for public consumption as a patriotic opportunity for young people to serve their socialist Motherland. While the program was nominally voluntary in nature, intense political and peer-group pressure was exerted on the students to sign up lest they appear selfish and unpatriotic. To drive this point home, those students who resisted such pressure often found their food ration cards cancelled.

Pre-departure rituals played upon the patriotic sentiments of the students. There were banquets and fireworks displays, and stirring send-off speeches by local officials. It was all very festive. And it's a measure of both the Red Guards' enduring faith in Chairman Mao and of the remarkable resiliency of their youthful optimism, that many (if not most) of the students welcomed their new assignments as a valuable opportunity to "serve the people." As their trucks departed, many of them happily sang revolutionary songs. Only later would they realize just how bleak their future prospects had become. By the late winter of 1969, the rustication movement had witnessed the largest human migration in Chinese history. Within six months, more than 10 million youngsters, ranging in age from 14 to 23, were sent from Chinese cities to rural areas and remote border regions. From Shanghai, half a million students were "sent-down" and from Beijing, more than 200,000.

For the vast majority of these young people, *xiaxiang* would be a one-way ticket. When they departed, the students carried with them their household registration certificates. Henceforth, they would be classified as rural dwellers, and could not return home to their original urban households. Because of this and because precious few of the "sent-down" youths would ever have an opportunity to pursue formal education again, these 10 million-plus sent-down youth have been collectively referred to as China's "lost generation." With the Red Guards effectively banished to the countryside, the next step in the Maoist restoration of political order was to revive the country's political institutions and administrative services. After two years of unremitting power struggles, the Communist Party was in a shambles. Between 1966 and 1968, hundreds of thousands of party officials had been overthrown, including almost 40 percent of the Central Committee members.

In rural counties, townships and villages, the assault on local power-holders was even more widespread, though reliable statistics on the extent of the damage have never been made available.

Among the civilian population at large, death and destruction were even more widespread. Years later, after Mao died, Jiang Qing and her Shanghai Clique would be officially charged with the murders of 34,800 people during the Cultural Revolution and the persecution of more than 729,000 others.

Most objective observers, however, including many leading Chinese scholars, believe these figures are far too low—orders of magnitude too low. And the most reliable estimates by Chinese scholars suggest that between 750,000 and 1.5 million people died as a result of Cultural Revolution violence, with a roughly equal number suffering permanent injury. After the Red Guards had been dispersed to the countryside, the next step in restoring political and administrative normalcy in China was to rebuild the badly damaged Communist Party apparatus. Under the circumstances, putting Humpty Dumpty back together again would be a daunting task. To whom would the job be entrusted? Because Lin Biao's PLA had survived the power struggles of the previous two years more-or-less intact, the army, almost by default, assumed a major role in party reconstruction. And as more and more provinces formed revolutionary committees in the last half of 1968, the vast majority of these new ruling bodies were dominated by uniformed military officers.

Along with the rise in military leadership in the provinces, substantial numbers of civilian party cadres who had been overthrown during the last two years were now cleared of allegations of wrongdoing and restored to active leadership. However, those on Mao's personal enemies list, people like Liu Shaoqi, his wife Wang Guangmei, Deng Xiaoping, Peng Dehuai, Peng Zhen, and Lo Ruiqing—just to name some of them—remained under a cloud of suspicion. Their exoneration would come only later, in some cases posthumously. For now, they remained condemned as bourgeois power-holders.

There was no small irony in this outcome: The Cultural Revolution had been fought in the name of unleashing the masses; yet when the dust settled, the masses were nowhere to be seen. To be sure, Mao had succeeded in toppling his worst enemies, both real and imagined. But not a single provincial revolutionary committee was headed by a member of Mao's cherished worker-peasant masses. And his little revolutionary generals, the Red Guards, were nowhere to be seen. To paraphrase the lyrics of a song made popular by The Who, the "new boss" looked a whole lot like the "old boss." The one big difference was that more often than not, the new boss wore a shiny green military uniform with brass stars on the collar.

When the Ninth National Party Congress met in the spring of 1969, it was the first such meeting to be held since the onset of the Great Leap Forward more than a decade earlier. Predictably, its main theme was "party rebuilding." Also not surprisingly, the army was highly conspicuous at the Party Congress. Almost 45 percent of the members and alternates of the newly selected Party Central Committee were uniformed military officers. At their head stood Lin Biao, who was now formally designated as Chairman Mao's successor, replacing the disgraced (and soon to be deceased) Liu Shaoqi. The state propaganda media now referred to Lin Biao glowingly as Chairman Mao's "best student" and "closest comrade-in-arms."

Along with the PLA, the other big winners to emerge from the Ninth Congress were members of the Central Cultural Revolution Group. Two members of that group, Mao's security chief, Kang Sheng, and the radical theoretician Chen Boda, were added to the Politburo's inner sanctum, the Standing Committee, to replace Liu Shaoqi and Deng Xiaoping. Although Jiang Qing was not included on the five-member Standing Committee of the Politburo, she and two other members of her Shanghai Clique were promoted to the Politburo itself.

A scattering of workers and peasants were also chosen to sit on the new Central Committee as tokens of the Maoist commitment to "mass democracy," but almost without exception, these mass representatives were excluded from leadership positions. In terms of its core leadership, the Chinese Communist Party was now overwhelmingly dominated by two major factional groupings, Lin Biao's army and the radical leftists of the Cultural Revolution Group. Soon enough, these two factions would become serious rivals for power. For now, however, they were allies, each with a major stake in defending the legacy of the Cultural Revolution.

Standing at the head of the reconstituted CCP were the only two holdovers from the party's pre-Cultural Revolution leadership group: Chairman Mao and Premier Zhou. When Lin Biao delivered the keynote address to the Ninth Party Congress, he declared that the Cultural Revolution had won a great victory against the forces of revisionism in China. Wrapping himself tightly in Mao's mantle, he declared that the "Thought of Mao Zedong" had achieved co-equal status with Marxism and Leninism as the main source of doctrinal orthodoxy throughout the world.

With the country having so recently drawn back from the edge of anarchy, Lin Biao was also extremely cognizant of the need to rebuild the shattered unity and morale of the Communist Party. So, even as he was trumpeting the brilliance of Chairman Mao, Lin held out an olive branch to Mao's defeated foes, welcoming their contribution to national healing. The healing process took on an even greater sense of urgency because of events that were taking place along China's northern border with the Soviet Union. After more than a decade of escalating verbal hostility between Beijing and Moscow, the two sides exchanged live gunfire in March of 1969. Once utterly unthinkable, war between the two Communist giants was growing increasingly possible—even likely. Next time we'll examine the beating of war drums on the Sino-Soviet border.

Timeline

B.C.E.

c. 600 .... Earliest hydraulic irrigation in China.

551 .... Confucius is born.

c. 500 .... Iron plow appears in China.

300 .... First Chinese dictionary.

221 .... China unified under Emperor Qin Shihuang Di.

220 .... Construction begins on Great Wall.

c. 190 .... Silk Road links China and Near East.

C.E.

c. 50 .... Buddhism introduced from Central Asia.

c. 605 .... First imperial civil service examinations.

609 .... Grand Canal completed.

c. 635 .... First Christian missionaries arrive from Persia.

650 .... Earliest record of Islam's arrival in China.

c. 850 .... First reference to gunpowder in China.

1265 .... Mongol leader Kublai Khan invades Sichuan.

1271 .... Voyages of Marco Polo.

1279 .... Mongols conquer China.

1368 .... Ming dynasty founded.

1405–1433 .... Maritime expeditions of Zheng He.

1516 .... First Portuguese contact with Macau.

1582 .... Jesuits begin missionary work in China.

c. 1620 .... Portuguese traders bring opium to China.

1644 .... Manchus overthrow Ming dynasty.

1721 .... Emperor Kangxi bans Christian teaching.

1793 .... Lord Macartney's trade mission arrive in Beijing.

1796–1799 .... White Lotus Rebellion.

1800–1820	Opium becomes leading Chinese import commodity.
1839	Commissioner Lin Zexu seizes British opium.
1839–1842	First Opium War.
1842–1843	Unequal treaties forced upon China.
1850–1864	Taiping Rebellion.
1853–1868	Nian Rebellion.
1856–1860	Second Opium War.
1860	Franco-British armies sack the Summer Palace; Treaty of Beijing further erodes Chinese sovereignty.
1862–1875	Self-Strengthening movement.
c. 1875–1885	Dowager Empress Cixi blocks reforms.
1894	Sun Yat-sen forms Revive China Society.
1898	Guangxu launches Hundred Days of Reform.
1899–1900	Boxer Rebellion.
1906–1911	Sun Yat-sen launches uprisings against Manchus.
October 1911	Local mutiny triggers collapse of Manchu dynasty.
1912	Sun Yat-sen inaugurated president of Provisional Republic of China and reorganizes Guomindang (GMD).
1912–1913	Sun Yat-sen forced into exile, succeeded by Yuan Shikai.
1915	Japan issues 21 Demands.
1916–1926	China enters warlord era.
November 1917	Bolshevik Revolution in Russia.
1918–1919	First Marxist study groups in China.
1919	May 4th movement; birth of modern Chinese nationalism.
1921	Chinese Communist Party (CCP) founded.
1923–1927	First CCP-GMD united front.
1925	Sun Yat-sen dies; Chiang K'ai-shek rises to power.

July 1926	Chiang K'ai-shek launches Northern Expedition.
April 1927	Chiang K'ai-shek attacks Chinese Communist Party; surviving Communists flee, form Red Army.
1927	Chiang K'ai-shek establishes Nationalist government in Nanjing.
1928–1934	Chiang K'ai-shek attacks Chinese Communist Party base area; Mao Zedong introduces "people's war."
September 1931	Japan occupies Manchuria.
October 1934	Chiang K'ai-shek forces Red Army out of South China.
1934–1935	Chinese Communist Party embarks on Long March, relocates in Yan'an.
December 1936	Zhang Xueliang kidnaps Chiang K'ai-shek.
Winter 1937	Chiang K'ai-shek forms second united front with Chinese Communist Party.
July 1937	Japan invades, occupies North and East China.
December 1937	Nanjing Massacre.
1938	Guomindang government retreats to Chongqing; Burma Road provides overland supply route for Guomindang.
1941–1942	Flying Tigers supply Chiang's army by air.
December 1941	Japan attacks Pearl Harbor.
1942–1945	U.S. naval power turns tide of war in Pacific.
1944	U.S. Dixie Mission establishes liaison with Mao in Yan'an.
August 1945	Japan surrenders.
December 1945	President Harry S. Truman sends General George C. Marshall to China.
1946	Mao Zedong and Chiang K'ai-shek talk peace, prepare for war.
1946–1947	Civil war breaks out in Manchuria.
1948–1949	Communists go on offensive, rout Chiang K'ai-shek's forces.

October 1949	Mao Zedong announces birth of People's Republic of China (PRC).
December 1949	Chiang K'ai-shek retreats to Taiwan.
February 1950	Mao Zedong signs treaty of friendship and alliance with Joseph Stalin.
1950–1952	Land reform conducted in rural China.
1950–1953	Korean War brings China and U.S. into military conflict.
1951–1952	Suppress Counterrevolutionaries and Three Anti campaigns launched.
March 1953	Joseph Stalin dies; Nikita Khrushchev eventually succeeds him.
July 1953	Cease-fire in Korea.
1953–1957	PRC launches 5-year economic plan with Soviet advice and money.
1956	China completes economic transition to socialism; Nikita Khrushchev denounces Joseph Stalin; popular unrest erupts in Hungary and Poland.
1956–1957	Mao Zedong introduces Hundred Flowers campaign.
May 1957	Stung by criticism, Mao Zedong halts Hundred Flowers campaign, punishes intellectuals.
Spring 1958	Great Leap Forward begins.
August 1959	Mao Zedong lashes out at critics of the Great Leap Forward.
1959–1961	Three Hard Years bring widespread famine.
1959–1962	Mao Zedong denounces Soviet "revisionism."
1961–1962	Liu Shaoqi and Deng Xiaoping reverse Mao Zedong's radical policies.
September 1962	Mao Zedong launches Socialist Education movement.
1964–1965	Lin Biao initiates Mao Study in People's Liberation Army and schools.

November 1965 .... Leftists criticize revisionist literary works.

August 1966 .... Mao Zedong unleashes Red Guards.

September 1966–1967 ..... Cultural Revolution spawns political violence.

Spring 1967 .... Liu Shaoqi denounced as "China's Khrushchev."

August 1968 .... Soviet troops invade Czechoslovakia.

March 1969 .... Fighting erupts on Sino-Soviet border.

Summer 1969 .... USSR threatens attack on Chinese nuclear facilities.

1969–1970 .... Richard Nixon and Mao Zedong begin to consider U.S.-China détente.

April 1971 .... Zhou Enlai invites U.S. ping-pong team to Beijing.

July 1971 .... Henry Kissinger makes secret trip to Beijing.

September 1971 .... Lin Biao dies in suspicious plane crash.

February 1972 .... Richard Nixon flies to China, signs Shanghai communiqué.

1973–1976 .... Succession struggle heats up as Mao Zedong's health fades.

August 1974 .... Richard Nixon resigns in wake of Watergate scandal.

April 1975 .... Chiang K'ai-shek dies, is succeeded by Chiang Ching-kuo.

January 1976 .... Zhou Enlai dies, is succeeded by Hua Guofeng.

April 1976 .... Deng Xiaoping purged for inciting "counterrevolutionary incident."

September 1976 .... Mao Zedong dies after naming Hua Guofeng his successor.

October 1976 .... Mao Zedong's widow, Jiang Qing, and three associates arrested for treason.

July 1977–
November 1978 .... Deng Xiaoping mounts political comeback.

November 1978 .... Deng Xiaoping supports free speech at Democracy Wall.

December 1978	Deng Xiaoping becomes "paramount leader," launches economic reforms; Deng and Jimmy Carter agree to normalize U.S.-PRC relations.
January 1979	Deng Xiaoping tours United States.
February 1979	Deng Xiaoping launches punitive counterattack against Vietnam.
Winter 1979	Democracy Wall closed; leading activists arrested.
April 1979	U.S. Congress passes Taiwan Relations Act.
Spring 1980	Chinese government authorizes decollectivization of agriculture.
1980	Four Special Economic Zones are created along China's southeast coast.
August 1980	Deng Xiaoping proposes major political reforms.
November 1980	Gang of Four tried for murder, treason.
December 1980	Stung by popular unrest, Deng Xiaoping shelves political reform.
1982	Rural people's communes abolished.
Fall 1983	Hard-liners launch campaign to stamp out spiritual pollution.
1984–1985	Sweeping urban economic reforms introduced by Zhao Ziyang.
November–December 1986	Student demonstrations support democracy.
January 1987	Hard-liners oust liberal Party chief Hu Yaobang.
October 1987	Zhao Ziyang proposes political reforms.
1987–1988	Rampant inflation and corruption undermine popular support for reforms.
April 15, 1989	Death of Hu Yaobang triggers student demonstrations.
April 26, 1989	Deng Xiaoping labels student movement "unpatriotic."
May 1–15, 1989	Student demonstrations grow larger; hunger strike begins.

May 19–20, 1989	Martial law imposed in Beijing; citizens block army convoys.
June 3–4, 1989	Deng Xiaoping orders People's Liberation Army to clear Tiananmen Square; hundreds killed.
June 14, 1989	Zhao Ziyang purged for "splitting party," replaced by Jiang Zemin.
August–December 1989	Communist regimes collapse in Eastern and Central Europe.
1990–1991	Conservatives attack Deng Xiaoping's reforms as "capitalistic."
1991	First McDonald's restaurant opens in Beijing.
December 1991	Soviet Union disintegrates; Boris Yeltsin replaces Mikhail Gorbachev.
January 1992	Deng Xiaoping undertakes Southern Tour to bolster support for reforms.
1993	Zhu Rongji named economic czar, applies brakes to overheated economy.
1994–1998	Banking and tax reforms launched; state enterprises restructured.
August 1995– March 1996	China conducts missile tests in Taiwan Strait.
March 1996	Lee Teng-hui becomes Taiwan's first elected president.
February 1997	Deng Xiaoping dies.
July 1, 1997	Britain returns Hong Kong to China.
April 1999	About 10,000 Falun Gong supporters "illegally" demonstrate in Beijing.
May 1999	U.S. accidentally bombs Chinese embassy in Belgrade, Yugoslavia.
2000	China introduces first Internet restrictions.
February 2000	Jiang Zemin calls for admitting capitalists into Chinese Communist Party.
March 2000	Chen Shui-bian elected president of Taiwan.
Summer 2000	George W. Bush's presidential campaign labels China as "strategic competitor."

Timeline

April 2001	U.S. spy plane forced down in China.
July 2001	Beijing awarded 2008 Summer Olympics.
September 2001	China enters World Trade Organization.
November 2002	Hu Jintao succeeds Jiang Zemin as Chinese Communist Party general secretary.
Winter 2003	SARS epidemic breaks out in China.
August 2003	Six-party talks begin on North Korean denuclearization.
June 2004	Scientists warn of major HIV/AIDS epidemic in China.
April 2005	Guomindang leader Lien Chan visits Beijing.
October 2005	First Chinese astronauts orbit Earth.
January 2006	Chinese agricultural tax abolished.
2006	Private autos exceed 30 million in China; China overtakes U.S. in carbon dioxide emissions.
2007	China surpasses Japan to become world's third-largest economy; annual U.S. trade deficit with China exceeds $250 billion.
December 2007	Internet users top 200 million in China.
March 2008	Ma Ying-jeou elected president of Taiwan; violent protest breaks out in Tibet and is suppressed by People's Liberation Army.
May 2008	Massive earthquake strikes Sichuan, killing 90,000.
July–September 2008	Tainted milk sickens 50,000 children; scandal is covered up.
August 2008	Beijing hosts Summer Olympics.
November 2008	China announces $586 million stimulus package.
December 2008	First direct flights from Taiwan to China.
July 2009	Ethnic violence erupts in Xinjiang: 187 killed, 2,000 arrested.
August 2009	China surpasses U.S. as largest producer of household garbage.

Glossary

antagonistic contradictions: Maoist reference to fundamental threats to state security posed by class enemies. Such contradictions are to be resolved through criticism and struggle. *See also* **contradictions among the people**.

Anti-Rightist Rectification movement (June 1957–1958): The struggle against "bourgeois intellectuals" and wayward CCP members following the termination of the Hundred Flowers campaign.

Autumn Harvest Uprisings (1927–1928): A series of ill-fated, armed insurrections carried out by the CCP in a desperate attempt to avoid annihilation by Chiang K'ai-shek's Nationalist army.

Awaken China Society: *See* **Xingzhong Hui**.

backyard blast furnaces (1958–1959): Indigenous kilns used in rural areas to smelt crude steel during the Great Leap Forward. Most of the steel was unusable.

Battle of Huai Hai (November 1948–January 1949): The turning point in the CCP-GMD civil war. PLA troops surrounded 500,000 GMD soldiers, decimating them in three stages.

Beida: Nickname for Peking University, a contraction of *Beijing Daxue.*

Belgrade embassy bombing (May 1999): The accidental destruction of the PRC embassy in Belgrade, Yugoslavia, by a U.S. stealth bomber. The United States claimed that outdated maps caused an error in targeting.

big-character posters: *See dazibao.*

black cats, white cats: Deng Xiaoping's 1962 thesis arguing that economic productivity is more important than political ideology. Taking exception, Mao Zedong purged Deng in the Cultural Revolution.

black jails: Informal detention centers set up in Beijing in 2007–2008 to hold unruly petitioners demanding fair compensation for pre-Olympic eviction.

bourgeois liberalization: A leftist epithet used to denounce the liberal reforms of Hu Yaobang and Zhao Ziyang in 1980s.

bourgeois powerholders: Those CCP officials accused by Maoists of undermining socialism and promoting capitalism in the mid-1960s. *See also* **capitalist road**.

Boxer Protocol (1901): The treaty that ended the Boxer Rebellion; it exacted large financial indemnities from the Manchus as punishment for their complicity in Boxer attacks on foreigners.

Boxer Rebellion (1899–1900): Insurrection by secret society of "harmonious fists" aimed at killing all foreigners and punishing the Manchus for China's weakness.

Brezhnev Doctrine: The Soviet doctrine of "limited sovereignty" promulgated after the 1968 Russian invasion of Czechoslovakia.

Burma Road (1938–1941): Overland supply route linking Rangoon with Kunming, enabling food and war matériel to reach embattled GMD forces in Chongqing.

capitalist road: Mao Zedong's mid-1960s allegation that many of his comrades were ignoring class struggle and following a "revisionist" path, leading to a restoration of capitalism in China. *See also* **bourgeois powerholders**.

CCP: Chinese Communist Party.

Central Committee: The executive committee of the National Party Congress. It meets annually to debate and enact major policy decisions.

China Alliance Society: *See* **Zhongguo Tongmeng Hui**.

"China's Khrushchev": Maoist epithet for Liu Shaoqi, around 1967–1968.

"Chinese learning as the foundation, Western learning for practical use" (*zhongxue weiti, yangxue weiyong*): The slogan of the Self-Strengthening movement. **civil society**: Nongovernmental associations and interest groups formed by concerned citizens to promote various societal causes.

collective farms (1955–1957): The highest stage of agricultural collectivization, marked by the abolition of private ownership and the large-scale pooling of land and labor among 100–200 families.

Communist International (**Comintern**): Organization founded by Vladimir Lenin in 1919 to promote revolutionary movements in colonial and semicolonial countries.

Confucianism: Classical Chinese philosophical doctrine holding that society is best regulated via internalized moral precepts of virtue and benevolence, rather than compulsion.

contradictions among the people: Maoist reference to the existence of nonantagonistic conflicts of interest among various different social classes and strata. Such contradictions are to be resolved through "patient education and persuasion," rather than coercion. *See also* **antagonistic contradictions**.

cooperative farms (1953–1954): The intermediate stage of agricultural collectivization, marked by the introduction of work points and year-round sharing of land and tools by 20–30 households.

dazibao (**big-character posters**): Large hand-written posters, often anonymous, espousing political principles or accusing others of wrongdoing. Widely used in the Hundred Flowers movement and later during the Cultural Revolution and Democracy Wall period.

Democracy Wall (a.k.a. **Xidan Wall**): The Beijing city wall west of Tiananmen Square that became a haven for free speech in the fall and winter of 1978–1979, as wall posters publicized various political ideas and personal grievances. It was closed by authorities in 1979.

Democratic Progressive Party (DPP): The proindependence Taiwan party that was legalized in 1987. Led by Chen Shui-bian, the DPP won presidential elections in 2000 and 2004.

dictatorship of the proletariat: The Soviet form of government introduced by Vladimir Lenin, which involved Communist Party dictatorship over all class enemies. *See also* **people's democratic dictatorship**.

Dixie Mission (1944): Wartime delegation of U.S. diplomats and military officers sent to Yan'an to liaise with CCP leaders.

East wind prevails over West wind: Coded Maoist thesis of 1958, claiming that the socialist camp had overtaken the imperialist camp in strategic military power.

edge-ball: Tactic used by investigative reporters to test governmental limits on free journalistic inquiry.

EP-3 incident (April 2001): A U.S. spy plane collided in midair with a Chinese fighter jet, forcing the U.S. plane to land in South China. The incident sparked anti-American protests in China.

floating population: Up to 150 million poor farmers who have migrated to Chinese cities since the 1980s. They are generally treated as second-class citizens.

Flying Tigers (1941–1943): Volunteer U.S. fighter pilots under Claire Chennault who assisted the GMD anti-Japan war effort.

Forbidden City: The imperial palace in Beijing, built early in the Qing dynasty.

Four Cleanups movement: *See* **Socialist Education movement**.

Four Modernizations: Slogan first coined by Zhou Enlai, and later revived by Hua Guofeng, calling for the rapid modernization of industry, agriculture, science and technology, and national defense.

four olds: The Red Guards were mobilized in 1966 to destroy "old habits, old ideology, old customs, and old culture."

free-rider problem: Classic dilemma posed when all members of a large group share equally in the benefits of membership without adequate monitoring of individual contributions.

Gang of Four: Radical clique led by Mao Zedong's wife, Jiang Qing, responsible for launching violent factional struggles during the Cultural Revolution. They were tried and convicted in 1980.

Gate of Heavenly Peace: The literal translation of *Tiananmen*, the southern entrance to Beijing's Forbidden City.

Gemingdang (Revolution Party): Organized by Sun Yat-sen while in exile in 1914, this party aimed at overthrowing the regime of Yuan Shikai.

"genocide Olympics": A term coined by activists seeking the boycott of the 2008 Beijing Olympics because of China's support for brutal regimes in Myanmar and Sudan.

***getihu* (individual households)**: The first private entrepreneurs permitted to engage in small-scale commerce in post-Mao China.

Gini coefficient: An index of the degree of inequality in income distribution. A coefficient of less than .30 indicates relatively modest inequality; greater than .45 indicates a high level of inequality.

granny police: Urban neighborhood watchdog groups, generally staffed by elderly women.

great firewall of China: The system of governmental regulations, automated Web filters, and human surveillance designed to censor unwanted Internet content.

Great Leap Forward (1958–1962): Mao Zedong's ill-fated attempt to reach Communism ahead of the USSR by relying on subjective factors—mass ideological mobilization, selfless devotion to labor, and "red" leadership. This movement resulted in great famine and 30 million deaths.

Green Gang: Criminal Shanghai underground society recruited to assist Chiang K'ai-shek govern Shanghai from 1927 to 1937.

guanxi: The Chinese cultural tradition characterized by reciprocal ties of mutual obligation and responsibility.

Guomindang (GMD; Nationalist Party): The republican political organization formed by Sun Yat-sen and Song Jiaoren in 1912, after the Xinhai Revolution. The GMD was forced to move to Taiwan in 1949.

Hai Rui Dismissed from Office: An allegorical 1961 opera by Wu Han likening the purge of Peng Dehuai to the Ming dynasty emperor's dismissal of a loyal minister, Hai Rui.

high-level equilibrium trap: Hypothesis holding that China's dramatic early successes in wet rice cultivation precluded later innovations in farming techniques.

Hong Kong Basic Law: The 1990 miniconstitution guaranteeing substantial local autonomy, political freedom, and institutional continuity for Hong Kong after the 1997 handover to China.

***hongyan bing* ("red-eye disease")**: The envy displayed by low-paid white collar workers in the state sector toward self-employed private entrepreneurs in 1980s.

household responsibility system: The system of contracting farmland to individual families for cultivation that was introduced by Deng Xiaoping in 1978–1979.

***hukou* system**: The system of household registration adopted in the early 1950s to prevent peasants from leaving rural areas. It has been modified since the 1980s to permit urban labor migration.

Hundred Days of Reform (1898): Abortive effort by Emperor Guangxu to reform the Manchu dynasty from within. Spearheaded by Liang Qichao and Kang Youwei, the reforms were blocked by Dowager Empress Cixi.

Hundred Flowers campaign (1956–1957): Mao Zedong's invitation to Chinese intellectuals to freely air grievances. When complaints turned to attacks on the CCP, Mao launched the Anti-Rightist Rectification movement.

information revolution: The rapid spread of new electronic means of communication since the 1980s, marked by the proliferation of cell phones and Internet use.

iron rice bowl: The policy of providing lifetime employment and welfare benefits to Chinese state employees. This policy was gradually restricted in the 1980s and eliminated in the 1990s.

Jiangxi (Kiangsi) Soviet Republic (1930–1934): The Red Army regional base in South China led by Mao Zedong, Zhou Enlai, and Zhu De.

Jinggangshan: The Red Army's mountainous revolutionary base along the Hunan-Jiangxi border, from 1927 to 1928.

Jingjing and Chacha: Pop-up cartoon police icons that appear on Chinese websites to remind Internet users to avoid controversial sites and subjects.

Joint Declaration on Hong Kong: The 1984 agreement signed by Britain and China promising that Hong Kong could retain its economic, administrative, and legal institutions for 50 years after reunification with China.

Keynesian stimulus: An economic policy geared to combat recession by pumping money into the economy via low interest rates, government jobs, and infrastructure investment.

Khmer Rouge: The radical Cambodian Communist movement that seized power in 1975 and then imposed a reign of terror, killing upward of 1 million people.

land reform: The Maoist policy of confiscating the land of wealthy landowners and distributing it to poor peasants. The policy was first introduced in Jiangxi Soviet in 1930–1934 and extended nationwide in 1950–1952.

laobaixing: Ordinary Chinese people (literally, "old hundred names").

Legalism: A classical Chinese philosophical doctrine that stresses the vital importance of laws, regulations, and punishments in regulating human society.

Lin Biao affair (September 1971): An aborted coup attempt allegedly masterminded by Lin Biao, which ended with Lin and his wife dying in a plane crash in Mongolia.

Little Red Book (a.k.a. ***Quotations from Chairman Mao Zedong***): A collection of Maoist sayings and writings that was distributed widely to soldiers and students in 1964 and 1965.

Lushan Plenum (July–August 1959): The party conference at which Mao Zedong angrily attacked critics of the Great Leap Forward and purged Peng Dehuai.

Macartney Mission (1793): The failed trade mission sent by King George III of England to open normal trade relations with China.

Malthusian crisis: A hypothesis by Thomas Malthus that holds that increases in human reproduction eventually outstrip increases in economic productivity, leading to rising human immiseration.

Manchu dynasty (a.k.a. **Qing dynasty**; 1644–1911): The last imperial dynasty, imposed by conquest from Manchuria.

Manchukuo (1931–1945): The puppet Japanese regime in Manchuria that was nominally headed by China's "last emperor," Puyi.

Mao Zedong Thought Propaganda Teams: Led by the PLA, these disciplinary teams entered schools and factories throughout China in August 1968 to suppress factional violence and punish recalcitrant Red Guards and rebels.

Marco Polo Bridge incident (July 1937): Gunfire erupted between Japanese and GMD soldiers at this bridge west of Beijing, providing a pretext for the Japanese invasion.

Marshall Mission (December 1945–January 1947): After Japan's defeat, Truman sent General George C. Marshall to Chongqing in a futile attempt to convince the CCP and GMD to form a coalition government.

May 4th movement (1919): Angry Chinese students and workers protested against the terms of the Versailles Treaty, marking the birth of modern Chinese nationalism.

middle characters: Literary reference in the early 1960s to ordinary people who are neither heroes nor villains; tacitly antithetical to socialist realism.

Middle Kingdom: This literal translation of "Zhongguo" (China) refers to the traditional Chinese belief in a Sinocentric universe.

migrant workers: *See* **floating population**.

modern revisionism: The Maoist charge that Nikita Khrushchev and his successors abandoned revolutionary Leninism in favor of peaceful coexistence and restoring capitalism in the USSR.

most-favored nation: A principle written into mid-19th century unequal treaties granting signatory foreign powers all rights and concessions granted to others in China.

mutual aid (1952–1953): The first stage of agricultural collectivization, marked by small-scale, seasonal sharing of tools, animals, and labor by six or eight neighboring families.

Nanjing decade (1927–1937): A shorthand term for the decade of GMD rule under Chiang K'ai-shek prior to the Japanese invasion.

Nanjing Massacre (a.k.a. **Rape of Nanjing**; December 1937): The invading Japanese army launched a brutal campaign of terrorism against civilians in which more than 100,000 people were murdered and thousands of women were raped and sexually mutilated.

National Party Congress: The highest policy-making body of the CCP, its functions are mainly ceremonial. It meets every four years to elect the Party Central Committee and Politburo.

National People's Congress (**NPC**): China's highest law-making body. Indirectly elected and led by the Communist Party, it lacks independent legislative power.

New Culture movement (1920s): An offshoot of the May 4th movement that witnessed the emergence of a Chinese literary renaissance.

Nian Rebellion (1853–1868): A massive peasant rebellion triggered by the extensive collapse of imperial flood-control works and subsequent famine in the Yellow River region.

Northern Expedition (1926–1927): Chiang K'ai-shek's successful military campaign, launched in cooperation with the CCP, to defeat the warlords and establish a unified government.

one-China principle: China's insistence that Taiwan is an integral part of China and can never be separated from it.

"one country, two systems": The slogan coined by Deng Xiaoping in the early 1980s, promising substantial autonomy for Taiwan and Hong Kong after reunification with China.

"one divides into two": The radical Maoist thesis that all antagonistic contradictions are zero-sum struggles, resulting in victory by one side or the other. *See also* **"two combine into one."**

open cities: Fourteen Chinese cities that in 1984 were granted discretionary authority to make trade and investment decisions without central authorization.

Open Door policy (1898): The policy initiated by President William McKinley that was designed to morally restrain foreign powers from dominating China and to maintain equal access among foreign countries.

Opium Wars: Wars launched by European powers in 1839 and 1856 to punish the Manchu government for restricting foreign commercial access to China.

parliamentary road to socialism: Nikita Khrushchev's thesis that socialism could be achieved without violent revolution in the age of nuclear weapons. Mao Zedong rejected this thesis as "revisionist."

peaceful evolution: China's fear that Western countries will undermine Communism by introducing bourgeois culture, values, and institutions.

people's democratic dictatorship: The Maoist form of government involving multiclass dictatorship over class enemies. *See also* **dictatorship of the proletariat**.

people's war: The Maoist doctrine of guerrilla warfare, which emphasizes tactical mobility, flexibility, and the benevolent treatment of the peasant population. *See also* **three-eight work style**.

Petitioners' movement: The protest movement organized by Fu Yuehua in the winter of 1979 to give voice to victims of Cultural Revolution persecution.

ping-pong diplomacy (April 1971): Term used for the U.S. table-tennis team's visit to Beijing at Zhou Enlai's invitation, which inaugurated the Sino-American détente.

PLA: People's Liberation Army, the army of the People's Republic of China.

poisonous weeds: Mao Zedong's 1957 characterization of art and literature that served to undermined socialism, CCP leadership, or Marxism-Leninism.

Politburo: The small executive body elected by the Party Congress that is the CCP's center of power. It meets frequently and exercises responsibility for party policies when the Central Committee is not in session.

PRC: People's Republic of China.

Qing dynasty (1644–1911): *See* **Manchu dynasty**.

Qingming Incident: *See* **Tiananmen Incident**.

Rape of Nanjing: *See* **Nanjing Massacre**.

Red Guards (a.k.a. *hongweibing*): High school and college students mobilized by Maoists in 1966 to launch attacks on "bourgeois powerholders."

Republic of China (ROC): The government founded by Sun Yat-sen in 1912 and transformed by Chiang K'ai-shek after 1927. The ROC was exiled to Taiwan in 1949.

Republican Revolution: *See* **Xinhai Revolution**.

responsible stakeholder: Term coined in 2005 by Deputy Secretary of State Robert Zoellick to describe the United States' preferred role for China in world affairs.

revolutionary rebels: Nonstudent activists in the Cultural Revolution, including workers and peasants.

rural people's communes: First introduced in 1958, these communes encompassed as many as 10,000 families, all of whom shared equally in communal income and contributed voluntary labor to backyard steelmaking and other nonagricultural tasks.

Rustication movement: *See* **"up to the mountains, down to the villages."**

sanmin zhuyi: *See* **Three People's Principles**.

SARS epidemic: The outbreak of Severe Acute Respiratory Syndrome that hit China in the winter of 2003, killing hundreds and causing brief panic.

scar literature: *See* **wounded literature**.

"seek truth from facts": The slogan used by Deng Xiaoping to attack Hua Guofeng's slavish devotion to the words of Mao Zedong.

Self-Strengthening movement (a.k.a. **Tongzhi Restoration**; 1862–1875): A reform movement initiated by Manchu Prince Gong, designed to defend China against foreigners by studying the secrets of Western military success.

Shanghai communiqué (February 1972): The document signed by Richard Nixon and Zhou Enlai establishing the one-China policy as the basis for normalizing U.S.-China ties.

Silk Road: The network of ancient trade routes linking western China to the Near and Middle East.

Singapore model: The Chinese goal of emulating Singapore by creating an affluent, orderly, law-abiding authoritarian society with few democratic checks and balances.

Socialist Education movement (a.k.a. **Four Cleanups movement**; 1962–1965): Mao Zedong's attempt to launch a mass campaign to inoculate peasants, workers, and cadres against class enemies seeking a "capitalist restoration."

socialist realism: The Stalinist notion, endorsed by Mao Zedong, that art and literature should glorify the working classes and expose the evil machinations of class enemies.

soft power: International influence gained through exemplary behavior, cooperativity, and moral suasion.

Son of Heaven (*tianzi*): The Chinese emperor's official title, implying an inclusive Sinocentric world order.

Southern Tour (*nanxun*): Deng Xiaoping's emergency five-city tour of prosperous coastal zones in January 1992, undertaken to rekindle support for his economic reforms and open policy.

Special Economic Zones: Four coastal ports in Southeast China—Shenzhen, Zhuhai, Xiamen, and Zhanjiang—became experimental export-processing zones in 1980 as part of Deng Xiaoping's "open policy."

spiritual pollution: In the early 1980s, CCP conservatives used this term to criticize Western cultural influences as decadent, immoral, and materialistic.

state-owned enterprises (**SOEs**): The backbone of China's socialist industrial economy. Under Zhu Rongji, SOEs were consolidated and converted to shareholding enterprises.

Taiping Heavenly Kingdom (1853–1864): A rebel state encompassing several provinces and tens of millions of uprooted peasants, with its capital in Nanjing. Founded by Christian zealot Hong Xiuquan.

Taiwan Relations Act (April 1979): The U.S. congressional act clarifying the nature of continuing U.S. economic, cultural, and military ties with Taiwan.

10,000-yuan households: The first group of affluent Chinese entrepreneurs to accumulate substantial private wealth in the 1980s.

Tet Offensive (February 1968): Ho Chi Minh's massive, unexpected offensive against South Vietnamese cities. Opposed by China as "premature," the offensive achieved a moral victory, demonstrating U.S. military vulnerability.

Third Plenum (December 1978): This historic Central Committee meeting is celebrated as the birthplace of Chinese "reform and opening up" under Deng Xiaoping.

Three Anti and Five Anti campaigns (1950–1953): Mass campaigns aimed at combating corruption, waste, tax evasion, bribery, and theft of state secrets, inter alia.

three-eight work style: The Maoist code of ethical conduct for Red Army soldiers and CCP cadres, first introduced in the 1930s. *See also* **people's war**.

Three-Family Village: A collective writing group in the early 1960s that published veiled satirical commentaries poking fun at Mao Zedong's personal foibles.

three hard years (1959–1961): The period of maximum rural hunger and starvation during the Great Leap Forward.

three links: In 2008–2009, direct shipping, postal, and communications links were established for the first time between China and Taiwan.

Three People's Principles (*sanmin zhuyi*): Sun Yat-sen's political platform, which calls for democracy, national independence, and people's livelihood.

Tiananmen Incident (a.k.a. **Qingming Incident;** April 1976): Funeral wreaths placed in Tiananmen Square in memory of Zhou Enlai were quietly removed, setting off angry demonstrations the next day. Jiang Qing blamed Deng Xiaoping for the disturbance.

Treaty of Beijing (1860): The treaty signed after Franco-British forces destroyed the Summer Palace in Beijing.

Treaty of Nanking (1842): The first of several unequal 19th-century treaties granting concessions to foreign powers.

tributary trade system: The traditional hierarchical system of Chinese external relations wherein foreign kings provided periodic gifts in exchange for benevolent Chinese treatment.

21 Demands (1915): The Japanese attempt to close the "open door" by demanding exclusive industrial and commercial rights in China.

"two combine into one": The philosophical premise promoted by liberal intellectuals in the early 1960s, holding that antagonistic contradictions could be peacefully reconciled. *See also* **"one divides into two."**

unequal treaties: Treaties imposed on the Manchu dynasty after the Opium Wars that granted major concessions to foreign powers.

united front: A Comintern tactic, later adopted by Mao Zedong, encouraging former enemies to unite against common foes. The first GMD-CCP united front (1923–1927) opposed warlords; the second united front (1937–1945) opposed Japan.

up to the mountains, down to the villages (*shangshan, xiaxiang*): The Maoist rustication movement of late 1968 that urged urban youths to resettle in the countryside to learn humility and discipline from peasants.

U.S.-Taiwan Mutual Defense Treaty: Signed in 1954, this treaty bound the United States to defend Taiwan. It was cancelled by the United States in 1979.

Velvet Revolution (1989–1991): The sudden, peaceful collapse of Communist regimes in Eastern and Central Europe, culminating in the disintegration of the USSR.

warlord era (1916–1926): The period after the death of Yuan Shikai during which regional militarists ruled independent provincial kingdoms. Warlord armies were defeated by Chiang K'ai-shek's Northern Expedition of 1926–1927.

Whampoa Academy: The military academy founded in Canton by Sun Yat-sen in 1924 to train the Revolutionary Army.

whatever faction: The sobriquet given to Hua Guofeng's supporters in 1977, referring to their habit of blindly upholding whatever Mao Zedong said or did.

White Lotus Rebellion (1796–1799): A peasant rebellion against excessive imperial grain taxes in Central China.

"With you in charge, I'm at ease" (*Ni banshi, wo fangxin*): Mao Zedong's April 1976 bequest to Hua Guofeng, anointing Hua as the his successor.

"women with bound feet": Classical Maoist reference to conservative cadres who are afraid to boldly innovate.

work teams: The traditional CCP method of solving social and organizational problems by sending teams of party and government workers to basic-level units to investigate local conditions. Criticized by Mao Zedong in 1966 for "suppressing the masses."

wounded literature (a.k.a. **scar literature**): Essays and novels published in the early 1980s depicting the suffering endured by the Chinese people during the Cultural Revolution.

Xi'an Incident (December 1936): GMD General Zhang Xueliang kidnapped Chiang K'ai-shek and held him hostage to end GMD-CCP hostilities and create an anti-Japan united front.

Xidan Wall: *See* **Democracy Wall**.

Xingzhong Hui (Awaken China Society): Organized by Sun Yat-sen in 1894, this society aimed at radical, Western-style reform of the Manchu dynasty.

Xinhai Revolution: On October 10, 1911, revolutionary agents in Wuhan's imperial garrison mutinied, triggering the collapse of the Manchu dynasty.

Yalta Conference (February 1945): The wartime meeting of Joseph Stalin, Winston Churchill, and Franklin D. Roosevelt that paved the way for the Soviet war declaration against Japan and postwar partition of Korea.

Yan'an Forum (1942): A lecture series by Mao Zedong that stressed the class content of art and literature, followed by the rectification of "incorrect ideas" within the CCP.

Yan'an spirit: Reference to the high morals, devotion to duty, and unity of leadership demonstrated by the CCP during the anti-Japanese War, 1937–1945.

Yinhe: A Chinese cargo ship suspected of carrying chemical weapons to the Middle East in 1993. The ship was searched at the behest of the U.S. CIA, but no weapons were found.

Yuanmingyuan: The Manchu Summer Palace in Beijing, which was destroyed by the British and the French in 1860.

Zhongguo Tongmeng Hui (China Alliance Society): Sun Yat-sen's renamed revolutionary movement, formed in 1904.

Zhongnanhai: The Beijing residential compound for top-level party and government leaders. Mao Zedong met Richard Nixon there in 1972.

Biographical Notes

Bo Yibo (1908–2007): One of eight original CCP "immortals." A top economic planner, Bo was among the first to concede the tragic death toll of the Great Leap Forward. He was imprisoned and beaten repeatedly by Red Guards during the Cultural Revolution.

Brzezinski, Zbigniew (b. 1928): President Jimmy Carter's national security advisor, Brzezinski championed the normalization of relations with China as a counterweight to rising Soviet expansionism.

Chen Duxiu (1879–1942): A leading intellectual in the May 4th era, Chen launched the influential *New Youth* magazine and cofounded the CCP (with Li Dazhao). Chen was expelled from the CCP in 1929 as a "Trotskyite."

Chen Gongbo (1892–1946): A founding member of the CCP, Chen quit the party in 1922 and joined the Guomindang. After the Japanese invasion, Chen collaborated with Japan. At war's end, he was tried as a traitor and executed by firing squad.

Chen Shui-bian (b. 1951): A vocal supporter of Taiwan independence and the president of the Republic of China from 2000 to 2008. His Democratic Progressive Party (DPP) ended a half-century of GMD rule in Taiwan, but his provocative proindependence rhetoric angered Beijing and irritated Washington. Chen and his wife were convicted of bribery and embezzlement in 2009 and sentenced to life in prison.

Chen Yun (1905–1995): A veteran party leader and top economic planner who in 1978 led the campaign to reinstate Deng Xiaoping. The two later split when the more conservative Chen rejected Deng's "capitalist" methods.

Chennault, Claire (1893–1958): A U.S. Air Force officer who formed a squadron of volunteer American fighter pilots known as the Flying Tigers in Chongqing during World War II.

Chiang Ching-kuo (1910–1988): The son of Chiang K'ai-shek, Chiang Ching-kuo became president of the Republic of China upon his father's death in 1975. He is best known for ending the civil war with the People's Republic of China and introducing democratic reforms in Taiwan in 1987.

Chiang K'ai-shek (1887–1975): The leader of the GMD after Sun Yat-sen's death, Chiang led the Northern Expedition to end warlordism. An ardent anti-Communist, Chiang sought to destroy the CCP at all costs—even while tolerating early Japanese encroachments. After World War II, Chiang suffered a humiliating defeat by Mao Zedong's PLA; Chiang fled to Taiwan in December 1949.

Cixi (1835–1908): This archconservative dowager empress dominated Manchu court politics in the late 19th century. Operating behind the scenes, she effectively manipulated youthful emperors and undermined all efforts at reform.

Deng Liqun (b. 1915): A leading CCP propagandist and hard-line opponent of liberal reform. Deng led the 1983 campaign to combat "spiritual pollution" and in 1991 spearheaded the drive to roll back Deng Xiaoping's "capitalistic" economic reforms.

Deng Xiaoping (1904–1997): A veteran CCP leader and economic pragmatist, Deng introduced sweeping market reforms after Mao Zedong's death. Twice purged as a "revisionist," Deng supplanted Hua Guofeng as China's top leader in December 1978. Best known for his 1962 slogan: "It doesn't matter if the cat is white or black, so long as it catches mice."

Elliot, George (1784–1863): Admiral who commanded the British naval force in Canton in 1839–1840. Seeking retribution for Lin Zexu's seizure of British opium, Elliot engaged his warships in a show of military force, precipitating the First Opium War.

Fang Lizhi (b. 1936): Former Professor of Astrophysics and vice president of China's University of Science and Technology. Fang's liberal political ideas inspired prodemocracy student demonstrations in 1986 and 1989. Expelled from the CCP in 1987, Fang sought asylum in the U.S. embassy in Beijing in June 1989.

Fu Yuehua (b. c. 1947): An unemployed female factory worker who organized the January 1979 Petitioners' movement among victims of leftist persecution in the Cultural Revolution. Fu was arrested and sentenced to three years in jail.

George III (1738–1820): The king of England who sent a high-level trade mission, led by Lord George Macartney, to the court of Emperor Qianlong in 1793.

Gong, Prince (1833–1898): The principal patron of the Self-Strengthening movement of the 1860s, Gong promoted educational reforms and foreign military technology, thereby running afoul of Cixi.

Guangxu (1871–1908): Influenced by liberal intellectuals Kang Youwei and Liang Qichao, this youthful Manchu emperor introduced 40 major domestic reforms in 1898. He was deposed and imprisoned by Cixi following the Hundred Days of Reform.

Hong Xiuquan (1814–1864): The charismatic founder and delusional leader of the Taiping Rebellion (1850–1864). Hong believed himself to be the brother of Jesus Christ and ruled the Taiping Heavenly Kingdom until his death in 1864.

Hu Jintao (b. 1942): A former party secretary in Tibet and Gansu Province, Hu has been the CCP general secretary since 2002. A colorless technocrat with a low-key leadership style, Hu is politically moderate and is a vocal supporter of the goal of a "harmonious society."

Hu Shih (1891–1962): An American-educated philosopher, Hu was a leading figure in China's literary renaissance during and after the May 4th era.

Hu Yaobang (1915–1989): A second-generation party leader and pre–Cultural Revolution head of the CCP Youth League. A liberal who actively supported Deng Xiaoping's reforms, Hu was tabbed to succeed Hua Guofeng as party chief in 1982. Hu was later forced out by hard-liners in 1987, and his sudden death in April 1989 triggered the Tiananmen student protests.

Hua Guofeng (1921–2008): An unheralded party secretary from Hunan, Hua rose to become the dark horse successor to both Zhou Enlai and Mao Zedong in 1976. He was eased out of power by Deng Xiaoping in 1978.

Hurley, Patrick (1883–1963): As President Franklin D. Roosevelt's personal representative in Chongqing from 1944 to 1945, Ambassador Hurley replaced the ascerbic General Joseph Stilwill.

Jiang Qing (1914–1991): Mao Zedong's fourth wife and a former movie actress, Jiang met and married Mao in Yan'an in 1938. She became China's culture czar during the Cultural Revolution, instigating Red Guards to attack "powerholders." She was convicted of murder and treason in 1980 and hanged herself in her prison cell in 1991.

Jiang Zemin (b. 1926): This former Shanghai party secretary was brought to Beijing in May 1989 to replace the discredited Zhao Ziyang as CCP general secretary. Jiang is best known for his 2001 "theory of the three represents," which encouraged Chinese capitalists to join the CCP. He retired in 2003.

Kang Sheng (1898–1975): The sinister head of Mao Zedong's internal security and intelligence apparatus, Kang gained influence by compiling confidential dossiers on thousands of party officials from the 1930s to the 1970s.

Kang Youwei (1858–1927): Kang was the leading liberal reformer in the last decades of the Qing dynasty. He persuaded Emperor Guangxu in 1898 to introduce major innovations in education, civil service exams, medical training, and foreign affairs.

Khrushchev, Nikita (1894–1971): The Soviet party leader after Joseph Stalin, Khrushchev drew Mao Zedong's ire as a "revisionist" for criticizing Stalin's personality cult and reversing Vladimir Lenin's theory of inevitable war with imperialism.

Kissinger, Henry (b. 1923): The national security advisor and later secretary of state under Richard Nixon, Kissinger initiated the U.S.-China rapprochement when he secretly flew to Beijing in July 1971 to meet with Zhou Enlai.

Lee Teng-hui (b. 1923): The first popularly elected president of the Republic of China. A native Taiwanese, Lee served as president from 1988 to 2000, presiding over Taiwan's democratic reforms and advocating Taiwan independence. Lee split from the GMD after the 2000 presidential election.

Lei Feng (1940–1962): This martyred PLA conscript typified Maoist virtues of self-sacrifice and "serving the people." When Lei's diary was published posthumously in 1962, he became a national hero.

Li Dazhao (1889–1927): Head librarian at Peking University, he was a cofounder of the CCP and an early mentor to Mao Zedong. When Chiang K'ai-shek turned against the CCP in 1927, Li was executed.

Li Hongzhang (1823–1901): Li fought alongside Zeng Guofan to suppress the Taiping Rebellion. During the Self-Strengthening movement, Li established China's first modern arsenals, copying Western designs.

Li Peng (b. 1928): A hydraulic engineer by training, Li was the Chinese premier from 1987 to 1998. A hard-liner, he criticized Zhao Ziyang's "wavering" attitude toward the 1989 student protests and urged a military crackdown on the demonstrators.

Liang Qichao (1873–1929): This student of Kang Youwei worked with Kang to enact the reforms of 1898. Both men fled to Japan in 1898 after Cixi suppressed the reforms and imprisoned Emperor Guangxu.

Lin Biao (1907–1971): A senior PLA general and longtime confidant of Mao Zedong, Lin became defense minister after Peng Dehuai's purge in 1959. Lin died in a plane crash in 1971 following an alleged attempt to assassinate Mao.

Lin Zexu (1785–1850): The imperial commissioner appointed by the Manchu emperor in 1838. Lin sought to suppress the British opium trade in Canton (Guangzhou). His efforts triggered the First Opium War in 1839.

Liu Shaoqi (1898–1969): A CCP organizational specialist and one of Mao Zedong's top lieutenants, Liu become Mao's heir apparent in the mid-1950s. Teaming with Deng Xiaoping to dismantle Mao's Great Leap Forward in 1961–1962, Liu was later accused of "taking the capitalist road." He was purged by Mao in 1966 and died in captivity in 1969.

Lo Ruiqing (1906–1978): As the PLA chief of staff, Lo criticized Mao Zedong's personality cult. During the Cultural Revolution, Lo was dismissed for calling the national fetish of reciting Mao's quotations "a needless exercise."

Lu Ping (b. 1927): As the president of Peking University, Lu was severely attacked by Red Guards in 1966 for "stifling the mass movement" at the outset of the Cultural Revolution.

Ma Ying-jeou (b. 1950): This Harvard-trained lawyer and former GMD mayor of Taipei was elected president of the Republic of China in 2008. Ma is opposed to both Taiwan independence and reunification with China and has forged closer economic ties with China.

MacArthur, Douglas (1880–1964): General MacArthur was the commander of UN forces in Korea from 1950 to 1951. Insisting on "total victory," he ran afoul of President Harry S. Truman, who fired him for insubordination in April 1951.

Macartney, George (1737–1806): The emissary who led the failed British trade delegation from King George III to the court of Qianlong in 1793. Lord Macartney offended the emperor by refusing to perform the traditional kowtow.

Mao Zedong (1893–1976): Political theorist, military strategist, and chairman of the CCP Central Committee from 1935 until his death, Mao adapted Vladimir Lenin's theory of proletarian revolution to the needs of China's rural society. He defeated Chiang K'ai-shek in China's civil war and led the People's Republic of China for 40 years. His radical policies in the 1950s and 1960s caused enormous suffering, leading to major reforms in the 1980s.

Marshall, George C. (1880–1959): Sent to China by President Harry S. Truman in December 1945, General Marshall tried without success to forge a coalition government between the CCP and the GMD.

Nie Yuanzi (b. 1921): A female philosophy instructor, Nie put up a wall poster at Peking University in May 1966, challenging the university's ban on wall posters and mass meetings. Mao Zedong endorsed her poster, praising her as a "true revolutionary."

Peng Dehuai (1898–1974): An outspoken PLA general and China's defense minister, Peng was purged by Mao Zedong in 1959 for criticizing the Great Leap Forward.

Peng Zhen (1902–1997): A veteran CCP revolutionary and mayor of Beijing. Peng was purged by Mao Zedong in 1966 for protecting Wu Han against leftist criticism. He was rehabilitated by Deng Xiaoping in 1978.

Puyi (1906–1967): China's "last emperor." As a toddler, he was placed on the Manchu throne as a figurehead by Cixi in 1908. Puyi was later installed by Japan as the puppet ruler of Manchukuo.

Qianlong (1711–1799): The fifth emperor of the Manchu (Qing) dynasty. He contemptuously rejected Lord Macartney's 1793 request for normal trade relations, citing China's "celestial supremacy."

Qin Shihuang Di (c. 259–210 B.C.E.): The first unifier of the Chinese empire. Known for his cruelty, he burned Confucian books and buried Confucian scholars alive. Mao Zedong once boasted that when it comes to cruelty, "we surpass Qin Shihuang 100 times."

Qishan (1790–1854): The Manchu imperial envoy known as the "manager of barbarians." His diplomatic efforts to limit British military forays in 1840–1841 failed, and he suffered permanent exile.

Qiying (1787–1858): Qiying replaced Qishan as the chief Chinese "barbarian handler" in 1841. He employed dilatory tactics to slow British encroachments. Failing to deter Britain, he was recalled in disgrace.

Song Jiaoren (1882–1913): An expert on parliamentary government, Song was the first prime minister of the Republic of China. A year after he orchestrated the GMD's first electoral campaign in 1912, he was assasinated on Yuan Shikai's orders.

Soong Ching-ling (1893–1981): The American-educated second wife of Sun Yat-sen. She was the daughter of Sun's key financial backer, Charlie Soong, and the sister of Soong Mei-ling (Madame Chiang K'ai-shek).

Soong Mei-ling (1897–2003): The younger sister of Soong Ching-ling, and wife of Chiang K'ai-shek. Educated in the United States, she acted as a go-between in the early 1940s, rallying the support of the American people for China's struggle against Japan.

Stilwell, Joseph W. (1883–1946): A much-decorated war hero, General "Vinegar Joe" Stilwell was sent by President Franklin D. Roosevelt to Chongqing in 1942 to train Chiang K'ai-shek's army. Increasingly critical of Chiang's ineffective performance, Stilwell was recalled in 1944.

Sun Yat-sen (1866–1925): A medical doctor trained in Hawaii and Hong Kong, Sun led efforts to overthrow the Manchu dynasty. When the dynasty collapsed in 1911, Sun founded China's first modern political party, the Guomindang, and became the first president of the Republic of China. He is revered as the father of modern China.

Tian Jiyun (b. 1929): A liberal reformer who was vice-premier under Zhao Ziyang in the 1980s. Tian gained notoriety in 1992 for his satirical critique of China's conservative hard-liners. Calling for creation of a "special zone" for opponents of reform, Tian promised them rigid state planning, rationing, long food lines, and no foreign travel.

Wang Dan (b. 1969): A leader of the Tiananmen student protest movement of 1989. Wang was arrested shortly after June 4 and served four years in prison before being granted compassionate release. He later earned a Ph.D. in History from Harvard University.

Wang Dongxing (b. 1916): Mao Zedong's principal bodyguard during the Cultural Revolution, Wang was subsequently put in charge of the Central Committee's archives. After Mao's death, he blew the whistle on Jiang Qing for attempting to usurp power.

Wang Guangmei (1921–2006): The glamorous wife of Liu Shaoqi, Wang was envied and resented by Jiang Qing. In 1967, Wang was tricked into leaving her Zhongnanhai sanctuary and was captured by Red Guards, who publicly humiliated her.

Wang Hongwen (1935–1992): A Shanghai factory security officer and revolutionary rebel, Wang rose during the Cultural Revolution to become vice chairman of the CCP Central Committee at age 35. He was arrested in 1976 as a member of the Gang of Four.

Wang Jingwei (1883–1944): He was initially a leader of the left wing of the GMD, but Wang's disdain for Chiang K'ai-shek led him to collaborate with the invading Japanese in 1937. Wang died in disgrace in Japan at the end of World War II.

Wang Ming (1904–1974): Mao Zedong's pro-Stalinist rival in the early 1930s. His policies were discredited by Mao at the start of 1934's Long March. After three decades in the USSR, Wang was publicly lauded in 1968 by the Soviets, who heralded him as the "true" leader of the CCP.

Wang Zhen (1908–1993): This foul-mouthed, hard-line PLA general was a stern critic of the student demonstrations in 1989. He was known as "Big Cannon" Wang.

Ward, Frederick Townsend (1831–1862): An American soldier of fortune hired to recruit and train foreign mercenaries to help suppress the Taiping Rebellion. Ward was fatally wounded at the battle of Cixi in 1862.

Wei Jingsheng (b. 1950): An electrician by training, Wei became active in the Democracy Wall movement of 1978, authoring a series of controversial wall posters, including a critique of Deng Xiaoping's "dictatorial tendencies." Wei was imprisoned in 1979.

Wen Jiabao (b. 1942): China's premier since 2003. His warm personality complements Hu Jintao's more detached style. Mentored by Zhu Rongji, Wen has a populist approach and preference for welfare economics over unrestrained capitalism that have endeared him to ordinary Chinese.

Wu Han (1909–1969): A playwright, historian, and deputy mayor of Beijing. His writing group published essays critical of Mao Zedong in 1961–1962. His 1961 opera *Hai Rui Dismissed from Office* was an allegorical criticism of Mao's 1959 purge of Peng Dehuai.

Wu Shuqing (b. 1932): A conservative who was appointed president of Peking University after the 1989 Tiananmen crackdown. Wu opposed renewed economic reforms he claimed would promote inflation, inequality, and unemployment.

Wu'er Kaixi (b. 1968): A college student of Uyghur ethnicity who gained prominence in the 1989 Tiananmen protests as a leader of the student hunger strike. Wu'er enraged Chinese premier Li Peng by rebuking him on national television.

Yang Kaihui (1901–1930): Mao Zedong's second wife and the daughter of Mao's favorite teacher. Yang joined the CCP in 1921. In 1930, she was captured, tortured, and executed by the GMD.

Yao Wenyuan (1931–2005): A member of the Gang of Four. Yao's November 1965 article attacking the Beijing Opera *Hai Rui Dismissed from Office* marked the beginning of the Cultural Revolution.

Yongle (1360–1424): The third emperor of the Ming dynasty (r. 1402–1424). He commissioned seven major oceanic expeditions, led by the great Chinese navigator Zheng He. With Yongle's death in 1424, maritime exploration ceased for 400 years.

Yuan Shikai (1859–1916): The last commander of the Manchu imperial army. Yuan transferred his loyalty to Sun Yat-sen after the revolution of 1911, only to seize power from Sun a few months later. Yuan died after an unsuccessful attempt to restore the dynastic system.

Zeng Guofan (1811–1872): The commander of the imperial Hunan army that defeated the Taiping Rebellion. Zeng later became a leading figure in the Self-Strengthening movement.

Zhang Chunqiao (1917–2005): The party secretary of Shanghai during the Cultural Revolution, and member of the Gang of Four. Under Jiang Qing's patronage, Zhang became the leading figure in the Central Cultural Revolution Small Group. He was imprisoned in 1976.

Zhang Tiesheng (b. 1951): In 1973, this aspiring college entrant from Liaoning Province turned in a blank entrance exam, claiming his proletarian birthright entitled him to a college education. He was lionized by radical leftists but imprisoned after Mao Zedong's death.

Zhang Xueliang (1901–2001): Son of the assassinated Manchurian warlord Zhang Zuolin, Zhang Xueliang was known as the Young Marshal. He led a mutiny against Chiang K'ai-shek in December 1936 (the Xi'an Incident), demanding a GMD-CCP united front to resist Japan.

Zhang Zuolin (1875–1928): This Manchu warlord ruled Manchuria from 1916 to 1928, when he was assassinated by a Japanese army officer. His son, Zhang Xueliang, famously kidnapped Chiang K'ai-shek in 1936.

Zhao Ziyang (1919–2005): The Chinese premier and general secretary of the CCP in the 1980s. He helped to design and implement Deng Xiaoping's market reforms. Zhao's prostudent sympathies during the 1989 Tiananmen protests angered Deng, resulting in Zhao's ouster and house arrest.

Zheng He (c. 1371–1433): A Hui Muslim and imperial eunuch, Zheng launched seven oceanic expeditions between 1405 and 1433. His fleet of 200 six-masted ships reached ports in Southeast Asia, India, Ceylon, the Persian Gulf, Arabia, and the Horn of Africa.

Zhou Enlai (1898–1976): The first premier and foreign minster of the People's Republic of China, Zhou was China's foremost diplomat. Ever loyal to Mao Zedong, he was the chairman's right-hand man and chief troubleshooter. Before succumbing to cancer, he paved the way for the Sino-U.S. détente.

Zhu De (1886–1976): Cofounder of the Chinese Red Army, Zhu helped turn the PLA into a well-disciplined guerrilla force. After 1949, he became the PLA's commander in chief and the CCP's vice chairman.

Zhu Rongji (b. 1928): As China's economic czar in the early 1990s, Zhu inherited a series of economic crises, including an excessive money supply, rising inflation, and chaotic financial markets. After achieving a successful soft landing, he was named premier in 1998. The unsung hero of China's economic miracle, Zhu restructured China's tax, banking, and state enterprise systems and steered China into the WTO.

Bibliography

Ash, Robert, Peter Ferdinand, Brian Hook, and Robin Porter, eds. *Hong Kong in Transition: One Country, Two Systems*. New York: RoutledgeCurzon, 2003. A wide-ranging collection of essays on the political, economic, and cultural consequences of Hong Kong's 1997 retrocession to China.

Barnett, A. Doak. *China on the Eve of Communist Takeover*. New York: Praeger, 1963. A correspondent in China during the latter stages of the GMD-CCP civil war faithfully records his impressions of a war-ravaged country on the eve of Communist "liberation."

Baum, Richard. *Burying Mao: Chinese Politics in the Age of Deng Xiaoping*. Princeton, NJ: Princeton University Press, 1996. A detailed analysis of China's shifting political dynamics, from the time of Mao Zedong's death in 1976 to the rise of Jiang Zemin in the early 1990s.

———. *China Watcher: Confessions of a Peking Tom*. Seattle: University of Washington Press, 2010. Part personal memoir, part travelogue, and part history of the field of modern Sinology, this book recounts the author's 40-year struggle to understand what makes China tick.

———. *Prelude to Revolution: Mao, the Party, and the Peasant Question, 1962–66*. New York: Columbia University Press, 1975. A study of China's Socialist Education movement, in the course of which Mao Zedong's festering quarrel with Liu Shaoqi and Deng Xiaoping erupted into open conflict, presaging the Cultural Revolution.

Bergère, Marie-Claire. *Sun Yat-sen*. Stanford, CA: Stanford University Press, 2000. The definitive biography of the widely revered founder of the Republic of China, this book reveals Sun's flaws as well as his brilliance.

Chang, Jung. *Wild Swans: Three Daughters of China*. New York: Simon and Schuster, 2003. A firsthand account of one family's efforts to cope with the turmoil and tragedy of the Chinese Revolution and its tumultuous aftermath.

Chang, Jung, and Jon Halliday. *Mao: The Unknown Story*. New York: Knopf, 2005. A well-researched, if ultimately unbalanced and polemical, attempt to illuminate Mao Zedong's dark side, including his alleged lifelong penchant for conspiracy, intrigue, and backstabbing and his cold-blooded indifference to human suffering.

Cheng, Nien. *Life and Death in Shanghai*. London: Grafton Books, 1986. A wrenching first-person account of a formerly well-to-do urban family's suffering inflicted in the course of Mao Zedong's ideological campaigns of the 1950s and 1960s.

Chesneaux, Jean. *Peasant Revolts in China, 1840–1949*. Paris: Curwen, 1973. A lively account of the history of agrarian unrest in early modern China, from the Taiping Rebellion to the Communist Revolution.

Chow, Tse-tsung. *The May Fourth Movement: Intellectual Revolution in Modern China*. Cambridge, MA: Harvard University Press, 1960. The definitive history of the birth of modern nationalism in China after World War I.

Deng, Yong. *China's Struggle for Status: The Realignment of International Relations*. Cambridge, MA: Cambridge Univerity Press, 2008. A comprehensive analysis of the shifting national priorities that have informed and underpinned Chinese foreign policy in the age of post-Mao reform.

Eastman, Lloyd E. *The Abortive Revolution: China under Nationalist Rule, 1927–1937*. Cambridge, MA: Harvard University Press, 1974. A classic analysis of the GMD's failure to create a viable national government under the conservative leadership of Chiang K'ai-shek.

Elvin, Mark. *The Pattern of the Chinese Past*. Stanford, CA: Stanford University Press, 1973. A highly original interpretation of China's 18th- and 19th-century decline from a powerful agrarian civilization to the brink of massive rural famine.

Esherick, Joseph, ed. *Lost Chance in China: The World War II Despatches of John Stuart Service*. New York: Vintage, 1974. Reviewing the work of the Dixie Mission, a U.S. military observer group in China in 1944, the editor argues that American mistakes and myopia prevented Washington from reaching détente with the CCP after 1945.

Fallows, James. *Postcards from Tomorrow Square: Reports from China*. New York: Vintage, 2008. With a veteran reporter's sharp eye and a non–China specialist's open mind, the author offers fresh new insights into the costs and benefits of China's rapid rise as an economic powerhouse.

Fenby, Jonathan. *Modern China: The Fall and Rise of a Great Power, 1850 to the Present*. New York: Harper-Collins, 2008. This lively, fascinating history of modern China is rich in insight and seasoned throughout with eyebrow-raising anecdotes of elite political intrigue and misbehavior.

Fewsmith, Joseph. *China since Tiananmen*. 2nd ed. Cambridge: Cambridge University Press, 2008. A thoroughgoing analytical history of Chinese political and economic development since the crushing of the student movement in 1989.

French, Patrick. *Tibet, Tibet: A Personal History of a Lost Land*. London: Knopf, 2003. A well-balanced narrative assessment of key events and personalities that have helped to shape Tibet's tragic modern history.

Friedman, Edward, Paul G. Pickowicz, and Mark Selden. *Chinese Village, Socialist State*. New Haven, CT: Yale University Press, 1991. A firsthand investigation into the experiences of the residents of a single rural Chinese county under Mao Zedong's agrarian revolution, from the 1930s to the collectivization drive of the mid-1950s.

―――. *Revolution, Resistance, and Reform in Village China*. New Haven, CT: Yale University Press, 2005. A continuation of the story told in the authors' *Chinese Village, Socialist State*, focusing on the period from the late 1950s to the present.

Gifford, Rob. *China Road: A Journey into the Future of a Rising Power*. New York: Random House, 2007. A fascinating travelogue written by a veteran National Public Radio correspondent, who takes the reader on a six-week, 3,000-mile journey along China's transcontinental Highway 312.

Gittings, John. *The Changing Face of China: From Mao to Market*. New York: Oxford University Press, 2005. A highly readable and well-balanced overview of Communism's impact on modern China, both positive and negative.

Goldman, Merle. *From Comrade to Citizen: The Struggle for Political Rights in China*. Cambridge, MA: Harvard University Press, 2005. The author analyzes the uphill struggle faced by China's intellectuals in their effort to progress from comrades expected to blindly obey the party to empowered citizens exercising political rights and freedoms.

Hsü, Immanuel C. Y. *The Rise of Modern China*. 6th ed. Oxford: Oxford University Press, 2000. For those who enjoy one-stop shopping, this massive, richly detailed but nonetheless readable textbook has become a standard reference on the history of China from 1644 through the end of the 20th century.

Huang, Ray. *1587, A Year of No Significance: The Ming Dynasty in Decline*. New Haven, CT: Yale University Press, 1981. An insighful examination of the manners and mores of Ming dynasty court life, revealing many continuities between imperial political rituals and political life in Mao Zedong's China.

Hughes, Christopher R. *Chinese Nationalism in the Global Era*. Oxon, UK: Routledge, 2006. An extended discourse on the continuities and changes in Chinese nationalism from the turn of the 20th century to the present.

Johnson, Chalmers A. *Peasant Nationalism and Communist Power: The Emergence of Revolutionary China 1937–1945*. Stanford, CA: Stanford University Press, 1962. An analysis of the CCP's success in mobilizing peasant support in North China during World War II by playing upon the patriotic sentiments evoked by Japan's brutal occupation policies.

Johnson, Kay Ann. *Women, the Family and Peasant Revolution in China*. Chicago: University of Chicago Press, 1983. The author persuasively shows how the CCP, starting in the 1930s, undertook to reform China's antiquated marriage laws and revamp its traditional patriarchal family structures.

Kynge, James. *China Shakes the World: The Rise of a Hungry Nation.* London: Weidenfeld and Nicolson, 2006. The author sharply challenges the comfortable notion that a rising China will readily be absorbed into the existing structure of global politics.

Li, Zhisui. *The Private Life of Chairman Mao.* New York: Random House, 1994. A unique and fascinating insight into Mao Zedong's character and erratic behavior in his later years, written by his personal physician.

Lifton, Robert Jay. *Thought Reform and the Psychology of Totalism: A Study of "Brainwashing" in China.* New York: W. W. Norton, 1961. The first major study of the CCP's so-called brainwashing techniques, as employed against suspected foreign spies and counterrevolutionaries in the early 1950s.

Ling, Ken. *The Revenge of Heaven: Journal of a Young Chinese.* New York: Ballantine, 1972. A vivid and at times disturbing firsthand account of the chaos and violence of the Cultural Revolution, as told by a former Red Guard leader.

Link, Perry. *Stubborn Weeds: Popular and Controversial Chinese Literature after the Cultural Revolution.* Bloomington: University of Indiana Press, 1985. A sensitive analysis of various modes of post–Cultural Revolution literary production, including the deeply revelatory wounded literature and scar literature of the early 1980s.

Lüthi, Lorenz M. *The Sino-Soviet Split: Cold War in the Communist World.* Princeton, NJ: Princeton University Press, 2008. A well-documented, richly detailed analysis of the growing schism between China and the USSR in the 1950s and 1960s, culminating in their border conflict of 1969 and the subsequent U.S.-China détente.

MacFarquhar, Roderick. *The Origins of the Cultural Revolution.* Vol. 1, *Contradictions among the People, 1956–1957.* New York: Columbia University Press, 1983. The definitive study of Mao Zedong's ill-fated Hundred Flowers campaign of 1956–1957 and the Anti-Rightist Rectification movement that followed it.

Bibliography

————. *The Origins of the Cultural Revolution.* Vol. 2, *The Great Leap Forward, 1958–1960.* New York: Columbia University Press, 1987. A pioneering assessment of the political dynamics that drove Mao Zedong first to launch, and later to intensify, his disastrous Great Leap Forward. Includes analysis of the purge of Peng Dehuai.

————. *The Origins of the Cultural Revolution.* Vol. 3, *The Coming of the Cataclysm, 1961–1966.* New York: Columbia University Press, 1999. The third and final volume of MacFarquhar's remarkable trilogy details Mao Zedong's preparations to attack his lieutenants and launch the Cultural Revolution.

MacFarquhar, Roderick, and Michael Schoenhals. *Mao's Last Revolution.* Cambridge, MA: Harvard University Press, 2006. The definitive political history of Mao Zedong's Cultural Revolution.

McGregor, James. *One Billion Customers: Lessons from the Front Lines of Doing Business in China.* New York: Wall Street Journal Books, 2006. A cautionary tale illustrating the many obstacles and illusions that continue to confound foreigners and serve to distort their ideas about prospering in the much-fabled China market.

Meisner, Maurice. *Li Ta-chao and the Origins of Chinese Marxism.* Cambridge, MA: Harvard University Press, 1967. A well-researched, sympathetic biography of the man who introduced Mao Zedong to Marxism-Leninism and later became a cofounder of the CCP.

Nathan, Andrew J., and Perry Link, eds. *The Tiananmen Papers.* New York: Public Affairs, 2001. A compilation of classified CCP documents pertaining to the origins, development, and bloody suppression of the Tiananmen Square student movement of 1989.

Naughton, Barry. *The Chinese Economy: Transitions and Growth.* Cambridge, MA: MIT Press, 2007. A clearly written, comprehensive guide to Chinese economic policy and performance from 1949 to the present.

Pan, Philip P. *Out of Mao's Shadow: The Struggle for the Soul of a New China.* New York: Simon and Schuster, 2008. A Chinese American investigative journalist tells the moving story of a handful of brave individuals who face political repression and legal prosecution for their efforts to speak truth to power in contemporary China.

Peerenboom, Randall. *China's Long March to the Rule of Law.* Cambridge: Cambridge University Press, 2002. Viewing China's flawed legal institutions in comparative perspective, the author concludes that China is actually making substantial progress toward instituting the rule of law.

Pei, Minxin. *China's Trapped Transition: The Limits of Developmental Autocracy.* Cambridge, MA: Harvard University Press, 2006. Viewing China's slow-paced political reforms with a critical eye, the author argues that in the absence of meaningful checks on CCP power, China's post-Mao regime is likely to founder and perhaps fail.

Pomeranz, Kenneth. *The Great Divergence: China, Europe, and the Making of the Modern World Economy.* Princeton, NJ: Princeton University Press, 2000. Arguing that China's economy easily rivaled that of the European powers until the mid-18th century, the author counters the conventional notion that China's quest for modernity was doomed to failure by its Confucian values and market-unfriendly institutions.

Preston, Diana. *The Boxer Rebellion: The Dramatic Story of China's War on Foreigners That Shook the World in the Summer of 1900.* New York: Walker, 2000. A vivid, comprehensive study of the Boxer uprising of 1899–1900, told from both Chinese and foreign perspectives.

Pye, Lucian W. *Warlord Politics: Conflict and Coalition in the Modernization of Republican China.* New York: Praeger, 1971. This fascinating study analyzes the remarkable (and at times bizarre) political behavior of China's regional military warlords, who held sway from 1916 to 1926.

Qiu, Jin. *The Culture of Power: The Lin Biao Incident in the Cultural Revolution.* Stanford, CA: Stanford University Press, 1999. A persuasive account of Lin Biao's growing conflict with Mao Zedong, and Lin's fatal plane crash of 1971, written by an insider who traces Lin's quarrel with Mao to a hostile rivalry between Lin's wife and Jiang Qing.

Romberg, Alan. *Rein in at the Brink of the Precipice: American Policy toward Taiwan and U.S.-PRC Relations*. Washington, DC: Henry L. Stimson Center, 2003. Arguably the best one-source reference work on the role of Taiwan as a sticking point in U.S.-China relations.

Schaller, Michael. *The United States and China: Into the 21st Century*. Oxford: Oxford University Press, 2002. A highly readable survey and overview of U.S.-China relations from the Boxer Rebellion to the presidency of George W. Bush.

Schell, Orville. *Discos and Democracy: China in the Throes of Reform*. New York: Pantheon, 1988. The author vividly captures both the manic excitement and the creeping disillusionment that marked the first frenetic decade of reform in post-Mao China.

Schram, Stuart R. *The Political Thought of Mao Tse-tung*. New York: Praeger, 1969. Through a careful study of Mao Zedong's revolutionary writings, the author distills the essence of Mao's populist, subjectivist political philosophy.

Schrecker, John. *The Chinese Revolution in Historical Perspective*. Westport, CT: Greenwood Press, 1991. A sociopolitical and intellectual history of modern China, focusing on 20th-century China's relation to its imperial past.

Schwartz, Benjamin. *Chinese Communism and the Rise of Mao*. Cambridge, MA: Harvard University Press, 1951. The classic account of the CCP's shift from an urban, worker-based labor movement in the first half of the 1920s to a rural, peasant-based guerrilla movement under Mao Zedong.

Seagrave, Sterling. *The Soong Dynasty*. New York: Harper Perennial, 1986. A lively family biography of Sun Yat-sen's top financial backer and confidant, Charlie Soong, and his remarkable offspring, who included the notorious Soong sisters—Ching-ling (Madame Sun Yat-sen), Mei-ling (Madame Chiang K'ai-shek), and Ai-ling.

Shambaugh, David, ed. *Deng Xiaoping: Portrait of a Statesman*. New York: Oxford University Press, 1995. A collection of essays by China specialists that highlights various aspects of Deng Xiaoping's life and political career.

Shirk, Susan. *China: Fragile Superpower*. New York: Oxford University Press, 2007. An engaging assessment of the major constraints, both foreign and domestic, that have served to shape Chinese foreign policy making in the post-Mao reform era.

Short, Philip. *Mao: A Life*. New York: John Murray, 2004. This is arguably the best of several available biographies of the late CCP Chairman Mao Zedong.

Snow, Edgar. *Red Star over China*. New York: Random House, 1938. This sympathetic, firsthand account of the rise of Chinese Communism in the 1930s was suppressed in the United States until the 1950s.

Spence, Jonathan D. *God's Chinese Son: The Taiping Heavenly Kingdom of Hong Xiuquan*. New York: W. W. Norton, 1996. An engrossing history of the rise and fall of the mid-19th century Taiping Rebellion.

———. *The Search for Modern China*. New York: W. W. Norton, 1990. A masterfully narrated history of late imperial and early modern China, from the Manchu dynasty to the reign of Mao Zedong.

Suettinger, Robert. *Beyond Tiananmen: The Politics of U.S.-China Relations, 1989–2000*. Washington, DC: Brookings Institution Press, 2005. A detailed analysis of the strategic and political calculations that helped to ensure continued forward momentum in U.S.-China relations despite many potential disruptions in the aftermath of the Tiananmen debacle.

Sun, Shuyun. *The Long March*. London: Harper, 2006. Based on interviews with survivors and witnesses, the author gives a gripping account of the travails experienced by the CCP during its 8,000-mile trek to escape annihilation at the hands of Chiang K'ai-shek in the mid-1930s.

Taylor, Jay. *The Generalissimo: Chiang Kai-shek and the Struggle for Modern China*. Cambridge, MA: Belknap, 2009. The definitive political

Bibliography

biography of one of the most enigmatic and ultimately tragic figures in modern Chinese history.

Teng, Ssu-yü, and John K. Fairbank, eds. *China's Response to the West.* Cambridge, MA: Harvard University Press, 1954. A marvelous collection of documents, with analysis, chronicling the responses of leading Chinese scholars and officials to Western encroachments in the late 18th and 19th centuries.

Tsai, Kellee. *Capitalism without Democracy: The Private Sector in Contemporary China.* Ithaca, NY: Cornell University Press, 2007. This study of the intimate relationship between Communist Party officials and successful commercial entrepreneurs in postreform China provides fresh insight into the absence of democratic aspirations among members of China's emerging bourgeoisie.

Tuchman, Barbara. *Stilwell and the American Experience in China, 1911–45.* New York: MacMillan, 1970. A vivid account of General Joseph Stilwell's efforts to upgrade the Guomindang's fighting capacity in World War II and the frustrations he encountered at the hands of Chiang K'ai-shek.

Tyler, Patrick. *A Great Wall: Six Presidents and China.* New York: PublicAffairs, 1999. A detailed, original study of the political forces that shaped U.S. policy toward China from the origins of normalization under Richard Nixon to the presidency of Bill Clinton.

Van Slyke, Lyman P. *Enemies and Friends: The United Front in Chinese Communist History.* Stanford, CA: Stanford University Press, 1967. The definitive study of Maoist united front tactics during the Chinese Revolution.

Wakeman, Frederic, Jr. *Strangers at the Gate: Social Disorder in South China, 1839–1861.* Berkeley: University of California Press, 1966. A thoughtful and highly original analysis of the powerful social and political forces unleashed by the Western imperialist assault on China in the 1840s and 1850s.

Waley, Arthur. *The Opium War through Chinese Eyes*. Stanford, CA: Stanford University Press, 1958. An assessment of the impact of Western imperialism in China from the 1830s to the 1850s, told from the perspective of the victims.

Whiting, Allen S. *China Crosses the Yalu: The Decision to Enter the Korean War*. New York: MacMillan, 1960. The classic study of China's calculus of deterrence as UN forces in Korea under General Douglas MacArthur marched northward toward the Chinese border in the early autumn of 1950.

Wright, Mary Clabaugh. *The Last Stand of Chinese Conservatism: The T'ung-Chih Restoration, 1862–1874.* Stanford, CA: Stanford University Press, 1957. The definitive study of Prince Gong's early efforts to modernize China after the Opium Wars and the efforts of reactionary officials, under Cixi, to thwart them.

Yang, Dali. *Remaking the Chinese Leviathan: Market Transition and the Politics of Governance in China*. Stanford, CA: Stanford University Press, 2004. Countering pessimistic assessments of an emerging legitimacy crisis in Chinese politics, the author argues that a more sensitive, responsive, and adaptive form of authoritarian governance has been emerging.

Zheng, Yi. *Scarlet Memorial: Tales of Cannibalism in Modern China*. Boulder, CO: Westview Press, 1996. A credible, disturbing account of several instances of people eating human flesh in contemporary China, either due to starvation (during the Great Leap Forward) or as a political act (in the Cultural Revolution).

Bibliography

Notes

Notes